About the Author

Jodie O'Rourke is an Interactive Developer living and working in central London, England. He specializes in producing rich client solutions using a variety of technologies, including Flash — which he's been using for 10 years. He has both a bachelor and masters degree from The Nottingham Trent University and is recognized in the Adobe developer community as a Community Professional and Certified Expert. He tweets (@jodieorourke) and blogs (http://jodieorourke.com) regularly about his daily adventures in technology and his less frequent adventures as trainee PADI Divemaster.

Dedication

To Joao for always being there and keeping me working, even when I was tired. Thanks for hanging in there.

I finished the book, Mum, so I can come and visit now!

Author's Acknowledgments

I couldn't have produced this book without the support of my family, friends, and colleagues. Thank you, Kelley, for being so tolerant during this long project, and to Moog for, well, being Moog!

Massive thanks to Matt Wagner at Fresh Books for approaching me with this title, and for working hard to keep the paperwork prim and proper!

I'd like to thank the team at Wiley for turning a pipe-dream into a reality. Thank you to Susan Christophersen and Katie Feltman for helping to keep the wheels on this project when they felt as though they might fall off — it was a bumpy ride, but the end result has made it seem worthwhile. I'd also like to thank Melanie Nelson, who allowed me to see through the eyes of a nontechnical reader and helped me to simplify some of the complicated subject matter covered in this book.

Thanks to everyone at Adobe who offered me tools, equipment, support, and insight. Adobe really does love its developers!

Publisher's Acknowledgments

We're proud of this book; please send us your comments at http://dummies.custhelp.com. For other comments, please contact our Customer Care Department within the U.S. at 877-762-2974, outside the U.S. at 317-572-3993, or fax 317-572-4002.

Some of the people who helped bring this book to market include the following:

Acqu ions, Editorial, and Vertical Webs s

Pr t Editor: Susan Christophersen

S or Acquisitions Editor: Katie Feltman

Development Editor: Melanie Nelson

Copy Editor: John Edwards

Technical Editor: Russ Mullen

Editorial Manager: Jodi Jensen

Vertical Websites: Richard Graves, Marilyn Hummel

Editorial Assistant: Amanda Graham

Sr. Editorial Assistant: Cherie Case

Cover Photo: © iStockphoto.com / Daniel Halvorson

Cartoons: Rich Tennant (www.the5thwave.com)

Composition Services

Project Coordinator: Nikki Gee

Layout and Graphics: Lavonne Roberts, Corrie Socolovitch

Proofreaders: Laura Albert, Dwight Ramsey, Toni Settle

Indexer: Potomac Indexing, LLC

Publishing and Editorial for Technology Dummies

> **Richard Swadley,** Vice President and Executive Group Publisher

> **Andy Cummings,** Vice President and Publisher

> **Mary Bednarek,** Executive Acquisitions Director

> **Mary C. Corder,** Editorial Director

Publishing for Consumer Dummies

> **Kathleen Nebenhaus,** Vice President and Executive Publisher

Composition Services

> **Debbie Stailey,** Director of Composition Services

Flash® Mobile
Application Development
FOR
DUMMIES®

by Jodie O'Rourke

WILEY

John Wiley & Sons, Inc.

Flash® Mobile Application Development For Dummies®

Published by
John Wiley & Sons, Inc.
111 River Street
Hoboken, NJ 07030-5774

www.wiley.com

Copyright © 2012 by John Wiley & Sons, Inc., Hoboken, New Jersey

Published by John Wiley & Sons, Inc., Hoboken, New Jersey

Published simultaneously in Canada

For general information on our other products and services, please contact our Customer Care Department within the U.S. at 877-762-2974, outside the U.S. at 317-572-3993, or fax 317-572-4002.

For technical support, please visit www.wiley.com/techsupport.

Wiley also publishes its books in a variety of electronic formats and by print-on-demand. Not all content that is available in standard print versions of this book may appear or be packaged in all book formats. If you have purchased a version of this book that did not include media that is referenced by or accompanies a standard print version, you may request this media by visiting http://booksupport.wiley.com. For more information about Wiley products, visit us at www.wiley.com.

Library of Congress Control Number: 2011940394

ISBN 978-1-118-01254-3 (pbk); ISBN 978-1-118-14632-3 (ebk); ISBN 978-1-118-14631-6 (ebk); ISBN 978-1-118-14633-0 (ebk)

Manufactured in the United States of America

10 9 8 7 6 5 4 3 2 1

WILEY

Contents at a Glance

Table of Contents

Introduction

Welcome to *Flash Mobile Application Development For Dummies.* This book will take you from knowing very little about mobile applications to having your own applications running on iPhone, iPod, and Android devices — all built with Flash.

You've made two good decisions: First, you bought my book — nice one! Second, you've opted to build your mobile application using Flash. You will not only find this a pleasant experience but also discover a way of building an app for all those devices in the time it would take you to build an app for just one of them, had you chosen to do it without Flash.

In this book, I show you everything you need to build your first app, impart pearls of wisdom I've picked up as I've built my own apps, and of course, crack a bad joke or two — it is a *Dummies* book after all!

About This Book

Flash Mobile Application Development For Dummies tells you everything you need to know to build an application on a computer that will run on a mobile phone. Without bombarding you with too much technical jargon, the book carefully offers the necessary details to build not just *an* app but a *good* app.

I explore three main areas of Flash mobile application development: the design and aesthetic considerations of a mobile app, the technical knowledge needed to actually build an app, and the administrative (and in some cases political) aspects of getting your app in front of a large audience.

Conventions Used in This Book

Most topics are explained in easy-to-follow steps. I found it easy to explain it this way, and I'm confident that you'll find things easier to understand as a result:

- ✓ I've used a bold typeface to denote text that you should type, **like this**.

- ✓ To save on repeating code I've already introduced, and improve the brevity of my examples, I use / / . . . to denote that additional code at this point has been removed in my example but should still be present in your version.

✔ When you should make a selection from a menu, the selection appears in the following format: Choose File⇨New. In this example, you should click File and then choose the New menu item that appears.

✔ When a web link (or URL) is specified, the following typeface (called monofont) is applied to distinguish it: `www.dummies.com`.

What You're Not to Read

This book is a reference, acting as a trusty companion long after you finish reading it. You can read the book from start to finish — quite conventional — or from back to front — less conventional, but just as helpful! Or you can jump around as needed.

Foolish Assumptions

Being a Brit, it's customary for me to apologize for something. In the case of this book, it's for some rather bold assumptions I've made about you.

I assume that you have access to an Android, iPhone, iPad, or iPod Touch device.

I assume that you have written code with a programming language or have used Flash. If you don't have a programming background or have never used Flash, don't worry. You'll discover loads from this book! If you've used Flash or programmed in another language, you'll find things just a little bit easier.

You *do not* need a Mac computer to develop Flash mobile applications and test them on your own devices. You do, however, need access to a Mac to submit apps to the Apple App Store (Android Market doesn't require a Mac). If you want to submit an app to the App Store, I assume that you have access to a Mac computer — you need only to have a friend who has a Mac to qualify!

Finally, I assume that you're able to obtain the tools needed to build Flash mobile applications. Flash Professional and Flash Builder are the tools that I use throughout this book. Both are available for a free, time-limited trial, allowing you to evaluate their capabilities to help you create great mobile apps before you shell out any money. You can download Flash Professional from `www.adobe.com/go/tryflash` and Flash Builder from `www.adobe.com/go/try_flashbuilder`.

How This Book Is Organized

Flash Mobile Application Development For Dummies is comprised of six parts, the first five addressing a specific portion of the application development process. You can read these parts forward, backward, in order, or out of order — whichever way makes sense for your own project and needs.

Part I: Getting Started

In Part I, I introduce you to mobile applications and explain what the deal is with Flash on mobile devices. I tell you the pros and cons of running your Flash application in the mobile web browser versus installing it on the device as a native app. I give you an appreciation of what happens under the hood when an application file is created. Finally, I introduce you to the development life cycle that I chose to follow.

Part II: Creating a Flash Application for Mobile Devices

There's no getting around it: Part II is where you get your hands really dirty. From the beginning, this part shows you how to start a new Flash mobile application and then gives you the know-how to create content and code within the app. After mastering the basics, you find out how to solicit input from the user, send data off to a server, and load data into your app.

Part III: Adding Extra Bells and Whistles

Basics are all well and good, but we all like to show off — even just a little bit! Go on, admit it: You're itching to make an all-singing, all-dancing application. It's a good thing then that this part made the final cut.

Animation, video, and audio are all examples of the bells and whistles that you find in a Flash mobile application. Part III shows you how to include these enhancements and how to use some unique features — such as geo-location and initiating calls — offered by the device on which your application runs. Later in this part, you discover how to use another tool — Flash Builder — to create Flash mobile applications.

Part IV: Getting Your App onto a Mobile Device

It would be a pretty unrewarding experience to show you how to build a mobile application and then not show you how to see it working on a mobile device. In fact, it would be worse than unrewarding; it'd be cruel! I could never put my name on a book that did such a thing, and checking the front cover again, I see my name on there, so you're in luck!

This part shows you how to install your Flash mobile application on your own Android or iOS device so that you can test it. First, I show you the easy steps of publishing your Android application to your device. Then I walk you through the steps of becoming a full-fledged member of the iOS Developer Program, obtaining the necessary bits from Apple, and finally putting the iOS app onto your device.

Part V: Testing and Sending Your App to Market

You picked up this book because you want to release your creations to the mobile app stores for the whole world to see. Having already showed you how to build a beauty of an app, I show you in Part V the nitty-gritty details of dotting the *i*s, crossing the *t*s, and making your app go live.

Part V covers the all-important aspect of testing your application, demonstrating where the bugs can arise and introducing some helpful tools along the way. After that, you find out how to release your application into the wild. I walk you through the step-by-step process of submitting an application to the Apple App Store and the Android Market.

Part VI: The Part of Tens

It wouldn't be a *For Dummies* book without a Part of Tens! Each of the three chapters in this part gives you ten tidbits of handy knowledge about getting the most out of your app, keeping the user happy, and getting through the App Store process unscathed. None of the lists are exhaustive, but I certainly exhausted myself in agonizing over the 20-or-so items in each list that I was forced to leave out!

Icons Used in This Book

When the Remember icon pops up, it signifies that you should keep a point in mind when progressing through a section of a particular chapter.

Life in a *Dummies* book carries on perfectly well without the additional technical blurb. If you're a little bit geeky or you're an experienced programmer, you'll like the technical stuff. If you want to skip the technical stuff, feel free to do so.

If there's an easier way to get something done, the Tip icon will alert you to it.

The Warning icon alerts you to something that could prove to be a show-stopper if it's missed. These icons are often there to help you avoid those annoying little quirks that can lead to hours of head scratching — or head-to-desk contact!

Where to Go from Here

Go forth and make brilliant apps with Flash Professional. When you're feeling comfortable with the code, step things up a notch by migrating your development practices over to Flash Builder, as explained in Chapter 12.

Don't stop at just one app. After you've cracked the basics, each successive app comes together just a little bit easier than the one before. Before long, you'll find yourself knocking out applications into both the Apple App Store and Android Market in a weekend!

I'm always ranting and raving on my blog — `http://jodieorourke.com/` — and on Twitter — `@jodieorourke`. If you have any (nicely worded) comments about this book or Flash development in general, feel free to drop me a message!

Part I
Getting Started

In this part . . .

"*A* little knowledge is a dangerous thing," as the saying goes, so in Part I, I tell you a lot about the technology and processes that underpin Flash mobile application development. Arming you with this knowledge in Part I will give you an enhanced understanding of the inner workings of your Flash mobile application when you start building it. Allow me some time to build the foundations, and you'll be amazed how quickly the project rises toward the sky.

Chapter 1 looks at defining the term Flash mobile application and then examines the characteristics of a good mobile application. Chapter 2 looks at the differences between browser-based Flash mobile applications, AIR for Android applications, and the cross-compilation of Flash applications to iOS — weighing each of them as a delivery strategy for your content. Chapter 3 looks at the technical processes that Flash applications undergo to become AIR for Android applications or native iOS applications.

Chapter 1

Exploring Flash on Mobile Devices

In This Chapter

▶ Understanding the truth behind Flash on mobile devices

▶ Looking at what makes a good mobile application

▶ Introducing an application you can build

Mobile applications have become the latest gold rush to sweep the technology sector. The mind-boggling sales figures of Android and iOS devices have lead to a surge in businesses wanting to reach these platforms with applications that users can install on their devices. Innovative apps have proven that, when built with the user in mind, they can be hugely successful.

For the developer, building apps leads to the complexities of understanding a number of platforms and programming languages. For the business, there comes the cost of maintaining multiple applications built in different technologies. This is where Flash steps in, acting as a way for the developer to build the application and then compile and deploy it for both Android and iOS devices. The developer benefits from requiring knowledge of only ActionScript to develop the application, and the business benefits from the reduced costs in building and maintaining a single application.

In this chapter, I introduce you to some basic terms related to Flash and mobile applications. Then I explain what Flash on mobile devices means, the various platforms you can reach with your content, and the delivery options available to you. I'll do my best to impress on you what makes a mobile app a good one, and I'll share a couple of my own choice picks. Finally, I introduce you to an old friend of mine, an app I developed called SpaceshipZapZap. I'll be referring to this app throughout the book.

Learning Flash and Mobile Application Terminology

Before I dive in to an explanation about what "Flash mobile application" means, it'd be rude of me not to first clarify some of the jargon that I'm likely to throw at you. With the terminology covered, you'll be catching all the phrases I throw and lobbing them back with gusto!

As with any technology, plenty of jargon is flying around in the mobile application space. Surprisingly, most of it actually means something, so allow me to introduce you to the essential terms:

- **Android OS:** This term is the name of the operating system software created by Google, which is installed on smartphones built by manufacturers such as Samsung, Motorola, HTC, and Sony Ericsson. Android OS is responsible for managing all aspects of the device's functionality, from making calls to establishing Internet connections. On top of this, the operating system also acts as the host for third-party applications that are installed on the device.

- **iPhone OS (iOS):** iOS is the name of the operating system software created by Apple to run on iPhone, iPad, and iPod touch devices. Initially called iPhone OS, it was shortened to iOS when the iPad was introduced, and the operating system became wider-reaching than just for the iPhone. As is true of its Android rival, iOS is responsible for controlling all the device's core functionality. iOS applications are installed onto the operating system and operate inside the confines of what the operating system allows.

- **Native application:** This term is used to describe an application that is installed locally on a device and runs as an integral part of the operating system software. Native apps can be preinstalled on devices — such as the calendar application on iOS and Android — or can be downloaded and installed — such as a game from the App Store or Android Market. Applications that don't install locally on the device and aren't trusted by the operating system — such as those that run in a web browser — are considered non-native.

- **Flash Player:** Adobe Flash Player is an application that allows Flash content to be viewed in web browsers. Flash applications are loaded from a remote web server when they're used. As well as being available for Windows, Mac, and Linux computers, Flash Player is also available for devices running the Android operating system and on the BlackBerry PlayBook tablet. Flash Player is *not* available on iOS mobile devices.

- **Flash Professional:** You use this Adobe software to build Flash mobile applications. Flash Professional is described in more detail in Chapter 4.

- **AIR:** Adobe AIR is another type of player — or *runtime* — that enables Flash content to run on the desktop in the same way that a native Windows or Mac OS application would. AIR applications are installed locally on the computer, instead of being served from a web server each time they are run. Running like a native application on the operating system means AIR applications can have features not available to the Flash Player, such as having access to write to local disk drives, loading web pages into Flash content, and invoking other applications installed on the computer.

✔ **Packager for iPhone:** This tool, which is built in to the Flash Professional software, converts a conventional Flash application into an application that can be installed to run natively on an iOS device.

✔ **AIR for Android:** This version of AIR is tailored for the Android mobile operating system. Adobe has worked with the Google engineers to make the runtime work as efficiently as possible on devices that are far more constrained in terms of processing power and memory than a conventional desktop computer. Running AIR on Windows or Mac OS gives the developer access to parts of the computer that aren't accessible from the Flash Player running in the browser. Similarly, AIR for Android also comes with benefits that are specific to mobile devices. Running like a native application, an AIR for Android app is able to access many restricted devices features, such as the location and local storage.

Clarifying Misconceptions about Flash on Mobile Devices

On the web, Flash evolved as the best way of delivering an application that runs on all major browsers and operating systems. Approaching mobile device operating systems with everything they know about the web, Apple and Google saw the potential for a model where developers could build applications that are installed and run natively on devices. Although Google sees Flash as an integral part of its mobile platform, Apple sees it as a threat and bans it from its iOS devices. Adobe's response was to create a tool that enabled Flash developers to convert their Flash applications to native iOS applications. Although initially annoyed by Adobe's apparent subversion of its platform, Apple later accepted that allowing Flash applications to be transformed into iOS applications was far from harmful.

Developing a mobile version of Flash to fit market and developer needs

In a world without politics and business objectives, you'd be able to view content in any format on any device. In the highly prized smartphone market, things are a little different, and two camps have formed: those who believe that users should be given the choice to have features like Flash on their mobile device and those who believe that such decisions should be made on the users' behalf.

It was almost impossible to have missed the spat between Adobe and Apple over Apple's decision not to allow Flash Player onto iOS devices. Much conversation occurred over whether the decision was based purely on Apple's claims of Flash performing poorly, or whether a business motivation existed to stop another application platform from challenging the App Store. Whatever the reason, Apple's competitors came running to the market proudly claiming to support Flash content on their devices. Both Google with its Android operating system and RIM with the BlackBerry PlayBook touted a "full web experience," citing the Internet without Flash as not quite being the full experience.

Apple's decision not to allow Flash apps on iOS devices wasn't the only issue, though. Developers recognized that being able to run their apps as native applications on mobile devices could provide benefits to the user (e.g., being able to play or access an app without using a browser or, in some cases, accessing Wi-Fi or accruing costs on their data plan) and to themselves (in the form of increased sales and exposure). Developers would jump at the chance to develop native apps if only they had the Java coding expertise for Android OS or sufficient knowledge of Objective-C to build an iPhone app.

In addressing these issues, Adobe realized that it needed offer a variety of deployment options for developers building Flash applications for mobile devices. Adobe responded to the challenges by creating a three-pronged solution that introduced improvements to the performance of Flash Player for mobile devices, opened iOS to Flash developers for the first time (via a non-Flash option), and provided a near-native application experience for Android.

Viewing Flash in a browser

Delivering content to the Flash Player plug-in running in a web browser has been the mainstay of the Flash delivery mechanism for years. You create your application and put the file on your web server, and then the user downloads it when he or she accesses it. Mobile devices running Android OS can view Flash content in this manner as well, requiring users to first install the Flash Player plug-in from the Android Market. The BlackBerry PlayBook ships with Flash Player already installed. Despite Adobe's continuous improvements to make Flash Player run faster and more efficiently on mobile devices, Apple refuses to allow Flash Player onto iOS devices. As such, it is not possible to deliver Flash content to the browser in iOS; the only viable approach is iOS cross-compilation.

Developing apps via iOS cross-compilation

You may be wondering how Flash can work on iOS mobile devices if Apple doesn't allow Flash applications. Well, the answer is that Flash applications for iOS devices are not actually Flash apps by the time they're compiled and packaged. Software integrated into Adobe's Flash authoring software — Flash Professional, the software that I'll be using throughout this book — translates the Flash code into native iOS code and places it inside a container that is recognizable to iOS. This conversion is called *cross-compilation,* and the result is a native app that can be installed on any iOS device. This conversion process is covered in more detail in Chapter 3. Once a cross-compilation app is submitted to the Apple App Store, Apple reviews the application as it would an iOS application developed using Objective-C, and, once approved, the app is placed in the Apple App Store alongside all the other iOS applications. The user is unaware that your iOS app started life as a Flash application, because it simply isn't Flash.

Initially, Apple's response to this work-around was to get pretty angry. Apple disliked the fact that developers were able to translate an application they'd already built for the web and put that app on iOS devices. Apple decided to change its terms and conditions for submission of apps to the Apple App Store, refusing to approve applications that weren't developed in Objective-C and using Apple software. Eventually, Apple relaxed this stance in the face of rising concern over its power and influence, and developers were once again able to make their converted Flash applications available in the App Store. This has been the status quo for a while, with a semblance of peace and productivity returning to the smartphone application market.

Using AIR for Android

Knowing full well that developers would also want to run native apps on Android, Adobe and Google worked together to build a version of the popular Adobe AIR desktop runtime specifically for Android. AIR for Android is an application much like Flash Player, only instead of requiring users to view Flash content in a web browser, the content runs as an Android app, like any other native application on the device. An important distinction is that the Android application is Flash and, unlike iOS, conversion to native operating system code isn't necessary. The application is installed on the Android device, and an icon appears on the menu. When the application is launched, the AIR for Android runtime is also launched; then your Flash application runs inside the AIR for Android container. The experience is seamless; your application looks and behaves like every other Android app. The only caveat is that the user must install the AIR for Android application, which is available for free in the Android Market. Having done it once, the user won't be asked to install it for other AIR for Android applications, and no other clues are provided to the user to hint that the application is in fact Flash.

Understanding the legality of cross-compilation

With all the arguments and press coverage, you'd be forgiven for thinking that cross-compilation is an insidious approach to application development that ranks alongside hacking and malware. This couldn't be further from the truth. Cross-compilation happens in many technologies to allow developers to write applications in programming languages that they know and are easier to read, and then to automatically translate the code to work on a device that doesn't normally run that type of code.

Cross-compiling doesn't require users to use a hacked copy of the iOS software on their device — a process known as *jail-breaking* — or breach any of the terms of the End User License Agreement (EULA) laid out by Apple. Apple approves cross-compiled Flash applications for the App Store. As such, iOS applications generated this way are legitimate.

Understanding What Makes a Good Mobile App

Building a successful mobile application requires a little more than an understanding of the technology involved. Understanding how users behave differently with a mobile device, compared to, say, a desktop computer, is pivotal in tailoring an experience that seems at home in a mobile context rather than one that appears to push against it. In explaining what makes a good mobile application, I cover the reasons for even bothering to target mobile devices, how to embrace a mobile device environment, and sources of inspiration for good mobile experiences.

Targeting mobile devices

These complicated boxes of wires and batteries that we all carry around in our pockets have become more important to us than remembering to leave the house with keys and wearing a pair of clean underwear! Our mobile devices are always with us and have become important tools for managing our lives, from calendar reminders to checking the status of public transportation. Increasingly, our mobile devices are becoming a source of addiction, with us whipping them out every few minutes to "get updated" on what's happening on social-networking services like Twitter and Facebook.

Many technology companies recognize the need to meet their customers where they are. Companies once saw desktop computers as their primary revenue stream, but they are finding that users now turn to their mobile devices. Creating and selling a successful app — and securing a place on as many mobile devices as possible — is a highly prized goal for technology companies.

Translating desktop apps to handset apps

One of the biggest travesties in mobile application development is when a company takes its website and performs an exact translation into a mobile app. Doing so places an application originally aimed at users in a stationary setting — at a desktop computer, with a mouse — in front of users who are on the move, have a smaller screen, and interact by touching the screen.

A few pitfalls that an application built this way could experience are as follows:

✔ **Performing irrelevant tasks:** When the users are on the move and using the app, they are doing so because the app serves them well for the tasks that they want to perform in this context.

For instance, if you're waiting on a bus and want to find out when the next one will arrive, you may open a transit app expecting to find a timetable or map. If instead you end up having to peruse a hierarchical list of the board of directors for the bus company that supplied the app, your current needs are not being met and the app is failing your expectations. Although a website may be a logical place to gather more information about a company, an app is not. Knowing the names and faces of the company directors has little relevance to you when you're out on the street trying to solve a problem. Other tasks, like getting to know the board of directors, can wait until you're home in front of a desktop computer.

✔ **Failing to embrace mobile user interface principles:** iPhones have been around since 2007, and since then, many competing touch-screen devices entered the market. In this time, tried-and-tested ways of navigating through menus, presenting lists of data, and dragging and dropping have all been established. Applications that attempt to port functionality directly from desktop to mobile — such as mouse-over buttons that have no relevance on a touch-screen device — risk missing out on incorporating proven mobile design standards, which could lead to the user's expectations being challenged when he or she uses the app.

✔ **Creating a cluttered and noisy user interface:** Less space on a smaller screen makes it imperative for the design of your user interface on a mobile device to be as simple as possible. Too much clutter — buttons placed too close to each other or graphical content detracting attention from text — can all cause users to become easily fatigued or frustrated with your app. Bring your user interface down to the basics by justifying the presence of every element in your application. If the feature lacks justification, it has no place in your application.

✔ **Failing to capitalize on the features of the device:** Users are wise to the capabilities of their mobile device and quickly become frustrated when they feel an application isn't doing the most it could to help them. Consider the bus stop example again. Imagine that you're visiting a new city and are trying to find a bus stop and are wondering what time the next bus will arrive. You launch the bus mobile application on your phone, and it asks you to enter a postal code so that the bus stop can be located. You've been tripped up at the first hurdle! You're out in town and don't know the postal code of the area you're in. As a savvy app user, you know that if the app had just integrated a GPS service into the application, you could have used it to automatically discover your location, the nearest bus stop, and the bus schedule. Had the developer of the application sought to capitalize on the features of the mobile device, he would have understood both that the user might not know his location and that the device would.

Exploiting the mobile device to its fullest extent is a continuing theme, and next I explain how to be sure of doing just that.

Exploiting the new user gestures

Mobile devices have a defining characteristic that separates them from their larger and more powerful desktop counterparts: They rely on a touch screen for user input, rather than a mouse and keyboard. Tailoring an experience around touch input is a crucial step in ensuring that your mobile application is usable. The following sections describe just a few of the user gestures — or *interaction metaphors* — that you can include in your mobile application.

Touch

A touch occurs whenever a finger is placed on the touch screen of the device. Rather than having to move a pointer to a place of interest and then click, the user just presses her finger on the point she wants to interact.

From a technology perspective, touch is the successor to a click. Where you may have used a point-and-click interaction before, this now becomes simply a touch. There is no pointing device to track the position of, rendering hover and rollover behaviors redundant on a mobile device.

Multitouch

This is like a touch, only with more fingers! Mobile devices support as many as five simultaneous touches, and you can also track the movement of these touches as digits slide around the touch screen. The ability to track interaction in this way is unique to touch-screen devices, and it opens some very exciting ways of interacting with an application.

Swipe

In addition to touch and multitouch comes a more complex interaction that also monitors how far, how fast, and in which direction a digit pressed on the screen moves. On almost all modern touch-screen devices, placing your finger on the screen, and then moving it rapidly to the left or right, instigates a *swipe gesture*. The most common use for this is moving between screens, as can be observed on any Android or iOS device home screen.

Taking advantage of being mobile

Being the pessimist that I am, I all too often focus on mobile devices introducing many limitations that don't present themselves in a desktop environment. Although this is true, it would be unfair not to point out that in addition to being highly portable, mobile devices also come with a load of extra features that you wouldn't find on a conventional desktop machine. The next sections discuss a few of them.

Geolocation

Modern mobile devices come with an integrated sensor that enables the device to triangulate its position using Global Positioning System (GPS) satellites. This allows you to build applications that incorporate location-based services for your user — such as finding the nearest bus stop or ice cream shop.

Accelerometer

Devices know when they're being moved! You might remember the story of Nokia putting an accelerometer sensor into the N95 smartphone and not telling anyone about it. When developers finally discovered it, they had a field day creating games that relied on the user's movement of the device, rather than entry on the keypad. Since then, device manufacturers realized that an accelerometer is a vital piece of kit in a mobile device. The ins and outs of the accelerometer are covered in more detail in Chapter 11.

Camera

The camera was an addition that arrived on mobile devices long before mass-market app development for devices did. Over time, cameras have grown in the resolution of images they can take and have evolved into being able to capture high-definition (HD) video too. As a mobile application developer, the camera is at your disposal, allowing your user to submit photos through your application or even capture a barcode for analysis by your application.

Finding examples of good apps

In giving an example of a couple of apps that offer a rewarding mobile experience to their users, I thought it appropriate to have an example of a game and an example of a utility application.

Flight Control

Having sold millions of copies, Flight Control (shown in Figure 1-1) is still one of the most successful games in the Apple App Store. The reason behind the success is not only the cleverly miniscule price point but also the simple yet effective game play that lends itself perfectly to a handheld touch-screen device.

Users guide aircraft in to land by drawing a line with their finger from the aircraft to the runway. The objective is simply to land as many aircraft as possible without having a single mid-air collision. It's extremely intuitive to play and ludicrously addictive. The graphics are bright and fun, without being overbearing. The user interface maximizes the available real estate on the screen by operating in landscape mode.

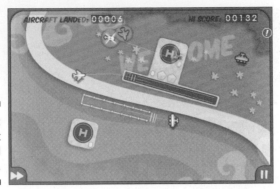

Because it doesn't require Internet connectivity to operate, Flight Control quickly became popular with commuters on underground transport systems, where a cellular network was unavailable.

TweetDeck

You can find many Twitter clients for mobile devices, but few have been able to pack such a large amount of functionality into a package that looks and behaves as well as TweetDeck, shown in Figure 1-2 as seen on an Android device. Originally built as an Adobe AIR application for the desktop, TweetDeck's unique feature has been the capability to separate a large amount of Twitter "noise" into meaningful columns. In their Android application, users switch between columns with left and right swipe gestures. They scroll lists of tweets in these columns with up and down swipe gestures. Further detail about the tweet is obtained by tapping them: right-to-left transitions indicating drilling down into a message and its author's details and left-to-right transitions signifying a return to the preceding screen.

TweetDeck's success is built around highly effective information architecture in an extremely constrained screen size.

As you may have sensed, the recurring principles throughout the two applications were making effective use of the space available and seeking to simplify the experience for the user as much as possible. If you can incorporate these two principles into your own mobile application design, you're halfway to success in the App Store and Android Market.

Figure 1-2:
The
TweetDeck
Android
app.

Introducing SpaceshipZapZap

Throughout the book, I refer to an example application that I've built to accompany your understanding. SpaceshipZapZap is a small arcade game that mirrors a tried-and-tested game-play format. It's available for free on the Android and iOS platforms, so feel free to install it on your device and have a play. The redirect links that follow allow you to view and download the application from either the Android Market or Apple App Store:

✔ Link for SpaceshipZapZap in the Android Market: `http://jodieorourke.com/zapzapandroid`

✔ Link for SpaceshipZapZap in the Apple App Store: `http://jodieorourke.com/zapzapios`

I intentionally made SpaceshipZapZap simple to allow you to grasp how it's assembled. However, I tried to include a decent number of features to help you appreciate what can be achieved in a Flash mobile application.

By the end of the book, I'll have given you a thorough walk-through of the majority of the features I've implemented in the SpaceshipZapZap application, but I'll be stopping short of giving a tutorial on how to build the app from the very start to the very end. My aim is to give you all the know-how around the complex bits so that you have the knowledge to not only build this app on your own but also to understand each of the features in isolation; that way, you can use them individually in future applications.

The source code for the entire SpaceshipZapZap app is available for you to download from `www.dummies.com/go/flashmobileappdevfd`. Feel free to modify and compile the application at your leisure, but please do not sell or redistribute it.

Chapter 2

Deploying Your Flash Application Natively or to the Browser

* *

In This Chapter

▶ Identifying the differences between the Flash Player and native app models

▶ Choosing a distribution method for Flash and native apps

▶ Understanding the differences in feature support between iOS and Android

* *

*N*ever before have there been so many credible ways to deliver content to mobile devices. In the past, there was only a single route to get Flash content onto a mobile device: Flash Lite. Now developers have a choice of how they decide to reach mobile device users with their Flash applications: They can deliver their application as Flash to the device's web browser or package the application to be installed and run natively on the device.

Deciding how to deploy your application almost always comes down to the target devices you're trying to reach with your application. As I mention in Chapter 1, devices such as the BlackBerry PlayBook tablet and phones running Android OS allow the use of the Flash Player in the browser, as well as allow Flash applications to be installed on the device as native applications using Adobe AIR runtime. Flash Player and AIR aren't available on iOS devices (but a work-around is available), so if your target audience includes this market segment, Flash Player alone cannot be your app's deployment vehicle. Quickly you see the decision-making process becoming a trade-off.

In this chapter, I present the three main methods used to distribute your Flash applications to mobile devices. I compare and contrast the approaches in terms of the technology used, the impact to the user, and the availability of device features.

Publishing with Flash Player or as a Native App

Before you decide to deliver native apps to your target devices, run your application in the Flash Player in the device browser, or even opt for both deployment routes to maximize the reach of your app, it helps to understand browser-based apps versus native apps.

In Chapter 1, you can find several key differences between Flash applications in the browser and applications compiled to run natively on the device. Here's a brief summary of those differences:

✔ Native apps are installed and stored on the device. Browser-based Flash apps are not installed on the device; they are stored on remote web servers.

✔ Whereas browser-based Flash applications have limited access to features on the device, native applications have full "trusted" access to the device, allowing them to use features such as local databases.

✔ Browser-based Flash applications cannot run on iOS devices, because Apple blocks Flash. Only native applications can be used to target iOS. Both native and browser-based Flash applications can be used to target Android devices.

A quick history lesson

The term *Flash mobile application* can mean a variety of things. For many years, it meant an application built to run on mobile devices via a stripped down version of Flash Player, called Flash Lite. The apps were diminished by the primitive features of the Flash Lite player, for the most part due to horrendously constrained resources on the mobile devices trying to run them. The biggest issue was that Flash Lite couldn't be installed by users — either the device shipped with it or it didn't. Things needed to change. Adobe then developed Adobe AIR and Adobe Flash Player 10.1.

The game changer

The Android operating system, Adobe AIR, and Adobe Flash Player 10.1 have vastly improved the relationship between Flash and mobile devices. Users can install the AIR and Flash Player runtimes on their mobile devices themselves — much as they can on a desktop computer. Thanks to the addition of the Packager for iPhone tool to the Flash Professional authoring tool, Flash applications can also be transformed into iOS applications that users of iOS devices can install and run natively.

Developers now have a choice of whether to distribute their content over the open Internet as Flash running in the mobile device's web browser, or package their application as a file that is installed on the mobile device's operating system as either a native Android application or a native iOS application.

Deciding which distribution mechanism (Flash Player or native app) is suitable for your application can be as simple as needing to target a specific OS (such as iOS, which requires you to distribute as a native app), though it is more likely that support for multiple platforms will form part of your strategy. The sections that follow help you weigh the pros and cons of browser-based (or Flash Player) and native deployments.

Distributing to the Flash Player

Distributing your app to run in a device's browser rather than as a native app has advantages and disadvantages in equal measures. The following sections explain what you should consider as you make your decision.

Advantages

The following is by no means an exhaustive list of the reasons to choose to deploy to Flash Player. Instead, the following points are at the top of my list:

- **No third-party approval required:** Putting your Flash application up on a web server and supplying the URL to your users are all you have to do to make your application available. You do not need to submit the app to a third party, such as Apple, to be vetted and approved at a time it determines. You retain full editorial control over your content and may publish whatever you see fit.

- **Consistent presentation on any Flash Player:** Flash Player is a platform that provides a ubiquitous experience regardless of the underlying browser or operating system. Building your application in Flash and distributing it to anyone with the Flash Player 10 runtime installed on his or her mobile device are sufficient to ensure a consistent look and behavior.

- **Ability to control who gets the application:** By delivering your app to the Flash Player in the mobile browser, you're able to use supportive technologies such as client-side JavaScript and server-side Java or .NET to determine user variables like the *user-agent string* — a string that is automatically sent with every HTTP request to the server. A user-agent string from a mobile device yields plenty of helpful information about the device requesting your application, such as the Android version and the device name, allowing you to decide whether you want to allow access. Here's a user-agent string sent from a Google Nexus One device with the Android version and device name in bold:

```
Mozilla/5.0 (Linux; U; Android 2.3.3; en-gb; Nexus One
        Build/GRI40) AppleWebKit/533.1 (KHTML, like
        Gecko) Version/4.0 Mobile Safari/533.1
```

Using server-side scripts, you can obtain the IP of the device making the request for your application. Then you can perform a geo-IP lookup of the IP address to discover where it is registered, and allow or prevent access depending on the location at the time the application is run. Controlling who gets your application may be necessary because the license for some of the content you're offering may not include your user's device type. For example, music and movie studios often separate tablets and phones into different device types requiring different licenses. Content is often licensed only to specific territories, so knowing the country in which your user is running the app may be vital in protecting your license agreements.

✔ **No digital certificates required:** Because a Flash application is distributed over the Internet using conventional web protocols and is run in the web browser with Adobe Flash Player, your application doesn't run directly on the device's operating system, where code-signing is mandatory. Because signing isn't required in this environment, you can skip the task of obtaining and including digital certificates. I discuss signing your AIR for Android and iOS applications with digital certificates in more detail in Chapters 13 and 16, respectively.

✔ **No fees or license agreements:** Directly distributing your Flash application to your users from your own web server exempts you from having to sign up with developer programs like those for iOS and Android. Both programs incur an enrollment fee and also require you to agree to sometimes lengthy terms of service. In Apple's case, this agreement can often dictate how you are allowed to monetize your application and what the app is allowed to do.

Disadvantages

As with all pleasures in life, there comes pain, and choosing to deploy to the browser brings a set of disadvantages that you may or may not be able to tolerate. The following are the most important ones to consider:

✔ **Internet connection required to use application:** Because your application is delivered from your web server to the mobile device's web browser each time a user wants to view it, the device must have an active Internet connection available. This can become a problem when the user is out of range of both a Wi-Fi signal and a cellular network, such as when traveling through a tunnel. Under these circumstances, the user wouldn't be able to use your application.

Another consideration is the amount of data that must be downloaded. A Flash application in the web browser has to be downloaded every time it's used. This behavior can result in the user waiting for the application to download and initialize and can use data from the user's data plan, possibly incurring extra costs. Users are far less likely to use an application that costs them money every time they run it.

✔ **Harder for users to find your content:** Deploying to the web browser means going it alone, outside the relative warmth of the app stores. Getting your app in an app store means the app is trumpeted to millions of interested users. As a browser-based app, your application is left in the vast expanse of the Internet. For example, the Apple App Store has more than 350,000 apps, which is a lot to sift through. Google indexes more than 40 billion web pages, which is even more to sift through. Your app is far less discoverable to your users when it's hosted outside an app store system.

Another reason why users will struggle to discover your content is that they'll first need to know they're looking for it. Using the web alone, no mechanism exists for them to browse to your application by purpose or genre. The closest you'll come is typing a search term into Google and hoping that your application comes up at the top of the page!

✔ **No icon or single-touch access:** Because your application isn't installed on the device's operating system, no application icon is placed in the menu system. Without this highly prized piece of real estate on a user's device, the user is unable to arrive at your application with a single touch of the application icon. Instead, he has to launch the web browser and type the URL of your application.

✔ **Restricted access to device features:** To deploy to the Flash Player, the browser places your application in a container — or security sandbox — isolated from the rest of the operating system. The mobile device's operating system doesn't trust content coming from the Internet as much as it would a signed application installed on the device. Because the application is held at arm's length, certain device features that would be available to the application if it were installed on the device aren't available to it in the browser, such as geolocation services provided by the device, preventing the device from going to sleep, and storing data on the device in a local database.

✔ **No access to iOS devices:** As mentioned, Apple bans Flash Player from iOS devices. This means that iOS users cannot view Flash applications in their web browser. A deployment of a Flash application to the web browser would not reach these users.

✔ **Browser may limit performance:** When using Flash Player to deploy your app, the application is embedded as an object in an HTML page, then the HTML page is rendered in the device's web browser. Although you can tweak the application to improve rendering performance in a web browser context, additional web browser processes are still running in conjunction with your Flash application that will have some effect on performance. For instance, all web requests that your application makes will be marshaled by the browser, adding an intermediary to every transaction with a remote server. The browser is also running code of its own concurrently with yours, so both will be vying for time on the device's limited hardware.

Distributing as a Native App

Much as distributing your application to the Flash Player has its pros and cons, distributing it as a native application brings its own set of advantages and disadvantages. The following sections summarize the key points.

Advantages

Distributing your application as a native app on the device operating system has plenty of advantages. The best of these follow:

- **Icon visible on device menu:** As a native application installed on a mobile device, you are awarded a place for your app's icon on the device's application menu where users can get to your application's content with a single touch of the app icon. Taking minimal steps to reach content is often seen as the holy grail of a good user experience. Having this kind of prominence for your app maximizes your chances of repeated use and creates a highly desirable degree of stickiness — the more sticky an experience, the higher the likelihood that a user will come back for a repeat experience.

- **Full access to device features:** Operating as a fully integrated and trusted application on the mobile device, your app is able to access the full suite of device features presented to you through the Flash application programming interface (API). For instance, your app can store data on the device in a local database, access the device's location through the geolocation services, and prevent the device from going to sleep when your application is being used.

- **No Internet access required to run the application:** After the application is downloaded and installed, no further downloads of the application file need to take place for the user to run it. The application might have dependencies on the Internet for the content it displays within, but the application itself will launch immediately irrespective of the presence of an active connection.

- **Better performance than in the browser:** Running directly on the mobile device's operating system affords the application better access to the device hardware to facilitate faster computation and improved graphics rendering performance.

- **Easier for users to find your content:** Looking again at Google's 40 billion web pages versus the App Store's 350,000 apps, the chances of being discovered in a smaller pond are higher. On top of this, App Store users are a captive and perfectly filtered set of individuals. By this I mean that they're iOS device users, looking for an app, fitting the keywords matching your app. The propensity to download is far greater than the average user coming across your application on Google — many of whom may not even be using a mobile device.

Disadvantages

Although the native application is the magic bullet for many budding Flash mobile application developers, this approach has a few disadvantages:

- **Developer program fees and agreements:** Both the iOS and Android developer programs cost money to join, and membership is compulsory if you want to publish your applications in their respective stores. In addition, you'll have to agree to be bound by fairly exhaustive terms and conditions that may restrict some of the things you planned to do with your application.

- **Limited control over who gets the application:** Distributing an application using a third-party app store gives you limited control over who can obtain your application. Although it's possible to restrict the territories your app is made available to, and preclude certain operating system versions, it isn't possible to use your own server-side code to preclude specific devices or mandate a highly customized set of system requirements.

   Controlling who gets your application may be necessary because your app may be subject to legislation that prevents you from delivering your content to certain territories.

- **Digital certificates required to sign the application:** Both Android OS and iOS require applications to be signed using a digital certificate. Although Android is slightly more relaxed about the whole affair, allowing developers to use an easier process of self-signing, Apple is extremely regimented and requires developers to obtain certificates from Apple. This process is time-consuming and, if done incorrectly, can lead to applications being rejected from app stores, particularly the Apple App Store.

- **Third-party control over availability of the application:** After your application is submitted to either the Android Market or Apple App Store, your application's availability is governed entirely by a third party (the store). If Apple decides it doesn't like your application, for whatever reason, it won't be available to users of iOS devices. Less likely, but worth mentioning, is that should Google take a dislike to your application, it reserves the right to remove it from the Android Market.

   The loss of control over the availability of your application can prove problematic when you're trying to release an update to your application. You may want your users to benefit from bug fixes you've made in the update as soon as you're ready to ship, but suddenly you're delayed indefinitely at the behest of the third party.

Supporting Native Features on iOS and Android

Before finally deciding whether to deploy as a browser-based application via Flash Player or a full-fledged native application, it's worth knowing what device features are made available to native applications targeting AIR for Android versus applications packaged for iOS — using the Packager for iPhone tool in Flash Professional. The AIR 2.5 SDK (Software Development Kit) comes bundled in Flash Professional CS5 — the software you use to build both browser-based and native Flash mobile applications. With version 2.5 of the SDK a number of features cannot be used on iOS. In the AIR 2.6 SDK update, which shipped with Flash Professional CS5.5 (a newer version of the Flash development software), Adobe filled in the blanks and created parity between Android and iOS support.

Table 2-1 provides a summary of what you can and can't do with your Flash mobile application on each mobile operating system, using the AIR 2.5 SDK.

Table 2-1	AIR 2.5 (Flash Professional CS5)	
Flash API	*Android Support*	*iOS Support*
Microphone	✓	
Camera	✓	
StageWebView	✓	
CameraRoll	✓	Add only
Accelerometer	✓	✓
File (Read/Write)	✓	✓
SQLite (Local)	✓	✓
Geolocation	✓	✓
Touch/Gesture	✓	✓

Table 2-2 shows the improvement in the support for mobile device features in your Flash mobile application when you use the AIR 2.6 SDK, made available with Flash CS5.5.

Table 2-2	AIR 2.6 (Flash Professional CS5.5)	
Flash API	*Android Support*	*iOS Support*
Microphone	✓	✓
Camera	✓	✓
StageWebView	✓	✓
CameraRoll	✓	✓
Accelerometer	✓	✓
File (Read/Write)	✓	✓
SQLite (Local)	✓	✓
Geolocation	✓	✓
Touch/Gesture	✓	✓

If you're using Flash Professional CS5, be mindful of the missing support for the Microphone, Camera, and StageWebView classes for iOS. If your app needs to use these elements, and you want to target iOS, you'll need to upgrade to AIR 2.6 (Flash Professional CS5.5 or better).

Chapter 3

Understanding the Process of Creating a Flash Mobile App

In This Chapter

▶ Preparing Flash applications for use on Android OS and iPhone OS (iOS)

▶ Planning the development lifecycle for a Flash mobile application

*T*he clever people at Adobe have toiled over the intricacies of both the iOS and Android platforms so that you don't need to worry about these details yourself when you build your application. You build mobile apps as you would any other Flash application: You select the device to target (iOS or Android), and then the development software (Flash Professional) decides what to do to make everything you've created work on the platform you're targeting.

It's easy to remain oblivious to what's happening behind the scenes when you see the finished application generated at the push of a button. I feel it's important to understand the underlying processes that are occurring, though, so that you are better informed when it comes to making decisions about performance, as well as to understand why API access might be limited — that is, why certain features you have in your application may work on one target platform but not another.

From this point forward, I focus your attention on the development of Flash mobile applications that run natively on the target mobile device. This "Flash in a browser" route is a lot simpler and more established than the native app route. Furthermore, the development practices that I cover later are fully transferrable to the development of Flash applications that run in the web browser. So if you are considering a browser-based app, all the development chapters remain highly relevant.

In this chapter, I dive under the hood of the compilation and packaging processes for both AIR for Android and iOS, before discussing how to plan your mobile application project.

Compiling and Packaging Flash Apps for Android OS

Flash applications that target the Android platform are actually Adobe AIR applications that run in the AIR for Android runtime. Before the application can be run on a mobile device, the user must first have installed the AIR for Android runtime (available for free from the Android Market) on his phone. When the user launches your application, it appears to be a native app.

To install an AIR for Android application file on an Android device, the file must be a recognizable Android file with the APK extension. To create this file, the application must be placed inside an APK file in a process called *packaging*. Figure 3-1 shows how packaging works for an AIR for Android application.

Following is an overview of the major — but largely hidden — actions that take an application from a Flash file on your desktop to an APK file running on an Android device:

1. Compile ActionScript.

   First, the Flash FLA file and any dependent ActionScript 3.0 files are fed into the Flash compiler. The compiler reads the contents of the FLA file and compiles them and all the ActionScript into ActionScript Byte Code (ABC) to create an SWF file. If a Flash application were to be deployed to a web browser, the compilation process would end here. Because the application isn't destined for an environment in which it can run in the Flash Player (that is, a web browser), the process must continue to further process the file.

2. Package for native installation.

   An application called the AIR Developer Tool (ADT) takes the SWF file that the ActionScript compiler generates and creates an APK file into which the SWF file is placed, along with some configuration files that tell the host device what to do with the file. ThisAPK file is often referred to as a *package*.

3. Install natively on the device.

   The APK file is installed on the Android device as any other Android application would be.

4. Invoke AIR for Android runtime.

   When the user runs the application, supplementary information in the native application file tells the Android operating system to run the SWF file stored inside using the AIR for Android app installed on the device. If the runtime hasn't yet been installed, the user is shown a screen inviting him or her to install it, as shown in Figure 3-2.

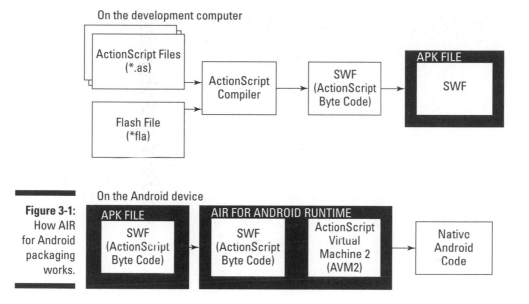

On the development computer

Figure 3-1: How AIR for Android packaging works.

5. Interpret with the ActionScript Virtual Machine.

The ActionScript Virtual Machine, Version 2 (AVM2) — a piece of software acting as an intermediary between your application and the Android operating system — running as a part of the AIR for Android runtime takes the ActionScript Byte Code (ABC) in the SWF file and makes on-the-fly translations of this code to native code that the Android operating system can understand. The output of this is the graphics that the user sees rendered on the screen and the sounds that he hears. At the same time, the AVM2 receives instructions from the Android operating system in native code, notifying your application of interactions with the device, location, and connectivity changes. AVM2 translates these to ABC to permit your application to be able to handle them.

The process is a lot to take in, but I'm sure that you feel a little less in the dark about what's going on behind the scenes to get your application running on an Android device. You might even be forgiven for thinking that it sounds a little brittle in its nature, though I can assure you it's anything but. The solution is sturdy and reliable from a development perspective. In addition, having installed the AIR for Android runtime once, the user is never pestered again, no matter how many AIR for Android apps she later goes on to install. To her, the process is seamless.

Compiling and Packaging Flash Apps for iPhone OS (iOS)

iPhone OS is a different paradigm than AIR for Android. As Apple does not permit the Flash Player or *interpreted code* — code that isn't native to the device and is interpreted using a third-party runtime — the Flash application must be entirely translated into native code for iPhone OS. This effectively means that the file you ship must be an iOS app written with iOS code. Don't worry, though, you're not being asked to do this! As I explain in Chapter 1, cross-compilation allows you to translate Flash code into native iOS code.

A supplementary piece of software that is bolted onto Flash Professional, called Packager for iPhone, is responsible for the unenviable task of translating the contents of a Flash application file, and its associated ActionScript documents, into a native iOS IPA file. The process that does this is shown in Figure 3-3.

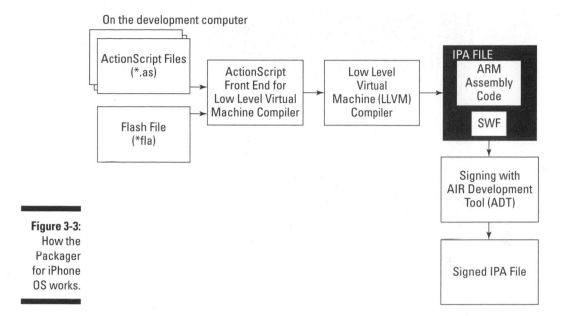

On the development computer

Figure 3-3:
How the
Packager
for iPhone
OS works.

Taking a closer look at the steps in the packaging process, here are the key hurdles that the Packager for iPhone software gallops over:

✔ **Preparation for the Low Level Virtual Machine:** The Flash FLA file and any dependent ActionScript 3.0 documents are fed into a *front end* — or preparation module — that enables a piece of licensed third-party software called the Low Level Virtual Machine (LLVM) to be able to understand ActionScript Byte Code (ABC).

✔ **Translation and optimization to native code:** The LLVM takes the ActionScript code and converts it into ARM — a make of processor found in iOS devices — assembly code, which can be run natively on iOS. The output of this process is an IPA file that contains the assembly code and an SWF file that contains the graphics used in the application. No ActionScript code exists beyond this point, as there is nothing in iOS that would be able to interpret it.

✔ **Signing the digital certificate:** The application must be signed with the appropriate digital certificate carried out by another discrete application called the AIR Development Tool. The output is an IPA file that installs and runs on iOS devices as a native application.

After reading that, I'd understand you holding on to the fear that things might get lost in translation. The reality is that you can forget the notion of "lost" and instead keep at the back of your mind the idea that some of your Flash-based behavior might not perform as well when executed on top of a completely different software architecture. Everything will be there, but you may have to fine-tune it.

Understanding the App Development Process

Creating an application from scratch can seem like a daunting process. By breaking the process down into a series of steps, you can be sure of not only making steady progress with a clear plan of attack but also ensuring that your tasks are performed in the right order. In application development, assembling a list of tasks in the right order prevents rework further down the line. Follow these steps sequentially, and you're well on your way to delivering your first mobile application on time and to the specifications required:

1. Design your app.

2. Develop your app.

3. Compile your app.

4. Package your app.

5. Sign your app's certificate.

6. Deploy your app on a mobile device.

7. Test your app on a mobile device.

8. Submit your app to an app store.

9. Put your app live.

Starting from the top, I'll now elaborate on what is meant by each of these terms and the functions that should be performed to satisfy them.

Designing your app

Design is more than drawing a picture on a piece of paper or mocking up your app's welcome screen in a graphics editing package. The design phase of your project should incorporate considerations such as the following:

- Why is an app being built? What problem is it trying to solve?
- Who is the audience?
- What fundamental tasks must the app perform to be considered complete?
- What criteria will be used to assess how successful the app is?

After you've established these points, you're safe to move on to thinking about the *information architecture* of the application. Information architecture is the detail of how information is presented to the user on the screen, and how the user is expected to interact with that information. Information architecture is not what color the screen is, what fonts are used, or the transitions from screen to screen. A common approach to information architecture is to create *wireframes*. Wireframes are very bland-looking skeletal sketches that serve to demonstrate the base dimensions of key elements. Wireframes also express the hierarchy of information in your application — displayed in a manner that focuses attention on the prominence, order, and functionality of content. The wireframe example shown in Figure 3-4 was generated using a handy tool called Balsamiq. You can download a time-limited trial of this software from `http://balsamiq.com`.

A wireframe is meant to evolve. As you progress, you'll move things around, increase and decrease the prominence of elements, and remove certain elements entirely.

After the wireframe is complete, you can begin to think about applying color and fonts to the wireframe, which leads to the first complete visual design. In addition, now is a good time to consider the transitions between screens and how to reveal or conceal information to help the user progress through the application efficiently. This process is often referred to as *interaction design*.

The design process can and should go through numerous iterations before being considered complete. Having designed the application to a high level of confidence, you can move on to the development phase of the project, knowing that a credible blueprint is on the table.

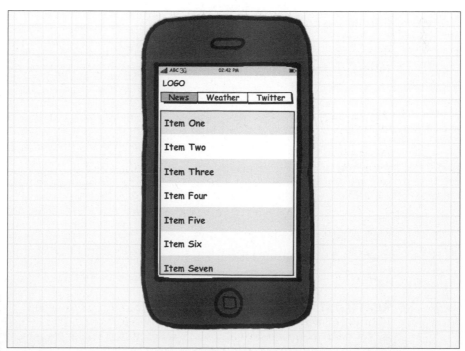

Figure 3-4:
A wireframe.

Developing your app

The fun begins! You fire up Flash Professional and code away until it's complete, right? To a degree, yes, but before you do, spend a little time answering these commonly overlooked questions:

- ✔ **Where are you keeping your code?** Hard drives are notoriously unfaithful beasts, letting you down at just the moment you need them to be there for you. Don't have your introductory foray into mobile application development with Flash marred by a drive failure, burglary, or meteor impact. Source control solutions, such as the one provided by Github (`https://github.com`), offer a secure way to remotely store any version changes you make to your application source. No matter what happens to your local development machine, as long as your code is in a remote source control system, you'll be able to recover easily from any disaster.

- ✔ **What is the milestone?** If you're working for a client, it's unwise to wait until you've finished the application before you show him or her anything. If the client doesn't like it, you might end up doing a lot of rework — and that's a very dirty word! Even if you're not building the app for someone else, it's worth laying down some objectives that you aim to achieve by a specific date. Much like marathon runners work to the next mile marker, your project will greatly benefit from being broken down into smaller chunks. Setting milestones also leads nicely into the next point of verifying that your app works.

- ✔ **Theoretically your app works, but does it work in reality?** Writing the code and creating the graphics in line with the recommendations of the document are all well and good, but you can only rely on that so far. Mobile application development involves myriad operating systems and hardware configurations, all of which can affect the way your application is expected to behave. It's a crying shame when a developer makes a great swath of changes to an application, only to find that one, or all of them, have broken the application when it's put onto a target device. The developer is left unpicking all the changes until things start working again. All of this is easily avoided by regularly deploying your application to target devices to test the changes. Device testing, whenever you try something experimental or when you reach a milestone in your project, ensures a pleasant conclusion to your development phase.

After reaching a logical point in the development of your application, you can compile it to see what it looks like and how well it functions.

Compiling your app

Compilation takes place on the development machine, using the tools in Flash Professional. Compilation alerts you to incomplete code or missing dependencies in your application, as well as provides you with a visual output that enables you to perform rudimentary testing of your application's features. For the most part, compilation will snag the majority of the big defects in your application.

Beyond validating the state of your application, compilation is the first step in the process of deploying a Flash application. After compilation, an SWF file is generated that can be used in browser-based distribution, but for native mobile application distribution, you must complete a process called *packaging*.

Packaging your app

Packaging your application comes about after it has successfully compiled as a Flash application. The Flash Professional software takes your application, cross-compiles it where necessary, and places it in the application container required for the target device's operating system. Compiling and packaging steps for Android are covered in Chapter 13 and for iOS in Chapter 16.

Signing your app's certificate

Applications that are installed natively on both the Android and iOS platforms must be signed with a digital certificate. This signing process is a way of guaranteeing that the code originated from you and has not been tampered with since it was signed. Although Flash Professional handles code signing for you, you must specify your certificates before the compiling and packaging processes can commence. After the application is compiled, any certificates you specified in Flash Professional are automatically applied. Signing your Flash mobile application is covered in detail in Chapter 13 for Android and Chapter 16 for iOS.

Deploying your app on a mobile device

Deployment is the act of releasing code into an environment that is either the live environment or representative of it. For Flash mobile application development, the deployment is to one or more test devices that you use to evaluate your application on. These devices are connected to your development computer, and the deployment process involves copying your application file onto the device and installing it. The deployment process is covered in full in Chapter 14 for Android and Chapter 17 for iOS.

Testing your app on a mobile device

With an application successfully deployed to your test device, you now need to make sure that features you're testing work as expected. Testing also involves assessing what the application does under stress, spotting where bottlenecks appear, and identifying scenarios that lead to a crash. Testing is integral to development for mobile devices, and neglecting to properly test your app will lead to headaches further down the line. Advice on how to test your app properly is covered in Chapter 18.

Submitting your app to an app store

Having gone through the sufficient iterations of developing and testing, you're ready to submit the application to either the Android Market or Apple App Store for distribution. The steps for submission to each store are covered in Chapters 19 and 20, respectively.

Putting your app live

After you've completed the submission process, and the necessary checks are performed by Apple or Google — who will distribute your application — your application becomes available to the world and is considered live. At this point, you can pat yourself on the back for a job well done and await the positive reviews — oh, and I should mention here that you could get negative ones too!

Beyond live comes further enhancements and bug fixes for your application that you release as updates. I'd recommend treating the process of developing an update for your application in the same manner as starting an application from scratch. Set clear goals again, go back to the design phase, and work forward from there.

Part II
Creating a Flash Application for Mobile Devices

The 5th Wave   By Rich Tennant

"You ever notice how much more streaming media there is than there used to be?"

In this part . . .

Part II is where you roll your sleeves up and get stuck in. Elbow grease and concentration are the order of the day, but there's a lot of fun to be had on the way, and the end result will be the apple of your eye.

Chapter 4 shows you how to begin a new Flash mobile application project. Chapter 5 looks at how to design and assemble a user interface, and Chapter 6 goes on to show you how to write the code of your application that makes it work on a mobile device. Chapter 7 looks at how you solicit and handle data that your users enter. Chapter 8 looks at how to transmit data between your application and remote web servers.

Chapter 4

Building a Mobile Flash Application with Flash Professional

*E*very task has a preferred tool that makes the overall job easier. If you're developing Flash mobile applications, your preferred tool is Flash Professional — sometimes referred to as *the Flash IDE,* or Integrated Development Environment.

From creating the base application file into which you store all your visual assets to compiling and packaging your completed application, Flash Professional will always be open on your desktop as you create your apps because it underpins the whole process.

In this chapter, I help you get familiar with Flash Professional so that you feel comfortable enough to start a brand new mobile application project. In subsequent chapters, you find out how to build upon this new application to eventually reach a state where you can deploy it to a mobile device.

Introducing Flash Professional

Flash Professional forms one element of a larger software package called Creative Suite (CS). This package includes graphics-editing tools such as Adobe Illustrator, Photoshop, and Fireworks, as well as code-editing tools such as Adobe Flash Builder and Dreamweaver. If you don't already have Creative Suite, you can download a full-featured, time-limited trial from Adobe at www.adobe.com/go/trywebpremium, or if you would rather install Flash Professional on its own without the rest of the products, you can obtain a trial of this application from `www.adobe.com/go/tryflash`. Having downloaded the chosen software package, you need to run through the relatively simple installation process for your operating system.

Flash Professional is the main authoring environment for creating Flash applications. It allows the developer to create content that renders consistently across a variety of web browsers, operating systems, and most recently, mobile devices. Built initially by Macromedia, Adobe acquired Flash Professional — along with the Flash runtime — when it bought Macromedia in 2005.

Flash Professional is certainly a unique tool in its class, allowing the creation of rich graphics in a *WYSIWYG* (What You See Is What You Get) — pronounced *wizzy-wig* — interface. In addition to strong graphics creation and manipulation, Flash Professional layers on rich frame-by-frame animation tools and offers the ability to program applications using a robust language called ActionScript 3.0. Combining the graphics, animation, and code is what has helped Flash to be what it is today on the web, and what has helped Flash Professional to be such a popular authoring environment.

Now that you are officially introduced to Flash Professional and the software is downloaded and installed, it's time to acquaint you with some of the nifty features it incorporates in its latest version.

Familiarizing Yourself with Flash Professional's New Features

The newest versions of Flash Professional focus heavily on being able to create applications for multiple mobile device platforms, such as Android and iOS, without needing the coding knowledge to develop for each of these different operating systems. The following sections provide a summary of the useful enhancements that Adobe has added to Flash Professional.

Packaging for mobile devices

Flash Professional introduced fully integrated development and packaging for both iPhone OS and AIR for Android applications in a single software application for the first time. If you wanted to build an app for the iPhone before these features were added to Flash Professional, you had to learn to code in Objective-C and use Apple's Xcode development software. If you wanted to target Android devices, you had to learn Java and use the Eclipse development tool. Even for an experienced developer, learning two distinct programming languages and two different development tools is quite an effort! Allowing developers to build applications that run natively on iOS and Android devices, in the same way that they build Flash applications for the web, created the potential for huge cost efficiencies — you effectively develop the app once and deploy it to multiple platforms using the built-in publishing tools.

Choice of code-editing environment

Creative Suite 5 saw Flash Builder 4 — Adobe's high-end code development tool — included for the first time as an integral part of the suite. Along with its inclusion came the integration between it and its older sister, Flash Professional. When choosing to create or edit ActionScript 3.0 classes — files that contain ActionScript 3.0 code — if you have Flash Builder 4 installed, Flash Professional now asks whether you would like to edit the class using the code editor in Flash Professional or the advanced code-editing capabilities offered by Flash Builder. For small snippets of code, you can opt to edit quickly in Flash Professional. For more involved application code, you can opt to step out of Flash Professional and into Flash Builder.

Auto-completion and code hinting

Editing code in Flash Professional has long been a painful and long-winded experience. The text editor into which you typed code was a primitive creature, doing very little to help you as you fumbled through the myriad ActionScript classes available to you. Fortunately, the product team behind Flash Professional finally heard the cries of the Flash community and improved the code editor in Flash Professional. As you type, the editor now offers code suggestions, or code hints, that you accept by pressing the Enter key — Flash Professional completes the code for you. In addition to the auto-completion of code as you type, Flash Professional also manages easily forgotten class import statements for you — removing the need to type all of these yourself. This automation has been a significant leap forward for code editing in Flash Professional, making it possible to write more complicated ActionScript code faster and with a greater sense of reliability.

Resource sharing

Resource sharing brings consistency and productivity gains to your Flash application development. Resource sharing allows visual assets, like graphics and buttons that would have conventionally been stored in a library inside an application source file, to instead be stored outside of the file. Storing assets this way allows developers to maintain a single set of assets and allows that set to be used by other application source files. This means, for example, that as the styling of a button is modified in the resource file, all the applications that reference that button receive the changes. This is really handy when you're managing one application file for your iPhone OS application and another for your AIR for Android application; both can draw from the same assets library.

Starting a Project in Flash Professional

A project in Flash Professional starts life when you create a new FLA — **FL**ash **A**pplication — file. This is a binary file format that is able to store graphics, code, and settings for your application. It's also the file that Flash Professional takes as the input when it compiles and packages your application into one of three output formats that I discuss in this book: an SWF (**S**hock**W**ave **F**lash) file for use in web browsers, an IPA (**IP**hone **A**pplication) file for use on iOS devices, and an APK (**A**ndroid **PacK**age) file.

When creating mobile Flash applications that target either a mobile web browser (Flash Player), the AIR for Android runtime, or the iPhone Operating System (iOS), you need to create a separate FLA file for each of them. At first, it might seem cumbersome and laborious to have separate FLA files for the three target platforms, but you can share code and assets across them all. This means that the FLA files merely act as the container for settings that are specific to their target platform. For example, my AIR for Android FLA file contains settings that are required only for Android applications, whereas my iPhone OS FLA file has settings relevant only to iOS. Both of my applications reference the same files containing code, requiring me to write code once for both of the applications. Suddenly it's sounding a little less cumbersome, right? In the following sections, I show you how to create three FLA files: one each for Flash Player, AIR for Android, and iOS.

Setting up a browser-based Flash application

By a browser-based Flash application, I'm referring to a Flash application that is packaged as an SWF file, embedded in an HTML page, and viewed in a web browser on the mobile device. This has been the traditional way of deploying Flash applications and has benefits over app-based distribution, as I discuss in Chapter 2.

Follow these steps to start a new browser-based Flash application in Flash Professional:

1. **Launch Flash Professional.**

   The application launches to the welcome screen, as shown in Figure 4-1.

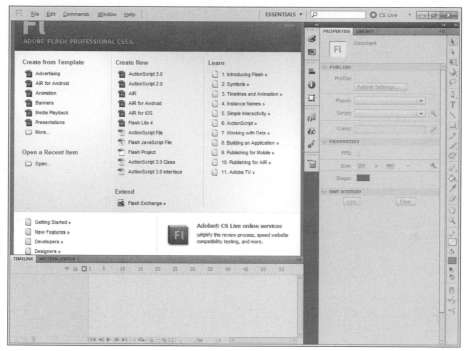

Figure 4-1:
The Flash
Professional
welcome
screen.

2. Click ActionScript 3.0 in the Create New list.

Alternatively, choose File➪New and then select ActionScript 3.0 from the General tab and click OK.

A new ActionScript 3.0 Flash application is created in the main window, as shown in Figure 4-2.

3. Choose File➪Publish Settings.

Alternatively, press Shift+Ctrl+F12 (Windows) or Shift+Fn+Option+F12 (Mac).

The Publish Settings dialog box opens. This is where you configure the settings specific to your Flash application.

4. Click the Flash (.swf) item in the list on the left.

The Flash Publish Settings dialog box is displayed, as shown in Figure 4-3.

5. Set the Player drop-down list to Flash Player 10.

This option should already be selected; if not, use the pull-down menu to change it.

6. Set the Script drop-down list to ActionScript 3.0.

This option should already be selected; if not, use the pull-down menu to change it.

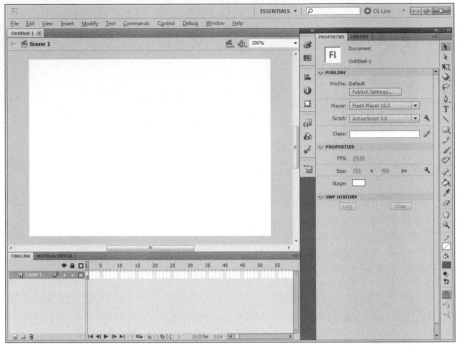

Figure 4-2:
A new Flash application created in Flash Professional.

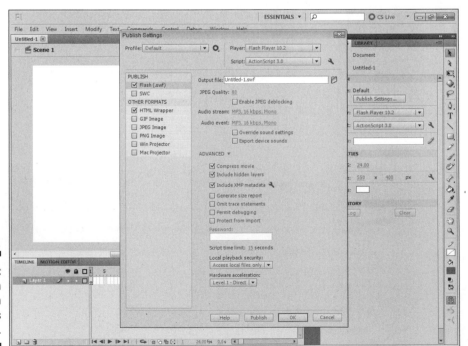

Figure 4-3:
The Flash Publish Settings dialog box.

7. **Set the Hardware Acceleration drop-down list to Level 1 - Direct.**

   By default, Flash Professional sets hardware acceleration to None. The application needs to able to allow Flash Player on a mobile device to draw directly on the screen instead of letting the browser do the drawing, so this setting should be changed.

8. **Click the HTML item in the list on the left.**

   Settings relating to the HTML file that Flash Professional generates during publishing are displayed.

9. **Select the Detect Flash Version check box.**

   The Version fields below it become enabled.

10. **Enter 1 in the first Version field and 0 in the second.**

    The Flash Player versions your app targets as 10.1.0. This is the lowest version of Flash Player that your browser-based Flash mobile application can target.

11. **Click OK.**

    The Publish Settings dialog box is closed and the settings are saved.

12. **Press Ctrl+S (Windows) or Command+S (Mac) to save your application FLA file.**

    The file system Save dialog box opens for you to choose a location to save your FLA file to.

13. **Enter a filename and click Save.**

    The FLA file and its settings are stored on your computer's file system.

The browser-based Flash application is now ready, and you can start adding code and graphics to it. Before you do that, however, you may want to skip to the "Changing Document Settings" section, later in this chapter, to see how to modify the default appearance of your application.

Setting up an AIR for Android application

Follow these steps to create a new AIR for Android application in Flash Professional:

1. **Launch Flash Professional.**

   The application launches to the welcome screen, as shown in Figure 4-1.

2. **Click AIR for Android in the Create from Template list.**

   An alternative is to choose File⇨New and then select AIR for Android from the Templates tab and click OK.

The New from Template dialog box displays, with the AIR for Android category selected and 800 x 480 Blank selected in the Templates box, as shown in Figure 4-4.

3. **Click OK.**

A new AIR for Android application is created in the main window.

4. **Press Ctrl+S (Windows) or Command+S (Mac) to save your application FLA file.**

The file system Save dialog box opens.

5. **Enter the filename** SpaceshipZapZapAndroid.fla **and click Save.**

The AIR for Android FLA file and its settings are stored on your computer's file system.

You can now start working in your AIR for Android application. Later in the chapter, in the "Changing Document Settings" section, I show you how to modify the default appearance of your application.

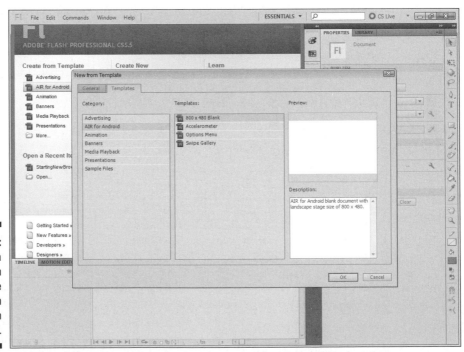

Figure 4-4:
Creating a
New from
Template
application
in Flash
Professional.

Setting up an iOS application

Follow these steps to start a new AIR for Android application in Flash Professional:

1. **Launch Flash Professional.**

   The application launches to the welcome screen, as shown in Figure 4-1.

2. **Click AIR for iOS in the Create New list.**

   Alternatively, select File⇨New and then select AIR for iOS from the General tab and click OK.

   A new iPhone OS application is created in the main window.

3. **Press Ctrl+S (Windows) or Command+S (Mac) to save your application FLA file.**

   The file system Save dialog box opens.

4. **Enter the filename** SpaceshipZapZapiOS.fla **and click Save.**

   The iOS FLA file and its settings are stored on your computer's file system.

Having created your three new application files in Flash Professional, the next step is to ensure that the applications' settings are configured the way that you need them.

Changing Document Settings

When you create an application with Flash Professional, a handful of default configurations are applied. Although these defaults serve most scenarios reasonably well, in some instances, they're not quite right. Most of the core settings for your Flash application, such as the background color, frame rate, and dimensions, can be altered quickly and easily in the Document Settings dialog box.

Setting the background color

The background color, as the name suggests, is the default color that Flash Player will use as the background of your application. By default, applications are assigned a white solid fill background color. Setting a suitable background color for your application, rather than drawing a shape the size of the background, causes less work for the application, and therefore causes less work for the mobile device on which it's running. Why? Any shape in the display list must be measured and drawn in each rendering cycle; one less shape means less computation to render the display. Less work for the mobile device means that your application runs smoother and doesn't hog the limited resources available to the device.

In the steps that follow, I show you how to change the background color to black:

1. **Choose Modify⇨Document.**

   Alternatively, press Ctrl+J (Windows) or Command+J (Mac).

   The Document Settings dialog box opens, as shown in Figure 4-5.

2. **Click the Background Color white square.**

   A color picker dialog box opens.

3. **Select the color #000000 (black).**

   The color picker closes and the Background Color square becomes black.

4. **Click OK to save the changes.**

   The Document Settings dialog box closes.

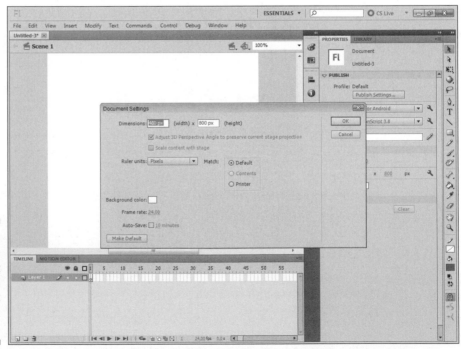

Figure 4-5:
The
Document
Settings
dialog box
in Flash
Professional.

Because you've changed the background color, anytime your application has redundant space — areas of your display where you haven't placed any graphical objects — it will be filled with the background color you configured. You can change the background color at any point in the development of your application by altering the Background Color value in the Document Settings dialog box.

Setting the frame rate

Flash applications run around the context of frames. Much like a video is comprised of frames that are played at a certain rate per second, a Flash application "plays" at a frame rate defined in the application settings. This frame rate governs the speed at which frame-by-frame animation runs in the Timeline, and also the speed at which events linked to frames being "played" execute at. For example, the default frame rate for a Flash application is 24 FPS (Frames Per Second). If you had a piece of code that was executed on each frame, the application would execute the code 24 times each second.

The best frame rate to use for your application is the lowest one. The higher the frame rate, the more tasks per second the central processing unit (CPU) on the mobile device has to execute. By keeping the frame rate as low as you can, you minimize the work that the CPU needs to do, thereby improving overall performance and reducing the device's battery usage. As a ballpark estimation, try to keep your frame rate at 24 FPS; increase this rate only if your application is unable to function correctly.

Here's how to modify the frame rate of your application (in this example, you will change from 24 FPS to 30 FPS):

1. **Choose Modify⇨Document.**

   Alternatively, press Ctrl+J (Windows) or Command+J (Mac).

   The Document Settings dialog box opens, as shown in Figure 4-5.

2. **Click the Frame Rate value and type** 30.

   You see the Frame Rate label at the lower-left corner of the dialog box. Next to this label is a text field that becomes editable when clicked.

3. **Click OK to save the changes.**

   The Document Settings dialog box closes. The frame rate for the application is now set to 30 FPS.

4. **Repeat Steps 1 to 3 to reset the frame rate back to 24 FPS.**

   Lower frame rates usually perform better. You now know how to increase or decrease the frame rate if your application requires it.

The frame rate modification applies to the entire application, and the setting is saved with the FLA file. Each FLA has its own configurable frame rate setting, so you can have one FLA saved with a frame rate of 24 FPS and another with a frame rate of 30 FPS.

Changing dimensions

Although width and height for iOS and AIR for Android applications are preconfigured by Flash Professional to correctly fit the screen of the device you're targeting, you will need to modify the dimensions of a browser-based Flash application yourself.

The following steps show you how to modify the width and height of a browser-based Flash application:

1. **Choose Modify⇨Document.**

   Alternatively, press Ctrl+J (Windows) or Command+J (Mac).

   The Document Settings dialog box opens (refer to Figure 4-5). Note that the dimensions of the document are specified as a width and a height value in pixels (px).

2. **Click the first Dimensions value (width) and type** 480.

3. **Click the second Dimensions value (height) and type** 800.

4. **Click OK to save the changes.**

   The Document Settings dialog box closes.

Changing the dimensions of your application can have a detrimental impact on the layout of visual elements when undertaken toward the completion of your application. Because of this, you should work out what the dimensions of the complete application will need to be before starting work.

With an FLA file started and configured in Flash Professional, now would be an appropriate time to walk you around the workspace in Flash Professional so that you know where all the important pieces are.

Finding Your Way around Flash Professional

With a new application open in Flash Professional, your default workspace is presented to you, as shown in Figure 4-6.

Main menu or application bar   Collapsed panel group   Library panel

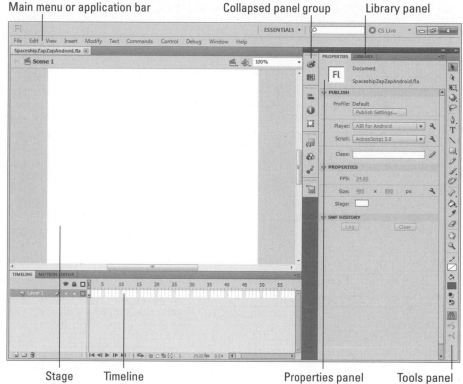

Figure 4-6:
The default
workspace
in Flash
Professional.

Stage   Timeline   Properties panel   Tools panel

The Essentials workspace satisfies most of the work that you'll be doing in Flash Professional, and it is selected for you by default. Working clockwise around the application from the left, you see the following:

✔ **Stage:** This is the largest part of the workspace and is the place where graphical elements are placed — either manually by you or using code. The stage is also where you create drawings.

✔ **Main menu or application bar:** This is where you can find all the menus and options relating to the Flash Professional application and all of its features.

✔ **Collapsed panel group:** Sandwiched between the stage and the neighboring Properties panel is a thin vertical strip of icons, with small, left-facing double arrows at the top of them. This is the collapsed state of the default panel group. Clicking the arrows expands the group so that you can see its entire contents. The expanded group pushes into the space occupied by the stage. Clicking the arrows again collapses the panels so that they don't get in the way when you're working on the stage.

- ✓ **Properties panel:** This panel contains all the available information about any object that is currently selected with the mouse. If no object is selected, the panel displays information about the application itself. Although some properties are read-only (that is, they can't be edited), the majority can be edited in place.

- ✓ **Library panel:** When you create visual assets in Flash Professional, they can be stored in the Library of your application's FLA file so that the assets can be used multiple times in your application. The Library panel is the visual representation of everything that is stored in the FLA's Library and allows you to drag and drop assets onto the stage. Storing visual assets in the Library also permits those assets to be placed on the stage programmatically with ActionScript 3.0 code.

- ✓ **Tools panel:** This is a fundamental panel in Flash Professional that you will use during every development session. It contains all the mouse tools you need to select objects on the stage, draw shapes, add text, and add or modify color. One of these tools is selected at all times, with the default selection being the Selection tool, which is topmost in the list.

- ✓ **Timeline:** Working your way along the bottom of the Flash Professional workspace, you see the Timeline on the left side. As you can imagine, this panel is responsible for organizing a Flash application's content over time. The major components of the Timeline are frames, layers, and the playhead. Flash applications divide lengths of time into frames, like a video would. Layers are like multiple film strips that can be placed on top of each other and contain different pieces of content that display on the stage. The playhead moves along the timeline during playback and represents what the user sees on a given frame.

That concludes the tour of the workspace in Flash Professional, leaving you aware of the constituent parts and the functions they perform. Later, when you further develop your application, I'll refer to the elements of the workspace using the names I've introduced here.

Clicking and dragging things around in Flash Professional is par for the course. Often you may find that you drag the wrong thing and start getting your panels in a bit of a mess. Fear not! If at any time you want to reset them to their original sizes and positions, just choose Window⇨Workspace⇨Reset 'Essentials', and Flash Professional will restore order to your workspace.

Chapter 5

Creating the User Interface

● ●

In This Chapter

▶ Doing a quick "Hello World"

▶ Designing and preparing the visual assets in Flash Professional

▶ Creating simple animations

▶ Drawing shapes with ActionScript 3.0 code

● ●

*T*he user interface (UI) is the part of your application that the users see and will most likely form an opinion on. A good UI almost always leaves a lasting impression; I'm sure one springs to mind right now. You can split Flash application UIs into two major parts: information architecture and interaction design. The information architecture is the look and layout, whereas the interaction design is how it responds or behaves to user interaction.

For mobile applications built with Flash, the majority of the components parts of the UI are built and assembled in Flash Professional, a highly visual tool for developing Flash applications that comes with a suite of drawing and animation tools. I discuss Flash Professional fully in Chapter 4.

In this chapter, I show you how to create the venerable "Hello, World" application, if you're eager to get ahead fast. You find out about preparing a variety of visual assets in the Flash Professional software, as well as understanding the importance of the iPhone Human Interface Guidelines and creating usable interfaces for your users.

Creating a Quick "Hello World"

I'm confident that one of the first things you're going to want to do is get something (anything!) built onto your Android or iOS device as soon as you can, to prove to yourself that it works. I don't blame you — even if you've skipped the last four chapters to get straight here — because this is the same thing I did when I got my hands on all this juicy new technology!

The best approach is almost always the "Hello World" application, which in case you've never built one before, displays "Hello World" on the screen, and nothing else. It's hardly exciting, but it's probably the smallest thing you can make in the shortest period of time. Use the following steps to get your very own "Hello World" working on your device. (As mentioned, you can understand these steps even if you've skipped chapters to get here.)

1. **Choose File⇨New.**

2. **Select either AIR for iOS from the General tab or AIR for Android from the Templates tab, and then click OK.**

   If you will be using AIR for Android, select the 800 x 480 Blank template, as shown in Figure 5-1. A new Flash file opens in Flash Professional.

3. **Select the Text tool from the Tools panel.**

4. **Draw a** `TextField` **instance on the stage.**

5. **Type** Hello World **into the** `TextField`.

6. **Select the** `TextField` **instance so that the blue bounding box appears around it.**

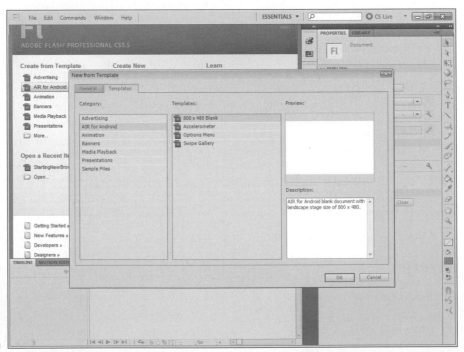

Figure 5-1:
Creating
a new
Flash file.

7. **In the Properties panel, select Classic Text from the topmost drop-down menu.**

   This sets the Text Engine — the rendering logic for text in the Flash Player.

8. **Set the character family to Arial.**

   The Arial font is available on both Windows computers and Macs.

9. **Choose the color, size, and font weight you want.**

10. **Set the anti-alias to Use Device Fonts.**

11. **Press Ctrl+S (Windows) or Command+S (Mac) to save the file as** `HelloWorld.fla.`

You're done with the development part of your "Hello World" application. Your Flash file now looks like the one in Figure 5-2. You can now hop over to Part V for the steps necessary to get your application onto your Android or iOS device. After you install your app on your mobile device, you can run it and see the fabled "Hello World" on your device's screen. If you'd rather continue learning about the design of the Flash mobile application user interface, read on!

Figure 5-2: The complete HelloWorld.fla file.

Complying with Apple's Human Interface Guidelines

When designing applications for the iPhone, you don't necessarily have free reign over the design of the user interface as you might be used to when designing applications for delivery through a web browser. Apple has laid down some standards and principles that it wants developers targeting the iPhone to incorporate into their applications. Apple has called them the *Human Interface Guidelines,* or HIG. Apple implemented HIG to ensure conformity between its iPhone OS user interface and various third-party applications, maintaining a continuous and therefore more intuitive user experience. Although it isn't a requirement that you read the guidelines from cover to cover, it is important that you understand the principles that Apple is trying to get across. In extreme cases, your application submission could be rejected from the App Store for insufficient compliance with the guidelines.

The guidelines are a comprehensive suite of online documentation, available freely through the iPhone OS Reference Library and downloadable from this site:

```
http://developer.apple.com/iphone/library/documentation/
         UserExperience/Conceptual/MobileHIG/
         MobileHIG.pdf
```

The one important thing to take away from the HIG document is the necessity not to challenge the user's expectations around how parts of your application should look and behave. This essentially means don't reinvent the wheel. If a tried-and-tested look and feel exist for various controls in your application, you should favor this over any bespoke design you think of. Equally, if iPhone users are already familiar with a way of transitioning from one screen to the next, you should aim to use the same transitions in your application. This isn't to say that you can't come up with new controls and interaction metaphors where the existing range doesn't suit your needs. Just be careful when redesigning common controls that already exist on the iPhone.

The HIG can be a minefield for developers who want to put cross-platform Flash applications onto the iPhone as well as a variety of other devices. I'd suggest steering clear of applications that require an "app-like" user interface — such as productivity and data-centric applications — that could be easily satisfied using the iOS software development kit (SDK). Instead, focus on gaming and creative applications to which the iOS SDK, and its suite of components, doesn't readily lend itself to. You can find out more about the iOS SDK at the iOS Dev Center (http://developer.apple.com/devcenter/ios).

To help you understand the range of UI controls available to the iOS SDK, some great guys at Teehan LAX have produced a Photoshop document that you can download and use when designing your iPhone applications. Download the

Photoshop PSD file from `www.teehanlax.com/blog/2009/06/18/` `iphone-gui-psd-30`.

Test!

It really is important to iteratively test your user interface as you're building it. This means not waiting until you've added the very last finishing touches to it before considering putting it on the target devices to see what it looks like. As you build, you should take breaks at sensible points to put your application onto your device to see how your changes render and how well they perform. The temptation is always there to "do just a little bit more" and put off testing your new application until it's "ready," but in the worst-case scenarios, your user interface could be so complicated or heavy that it crashes the device, or so sluggish that it's simply unusable. It would be a shame for this to happen so far into your project, so it pays to test iteratively. Each time that you add a new screen or procedure, drop it onto the device and see whether it behaves exactly as you planned.

Another part of iteratively testing your user interface is ensuring that it is usable in the sense that a user will know how to use it. Usability testing can be done at many stages in your project — even with drawings before you start development. I guarantee that you will have occasions where, despite the best planning and research, a screen or interaction you designed just doesn't seem right when you test it on the device. Trapping these usability problems as early as you can will save you from a world of pain later, when changing something may have a huge effect on the rest of your application and cost you days of extra work. Simple drawings, or paper prototypes, can be made quickly and can often expose problems with the layout of your user interface and the relationship between different parts of your application long before you go to the hassle and expense of developing it.

Don't forget to rope in friends to test your user interface for you. Although you might think your design is beautiful — of course it is, it's your masterpiece — other people might not agree. It's useful to gain a consensus of opinion on your proposed design before you start work. Your friends and colleagues can also be great guinea pigs when it comes to testing the interactive parts of your application. If four out of your five test candidates can't work out how to do an important task, you have a good idea that a large percentage of your real users are likely to have the same problem. The great thing is that your test candidates are going to be constructive about it, whereas your customers on the Marketplace or App Store will be less forgiving and likely to hammer you with scathing reviews and the dreaded 1-star rating! By accepting usability testing as a valuable tool in your design armory, you'll be more assured of success than you can be by simply imagining that you know what your user will like.

Preparing the Visual Assets in Flash Professional

Flash Professional has an extensive set of drawing tools that allow you to create vector graphics for inclusion in your application. Conventionally, the approach with graphics in Flash applications targeted at desktop computers has always been to draw what you can as vectors and reserve imported bitmap images, such as PNGs, for complex graphics that are difficult to create with the tools available to you in Flash Professional. The reason for this approach is that the use of vector drawings creates a smaller resulting SWF file size than embedding bitmaps, making the application smaller for download.

For mobile application development, the same is less true. It's still important to keep file size to a minimum by choosing the image compression format — such as PNG — but more important than that is ensuring that the rendering of the graphics doesn't kill your application when it's running. Crashes annoy your users and will most likely prevent your app from being accepted into the Android Marketplace or the Apple App Store.

If you have a complex logo with intricate effects and fonts, it's better to create it as a PNG image and then import that file into your Flash FLA file as a bitmap. (Importing external graphic files with Flash Professional is covered later in the chapter.) Your resulting application will be configured by default to expedite the rendering of bitmaps using a process known as *bitmap caching* (explained in more detail in Chapter 6). Bitmaps don't scale well, so bear in mind that they should be imported at the exact size you intend to display them, or you'll suffer pixilation.

Conversely, if you want to create a simple shape with a solid fill, it is better to create that image as a vector drawing in Flash Professional. The benefits are a much shorter workflow to create the graphic, easier modification, and a smaller file size than an imported bitmap. A vector drawing can also be scaled either using the Transform tool in Flash Professional or at runtime with ActionScript code, without causing pixilation.

Somewhere in the middle are the majority of graphics you'll be using in your application — something I like to refer to as the gray area. You'll need to assess these images on a case-by-case basis, and in some cases, you might need to do some performance testing to determine whether they should be sourced from bitmaps or drawn in Flash as vectors.

With the necessary pros and cons to drawing covered, I'll show you how to create the component parts of the SpaceshipZapZap game user interface.

In the following few pages, you get a feel for the common workflow of

✔ Drawing graphical elements

✔ Creating dynamic ActionScript Linkages

✔ Linking the graphical elements to code-behind ActionScript 3.0 classes that can control the graphical elements

The Library is where all your visual assets are stored inside your Flash file. The symbols — MovieClips, Buttons, and Bitmaps — that you import into your application are all visible in this Library panel. MovieClips are graphical elements that can have animation running inside them. Buttons have three visual states — mouse up, mouse over, and mouse down — to which you can apply graphics. Bitmaps are images, such as PNG files, that have been imported into your application.

Creating a new empty MovieClip

Follow these five short steps to create an empty MovieClip symbol in your application Library:

1. **Open the iOS or Android application FLA in Flash Professional.**

   In Chapter 4, I show you how to start new AIR for Android and iOS FLA files. If you haven't done that yet, no worries! Just head back there now and read the section "Starting a Project in Flash Professional." Then jump back here when you're done.

2. **From the menu bar, choose Insert➪New Symbol.**

   Alternatively, press Ctrl+F8 (Windows) or Command+F8 (Mac). The Create New Symbol dialog box opens, as shown in Figure 5-3.

3. **Type the name for the MovieClip.**

   This is the friendly name that your MovieClip will appear as in the Library.

4. **Choose the type MovieClip.**

5. **Click the Advanced arrow in the bottom left of the dialog box.**

   You see the advanced settings for the MovieClip.

6. **Click to select Export for ActionScript under the ActionScript Linkage section.**

   This option allows the MovieClip to be referenced from the Library using ActionScript code.

7. **Click OK.**

   A MovieClip with the name you assigned in Step 3 is created in the Library, and the Create New Symbol dialog box opens. From here, you can edit the contents of the MovieClip.

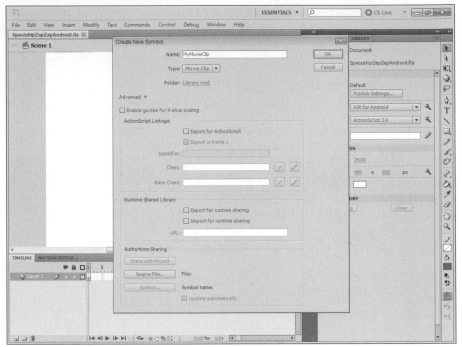

Figure 5-3:
Creating a
new empty
MovieClip.

Creating the Bullet and the Bomb MovieClips

A shoot-'em-up game would be rather boring without projectiles flying around the screen. In the SpaceshipZapZap game, both the defender and the alien invaders fire projectiles. These projectiles are actually MovieClips that are animated across the screen with code.

Continue working in the AIR for Android or iOS FLA file you were working in to create a new empty MovieClip — in the preceding section — and follow these steps to create the bullet MovieClip:

1. **Create a new** MovieClip **called** Bullet.

   Follow the previous steps to create a new empty MovieClip in your application Library.

   The view changes to show the timeline of the new bullet MovieClip.

2. **Select the Line tool from the Tools panel.**

3. Position the mouse centrally over the crosshair that marks the 0,0 coordinate of the `MovieClip`.

4. Hold down the left mouse button and drag a line down by around 10 pixels.

5. Release the left mouse button.

6. Switch to the Selection tool in the Tools panel.

7. Select the line drawn on the stage, and then toggle to the Properties panel.

8. Under the Fill and Stroke section of the Properties panel, change the stroke color — denoted by a Pencil icon — to yellow by clicking the current color and then selecting a new color from the selector that appears.

9. Under the Fill and Stroke section, modify the stroke weight value to be 7.00.

   This makes the line you've just drawn fatter, as shown in Figure 5-4.

10. Press Ctrl+S (Windows) or Command+S (Mac) to save the file.

   It's good practice to save your work regularly!

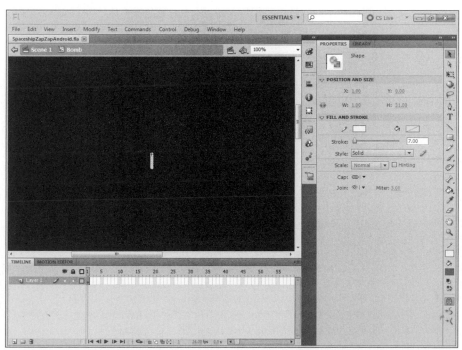

Figure 5-4: Modifying the properties of a line.

The Bomb MovieClip is largely the same as the Bullet, except this time, you use the Brush tool instead of the Line tool to draw the MovieClip contents. To create the Bomb MovieClip, follow these steps:

1. **Create a new** MovieClip **in your Library called** Bomb.

2. **Select the Brush tool from the Tools panel.**

3. **Position the mouse centrally over the crosshair that marks the 0,0 coordinate of the** MovieClip.

4. **Hold down the left mouse button and draw a Z shape that's around 10 pixels tall — it doesn't matter if it's not perfect.**

5. **Release the left mouse button.**

6. **Switch to the Selection tool in the Tools panel.**

7. **Select the Z shape you drew on the stage, and then toggle to the Properties panel.**

8. **Under the Fill and Stroke section of the Properties panel, change the fill color — denoted by a Bucket icon — to white by clicking the current color and then selecting a new color from the selector that appears.**

9. **Press Ctrl+S (Windows) or Command+S (Mac) to save your work.**

That's it! Both the Bullet and Bomb MovieClips are now prepared and waiting in the Library for use by the ActionScript code that you'll write later in Chapter 6.

If you're unsure whether a symbol in the Library is being exported for ActionScript, select the symbol in the Library, right-click (Windows) or Control+click (Mac), and then choose Properties from the contextual menu that appears. If the Export for ActionScript check box is selected, the symbol will be available to your ActionScript code to access from the Library at run-time. The Symbol Properties dialog box that appears allows you to modify not only the ActionScript Linkage properties but also the symbol's name and type.

Using the Gradient Tools

The Header MovieClip is a graphic that sits at the top of a screen and represents the navigation bar that is common to a lot of iPhone applications. Although apparently sophisticated in its appearance, the bar is little more than a rectangle with a gradient fill applied to it. You can create your own using the following steps:

1. **Create a new** MovieClip **symbol and name it** Header.

2. **Click Fill Color in the Tools panel.**

3. **Select the white-to-black linear gradient shown at the bottom of the color palette.**

4. **Select the Rectangle tool from the Tools panel.**

5. **Click Stroke Color and select the white square that has a red line through it.**

   Setting the Stroke Color to empty — top right in the color picker — ensures no key-line is drawn around the rectangle you're about to create.

6. **On the stage, hold down the left mouse button down and drag out a rectangle that's about 480 pixels wide and 50 pixels high.**

   When you're done, your rectangle will look like Figure 5-5.

   Mind those pixels! When positioning objects with your mouse in Flash Professional, it's very easy to place the objects so that either the x or y value is not a whole number. The result? When you run your application, you may experience broken lines, poorly rendered text, or incorrectly aligned assets. You can avoid these issues by ensuring that any asset you position on the stage has an x and y value that is an integer. If it doesn't, modify the position of the object using the Properties panel.

7. **Switch to the Selection tool and select the filled rectangle.**

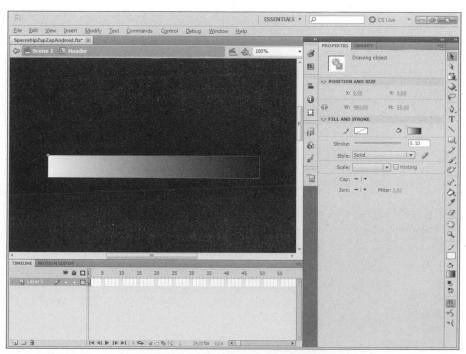

Figure 5-5:
Filled rectangle with a linear gradient.

8. **Select the Gradient Transform tool.**

   This tool is the third option on the Tools panel; if it is currently set as the Free Transform tool, click it to reveal hidden options.

9. **Grab the circular handle at the upper-right corner of the rectangle and move it downward to rotate the gradient 90 degrees clockwise.**

   Your screen appears as shown in Figure 5-6.

10. **Grab the handle that has a right-facing arrow on it and slowly move it upward so that the blue selection line is flush with the bottom edge of your rectangle.**

    The top selection line moves so that it becomes flush with the top of the rectangle too. Your gradient now runs from white at the top to black at the bottom.

Your rectangle with a gradient fill is done, although it probably doesn't look that nice with default colors, so adjust them to achieve the right effect using this method:

1. **Select the rectangle using the Selection tool.**

2. **Open the Color panel by choosing Window⇨Color or by clicking the Palette icon in the expanded panel.**

   The Color panel opens, as shown in Figure 5-7.

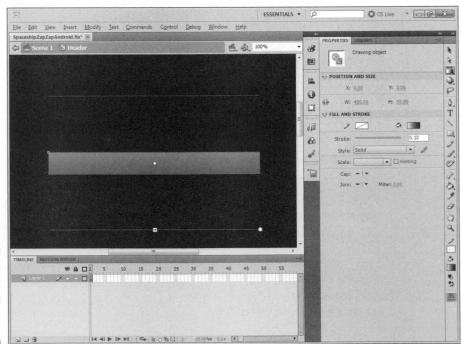

Figure 5-6:
Using the
Gradient
Transform
tool.

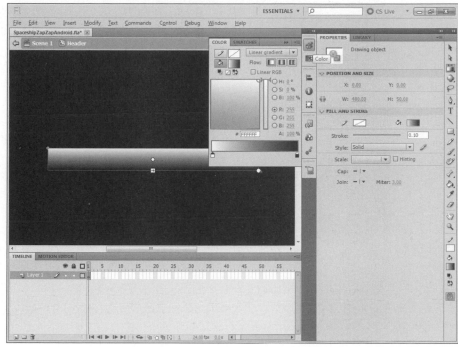

Figure 5-7:
A gradient
shown in
the Color
panel.

3. **Add two additional points to the middle of the gradient scale as follows:**

   a. **Click just below the scale at the point where you want to insert the points.**

   The cursor displays a plus sign (+).

   b. **Insert two new points side by side, at the midway point on the scale.**

4. **Select the first gradient point on the left by clicking it. Set the color to #434343 (dark gray).**

5. **Select the second gradient point and set the color to #9C9C9C (light gray).**

6. **Select the third gradient point and set the color to #7D7D7D (dark gray).**

7. **Select the last gradient point on the right and set the color to #000000 (black).**

8. **Press Ctrl+S (Windows) or Command+S (Mac) to save your work.**

Experiment with a gradient of your choice. In my example, the bottom half blends from #000000 to #7D7D7D, and the lighter top gradient blends from #434343 to #9C9C9C in the center. Now your `Header MovieClip` is complete and should look like Figure 5-8.

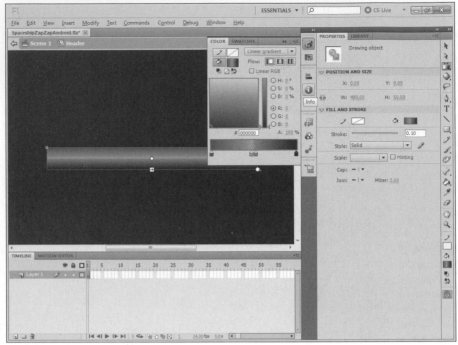

SpaceshipZapZapAndroid.fla*

Figure 5-8:
The
complete
Header
MovieClip.

TIP

To remove gradient marker points from the gradient scale, just click and drag them off the Color panel.

Importing External Graphics

Some assets in your application are either too complicated or simply impossible to draw using the tools available in Flash Professional. For these situations, you can import graphics generated as PNG files into your application FLA file. The PNG files are then compiled into your application and rendered as bitmaps.

The graphics that I use in my SpaceshipZapZap game are reasonably intricate with lots of corners. Rendering these as vector graphics in Flash would be computationally more intensive than if they were imported and presented as bitmap images. I chose to draw them in Fireworks, a graphics authoring package from Adobe (included in the Creative Suite as explained in Chapter 4), and then export them as PNG files. My completed graphics are shown in Figure 5-9.

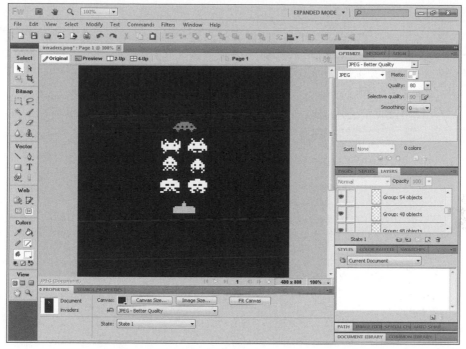

Figure 5-9:
Graphics
drawn in
Fireworks
ready to be
exported as
PNG files.

You can download the images to use with the source of the SpaceshipZapZap
application from www.dummies.com/go/flashmobileappdevfd. Save them
to your development computer. alien1a.png represents the up-swing of
Alien1's animation, whereas alien1b.png is the down-swing of the animation.
When you come to animate Alien1, you'll cycle between these two images. The
same is true for alien2a.png and alien2b.png, which represent the two
animation states of Alien2. The third alien type is Alien3, and it needs to animate using alien3a.png and alien3b.png. Placing the images on different
frames of the MovieClip causes the MovieClip to appear to flicker from one
image to the next, and back again, giving the illusion of motion. Because the
graphics for my aliens are external image files, I have to import them into the
Library in Flash Professional before I can start using them. Follow these steps
to import the alien images into the Library in Flash Professional:

1. **Choose File⇨Import⇨Import to Library.**

   The Import to Library dialog box appears.

2. **Browse to the location on your computer where you've saved the
   images. Hold down the Ctrl key (Windows) or Command key (Mac)
   and click each file you want to import.**

3. **Click Open.**

   An Import Fireworks Document dialog box appears, as shown in Figure 5-10.

4. **Select the Import as a Single Flattened Bitmap check box.**

5. **Click OK.**

   The PNG files are added to the Library. Also observe that Flash Professional automatically creates a Graphic symbol in the Library for each of the imported images. You use these symbols in your application.

Now that you've imported your PNG files, the next task is to create three new `MovieClips` in the Library. Each `MovieClip` represents a type of alien.

Follow the steps for creating an empty `MovieClip` covered earlier in this chapter, in the "Creating a new empty MovieClip" section. (In Chapter 6, you find out how to create a fleet of aliens using these three `MovieClips`.) Name them **Alien1**, **Alien2**, and **Alien3**, respectively. After you've created your empty `MovieClip` files, remember to select Export for ActionScript in the ActionScript Linkage section for each one.

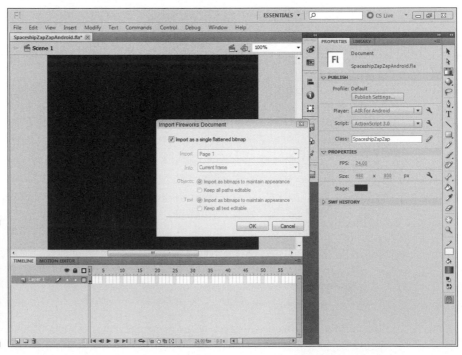

Figure 5-10:
The dialog box displayed when importing PNG files.

After your three empty MovieClips are in the Library, you need to add image contents to frame 1 and frame 30. Follow these steps:

1. **In the Library, double-click one of the empty MovieClips you created to open it for editing.**

2. **Select the first of the three alien images in the Library and drag it to the crosshair on the stage that marks the 0,0 coordinate of the MovieClip.**

   Ensure that the x and y coordinates of the image are 0.00 and 0.00, respectively. Click the values for x and y and enter new ones if necessary. If they aren't set exactly to 0, the positioning of the graphic on the stage at runtime could be affected.

3. **On the MovieClip's timeline, right-click (Windows) or Control+click (Mac) frame 30 and select Insert Keyframe from the context menu that appears.**

   A black dot appears on the selected frame, denoting that it's now a keyframe.

4. **With the playhead still on frame 30, select the second image in the Library and drag it to the crosshair that marks the 0,0 coordinate of the MovieClip.**

   With the image on the stage selected, ensure that the x and y coordinates of the image are 0.00 and 0.00, respectively. Click the values for x and y and enter new ones if necessary.

5. **On the timeline, right-click (Windows) or Control+click (Mac) frame 60 and select Insert Frame from the context menu that appears.**

6. **Repeat the previous steps for the other two empty alien MovieClips in the Library, Alien2 and Alien3.**

   The timeline of each complete MovieClip will look like the one shown in Figure 5-11.

To test the effect, simply drag one of your new alien MovieClips to the stage from the Library. Then press Ctrl+Enter (Windows) or Command+Enter (Mac) to preview the Flash application. You see that the MovieClip continuously loops between the two images, switching every second or so.

Figure 5-11:
The
completed
MovieClip
timeline.

Creating Buttons with Dynamic Labels

You often want to be able to create a button component that allows you to configure the label displayed on the button at runtime. Doing this affords you the convenience of needing to build the button only once, yet use it in many places in your application. If you later need to modify the appearance of the button, you need to perform the modifications once for them to permeate throughout the application.

To create buttons like this, you cannot use the Button symbol, as it prevents you from dynamically modifying properties in it at runtime. Instead, you have to create a MovieClip symbol and make it behave like a button. It's not particularly hard; you just have to manually code the up- and down-state logic yourself, rather than letting the software handle it for you. The big advantage of creating a button with a dynamic label is that you can have a dynamic TextField inside the MovieClip symbol that you can update while the application is running.

In my SpaceshipZapZap application, I decided to create my own button component that I could use repeatedly in my code. The LabelButton is a representation of a regular Rectangle button defined in the iOS Human Interface Guidelines. It appears on screens where a selection is to be made by the user that isn't on the navigation bar. Its key characteristics are a key-line around the outside, a gradient fill (giving a glass effect), and a solid down state when the button is pressed.

Here are the steps to create a button `MovieClip` with a dynamic text label:

1. **Press Control+F8 (Windows) or Command+F8 (Mac) to open the Create New Symbol dialog and create a new `MovieClip` symbol with the name** LabelButton.

   Remember to select Export for ActionScript under the ActionScript Linkage section.

2. **Select a solid Fill Color and Line Color in the Tools panel.**

3. **Select the Rectangle tool.**

4. **Change the Stoke height to 2.00.**

5. **Under Rectangle Options, choose Rectangle Corner Radius and modify the rectangle corner radius to 10.00.**

6. **In frame 1, starting at the crosshair marker on the stage, draw a rectangle that is 300 pixels wide and 45 pixels high.**

   If necessary, modify the x and y position of the rectangle in the Properties panel to ensure that it's exactly 0.00 and 0.00, respectively. You now have a filled rectangle drawn on the stage.

7. **Apply a gradient fill to the rectangle.**

   You can follow the steps discussed in the section "Using the Gradient Tools," earlier in this chapter, to accomplish this. Alternatively, you can stick with a solid fill color of your choice.

8. **In frame 2, right-click (Windows) or Control+click (Mac) and select Insert Keyframe.**

9. **With the rectangle shape selected, select Window⇨Color or click the Palette icon in the expanded panel.**

10. **From the Color menu, select Solid Color from the Color Type drop-down menu.**

    I chose a dark gray color (#333333) in my application.

11. **Insert a new layer.**

    The quickest way to do this is to click the New Layer icon at the lower-left corner of the screen. Alternatively, choose Insert⇨Timeline⇨Layer.

    A new layer appears in the timeline directly above the layer you've just been working with, as shown in Figure 5-12.

12. **Using the Text tool, draw a new `TextField` on the new layer.**

    Make it 280 pixels wide and position it centrally on the rectangle shape.

    A fast and accurate way of aligning objects with each other is to use the Align panel. You can open the Align panel by pressing Ctrl+K (Windows) or Command+K (Mac) or by choosing Window⇨Align. Select the object you want to align, simultaneously select the object you want to align it against, and then select the horizontal and vertical align options from the Align panel.

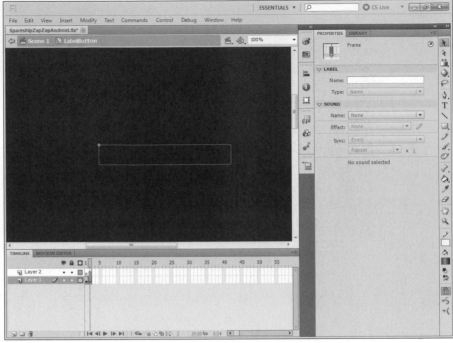

Figure 5-12:
The new layer is added to the LabelButton MovieClip.

13. **In the Properties panel, modify the properties as follows:**

   a. **Assign it the instance name** buttonText.

   b. **Ensure that the Text Engine selected is Classic Text.**

   c. **Ensure that the text type is Dynamic Text.**

   d. **Set the Character Family as Arial, the Style as Bold, and the Size as 18pt.**

   e. **Assign a color of your choice.**

   f. **Set the anti-alias to Use Device Fonts.**

   g. **Ensure that the Selectable button is deselected.**

   h. **Set the paragraph format as Align Center and the behavior as Single Line.**

The graphical part to the LabelButton is now complete, as shown in Figure 5-13. In Chapter 6, I explain the ActionScript code required to make the MovieClip behave like a button and describe how to update its text at runtime. Next, I continue the assembly of the user interface components by introducing you to the art of font rendering on mobile devices.

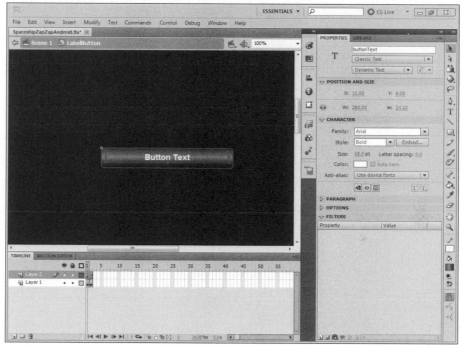

Figure 5-13:
The
completed
LabelButton
MovieClip.

Rendering Text and Font

Mobile phone screens aren't the biggest in the world, so it's important to pay particular attention to the way your font will look — or *render* — on the screen. Illegible text not only makes your application look scruffy and dissatisfies your users but also can lead to rejection from the Android Marketplace or Apple App Store.

As far as target platforms go, both Android and iOS render their preinstalled fonts very well, so it makes sense to use those in your application wherever possible. With this in mind, I always choose to use device fonts as the anti-alias setting for all my `TextFields`. This means that the font will be sourced and rendered by the host operating system, rather than by fonts embedded inside your application. You should strive to always use a point size of 12 or greater for your text; otherwise, your user will need a magnifying glass to read it!

Android offers three preinstalled fonts: Droid Sans (sans), Droid Sans Serif (serif), and Droid Sans Mono (monospace). Droid Sans is the default.

You can safely use Arial, Helvetica, and Verdana on the iPhone, but for an up-to-date list of the supported fonts, you can download the free Fonts iPhone application, which tells you which fonts you have on your device. You can download it from here:

```
http://itunes.apple.com/app/fonts/id285217489?mt=8
```

Applications occasionally distribute and install fonts, so you should approach fonts other than the preinstalled ones just listed with caution. If the font you reference is not installed on a user's device, there will be problems rendering the text in your application.

You can embed fonts with your application, but these do increase the overall file size of the packaged application significantly. You also need to be aware of distribution restrictions that govern licensed font sets. Please refer to the creator or distributor of the font you want to use to find out if your license allows you to redistribute it.

Just remember these three points, and you shouldn't run into too many problems:

- ✔ Use device fonts.
- ✔ Use a minimum 12pt font size for text.
- ✔ Specify your font as Arial.

If you follow those three rules, where Arial is present (on iPhone), your font will render as Arial; otherwise, it will render on Android as Droid Sans, which is a reasonably pretty font itself.

Now that you have a grasp of the basics of text display on mobile devices, you can put your newly acquired knowledge to work in the next section by creating a text-input component that you can reuse.

Creating the TextEntry MovieClip

In the SpaceshipZapZap application I want the users to be able to enter their name when they achieve a high score. Although Flash has a component for text input, it's visual appearance isn't sufficiently complete to use it in an application. We can improve the aesthetics and the application's usability by adding a background and a border — perhaps with rounded corners — as well as clearing the text when the user wants to add new text. First, you need to create a new MovieClip that adds these features to the basic Input TextField.

The TextEntry MovieClip is simply an Input TextField component with a background shape behind it for aesthetic purposes. It's also a MovieClip so that you can later put some code behind it to control how it behaves when the user selects it. The following steps show you how to create a TextEntry MovieClip:

1. **Create a new** `MovieClip` **symbol called** TextEntry.

   Remember to select Export for ActionScript in the ActionScript Linkage section.

2. **In the Tools panel, set the fill color to #FFFFFF and the stroke color to #CCCCCC.**

3. **Select the Rectangle tool, modify the stroke weight to 2.00 and the rectangle corner radius to 10.00; then drag out a rectangle shape onto the stage on frame 1.**

   Make the rectangle 300 pixels wide and 36 pixels high.

4. **Click the New Layer icon at the lower-left corner of the screen to insert a new layer and name it** Text.

   While you're there, you can double-click the Layer 1 label and rename it **Background**.

5. **Select the Text tool and draw a** `TextField` **instance on top of your background and to similar dimensions.**

6. **In the Properties panel for your** `TextField`, **modify the properties as follows:**

   a. **Assign it the instance name** input.

   b. **Ensure that the Text Engine selected is Classic Text.**

   c. **Ensure that the text type is Input Text.**

   d. **Set the character family as Arial, the style as Bold, and the size as 16pt.**

   e. **Assign a text (fill) color of #000000 (black).**

   f. **Set the anti-alias to Use Device Fonts.**

   g. **Set the paragraph format to Align Left and the behavior as Single Line.**

7. **Click the** `TextField` **instance on the stage and type the text** Your Name.

   This is the default text displayed in the `TextField`. In Chapter 6, I show you how to clear this text when the user enters new text.

Your complete `TextEntry MovieClip` now looks like Figure 5-14 and is ready to be included in your application's user interface. You learn how to display `MovieClips` stored in the Library on the stage using code in Chapter 6.

Figure 5-14:
The complete TextEntry MovieClip.

Assembling a StartScreen MovieClip

The StartScreen MovieClip is the first screen that is displayed to a user when he or she runs the application for the first time. It contains helpful information to get the user up and running with your app and is just a display object that contains a number of the other MovieClips you've created as its component parts. In the SpaceshipZapZap game you're building the StartScreen MovieClip comprises the following:

- ✔ Two single-line TextFields
- ✔ One multiline TextField
- ✔ A LabelButton, which you created in the Library a little earlier in this chapter
- ✔ Eight Alien1 MovieClips; you created the Alien1 MovieClip earlier in this chapter using imported graphics

The following steps show you how to create a new StartScreen MovieClip that includes some graphics from the Library and a logo made from two TextFields.

1. **Create a new** MovieClip **symbol called** StartScreen.

   Remember to select Export for ActionScript under the ActionScript Linkage section.

2. **Drag a new** Alien1 MovieClip **instance from the Library to the stage.**

   You imported these to the Library earlier in this chapter, in the "Importing External Graphics" section.

3. **Create seven more instances of the** Alien1 MovieClip.

   The easiest way to do this is to use the Copy and Paste commands on the MovieClip you just dragged from the Library. Select the MovieClip, press Ctrl+C (Windows) or Command+C (Mac) to copy it, and then deselect it and press Ctrl+V (Windows) or Command+V (Mac) to paste a copy. Repeat this action to create the required number.

4. **Position the eight alien** MovieClips **into a single line spreading horizontally across the screen starting at an** x **coordinate of around** 48.00 **and a constant** y **coordinate of** 130.00.

   Give them a 10-pixel gap in between. Don't worry about giving them instance names.

5. **Create a new** TextField.

6. **In the Properties panel for your** TextField, **modify the properties as follows:**

   a. **Ensure that the Text Engine selected is Classic Text.**

   b. **Ensure that the text type is Static Text.**

   c. **Set the character family as Arial, the style as Bold, and the size as 40pt.**

   d. **Assign the text (fill) color as white (#FFFFFF).**

   e. **Set the anti-alias to Use Device Fonts.**

   f. **Make sure that the Selectable button is deselected.**

   g. **Set the paragraph format as Align Left and the behavior as Single Line.**

7. **Duplicate the** TextField **by selecting the** TextField **you just created, press Ctrl+C (Windows) or Command+C (Mac) to copy it, and then deselect it and press Ctrl+V (Windows) or Command+V (Mac) to paste a copy.**

   Move it with the mouse so that it lies over the top of the first TextField.

8. **Select the** TextField, **and then in the Properties panel, assign the text (fill) color gray (#666666).**

9. **Move the gray** `TextField` **3 pixels upward and 3 pixels to the left of the white** `TextField`.

   You see that an extruding effect is mimicked. This is a cheap way of creating a text effect without needing to use computationally expensive programmatic filters, which are covered in detail in Chapter 6.

10. **Group the two** `TextFields` **into a single Graphic Symbol by selecting both of the** `TextFields`, **and then pressing F8 to launch the Convert to Symbol dialog box.**

11. **Name the new symbol** Logo **and select** `Graphic` **from the Type dropdown menu.**

12. **Click OK to confirm.**

    The two `TextFields` you created are now contained inside a graphic object on the stage.

The `StartScreen MovieClip` is ready, with the logo and graphics included. In the next steps, you add to the `StartScreen MovieClip` by creating a `TextField` instance to provide some instructions to your user and a `LabelButton` instance that the user can click to start the game:

1. **Select the Logo Graphic, and then in the Properties panel, adjust the** x **and** y **values to be** 50.00 and 214.00, **respectively.**

2. **Drag out a new** `TextField` **on the stage of the** `StartScreen MovieClip`.

   This is a new multiline `TextField` for the game instructions.

3. **In the Properties panel for your** `TextField`, **modify the properties as follows:**

   a. **Ensure that the Text Engine selected is Classic Text.**

   b. **Ensure that the text type is Static Text.**

      Don't worry about giving it an instance name because the text doesn't need to be altered with ActionScript.

   c. **Set the character family as Arial, the style as Bold, and the size as 20pt.**

   d. **Assign the text (fill) color as white (#FFFFFF).**

   e. **Set the anti-alias to Use Device Fonts.**

   f. **Make sure that the Selectable button is deselected.**

   g. **Set the paragraph format as Align Left and the behavior as Multiline.**

4. **Enter instruction text for your user in the** `TextField`.

   The most important information you can provide your users is how they interact with the game. Don't go overboard. Your users don't want a blow-by-blow account of what happens under the hood, but they will want to know the object of the game and the ways to move and fire.

5. **Drag a new** `LabelButton MovieClip` **instance from the Library to the stage and position it centrally below the instruction** `TextField`.

6. **Assign the new** `LabelButton` **the instance name** startButton **in its Properties panel.**

Your `StartScreen MovieClip` now looks like what is shown in Figure 5-15, and you have a `MovieClip` comprised of `TextFields`, graphic symbols, and `MovieClips`. You can preview your `StartScreen MovieClip` by dragging it from the Library to the stage and then pressing Ctrl+Enter (Windows) or Command+Enter (Mac) to quickly publish and preview your Flash application. The application will launch in the AIR Debug Launcher (ADL).

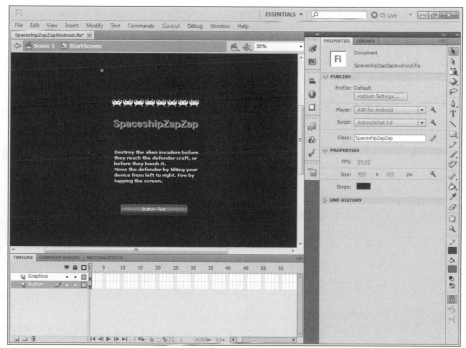

Figure 5-15:
The complete StartScreen MovieClip.

Creating the LoadingGraphic MovieClip

The `LoadingGraphic MovieClip` is displayed to the user when loading operations are taking place that need to complete before the user can continue to interact with the application. Generally, the `LoadingGraphic MovieClip` is a spinning object or a progress bar, and it can be created as a `MovieClip` in the Library and then hidden or displayed as needed.

I'll show you how to create a spinning object as your loader graphic. That way, you can see how easy it is to animate using frames on the timeline in Flash

Professional! You can find on the Internet many stock PNG images of loading graphics that you can freely use, or you can create your own PNG image in an application such as Adobe Fireworks or Photoshop. After you've found an image, save it on your computer so it's ready for use in the next set of steps.

Follow these steps to import an image stored on your computer into Flash Professional and then create a rotation animation with it:

1. **Create a new** `MovieClip` **symbol called** LoadingGraphic.

2. **Remaining inside** `LoadingGraphic`**, choose File⇨Import⇨ Import to Stage, then select your PNG file.**

   The imported bitmap is placed on the stage.

3. **Right-click (Windows) or Control+click (Mac) frame 1 in the** `MovieClip's` **timeline panel — the frame with the solid black dot — and select Create Motion Tween from the context menu.**

   A Convert Selection to Symbol for Tween warning dialog box appears.

4. **Click OK.**

   A new `MovieClip` symbol is created in the Library that contains your imported bitmap image. The frames in Layer 1 also turn blue and extend to frame 24 — equivalent to 1 second of time when your application is running.

5. **Right-click (Windows) or Control+click (Mac) and select Insert Keyframe⇨Rotation from the context menu.**

6. **Select frame 25, then click the Properties panel.**

   You are presented with properties for the current motion tween.

7. **Click the value set for Rotate, and enter** 1 **as its value.**

   The `MovieClip` on the stage will visibly rotate to the new rotation value.

   If you increment the Rotate value to 2 in the Properties panel, the graphic will rotate twice over the same period on the timeline. Increment it to 3, and it rotates three times, and so on.

If you move the playhead forward and backward with your mouse cursor, you can see the graphic rotating. Pressing Enter with the timeline selected causes Flash Professional to simulate playback in-place on the stage — as shown in Figure 5-16.

Place the `LoadingGraphic` on the main application stage and test the Flash movie by pressing Ctrl+Enter (Windows) or Command+Enter (Mac). You see the `LoadingGraphic MovieClip` rotating in perpetuity.

Figure 5-16:
The Loading
Graphic
MovieClip.

Using the Drawing API

The Drawing API is a feature of the ActionScript 3.0 `Graphics` class that allows you to programmatically draw lines and shapes in your display list. It is very convenient for drawing graphics on the fly, like when you're unsure of how big to draw something until some data has loaded, or when a user interacts with a display object, requiring its shape to change. This kind of convenience comes at a price: The Drawing API is processor intensive and can therefore cause significant performance problems, or even crashes, if its use isn't carefully managed. I'm not going to scare you off from using the Drawing API. I'm just going to suggest that you ask yourself the following questions to ensure that you're choosing the right tool for the job:

- ✔ Could you draw these graphics in advance in Flash Professional and just reference them as `MovieClips` at runtime? If yes, you don't need to use the Drawing API.

- ✔ How frequently are the graphics likely to change shape during the application's lifetime? If the answer is never, you don't need to use the Drawing API.

After asking yourself these questions, if you're still of the view that the Drawing API is the only solution that will work for your application, you can continue safely in the knowledge that you've picked the right tool for the job. Remember, performance is almost always better with predrawn graphics, so you have no additional points to be gained here with complex dynamic drawing routines! You're choosing the Drawing API because it's the only way to get the job done.

You can draw in any object that extends, or *subclasses*, `Sprite`. This includes `MovieClip`. In the example that follows, I show you how to draw a rounded rectangle in a `MovieClip`:

1. **Create a new** `MovieClip` **symbol called** RoundedRectangle.

2. **In the ActionScript Linkage section, select Export for ActionScript and then click OK.**

3. **Right-click (Windows) or Control+click (Mac) the** `RoundedRectangle` `MovieClip` **in the Library and select Edit Class.**

   The ActionScript code editor opens and contains the `RoundedRectangle` class code.

4. **Under the line that denotes where to insert constructor code, place the following code to set the fill color (new code is in bold):**

   ```
   package
   {
       import flash.display.MovieClip;

       public class RoundedRectangle extends MovieClip
       {
           public function RoundedRectangle()
           {
               // constructor code
               graphics.beginFill( 0xFF6600 );
           }
       }
   }
   ```

5. **Set the line thickness and color of the shape's line with this code:**

   ```
   public function RoundedRectangle()
   {
       // constructor code
       graphics.beginFill( 0xFF6600 );
       graphics.lineStyle( 2, 0xCCCCCC );
   }
   ```

6. **Invoke the Draw Rounded Rectangle method with this code:**

```
public function RoundedRectangle()
    {
        // constructor code
        graphics.beginFill( 0xFF6600 );
        graphics.lineStyle( 2, 0xCCCCCC );
        graphics.drawRoundRect( 0, 0, 150, 150, 10,
        10 );
    }
```

The first two parameters set the x and y position of the rectangle. You want it to be drawn at the origin of your MovieClip, so set these to 0,0.

The second two parameters are the width and height of the rectangle being drawn; here they're both set to 150.

The final two parameters are the ellipse width and height of the rounded corners. I've chosen a uniform curve for the corners, so set them to 10 each.

7. **Save the class file as** RoundedRectangle.as.

8. **Drag the** RoundedRectangle MovieClip **from the Library to the stage.**

Because the RoundedRectangle MovieClip is empty, it appears as a small white circle with a crosshair on it.

9. **Run the application by pressing Ctrl+Enter (Windows) or Command+Enter (Mac).**

The application launches in the AIR Debug Launcher (ADL) and appears as shown in Figure 5-17.

When using the Drawing API, it is critical to define all the line and fill properties before the drawing action takes place. If you were to put the drawRoundRect() command before the beginFill() and lineStyle() instructions, the rounded rectangle would simply be drawn with default colors and line thicknesses.

Figure 5-17:
Rounded
Rectangle,
courtesy of
the Drawing
API.

Chapter 6

Writing the Code

*Y*ou must write Flash applications for Android and iOS in ActionScript 3.0 — using Flash Professional or an alternative code editor — so a base requirement exists for you to have a certain amount of exposure to this language. Don't worry if you're not an expert — few are. Even so, many developers are able to create great applications on the Flash platform with only a modest knowledge of ActionScript 3.0.

When it was introduced, the ActionScript coding language brought to Flash's impressive animation capabilities the ability to perform logic and decision making at runtime. In 2006, Adobe released ActionScript 3.0, a powerful update to the scripting language, and underpinning this update was a brand-new Flash Player and virtual machine.

In this chapter, I walk you through constructing the core ActionScript 3.0 code for my familiar arcade game SpaceshipZapZap, before looking at how to knit it together with user interface elements that allow your user to interact with your app.

Creating the Document Class

Although it is possible to place code directly on key frames in your application's main Timeline, a better way is to associate a *Document Class* with your FLA file. A Document Class is an ActionScript class that must *subclass* — inherit all the credentials of — a `Sprite` or `MovieClip`. Associating a Document Class with your FLA file separates the graphical elements of your binary FLA file and the code behind that controls them, and stores all code in text files.

A benefit of keeping all your code separate in text files is that you can use source control software, such as Subversion (`http://subversion.apache.org`) or Git (`http://git-scm.com`), which allows you to track your changes, merge changes with other developers, and revert to an older version in the event of a mistake.

If you plan to sell your apps, or even submit them to the Android Market or Apple App Store, source/version control software will save your bacon at least once! Don't let a silly late-night mistake cause you to lose hours of work. Get into the habit of regularly tracking your changes via a source control system so that if you do make a mistake, you can revert to a previous version and continue as if the mistake never happened.

Because an application created in Flash Professional has a root Timeline, you're almost always better off opting to subclass a `MovieClip` (which has a Timeline) rather than a `Sprite` (which does not have a Timeline), so that you can control the root Timeline from the Document Class. Although a `Sprite` is lighter weight, any calls to frame actions like `stop()` and `play()` are going to result in compilation errors.

In the following instructions, I demonstrate how to create a basic Document Class that extends `MovieClip` to be associated with the SpaceshipZapZap application. Open Adobe Flash Professional, and then follow these instructions to create a Document Class (you'll see that all new code being added is in bold):

1. **Open your iOS or Android application FLA in Flash Professional.**

   In Chapter 4 I show you how to start new AIR for Android and iOS FLA files. If you haven't done that yet, no worries! Just head back there now and read the section on starting a project in Flash Professional. Then jump back here when you're done.

2. **In the Properties panel, click the wrench icon next to the Class field.**

   The Create ActionScript 3.0 Class dialog box opens, as shown in Figure 6-1.

3. **Choose Flash Professional as the application that should create the ActionScript 3.0 class.**

4. **Type the Class name** SpaceshipZapZap, **and then click OK.**

   A new ActionScript 3.0 class opens in Flash Professional.

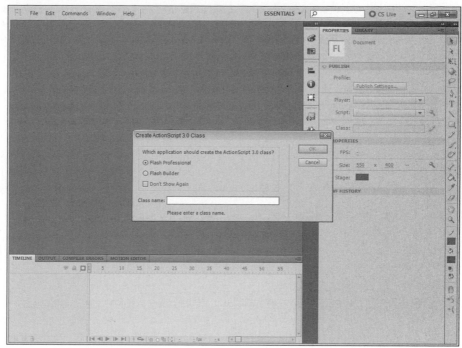

Figure 6-1:
The Create
ActionScript
3.0 Class
dialog box.

5. **Add a call to the** `trace()` **function inside the** `SpaceshipZapZap` **function — the class constructor:**

```
package
{
    import flash.display.MovieClip;
    public class SpaceshipZapZap extends MovieClip
    {
        public function SpaceshipZapZap()
        {
            trace( "Document class initialized" );
        }
    }
}
```

The `trace()` function writes to the Flash Professional output console a message you type (for example, *Document Class initialized*). In this way, you can see what your application is doing behind the scenes.

6. **Press Ctrl+S (Windows) or Command+S (Mac) and save the file as** SpaceshipZapZap.as.

7. **Click the SpaceshipZapZap.fla tab, at the top left of the stage.**

   The focus switches from the `SpaceshipZapZap.as` class to the `SpaceshipZapZap.fla` file.

8. **Press Ctrl+S (Windows) or Command+S (Mac) to save the FLA file.**

   The FLA application is now associated with the Document Class entered in the Class text field, as is shown in Figure 6-2. When you run the application, the Document Class runs as the controller of the FLA.

Every ActionScript 3.0 class has a function inside that is the same name as the class. This function is known as the *constructor* and is run when the class is first needed by the application. Classes can have only one constructor, and after the constructor has been run, it cannot be run again. The class is said to be *initialized* after the constructor function of a class has been run.

You just created a Document Class and linked it to your FLA. If you perform a quick-publish by choosing Control➪Test Movie, you see `Document Class initialized` in the console window. The compiler successfully located your class and compiled it into the application, and Flash Player executed the code inside this class when the application was run.

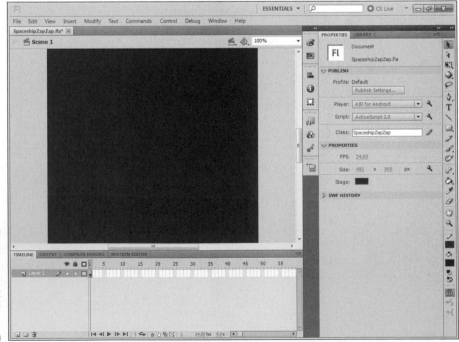

Figure 6-2: Specifying the Document Class for an FLA.

Code hinting and autocompletion in Flash Professional are considerably better than in previous versions. Code completion can now detect properties and methods on your custom classes as well as hinting method parameters. As you type, the code editor will often offer suggestions that you can select by using the arrow keys and pressing Enter. If at any time you want to invoke the code completion dialog box, press Ctrl+spacebar (Windows) or Command+spacebar (Mac) to see the list of available properties and methods.

Initializing the Application

For the moment, when your application starts, nothing really happens that entices the user's interest. A few items are on the stage, a few others are in the library, and then a Document Class traces something to the console window. This is the point where a metaphorical spark is needed to kick everything into life. This spark needs to be a useful event during the application's startup process that lets you know that everything is ready. The best candidate for this task is the ADDED_TO_STAGE event.

When a Document Class is initialized after it has completed executing its constructor, it is automatically added to the *display list* — the term given to the full list of visible objects in your Flash application. When the Document Class is added to the stage, because it is a MovieClip, it dispatches an *event* to notify any other object or class that may be *listening* that this happened. You can assign a listener in the Document Class for this event and use it as a cue to start performing some initialization logic.

This section explains how to add an import directive for the Event class, register an event listener for the ADDED_TO_STAGE event — the event that fires when an object is added to the display list — and create a new method to handle the ADDED_TO_STAGE event. When the code for these actions is added to the Document Class SpaceshipZapZap.as (which the previous section shows you how to create), it looks like this:

```
package
{
    import flash.events.Event;
    import flash.display.MovieClip;
    public class SpaceshipZapZap extends MovieClip
    {
        public function SpaceshipZapZap()
        {
            trace( "Document Class initialized" );
            addEventListener( Event.ADDED_TO_STAGE,
              initialize);
        }
        private function initialize( e:Event ) :void
```

```
        {
            removeEventListener( Event.ADDED_TO_STAGE,
              initialize);
        }
    }
}
```

I walk you through snippets of the code, showing each of the added parts (boldface in the code), to help you understand what they do. To follow along, open the Document Class `SpaceshipZapZap.as` that you created in the previous section (or create it now). Then follow these steps:

1. **Register an event listener for the** `ADDED_TO_STAGE` **event that calls a function called** `initialize`.

   The listener registration goes below the `trace` statement you created, in the `SpaceshipZapZap` function — the constructor:

   ```
   public function SpaceshipZapZap()
   {
       trace( "Document class initialized" );
       addEventListener( Event.ADDED_TO_STAGE, initialize
           );
   }
   ```

As you begin typing **Event**, press Ctrl+spacebar (Windows) or Command+spacebar (Mac). A context menu appears listing the `Event` type. If you select `Event` from the list — using either your keyboard's up and down arrow keys or your mouse — Flash Professional completes the word you were typing, and automatically adds the `import flash.events.Event` directive to the top of your ActionScript 3.0 class. You can use this autocompletion shortcut with most of the default Flash classes. See a full list of Flash API classes at `http://help.adobe.com/en_US/FlashPlatform/reference/actionscript/3/index.html`.

2. **Create a new function — or class method — called** `initialize` **to handle the** `ADDED_TO_STAGE` **event:**

   ```
   trace( "Document Class initialized" );
           addEventListener( Event.ADDED_TO_STAGE,
             initialize);
       }

       private function initialize( e:Event ) :void
       {}
   }
   ```

The `initialize` function is called when the `ADDED_TO_STAGE` event is "heard" by your event listener. When called at runtime, the function receives an `Event` object as a parameter, so this is declared as `e` between the parentheses and is assigned the `Event` type.

3. **Remove the** `ADDED_TO_STAGE` **event listener after it has been handled:**

```
private function initialize( e:Event ) :void
{
    removeEventListener( Event.ADDED_TO_STAGE,
        initialize );
}
```

The `initialize` method you just created handles the `ADDED_TO_STAGE` event — it's the *event handler.* After the event has been handled, it doesn't need to be listened for a second time, so the listener registration should be removed inside the `initialize` method. You remove it by adding the code indicated in bold.

Tidying up by removing listeners is worthwhile. Anything you don't get rid of can linger in memory, and in large quantities, this waste can cause performance problems.

You now have an initialization method that is called at a suitable point during the application's startup process. Now you can begin to wire up the various component parts.

Referencing Components in the Library

At times, the stage becomes too cluttered to a have all your display objects (`MovieClips`, `Sprites`, and `Buttons`) placed on it at compilation time. Often, the nature of an application means that it is impossible to know which and how many items should appear on the stage until the application is running. Because of this, it is usually a good idea to keep everything in the Library and then add it to the stage at runtime through a technique that uses a *pseudo-class name.* A Library object is referenced through a pseudo-class name when you assign it a class name in the Library in Flash Professional (refer to Chapter 5), but you haven't created an ActionScript class file bearing the same name. When the application is compiled, Flash Professional treats the object as though it were an ActionScript class that can be initialized.

In Chapter 5, I walk you through the creation of a `MovieClip` called `StartScreen` in the Library of the application FLA. I'm now going show you how to create a class to associate with this display object that will be responsible for controlling its behavior — a technique also known as *code-behind:*

1. **Open the application FLA file in Flash Professional.**

2. **Locate the** `StartScreen MovieClip` **in the Library.**

3. **Right-click (Windows) or Control+click (Mac) and select Edit Class.**

4. **Select Flash Professional as the application that should edit the ActionScript class.**

A new ActionScript class document opens with the following code in it:

```
package
{
    import flash.display.MovieClip;
    public class StartScreen extends MovieClip
    {
        public function StartScreen()
        {}
    }
}
```

5. **Save the document as** StartScreen.as.

6. **Add a** stop **action to the class constructor to halt the** MovieClip's **internal playhead:**

```
public class StartScreen extends MovieClip
{
    public function StartScreen()
    {
    stop();
    }
}
```

7. **Set the** MovieClip's cacheAsBitmap **property to** true:

```
public function StartScreen()
{
    stop();
    cacheAsBitmap = true;
}
```

This code turns on bitmap caching for the StartScreen MovieClip, which speeds up rendering on the mobile device. The reasons for this are explained a little later in this chapter.

8. **Save the document.**

That's it! Your StartScreen MovieClip now has a code-behind ActionScript class associated with it.

In the SpaceshipZapZap.as Document Class you created earlier in this chapter, you can now add another method that will be responsible for adding items to the display list and invoke it from the initialize method. To do that, follow these instructions:

1. **Open** SpaceshipZapZap.as **in Flash Professional.**

2. **Create a new private function, or method, in the class called**
   displayStartScreen:

```
        removeEventListener( Event.ADDED_TO_STAGE,
      initialize );
   }
   private function displayStartScreen() :void
   {}
   }
}
```

3. **Invoke the** displayStartScreen() **method from the** initialize()
   method:

```
private function initialize( e:Event ):void
{
   removeEventListener( Event.ADDED_TO_STAGE,
      initialize );
   displayStartScreen();
}
```

You now have a placeholder for the code that will display the StartScreen
MovieClip in your app. The next step is to create an instance of the
StartScreen MovieClip inside the displayStartScreen() method and
assign it to a class member variable. I show you how with these instructions:

1. **Declare a new class member variable called** _startScreen:

```
package
{
   import flash.events.Event;
   import flash.display.MovieClip;

   public class SpaceshipZapZap extends MovieClip
   {
      private var _startScreen:StartScreen;
      public function SpaceshipZapZap()
      {
         //...
```

2. **Inside the** displayStartScreen() **method, assign the** _startScreen
   variable a new instance of the StartScreen MovieClip — **the**
   StartScreen **is dynamically linked from the Library:**

```
private function displayStartScreen() :void
{
   startScreen = new StartScreen();
}
```

3. **Use the** `addChild()` **method to add the new** `StartScreen` **instance to the display list:**

```
private function displayStartScreen() :void
{
    _startScreen = new StartScreen();
    addChild( _startScreen );
}
```

Initializing Many Display Objects with Code

In the SpaceshipZapZap application, you'll notice five rows of invading aliens, with seven aliens per row, as shown in Figure 6-3. I refer to this collection as my "alien fleet."

You could create the alien fleet by manually dragging the desired numbers of each of the three alien types from the Library, positioning them on the stage, and then assigning each of them a unique instance name in the Properties panel. That method would not only be labor intensive from the outset but also cause problems later when you need to be able to track the positions of each of the alien `MovieClips` during game play. Furthermore, if you need to alter the layout of your invading alien fleet depending on the screen size of the device that SpaceshipZapZap is played on, you would need to adopt a programmatic approach to initializing and positioning my alien fleet.

Creating the alien fleet programmatically from the beginning enables you to track each alien object at any time during game play and allows you to make adjustments to the layout based on the computed width and height of the device's screen, which is known only when your application is running.

Although you can configure the width and height of your application FLA file in the Properties panel of Flash Professional, this setting simply dictates the *preferred* width and height of your application's display. If your application loads onto a device with screen dimensions that are larger than those specified by your application, your application may not use all the device's screen real estate. By using two properties in your ActionScript 3.0 code — `Capabilities.screenResolutionX` and `Capabilities.screenResolutionY` — you can find out the true width and height (in pixels) of the device's screen. For example, the following code snippet uses `Capabilities.screenResolutionX` and `Capabilities.screenResolutionY` to determine the number of aliens per row to have in a game:

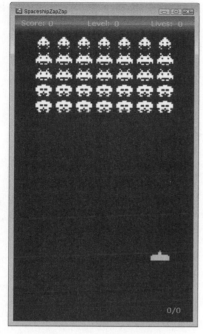

Figure 6-3:
The rows
of invading
aliens in the
Spaceship-
ZapZap
game.

```
var aliensPerRow:int = 5;
if( Capabilities.screenResolutionX > 479 && Capabilities.
          screenResolutionY > 600 )
{
    aliensPerRow = 8;
}
```

If the width of the screen is greater than 479 pixels and the height is greater than 600 pixels, 8 aliens per row is set. If the device's screen dimensions fall at or below 479x600 pixels, the number of aliens per row is set at 5.

To create the alien fleet programmatically, you first need to create a Sprite that will act as the container and add it to the display list. You then create a Vector object into which you add each alien MovieClip that forms the fleet by using a looping technique in ActionScript. Finally, you add all the alien MovieClips to the Sprite container so that they're visible in the display list. Adding the aliens inside a Sprite rather than directly to the display list makes moving them around the screen easier because you need to move only the Sprite to move them all.

In the following steps, I explain how you can programmatically build the alien fleet referencing the `MovieClips` from the Library (all added code is shown in bold). Before you begin, reopen the `SpaceshipZapZap.as` file that I explained how to create a little earlier in this chapter:

1. **In the** `SpaceshipZapZap` **Document Class, declare a new** `Vector` **variable called** `_aliens` **and a new** `Sprite` **variable called** `_fleetContainer`:

```
package
{
    import flash.events.Event;
    import flash.display.MovieClip;

    public class SpaceshipZapZap extends MovieClip
    {
        private var _fleetContainer:Sprite;
        private var _aliens:Vector.<MovieClip>;
        private var _startScreen:StartScreen;
        public function SpaceshipZapZap()
        {
            trace( "Document Class initialized" );
            addEventListener( Event.ADDED_TO_STAGE, init
            );
            //...
        }
    }
}
```

The `.<MovieClip>` notation states that the `Vector` can accept only objects that either are or inherit from the `MovieClip` class.

2. **Declare a new constant** `int` **variable called** `ALIENS_PER_ROW` **and assign it the value** 6:

```
public class SpaceshipZapZap extends MovieClip
{
    private const ALIENS_PER_ROW:int = 7;
    private var _fleetContainer:Sprite;
    private var _aliens:Vector.<MovieClip>;
```

3. **Declare a new constant** `int` **variable called** `ALIEN_PADDING` **and assign it the value** 10:

```
public class SpaceshipZapZap extends MovieClip
{
    private const ALIEN_PADDING:int = 10;
    private const ALIENS_PER_ROW:int = 7;
    private var _fleetContainer:Sprite;
```

The `const` keyword means that the value of the variable cannot be altered at runtime.

The ALIEN_PADDING value is the amount of space in pixels that will be left around each alien MovieClip object when displayed.

4. **Create a new function, or method, called** buildAlienFleet **in the Document Class after the** StartScreen **instance:**

```
public class SpaceshipZapZap extends MovieClip
{
   //...
   private function displayStartScreen() :void
   {
      startScreen = new StartScreen();
      addChild( _startScreen );
   }
   private function buildAlienFleet() :void
   {}
}
```

5. **Create a** for **loop that loops until** i **equals the value of** ALIENS_ PER_ROW**:**

```
private function buildAlienFleet() :void
{
   for( var i:int = 0; i<ALIENS_PER_ROW; i++ )
   {}
}
```

Each loop iteration creates a row of aliens. Because ALIENS_PER_ROW has been initialized with a value of 7, this loop iterates seven times before it completes execution.

6. **Declare and initialize an** Alien1 **instance as a local variable called** row1 **inside the** for **loop:**

```
private function buildAlienFleet() :void
{
   for( var i:int = 0; i<ALIENS_PER_ROW; i++ )
   {
      var row1:Alien1 = new Alien1();
   }
}
```

7. **Declare and initialize two** Alien2 **instances as local variables named** row2 **and** row3, **respectively:**

```
for( var i:int = 0; i<ALIENS_PER_ROW; i++ )
{
   var row1:Alien1 = new Alien1();
   var row2:Alien2 = new Alien2();
   var row3:Alien2 = new Alien2();
}
```

8. Declare and initialize two `Alien3` **instances as local variables named** `row4` **and** `row5`**:**

```
for( var i:int = 0; i<ALIENS_PER_ROW; i++ )
{
    var row1:Alien1 = new Alien1();
    var row2:Alien2 = new Alien2();
    var row3:Alien2 = new Alien2();
    var row4:Alien3 = new Alien3();
    var row5:Alien3 = new Alien3();
}
```

Unlike member variables, *local variables* — variables declared inside functions — do not need to be given access modifiers (`private` or `public` keywords). Their scope is implicitly localized to the function in which they are declared and cannot be accessed from outside the function. For example, a local variable declared in one function can't be accessed from a different function.

You're now at the halfway point. You have a programmatic loop that iterates seven times, creating 5 individual alien `MovieClips` on each iteration — 35 aliens, total, have been created when the loop exits.

The final parts of creating the alien fleet using code are to initialize both the `_fleetContainer Sprite` and the `_aliens Vector` object, add each of the aliens to the `_aliens Vector` object, and then position the aliens in a grid formation. Follow these steps to do that (all added code is shown in bold):

1. Initialize the `_fleetContainer Sprite` **as a new** `Sprite` **instance:**

```
private function buildAlienFleet() :void
{
    _fleetContainer = new Sprite();
    for( var i:int = 0; i<ALIENS_PER_ROW; i++ )
    {
```

2. Initialize the `_aliens Vector` **as a new** `Vector` **instance:**

```
private function buildAlienFleet() :void
{
    _aliens = new Vector.<MovieClip>();
    _fleetContainer = new Sprite();
    for( var i:int = 0; i<ALIENS_PER_ROW; i++ )
    {
```

3. Add each of the new alien instances that are created in the `for` **loop to the** `_aliens Vector` **instance:**

```
for( var i:int = 0; i<ALIENS_PER_ROW; i++ )
{
    //...
```

```
    _aliens.push( row1 );
    _aliens.push( row2 );
    _aliens.push( row3 );
    _aliens.push( row4 );
    _aliens.push( row5 );
}
```

4. **Add each of the new alien instances to the** _fleetContainer Sprite:

```
for( var i:int = 0; i<ALIENS_PER_ROW; i++ )
{
    //...
    _aliens.push( row4 );
    _aliens.push( row5 );

    _fleetContainer.addChild( row1 );
    _fleetContainer.addChild( row2 );
    _fleetContainer.addChild( row3 );
    _fleetContainer.addChild( row4 );
    _fleetContainer.addChild( row5 );
}
```

5. **Declare an** int **variable outside the** for **loop called** xOffset **to store the horizontal offset position:**

```
private function buildAlienFleet() :void
{
    var xOffset:int;
    _aliens = new Vector.<MovieClip>();
    _fleetContainer = new Sprite();
    for( var i:int = 0; i<ALIENS_PER_ROW; i++ )
```

The grid is built from left to right, with each iteration of the for loop creating a vertical column of alien MovieClips.

6. **Inside the** for **loop, set the** x **property for** row1 **to** row5 **of the alien** MovieClips **to the value of** xOffset:

```
private function buildAlienFleet() :void
{
    //...
    _fleetContainer.addChild( row4 );
    _fleetContainer.addChild( row5 );

    row1.x = xOffset;
    row2.x = xOffset;
    row3.x = xOffset;
    row4.x = xOffset;
    row5.x = xOffset;
}
```

7. **Set the** y **property of** row2 **to be the sum of** row1**'s** y **property,** row1**'s** height **property, and the** ALIEN_PADDING **variable:**

```
row4.x = xOffset;
row5.x = xOffset;
row2.y = row1.y + row1.height + ALIEN_PADDING;
```

Each MovieClip is positioned on the y-axis below its predecessor, with the addition of some padding to space them out a little. On the x-axis, each is positioned using the same value stored in the xOffset variable.

8. **Set the** y **property of** row3, row4, **and** row5 **to be the sum of the previous row's** y **property,** height **property, and the** ALIEN_PADDING **variable:**

```
row2.y = row1.y + row1.height + ALIEN_PADDING;
row3.y = row2.y + row2.height + ALIEN_PADDING;
row4.y = row3.y + row3.height + ALIEN_PADDING;
row5.y = row4.y + row4.height + ALIEN_PADDING;
```

You may be asking why I didn't set row1's y property. The reason is that I want it to be positioned at 0. The default x and y values for a display object are 0, and because I want to place row1 at 0 on the vertical axis, I don't need to change the default.

9. **Increment the** xOffset **variable for the next column in the grid.**

So that the next column of alien MovieClips isn't positioned directly over the top of the others that have just been positioned, the xOffset variable is incremented by the width of the Alien3 MovieClip, which is referenced through the row5 variable, plus a little padding:

```
    row4.y = row3.y + row3.height + ALIEN_PADDING;
    row5.y = row4.y + row4.height + ALIEN_PADDING;
    xOffset += row5.width + ALIEN_PADDING;
}
```

10. **After the closure of the** for **loop, add the code to change the** _fleet-Container Sprite's x **property so that the** Sprite **is horizontally centered:**

```
    for( var i:int = 0; i<ALIENS_PER_ROW; i++ )
    {
        //...
        xOffset += row5.width + ALIEN_PADDING;
    }
    _fleetContainer.x = ( stage.stageWidth * .5 ) - (
        _fleetContainer.width * .5 );
}
```

11. **Use the** `addChild()` **method to add the** `_fleetContainer` `Sprite` **to the display list:**

```
for( var i:int = 0; i<ALIENS_PER_ROW; i++ )
{
    //...
}
_fleetContainer.x = ( stage.stageWidth * .5 ) - (
    _fleetContainer.width * .5 );
addChild( _fleetContainer );
}
```

Here's what your `buildAlienFleet()` method now looks like in its entirety:

```
private function buildAlienFleet() :void
{
    _aliens = new Vector.<MovieClip>();
    _fleetContainer = new Sprite();

    var xOffset:int;

    for( var i:int = 0; i<ALIENS_PER_ROW; i++ )
    {
        var row1:Alien1 = new Alien1();
        var row2:Alien2 = new Alien2();
        var row3:Alien2 = new Alien2();
        var row4:Alien3 = new Alien3();
        var row5:Alien3 = new Alien3();

        _aliens.push( row1 );
        _aliens.push( row2 );
        _aliens.push( row3 );
        _aliens.push( row4 );
        _aliens.push( row5 );
        _fleetContainer.addChild( row1 );
        _fleetContainer.addChild( row2 );
        _fleetContainer.addChild( row3 );
        _fleetContainer.addChild( row4 );
        _fleetContainer.addChild( row5 );

        row1.x = xOffset + 5;
        row2.x = xOffset;
        row2.y = row1.y + row1.height + ALIEN_PADDING;
        row3.x = xOffset;
        row3.y = row2.y + row2.height + ALIEN_PADDING;
        row4.x = xOffset;
        row4.y = row3.y + row3.height + ALIEN_PADDING;
        row5.x = xOffset;
        row5.y = row4.y + row4.height + ALIEN_PADDING;
```

```
     xOffset += row5.width + ALIEN_PADDING;
  }
  _fleetContainer.x = ( stage.stageWidth * .5 ) - ( _
        fleetContainer.width * .5 );
  addChild( _fleetContainer );
}
```

You're done! You can test now to check that it all works fine. Just comment out the line that calls `displayStartScreen()` in your `initialize` method, and add a call to the `buildAlienFleet()` method:

```
private function initialize( e:Event ):void
{
   removeEventListener( Event.ADDED_TO_STAGE, initialize
        );
   //displayStartScreen();
   buildAlienFleet();
}
```

Press Ctrl+Enter (Windows) or Command+Enter (Mac) to run the application. You'll see 35 alien `MovieClip` objects stacked in five rows of seven on the stage (refer to Figure 6-3).

Don't forget to remove the comment in front of the `displayStartScreen()` call and delete the `buildAlienFleet()` line, as those changes were just to test the feature you've just built.

By simply altering the value of the `ALIENS_PER_ROW` constant from 6 to 12, you can create 70 `MovieClip` instances in the display list. Make it 24 and you'll find 140 are created. Useful stuff!

Registering for User Interaction Events

On both Android and iOS devices, users interact with an object in the display list via touch. The Flash Player API provides an extended set of classes that allow touch events to be handled in your Flash application. However, unless the application is explicitly "listening" for these interaction events, they go unnoticed, and the user gets no noticeable feedback or response. To have the application respond to user interaction, you first need to assign event listeners to the display objects you want the user to interact with.

In the following steps, I show you how to add code to the `StartScreen.as` class you created earlier in this chapter to assign an event listener for when the user touches the `StartButton` display object. I've bolded all the new code so that you can see where to place it within the existing code:

1. **Open** `StartScreen.as` **for editing in Flash Professional.**

2. **Register a** `MouseEvent.CLICK` **event listener to the** `StartButton`
instance:

```
public class StartScreen extends MovieClip
{
    public function StartScreen()
    {
        stop();
        cacheAsBitmap = true;
        startButton.addEventListener( MouseEvent.CLICK,
          onStartClick );
    }
}
```

3. **Create a new method called** `onStartClick` **that handles the**
`CLICK` **event:**

```
public class StartScreen extends MovieClip
{
    public function StartScreen()
    {
        //...
    }
    private function onStartClick( e:MouseEvent ) :void
    {}
}
```

4. **Dispatch an** `Event.SELECT` **event from the** `onStartClick()` **method.**

```
private function onStartClick( e:MouseEvent ) :void
{}
```

This code allows an application that implements the `StartScreen`
`MovieClip` to register for the `Event.SELECT` event to know when the
game needs to start.

The code inside the `StartScreen` class is complete. Next, I show you how
to register a listener for `Event.SELECT` in the Document Class against the
`StartScreen` instance so that the user will receive start notifications from
the `StartScreen`:

1. **Open** `SpaceshipZapZap.as` **in Flash Professional.**

2. **Register a** `SELECT` **event listener to the** `StartScreen` **instance, inside
the** `displayStartScreen()` **method:**

```
private function displayStartScreen() :void
{
    _startScreen = new StartScreen();
    addChild( _startScreen );
    _startScreen.addEventListener( Event.SELECT,
        onStartSelect );
}
```

3. **Create a new method called** `onStartSelect` **to handle the**
   `SELECT` **event.**

```
public class SpaceshipZapZap extends MovieClip
{
    //...
    private function buildAlienFleet() :void
    {
        //...
    }
    private function onStartSelect( e:Event ) :void
    {}
}
```

4. **Call** `removeChild()` **from inside the** `onStartSelect()` **method to**
   remove `_startScreen` **from the display list:**

```
private function onStartSelect( e:Event ) :void
{
    removeChild( _startScreen );
}
```

5. **Invoke the** `buildAlienFleet()` **method from inside the**
   `onStartSelect` **handler:**

```
private function onStartSelect( e:Event ) :void
{
    removeChild( _startScreen );
    buildAlienFleet();
}
```

Do a quick-publish of your application by pressing Ctrl+Enter (Windows) or
Command+Enter (Mac), and then click the Start button in your application.
The `MouseEvent.CLICK` event is raised when the user touches the object
with his or her finger — or clicks it with the mouse in your test — so this is a
fair simulation of the behavior you'd expect to see when you get the application onto a mobile device.

Moving objects around

With touch-screen devices, you'll often want your user to be able to touch
a display object and move it with his or her finger to another part of the
screen. To many, this behavior is better known as drag and drop and was
once one of the key differentiators between the Flash platform and other
browser-based technologies. Although the example you work through
here won't necessarily be the behavior that'll be used in the completed
SpaceshipZapZap application, you will use the techniques demonstrated to
create more complex movement gestures, so treat this as practice for now.

For the device to detect movement, you need to first register for an event that tells the device that contact with an object has been made and then register to follow the movement of that contact until the contact ends. Three `MouseEvents` satisfy the criteria for this: MOUSE_DOWN, MOUSE_MOVE, and MOUSE_UP.

Follow these steps to establish these event listeners, and then create the methods that can handle them:

1. **Open your iOS or Android application FLA in Flash Professional.**

   In Chapter 4, in the section on starting a project in Flash Professional, I show you how to start new AIR for Android and iOS FLA files.

2. **In the Properties panel, delete the text in the Class field, type MyDragTest, and then click the wrench icon next to the Class field.**

   The ActionScript Class Warning dialog box appears, stating that a definition for the class cannot yet be found.

3. **Click OK.**

4. **Click the wrench icon next to the Class field again.**

   The Edit ActionScript Class dialog box appears.

5. **Choose Flash Professional as the application that should create the ActionScript 3.0 class, and click OK.**

   A new ActionScript 3.0 class opens in Flash Professional.

6. **Initialize an instance of the `Alien2 MovieClip` from the Library and add it to the display list as follows:**

```
package
{
    import flash.display.MovieClip;
    public class MyDragTest extends MovieClip
    {
        public function MyDragTest()
        {
            var object:Alien2 = new Alien2();
            addChild( object );
        }
    }
}
```

7. **Register event listeners to the `Alien2` instance for the MOUSE_DOWN, MOUSE_UP, and CLICK events:**

```
public function MyDragTest()
{
    var object:Alien2 = new Alien2();
    addChild( object );
```

```
object.addEventListener( MouseEvent.MOUSE_DOWN,
    onItemDown );
object.addEventListener( MouseEvent.MOUSE_UP,
    onItemUp );
object.addEventListener( MouseEvent.CLICK,
    onItemClick );
}
```

8. **Create new methods called** onItemDown, onItemUp, **and**
   onItemClick **to handle each of the event types:**

```
package
{
    public class MyDragTest
    {
        public function MyDragTest()
        {
            //..
        }
        private function onItemDown( e:MouseEvent )
            :void
        {}
        private function onItemUp( e:MouseEvent ) :void
        {}
        private function onItemClick( e:MouseEvent )
            :void
        {}
    }
}
```

9. **In the** onItemDown **method, register a listener to the stage to receive
   notifications of the** MOUSE_MOVE **event:**

```
private function onItemDown( e:MouseEvent ) :void
{
    stage.addEventListener( MouseEvent.MOUSE_MOVE,
        onItemMove );
}
```

This listener is assigned to the stage, not to the item itself, so that the
event will continue to trigger even if the user accidentally moves his or
her finger away from the item while still pressing down.

10. **Create a new method called** onItemMove **to handle the** MOUSE_MOVE
    event called:

```
        private function onItemClick( e:MouseEvent )
            :void
                {}
        private function onItemMove( e:MouseEvent )
            :void
        {}
    }
}
```

11. Remove the stage listener from inside the `onItemUp` **handler:**

```
private function onItemUp( e:MouseEvent ) :void
{
    stage.addEventListener( MouseEvent.MOUSE_MOVE,
        onItemMove );
}
```

You won't need the listener after the `MOUSE_UP` event has fired, signaling that the user is no longer touching the item.

Having rigged up all the events, it's time to apply the logic that will update the position of the item that the user is moving with his or her finger. A slight "gotcha" here is that the `MOUSE_MOVE` listener is assigned to the stage, not the item itself, so you have no reference to it in the `onItemMove` handler. That is, the `currentTarget` property of the event object passed to the handler is the stage itself, not the item that the user is moving. To get around this, you can store a reference to the item when the `MOUSE_DOWN` handler is invoked. Here's how:

1. In `MyDragTest.as`, **declare a new member variable called** `item`:

```
package
{
    public class MyDragTest
    {
        private var item:MovieClip;
        public function MyDragTest()
        {
            //..
```

2. In the `onItemDown()` **method, assign the** `currentTarget` **property of the** `MouseEvent` **object to the** `item` **property:**

```
private function onItemDown( e:MouseEvent ) :void
{
    item = e.currentTarget as MovieClip;
}
```

3. Inside the `onItemMove()` **method, position** `item` **by using the stage's** `mouseX` **and** `mouseY` **properties (the current mouse position on the stage):**

```
private function onItemMove( e:MouseEvent ) :void
{
    item.x = stage.mouseX;
    item.y = stage.mouseY;
}
```

At this point, your application will compile and execute just fine; press Ctrl+Enter (Windows) or Command+Enter (Mac) to test it. However, you'll find two annoyances here. First, the item seems to jump when you first move it, as if it's not being dragged from the position that you pressed down on. Second, and far more noticeable, is that the click event fires when you release the item. This is far from ideal!

Fortunately, you can prevent both of these undesirable outcomes by adding and tracking a couple of additional properties in the class. The following instructions explain how:

1. **Declare and initialize a constant** int **variable called** CLICK_TOLERANCE **with the value** 250:

```
package
{
    public class MyDragTest
    {
        private const CLICK_TOLERANCE:int = 250;
        private var item:MovieClip;
        public function MyDragTest()
        {
            //..
```

The CLICK_TOLERANCE property is a constant that is initialized with the value of 250. This value is the limit in milliseconds within which a CLICK event will be allowed to occur. Should the user release an item within 250 milliseconds, the click event will be handled.

2. **Declare an** int **variable called** lastClick:

```
public class MyDragTest
{
    private var lastClick:int;
    private const CLICK_TOLERANCE:int = 250;
    private var item:MovieClip;
    public function MyDragTest()
    {
        //..
```

3. **Declare a** Point **variable called** mouseOffset:

```
public class MyDragTest
{
    private var mouseOffset:Point;
    private var lastClick:int;
    private const CLICK_TOLERANCE:int = 250;
```

4. **Within the** onItemDown() **method, assign the** lastClick **variable the value of Flash's** getTimer() **global method:**

```
private function onItemDown( e:MouseEvent ) :void
{
    stage.addEventListener( MouseEvent.MOUSE_MOVE,
        onItemMove );
    lastClick = getTimer();
}
```

5. **In the** `onItemDown()` **method, initialize the** `mouseOffset` **variable with the value of the** `MouseEvent` **object's** `localX` **and** `localY` **properties:**

```
private function onItemDown( e:MouseEvent ) :void
{
    stage.addEventListener( MouseEvent.MOUSE_MOVE,
        onItemMove );
    lastClick = getTimer();
    mouseOffset = new Point( e.localX, e.localY );
}
```

The `localX` and `localY` properties are the on-screen coordinates at which the `MOUSE_DOWN` event occurred, localized to the object on which they occurred. You store them as a `Point`, as it's a suitable object to store coordinates in.

6. **Replace the positioning code in the** `onItemMove` **method to offset the** `stage.mouseX` **and** `stage.mouseY` **values by the** x **and** y **values stored in the** `mouseOffset` **Point:**

```
private function onItemMove( e:MouseEvent ) :void
{
    item.x = stage.mouseX - mouseOffset.x;
    item.y = stage.mouseY - mouseOffset.y;
}
```

This change positions the item relative to the point that the user made contact with it, rather than from its 0,0 registration point.

7. **Add an** `if` **statement to the** `onItemClick()` **method to check whether the time elapsed since the last click is less than the value of the** `CLICK_TOLERANCE` **variable:**

```
private function onItemClick( e:MouseEvent ) :void
{
    if( getTimer() - lastClick < CLICK_TOLERANCE )
    {}
}
```

This code checks whether the time between the `MOUSE_DOWN` event occurring and the `CLICK` event being handled is within the 250-millisecond threshold assigned in Step 1.

8. **Use the** `navigateToURL()` **global method to open** `http://www.bbc.co.uk` **in the device web browser:**

```
private function onItemClick( e:MouseEvent ) :void
{
    if( getTimer() - lastClick < CLICK_TOLERANCE )
    {
        navigateToURL( new URLRequest( "http://www.bbc.
            co.uk" ) );
    }
}
```

That's it! Now try running your application again, and observe the difference those changes have made. You can move the object around the screen with the mouse — a finger on an Android or iOS device — and only a rapid press-and-release motion will invoke the browser to open and navigate to the supplied URL.

Here's what the complete MyDragTest class should now look like:

```
package
{
    import flash.display.MovieClip;
    import flash.events.MouseEvent;
    import flash.geom.Point;
    import flash.net.navigateToURL;
    import flash.net.URLRequest;
    import flash.utils.getTimer;

    public class MyDragTest extends MovieClip
    {
        private const CLICK_TOLERANCE:int = 250;
        private var item:MovieClip;
        private var lastClick:int;
        private var mouseOffset:Point;

        public function MyDragTest()
        {
            var object:Alien2 = new Alien2();
            addChild( object );
            object.addEventListener( MouseEvent.CLICK,
              onItemClick );
            object.addEventListener( MouseEvent.MOUSE_DOWN,
              onItemDown );
            object.addEventListener( MouseEvent.MOUSE_UP,
              onItemUp );
        }

        private function onItemDown( e:MouseEvent ) :void
        {
            lastClick = getTimer();
            item = e.currentTarget as MovieClip;
            mouseOffset = new Point( e.localX, e.localY );
            stage.addEventListener( MouseEvent.MOUSE_MOVE,
              onItemMove );
         }

        private function onItemUp( e:MouseEvent ) :void
        {
            stage.removeEventListener( MouseEvent.MOUSE_MOVE,
              onItemMove );
        }

        private function onItemMove( e:MouseEvent ) :void
```

```
        {
            item.x = stage.mouseX - mouseOffset.x;
            item.y = stage.mouseY - mouseOffset.y;
        }

        private function onItemClick( e:MouseEvent ) :void
        {
            if( getTimer() - lastClick < CLICK_TOLERANCE )
            {
                navigateToURL( new URLRequest( "http://www.
            bbc.co.uk" ) );
            }
        }
    }
}
```

 Don't forget to switch the Document Class for your SpaceshipZapZap application back to `SpaceshipZapZap.as`; you don't need `MyDragTest.as` beyond this example.

Bubbling your events is expensive

The event model introduced with ActionScript 3.0 gave you the ability to bubble events up through a set of nested children and listen for them on the outer parent. Although this is handy, event bubbling affects performance on devices with lower processing power, so you must eliminate event bubbling where it isn't necessary for your application to function.

The `TextField` class dispatches `Event.CHANGE` every time the value in the control changes. So as a user types **four** into an input `TextField`, the change event is dispatched no less than four times! To add insult, the event is also configured to bubble by default. `MouseEvent`s are also a common culprit, as they too bubble by default.

To stop any `Event` object bubbling beyond the current handler method, you can use the `stopPropagation()` method:

```
private function onMouseClick( e:MouseEvent ) :void
{
    e.stopPropagation();
}
```

After calling the `stopPropagation()` method, any further bubbling beyond the current event execution thread will not occur, effectively stopping the event in its tracks.

To prevent a `TextField` from bubbling, change events up to the main application. The best approach is to encapsulate the `TextField` itself inside a `MovieClip` or `Sprite` object. By then applying a code-behind class to the `MovieClip`, you can capture the `CHANGE` events each time they're dispatched by the `TextField` and stop them from propagating. I show you how to do that in the following steps:

1. **Choose Insert➪New Symbol to create a new** `MovieClip` **in the Library.**

   Alternatively press Ctrl+F8 (Windows) or FN+Command+F8 (Mac).

   The Create New Symbol dialog box appears.

2. **Select the Export for ActionScript check box in the Linkage section.**

3. **Give your** `MovieClip` **any name you like.**

   I named mine MyMovieClip.

4. **Select the Text tool from the Tools panel and draw a dynamic** `TextField` **in the** `MovieClip`.

5. **Select the new** `TextField`.

6. **In the Properties panel:**

   a. **Set the** `TextField` **instance name to** myTextField.

   b. **Set the TextField text engine to Classic Text.**

   c. **Set the text type to Dynamic Text.**

7. **Right-click (Windows) or Control+click (Mac) and select Edit Class.**

   The ActionScript class for `MyMovieClip` opens for editing.

8. **Register an event listener to the** `myTextField` **instance for a** `CHANGE` **event and assign the handler name as** `onTextChange`:

```
package
{
    import flash.display.MovieClip;
    import flash.events.Event;

    public class MyMovieClip extends MovieClip
    {
        public function MyMovieClip()
        {
            myTextField.addEventListener( Event.CHANGE,
            onTextChange );
        }
    }
}
```

9. **Create a new method called** `onTextChange` **to handle the** `CHANGE` **event:**

```
private function onTextChange( e:Event ) :void
{}
```

The method immediately kills the event bubbling phase.

10. **Call the** `stopPropagation` **method on the** `Event` **object:**

```
private function onTextChange( e:Event ) :void
{
    e.stopPropagation();
}
```

Although this is enough to know for the purposes of keeping event management in check for mobile application development, the intricacies of the event model in Flash are vast. If you'd like to discover more about the event system in Flash, read Trevor McCauley's article on the Adobe Developer Connection, which you can find at: `http://www.adobe.com/devnet/actionscript/articles/event_handling_as3.html`.

Applying Programmatic Filters Properly

Developers have been using ActionScript code to apply filters to display objects at runtime since the release of Flash Player 8. ActionScript allows you to add adjustments such as blur and drop shadow to an instance with just a couple of lines of code, and you can remove them just as easily.

With the introduction of a faster and more efficient virtual machine in Flash Player 9, developers have been able to use filters far more liberally throughout their applications, with little need to worry about performance. When you target a resource-constrained device, such as a mobile phone, it's important to consider the impact that programmatic adjustments to display objects can have on the overall performance of your application. Filters are computationally intensive, so when building applications targeting Android and iOS, the general rule is to use them only where you need to. An application with filters applied to many of the child display objects, particularly ones that are intended to move around, will not perform as well as an application that has just a few filters. I also want to note that filters can often be substituted with enhancements to the base graphic or shape. For example, you can easily apply a drop shadow to a shape by adding another drawing layer rather than applying it via a filter (I demonstrate how to create a drop shadow effect using the drawing tools in Flash Professional in Chapter 5).

Although it's important to use filters sparingly, I think it's equally important to know how filters work. Try applying a `BlurFilter` to a display object at runtime. In the Document Class you've been working on, follow these instructions to add some code at the point where you dynamically create the alien fleet objects:

1. **Open** `SpaceshipZapZap.as` **in Flash Professional.**

   I show you how to create this class near the start of this chapter.

2. **Create a new** `BlurFilter` **instance in the** `buildAlienFleet()` **method:**

```
private function buildAlienFleet() :void
{
    var blur:BlurFilter = new BlurFilter();
    //...
}
```

3. **Apply the** `BlurFilter` **instance to the** `row1` **filters property (which contains an instance of** `Alien1`**):**

```
private function buildAlienFleet() :void
{
    var blur:BlurFilter = new BlurFilter();
    //..
    row5.y = row4.y + row4.height + ALIEN_PADDING;
    xOffset += row5.width + ALIEN_PADDING;
    row1.filters = [ blur ];
}
```

The square brackets, [ ], are placed around the `blur` instance because the `filters` property expects an Array to be assigned to it; the square brackets are a shortcut for wrapping an object inside an Array.

Now test the application again by pressing Ctrl+Enter (Windows) or Command+Enter (Mac). The `Alien1` instances added to the display list are now blurry.

Great! You can apply filters to display objects, evaluate where they should be used, and see where you can substitute their use for a more efficient approach using predrawn graphics.

Bitmap Caching All the Way!

Graphics rendering is one of the most processor-intensive operations that occurs throughout your application's execution on a mobile device. You can gain great performance improvements from delegating some of the responsibility for rendering to the device's graphics processing unit (GPU). ActionScript 3.0 can help with this. ActionScript 3.0 offers a relatively unfamiliar, but highly effective, display objects property called `cacheAsBitmap`. Setting the `cacheAsBitmap` property to `true` causes an application that is able to delegate rendering to the GPU to take a snapshot of the display object and store a bitmap representation of it in memory. This makes rerendering the object much faster than if it is drawn normally because the application just uses the prerendered snapshot.

Here's how you set the `cacheAsBitmap` property to `true` on a display object:

```
var mySprite:Sprite = new Sprite();
mySprite.cacheAsBitmap = true;
```

Earlier in the chapter, you created the code-behind class for the `StartScreen` `MovieClip` and set the `cacheAsBitmap` property to `true` in the constructor. You did that to automatically turn on bitmap caching whenever an instance of the `MovieClip` object is created. This demonstrates another benefit of having an ActionScript class behind your `MovieClip` objects: Developers who later come to use your `MovieClips` won't need to decide whether it is appropriate to turn on bitmap caching.

If your display object will be rotated or scaled during its lifetime, your display object will need another property set on it called `cacheAsBitmapMatrix`. Setting this property allows the application to perform transformations on the object using the device's GPU, which is able to perform these transformations far faster than if the same was done on the device's CPU. Even with `cacheAsBitmap` turned on, an object that undergoes a transformation won't be rendered on the GPU without the `cacheAsBitmapMatrix` property also set.

For both `cacheAsBitmap` and `cacheAsBitmapMatrix` to work correctly, you must select GPU rendering on the Publish Settings page in Flash Professional. For Android, this is covered in Chapter 13, and for iOS, in Chapter 16.

You can enable the `cacheAsBitmapMatrix` feature by using the following code:

```
var mySprite:Sprite = new Sprite();
mySprite.cacheAsBitmap = true;
mySprite.cacheAsBitmapMatrix = new Matrix();
```

Caching display objects that are likely to change frequently is usually a bad idea because caching an image is processor-intensive, and the GPU has to cache the image again each time it changes. Examples of objects where you should not set `cacheAsBitmap=true` are

- Dynamic text fields and text input fields
- `Sprites` that draw frequently using their graphics property
- `DisplayObjectContainers` that alter or move their children frequently

The `cacheAsBitmap` and `cacheAsBitmapMatrix` properties are simple, but both are highly effective ways of improving the performance of the graphics. Often property tweaks like these are sufficient to get performance bottlenecks in your application down to an acceptable level.

Cleaning Up After Yourself

Imagine living in a mansion where you never took the trash out. After a while, you might start tripping over rubbish, but it's going to take a while before things get really bad because you have so much space. Now imagine doing the same in a very small apartment. The environment deteriorates in a much shorter period of time. If you're going to be able to carry on living there, you have to take the trash out. The same is true for memory management on resource-constrained devices like an iPhone or Android device: As objects implemented in an application cease to be useful, the app needs to perform a few housekeeping tasks to ensure that those objects don't linger and start making the application fall over. In software development, this lingering is known as a *memory leak*.

Although memory usage should be a consideration for all Flash developers, those working on applications that target conventional computers are spoiled with vast amounts of available memory and fast processing capabilities. It's easy to understand why memory management becomes a low priority to these developers — why worry about running out of memory when you have so much? Development for mobile devices is different and mandates that you write code in a way that it cleans up after itself.

ActionScript gives Flash developers a very effective automatic memory management system called the Garbage Collector that can "sweep away" objects that are no longer referenced in your application, freeing memory on the device. If you imagine it as a little robot with a vacuum cleaner working invisibly inside your application — clearing up things marked as rubbish — you won't be far wrong! Using ActionScript Garbage Collector is far easier than using some other programming languages, such as the iPhone's native Objective-C language, which requires the developers to manage all memory allocation themselves — a real headache if you're not used to it!

Two circumstances stop the Garbage Collector from sweeping up an object and freeing the memory it occupied: having a reference to the object stored in a variable or leaving an event listener registered to the object. By default, a listener reference remains in memory until it is explicitly removed using the `removeEventListener` method. Even after the object the listener was registered to has been set to `null` — the way a variable is emptied of its current object instance in ActionScript 3.0 — the listener will continue to persist and won't be removed by the Garbage Collector. This type of listener persistence is a common cause of memory leaks.

In the next sections, I introduce you to some practices that you can implement to avoid garbage from building in your application. As an added benefit, all the practices I mention can be used in regular Flash applications (not just mobile apps) to improve their performance too. I'll try not to nag too much, but suffice it to say that resource management is an important part of developing for mobile devices and other devices that have limited memory.

Null the objects you don't need and recycle those that you do

It's great practice to `null` objects that you don't need anymore — allowing the garbage collector to free the memory — but on mobile devices, you have the additional consideration of the CPU resources required for the creation of a new object (something you'd seldom need to worry about on a regular computer). To address this, you can implement an object recycling technique known as *object pooling,* where, instead of completely destroying the object you were using, you can leave it in a "pool" — such as a `Vector` object — for reuse the next time you need an object like it. The references remain the same, and therefore you avoid the overhead of object instantiation. For example, a game like SpaceshipZapZap, which has many repeating display objects — in the form of alien spaceships appearing and being blown up — would benefit from object pooling. If no more than 35 alien craft are on the screen, the maximum that ever needs to be created in the application's lifetime is 35.

Looking back at the SpaceshipZapZap Document Class created at the start of the chapter, you recall that as well as creating the 35 alien `MovieClips`, a reference to each was pushed onto a `Vector` object. This was quite a handy thing to do, as this is half the work of object pooling. Now you just need to write the logic that determines whether objects are in the pool, and what to do if they are — you already have the code to create a new alien fleet if they aren't.

Open SpaceshipZapZap.as in Flash Professional, then follow these steps to implement object pooling for the `buildAlienFleet` method in the SpaceshipZapZap Document Class:

1. **Wrap all the code inside the** `buildAlienFleet()` **method with an** `if...else` **statement to check whether the** `_aliens` Vector **is not initialized:**

```
private function buildAlienFleet() :void
{
    if( !_aliens )
    {
        xOffset:int;
        _aliens = new Vector.<MovieClip>();
        _fleetContainer = new Sprite();
        for( var i:int = 0; i< ALIENS_PER_ROW; i++ )
        //...
        addChild( _fleetContainer );
    }
    else
    {
        // new code will go here
    }
}
```

2. **Create a** `for...each` **loop that adds all existing alien** `MovieClips` **in the** `_aliens` `Vector` **to the** `_fleetContainer`.

Using the `for...each` loop against the `_aliens` `Vector`, you can iterate through all the contents of a `Vector` object, performing a routine on each item. In this instance, the routine is simply to add `MovieClips` already initialized in the `Vector` to the display list:

```
private function buildAlienFleet() :void
{
    if( !_aliens )
    {
        //..
    }
    else
    {
        for each( var item:MovieClip in _aliens )
        {
            _fleetContainer.addChild( item );
        }
    }
}
```

3. **Move the two lines of code responsible for the display and positioning of the** `_fleetContainer` `Sprite` **outside the** `if..else` **statement, placing them at the end of** `buildAlienFleet()` **method:**

```
private function buildAlienFleet() :void
{
    if( !_aliens )
    {
        //...
    }
    else
    {
        //...
    }
    _fleetContainer.x = ( stage.stageWidth * .5 ) - (
        _fleetContainer.width * .5 );
    addChild( _fleetContainer );
}
```

Your object pooling code is complete, and your application is now recycling! You can test that it's working by temporarily adding some code to the `initialize` method of your Document Class:

```
private function initialize( e:Event ):void
{
    removeEventListener( Event.ADDED_TO_STAGE, initialize
            );
    displayStartScreen();
    buildAlienFleet();
    trace( System.privateMemory );
    buildAlienFleet();
```

```
    trace( System.privateMemory );
    buildAlienFleet();
    trace( System.privateMemory );
}
```

The code that you added here repeatedly calls the `buildAlienFleet()` method, and after each call, it traces out to the console window the amount of memory (in bytes) being used by the Flash application, which is accessed using the `System.privateMemory` property in ActionScript.

Run the application in Flash Professional by pressing Ctrl+Enter (Windows) or Command+Enter (Mac). Notice how the value traced out barely changes. This demonstrates that little to no new memory is being allocated to the application during the repeated build and rebuild of the alien fleet `MovieClip` assets — the recycling is working!

Assign listeners with weak references

An alternative to manually removing all the listener registrations that you assigned to an object is to change the way that you assign them in the first place.

A weakly referenced listener can never hold on to a reference to an object if the object is null or goes out of scope. This means you can set an object to `null`, safe in the knowledge that the listener won't prevent the Garbage Collector from sweeping up the disused object. Here's how you assign a listener with a weak reference:

```
myButton.addEventListener( MouseEvent.MOUSE_DOWN,
        onTouchBegin, false, 0, true );
```

In the listener assignment, you can see the addition of three new parameters to the `addEventListener` method, which appear as `false`, `0` and `true`, after the `onTouchBegin` handler parameter. Here's what each of them does:

✔ `useCapture` is a Boolean parameter that determines whether the listener works in the capture or the target and bubbling phases. Changing this isn't a priority right now, so set it as `false` (its default).

✔ `priority` is an integer that you can set to change the priority of an event listener. If you wanted to make a listener receive the event before any other listeners registered against the same event type, you would set this parameter to a value greater than 1. In this case, changing the priority of the listener isn't important, so set it as 0.

✔ `useWeakReference` is a Boolean value that determines whether the listener is assigned with a weak reference or a strong one. By default, this parameter is `false`. You want a weak reference, so set this to `true`.

Writing Code That Performs

There's more than one way to skin a cat, and when it comes to writing code that performs well, you have myriad tricks and tweaks that every ActionScript developer can share. By no means an exhaustive list, following are some optimizations you should consider including in your code to improve the execution speed of your application:

✔ **Square bracket notation executes slowly.** Minimize their use by storing a reference in a local variable before trying to modify its properties. Instead of

```
_aliens[ i ].x = 0;
_aliens[ i ].y = _aliens[ i ].height * i;
```

it's better to use

```
var item:MovieClip = _aliens[ i ];
item.x = 0;
item.y = item.height * i;
```

✔ **Append text to** `TextFields` **rather than using the** `+=` **notation.** Instead of

```
myTextField.text += "some more text";
```

or

```
myTextField.text = myTextField.text + "some more
        text";
```

it's better to use

```
myTextField.appendText( "some more text" );
```

✔ **Evaluation in loops is costly.** Localize `Array` lengths and other properties you're going to evaluate in the `for` loop to prevent evaluation having to occur on each iteration. Instead of

```
for( var i:int=0; i<_aliens.length; i+=1 )
{}
```

it's better to use

```
var len:int = _aliens.length;
for( var i:int=0; i<len; i+=1 )
{}
```

✔ **ActionScript 3.0 is a strongly typed language.** Providing strong references to everything speeds execution. Instead of

```
var myValueObject:Object = new Object();
myValueObject [ "counter" ] = 52;
myValueObject [ "color" ] = 0xFF6600;
var myCounter:int = myValueObject [ "counter" ];
```

you should create a strongly typed value object class that you can then use dot notation to access the properties through:

```
package
{
    public class ValueObject
    {
        public var counter:int;
        public var color:uint;
        public function ValueObject(){}
    }
}
```

You'd then implement it like this:

```
var myValueObject:ValueObject = new ValueObject();
myValueObject.counter = 52;
myValueObject.color = 0xFF6600;
```

✔ **Adding is faster than multiplying.** If you want to multiply by 2, it's faster to add the two numbers together. Instead of:

```
var myMultiple:Number = 5 * 2;
```

It's better to use

```
var myMultiple:Number = 5 + 5;
```

✔ **Multiplying is faster than dividing.** If you want to divide a number by 2, it's faster to multiply the number by 0.5. Instead of

```
var myHalf:Number = 4 / 2;
```

it's better to use

```
var myHalf:Number = 4 * .5;
```

✔ `Math.floor` **is slower than casting the number an** `int`, **and both are slower than the** `bitwise` **>> operator.** These all yield the same value:

```
var scale:int = Math.floor( 5.4 );
scale = int( 5.4 );
scale = 5.4 >> 0;
```

All three round 5.4 down to 5, but `int()` is faster than `Math.floor`, and the right-shift bitwise operator is the fastest of all.

✔ **Be sure that your performance issue is not actually a problem with available memory.** You can see how much memory your application is using by writing the `System.privateMemory` property to the Output panel in Flash Professional like this:

```
trace( System.privateMemory );
```

These are just a few of the enhancements you can make to the way you write ActionScript code to improve its efficiency. Bear in mind that optimization is something that you layer onto your application after you've arrived at something that works satisfactorily, but could use tweaks on the performance side. A notable computer scientist, Donald Knuth, once said, "Premature optimization is the root of all evil," making the point that until you've identified the parts you need to optimize, how do you know you're optimizing anything? Don't let best practices get in the way of laying down your ideas and writing the code for your application — the time to optimize will present itself in due course.

Testing Your Code

Testing your code to confirm that it's working as intended, and as efficiently as possible, is the best way to ensure that your app will function well on your target mobile devices and pass the vetting process for the Apple App Store and Android Market. The next sections introduce a few ActionScript tools that you can use to test the performance of your code.

PerformanceTest

You don't really want to take my word for it when I say that some ways of writing code execute faster than others — never listen to other developers; they know nothing. You need to test it and see it for yourself! To that end, ActionScript performance expert Grant Skinner has created a handy class called PerformanceTest that allows you to run performance tests yourself. You can download it from `http://gskinner.com/blog/assets/PerformanceTest.zip`.

Using PerformanceTest, try testing and comparing `Math.floor` and casting as an `int` to see which one is faster. I walk you through that process here (new code is in bold):

1. **Place the PerformanceTest ActionScript class file in the directory structure** `com/gskinner/utils` **relative to your application FLA.**

2. **In Flash Professional, choose File➪New➪ActionScript 3.0 Class.**

3. **Select Flash Professional as the application with which to edit the class.**

4. Enter the class name PerfTest **and click OK.**

A new ActionScript 3.0 class document opens in Flash Professional, with the following code already added:

```
package
{
   public class PerfTest
   {
      public function PerfTest()
      {
         // constructor code
      }
   }
}
```

5. Type extends MovicClip **next to the class name:**

```
package
{
   import flash.display.MovieClip;
   public class PerfTest extends MovieClip
   {
      public function PerfTest()
```

6. Declare a new local variable called perfTest **and assign it the value of** PerformanceTest.getInstance().

As you type **PerformanceTest**, Flash Professional will offer to auto-complete the name for you. By accepting the autocomplete suggestion, Flash Professional will automatically add the import com.gskinner. utils.PerformanceTest directive to the top of the class like this:

```
function PerfTest()
{
   var perfTest:PerformanceTest = PerformanceTest.
      getInstance();
}
```

7. Set the perfTest out **property to** trace.

The out property is the output location — the place where all the text output from the performance tests will be put. Setting it to trace means that all output will go straight to the output panel, when the application is run in Flash Professional:

```
public function PerfTest()
{
   var perfTest:PerformanceTest = PerformanceTest.
      getInstance();
   perfTest.out = trace;
}
```

8. Save the file as PerfTest.as **in the same directory as your application FLA.**

That's the initialization of PerformanceTest. Now you need to define some tests for it to run. The next set of steps show you how to define two tests in your new `PerfTest` class:

1. **Create a new method in the** `PerfTest` **class called** `floor`:

```
public class PerfTest extends MovieClip
{
    public function PerfTest()
    {
        var perfTest:PerformanceTest = PerformanceTest.
          getInstance();
        perfTest.out = trace;
    }
    private function floor() :void
    {}
}
```

2. **Add a** `for` **loop to the** `floor()` **method that iterates 100,000 times:**

```
private function floor() :void
{
    for( var i:int=0; i<100000; i++ )
    {}
}
```

3. **Inside the** `for` **loop, apply** `Math.floor` **to the value 3.5.**

The effect of the `floor` function is to round 3.5 down to 3 — using the `Math.floor` method — 100,000 times:

```
private function floor() :void
{
    for( var i:int=0; i<100000; i++ )
    {
        Math.floor( 3.5 );
    }
}
```

4. **Create a new method in the** `PerfTest` **class called** `cast`:

```
        private function floor() :void
        {
            for( var i:int=0; i<100000; i++ )
            {
                Math.floor( 3.5 );
            }
        }
        private function cast() :void
        {}
    }
}
```

5. Add a `for` loop to the `cast()` method that iterates 100,000 times:

```
private function cast() :void
{
    for( var i:int=0; i<100000; i++ )
    {}
}
```

6. Inside the `for` loop, cast the value 3.5 to an `int`.

The effect of the `cast` function is to cast 3.5 to an integer — effectively rounding it down to 3 — 100,000 times:

```
private function cast() :void
{
    for( var i:int=0; i<100000; i++ )
    {
        int( 3.5 );
    }
}
```

7. Call the `testFunction()` method with parameters specifying `floor` as the function to call, the number of times to call it as `5`, the function name to trace to the output console as `floor`, and a description to trace out as `Test of Math.floor`.

This is the code that causes a test to be executed on the `floor` method. The first two parameters are the most important as they indicate to the `PerformanceTest` class what function to call and how many times to call it:

```
public function PerfTest()
{
    var perfTest:PerformanceTest = PerformanceTest.
        getInstance();
    perfTest.out = trace;
    perfTest.testFunction( floor, 5, "floor", "Test of
        Math.floor" );
}
```

8. Call the `testFunction()` method with parameters specifying `cast` as the function to call, the number of times to call it as `5`, the function name to trace to the output console as `cast`, and a description to trace out as `Test of casting as int`.

This is the code that causes a test to be executed on the `cast` method:

```
public function PerfTest()
{
    var perfTest:PerformanceTest = PerformanceTest.
        getInstance();
    perfTest.out = trace;
    perfTest.testFunction( floor, 5, "floor", "Test of
        Math.floor" );
```

```
perfTest.testFunction( cast, 5, "cast", "Test of
    casting as int" );
}
```

9. **Open the SpaceshipZapZap application FLA file.**

10. **Update the Document Class in the Properties panel to be** `PerfTest`.

11. **Press Ctrl+Enter (Windows) or Command+Enter (Mac) to test the application.**

    Observe the results of the two performance tests in the console output window. The results demonstrate that casting to `int` executes faster than using `Math.floor`.

That's your performance testing at work! You can test any number of functions, or you can test entire classes using the `testSuite` method. If you'd like to find out more about testing with PerformanceTest, the software's documentation is very useful, and of course you can visit Grant Skinner's website at `http://gskinner.com`.

Stats

Stats is a handy utility that you can use during the development of your mobile application. Stats places a postage stamp–sized window in the upper-left corner of your application that displays the output of a number of tests that it runs on each frame. You can download it from `http://mrdoob.com/80/Stats`.

Use these Stats tests to see how your app stacks up:

- ✔ **FPS: Frame per second** shows how many frames are being rendered per second in your application.

- ✔ **MS: Milliseconds** shows the number of milliseconds taken to render a frame.

- ✔ **MEM: Memory** shows the amount of memory your application is using.

- ✔ **MAX: Maximum Memory** shows the maximum amount of memory allocation your application has reached.

To include Stats in your application is simple indeed. Just follow these steps:

1. **Place the Stats ActionScript class file in the directory structure** `net/hires/debug` **relative to your Flash mobile application FLA.**

2. **Open the** `SpaceshipZapZap.as` **Document Class in Flash Professional.**

3. **Add an** `import` **directive for the** `Stats` **class, placing it with all the other** `import` **directives, like this:**

```
package
{
    import net.hires.debug.Stats;
    import flash.events.Event;
    import flash.display.MovieClip;

    public class SpaceshipZapZap extends MovieClip
    {
        //...
    }
}
```

4. **Add a** `Stats` **instance to the display list:**

```
package
{
    import net.hires.debug.Stats;
    import flash.events.Event;
    import flash.display.MovieClip;

    public class SpaceshipZapZap extends MovieClip
    {
        public function SpaceshipZapZap()
        {
            trace( "Document Class initialized" );
            addChild( new Stats() );
            addEventListener( Event.ADDED_TO_STAGE, init
            );
        }
```

That's it! Now press Ctrl+Enter (Windows) or Command+Enter (Mac) to see Stats running in your application. Important things to observe are the number of milliseconds (MS) taken to render a frame when you perform certain operations — a higher value of milliseconds usually indicates a performance bottleneck (that is, loads of things going on at one time). Also look closely at the current memory usage (MEM). If this value is gradually increasing on each frame — visualized by a steadily upward sloping line — it suggests that objects aren't being swept up by Garbage Collector effectively, causing the application to leak memory.

PerformanceTest and Stats are two great classes that can provide an insight into what's going on with your code when it's running. If testing is something you're particularly interested in, you can take things even further with a unit test framework such as FlexUnit (download it at http://docs.flexunit.org).

You now have an application that can dynamically instantiate `DisplayObjects` in the library and respond to gestures from the user interface, and most importantly, you can keep things ticking along efficiently! I have only scratched the surface of what is possible with ActionScript 3.0. You can take your ActionScript 3.0 knowledge further through plenty of specialist texts, such as *ActionScript 3.0 Bible,* 2nd Edition, by Roger Braunstein.

Chapter 7

Entering and Managing Data

*I*f your mobile application doesn't require any user input to be successful, you're doing better than the rest of us! User input gives the app the data needed to provide a response to the user. The input can be a simple tap on the screen or some text that the user has typed using the device keyboard. As the app developer, you might take the data entered by the user and either send it to a remote server for storage or store it locally on the device. Although in many scenarios, filling out forms on a mobile device can be a fallback for when the services provided by the extended Flash Player mobile APIs aren't available — such as location services — those forms end up needing to be there nonetheless.

If you've jumped straight to this chapter, you're probably flying ahead with your application and looking for some tips on how to start getting user input. In this chapter, I show you how to add some more parts to the SpaceshipZapZap game (such as adding the code behind the `TextEntry` component you create in Chapter 5) and some additional tricks and techniques, such as storing data that is available to the app after it restarts, that you might want to incorporate into your future applications.

Creating a Simple Form

In the SpaceshipZapZap game, users are required sometimes to enter text using the keyboard on the device, such as entering names into the high-score leader board or manually enteringlocations for apps that have a geolocation option.

In Chapter 5, I show you how to create a component called `TextEntry`, which facilitates soliciting and temporarily holding the text the user enters. The next step in the evolution of the `TextEntry` component is to provide some logic to it in the form of a code-behind class, which is what I explain in the next section.

Putting the code behind TextEntry

In Chapter 5, you create the user interface of a `MovieClip` called `TextEntry`. This `MovieClip` provides a clear and easy-to-use method for the user to input text into your Flash mobile application. If you haven't created this `MovieClip` yet, turn to Chapter 5 and then come back here when you're done. To improve the usefulness of the `TextEntry MovieClip`, it needs ActionScript code behind it to allow it to be populated with a label or example text, as well as clear the input field when it receives *focus* — that's when the user presses it to begin typing into it. Because space is limited on a mobile device screen, often room isn't available to put labels alongside text input fields. A workaround is to put the label inside the input field and then clear it when the user is ready to type in the field.

When a `TextField` receives focus, it sends an ActionScript event called `FOCUS_IN`. When the `TextField` loses focus to another part of the application — meaning the user's keypresses no longer cause text to be typed in the `TextField` — the `FOCUS_OUT` event is sent. You can register event listeners for these two events that allow your code to know when the user is interacting with a `TextField`.

In the steps that follow, I show you how to register for the `FOCUS_IN` and `FOCUS_OUT` events, populate the `TextField` inside the `TextEntry MovieClip` with a label, and clear it when the users press the `TextField` to enter their own text:

1. **Open the SpaceshipZapZap FLA file.**

   In Chapter 4, I show you how to create `SpaceshipZapZapiOS.fla` and `SpaceshipZapZapAndroid.fla`.

2. **Right-click (Windows) or Ctrl+click (Mac) the** `TextEntry MovieClip` **in the Library.**

3. **Click Edit Class.**

   A new `ActionScript 3.0` class document is opened for editing.

4. **Save the document as** TextEntry.as.

5. **Create a new variable called** `fieldValue` **and type it as a String:**

```
package
{
    import flash.display.MovieClip;

    public class TextEntry extends MovieClip
    {
        private var _fieldValue:String;
        public function TextEntry()
        {
            //constructor code
        }
    }
}
```

6. **Register event listeners for the** FOCUS_IN, FOCUS_OUT, **and** CHANGE **events:**

```
package
{
    import flash.display.MovieClip;
    import flash.events.FocusEvent;
    public class TextEntry extends MovieClip
    {
        private var _fieldValue:String;
        public function TextEntry()
        {
            //constructor code
            input.addEventListener( Event.FOCUS_IN,
            onChange );
            input.addEventListener( FocusEvent.FOCUS_IN,
            onInputFocusIn );
            input.addEventListener( FocusEvent.FOCUS_OUT,
            onInputFocusOut );
        }
    }
}
```

The FOCUS_IN event occurs when a DisplayObject receives a mouse or touch interaction. The FOCUS_OUT event is dispatched when users click their mouse or touch elsewhere, causing the DisplayObject to lose focus to another object.

7. **Create an event handler method for the** FOCUS_IN **event that stores the value of the input** TextField **in the** fieldValue **variable (created in Step 5) and then clears the input** TextField**:**

```
package
{
    import flash.display.MovieClip;
        import flash.events.FocusEvent;
    public class TextEntry extends MovieClip
    {
        private var _fieldValue:String;
        public function TextEntry()
        {
            //constructor code
            input.addEventListener( Event.FOCUS_IN,
            onChange );
            input.addEventListener( FocusEvent.FOCUS_IN,
            onInputFocusIn );
            input.addEventListener( FocusEvent.FOCUS_OUT,
            onInputFocusOut );
        }

        private function onInputFocusIn( e:FocusEvent )
          :void
        {
            fieldValue = input.text;
            input.text = "";
        }
    }
}
```

The code in the event handler clears the TextField so that the user doesn't need to first delete the previous entry before typing. The value that the user previously entered is stored for safekeeping in the field-Value property.

8. **Add the event handler method for the** FOCUS_OUT **listener that restores text saved in** fieldValue **to** TextField **if the user didn't enter any text, or overwrites text in** fieldValue **if the user did enter some text:**

```
package
{
    import flash.display.MovieClip;
        import flash.events.FocusEvent;
    public class TextEntry extends MovieClip
    {
        private var _fieldValue:String;
        public function TextEntry()
        {
            //...
```

```
        }

        private function onInputFocusIn( e:FocusEvent )
          :void
        {
            //...
        }
        private function onInputFocusOut( e:FocusEvent )
          :void
        {
          if( input.text == "" )
          {
              input.text = fieldValue;
          }
          else
          {
              fieldValue = input.text;
          }
        }
    }
}
```

When focus leaves the TextField, the FOCUS_OUT code checks to
see whether anything was entered. If the TextField.text property is
empty, the previous string that you put away for safekeeping is used to
restore the TextField to its pre-edit state. If the user did actually enter
something, it is this value that is stored in the fieldValue property.

9. **Create an accessor/mutator (getter/setter) pair for the** fieldValue
property.

This step allows you to retrieve the value that the user entered, as well
as to update what's displayed in the TextField:

```
package
{
    import flash.display.MovieClip;
        import flash.events.FocusEvent;
    public class TextEntry extends MovieClip
    {
        private var _fieldValue:String;
        public function TextEntry()
        {
            //...
        }

        private function onInputFocusIn( e:FocusEvent )
          :void
        {
            //...
        }
```

```
        private function onInputFocusOut( e:FocusEvent )
          :void
        {
          //...
        }

        public function set inputText( text:String )
          :void
        {
          input.text = fieldValue = text;
        }

        public function get inputText() :String
        {
          return fieldValue;
        }
      }
    }
```

10. Add a handler method for the CHANGE **event.**

In Chapter 6, I discuss how certain events bubble by default through the varying layers of your Flash application. The CHANGE event on TextField instances is one such event. By handling the event in the TextEntry class and stopping immediate propagation, you can prevent unnecessary bubbling of these events:

```
package
{
    import flash.display.MovieClip;
    import flash.events.FocusEvent;
    public class TextEntry extends MovieClip
    {
        private var _fieldValue:String;
        public function TextEntry()
        {
            //...
        }

        private function onInputFocusIn( e:FocusEvent )
          :void
        {
            //...
        }
        private function onInputFocusOut( e:FocusEvent )
          :void
        {
            //...
        }

        public function set inputText( text:String )
          :void
```

```
    {
        input.text = fieldValue = text;
    }

    public function get inputText() :String
    {
        return fieldValue;
    }

    private function onChange( e:Event ) :void
    {
        e.stopImmediatePropagation();
    }
  }
}
```

You now have a completed `TextEntry` control! No matter how many of these you put in your application, they'll all behave in the same way, as they all use the user interface elements defined in the `TextEntry MovieClip` and the behaviors controlled by the `TextEntry.as` class.

Putting the code behind LabelButton

Back in Chapter 5, I show you how to create the visual elements of a `MovieClip` called `LabelButton`. It consists of a button-shaped background with a dynamic `TextField` instance on top. By adding code-behind to `LabelButton`, the text displayed can be changed at runtime using code. This functionality means you can create many instances of a single `LabelButton` in your Library, setting a unique label for each.

The `LabelButton MovieClip` requires some code to be able to mimic the behavior of a `SimpleButton` object, while you retain the flexibility afforded to an object that subclasses a `MovieClip` — such as being able to update properties on the object at runtime. In the following steps, you learn how the dynamic button label is wired up and how interaction events change the button's appearance:

1. **With your SpaceshipZapZap application FLA file open in Flash Professional, right-click (Windows) or Control+click (Mac) the** `LabelButton MovieClip` **in the Library.**

2. **Click Edit Class.**

   A new ActionScript class document opens for editing.

3. **Save the document as** LabelButton.as.

4. Add a `stop();` **action to the** `LabelButton` **class constructor:**

```
public function LabelButton()
{
    stop();
}
```

This code prevents the `MovieClip` from playing all its frames repeatedly.

5. Register event listeners for the `MOUSE_DOWN` **and** `MOUSE_UP` **events:**

```
addEventListener( MouseEvent.MOUSE_DOWN, onButtonDown
        );
addEventListener( MouseEvent.MOUSE_UP, onButtonUp );
```

6. Create a handler method for the `MOUSE_DOWN` **event.**

The `MOUSE_DOWN` event moves the `MovieClip`'s playhead to frame 2:

```
private function onButtonDown( e:MouseEvent ) :void
{
    gotoAndStop( 2 );
}
```

7. Create a handler method for the `MOUSE_UP` **event.**

The `MOUSE_UP` **event moves the** `MovieClip`'**s playhead back to frame 1:**

```
private function onButtonUp( e:MouseEvent ) :void
{
    gotoAndStop( 1 );
}
```

8. Add a mutator (setter) method called `buttonLabel`.

The mutator method allows you to set the label on the button at runtime:

```
public function set buttonLabel ( label:String ) :void
{
        buttonText.text = label;
}
```

Your `LabelButton` component is now ready to ship. When you create instances of it, you can call the `buttonText` property to change the label whenever you need to. For example, if pressing your `LabelButton` started an animation, you need to display a button to stop it. Rather than create two buttons and have to worry about hiding and showing them at the right times, you could use the `LabelButton` and switch the label from *Start* to *Stop* using code.

Assembling the HighScoreSubmit MovieClip

In the SpaceshipZapZap application — I've been showing you some of the key features throughout the book — the `HighScoreSubmit MovieClip` is displayed when the user achieves a score that ranks in the top-ten scores stored by the application. The `HighScoreSubmit MovieClip` is comprised of a `TextEntry MovieClip` and the `LabelButton MovieClip`. You create the user interface (UI) for both in Chapter 5, and complete the code-behind for both in this chapter. Here I explain how to assemble the `HighScoreSubmit MovieClip` and apply the code that controls it. Follow these steps:

1. **With your SpaceshipZapZap application FLA file open, press Ctrl+F8 (Windows) or Fn+Command+F8 (Mac).**

   The Create New Symbol dialog box opens.

2. **Enter the name** HighScoreSubmit.

3. **Select the Export for ActionScript check box in the Linkage section and then click OK.**

   The view switches to display the contents of the new `HighScoreSubmit MovieClip`, which is currently empty.

4. **Drag an instance of** `TextEntry` **to the stage from the Library panel.**

5. **Highlight the** `TextEntry MovieClip` **by clicking it, and type** name-Field **as the instance name in the Properties panel.**

6. **Drag an instance of** `LabelButton` **to the stage from the Library panel.**

7. **Highlight the** `LabelButton MovieClip` **by clicking it, and type** sub-mitButton **as the instance name in the Properties panel.**

8. **Highlight the** `TextEntry MovieClip` **on the stage, and then set the** *x* **position to** 0.00 **in the Properties panel.**

9. **Highlight the** `LabelButton MovieClip` **on the stage, and then set the** *x* **position to** 0.00 **in the Properties panel.**

10. **Move the** `LabelButton` **instance below the** `TextEntry` **instance.**

    Your `HighScoreSubmit MovieClip` looks like Figure 7-1.

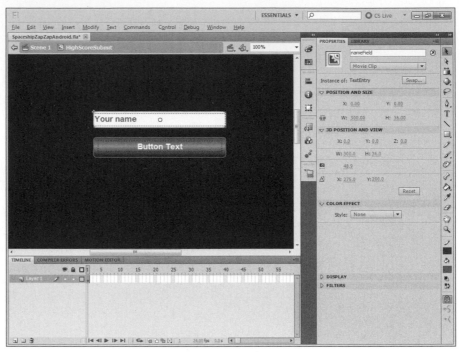

Figure 7-1:
The
HighScore
Submit
MovieClip.

Now you need to edit the `HighScoreSubmit MovieClip` class so that it assigns the label `"Submit"` to the `LabelButton` instance, as well as register and handle the `CLICK` event. Follow these steps to modify the code that will operate behind the `HighScoreSubmit MovieClip`:

1. **Open the SpaceshipZapZap FLA file.**

   In Chapter 4, I show you how to create `SpaceshipZapZapiOS.fla` and `SpaceshipZapZapAndroid.fla`.

2. **Right-click (Windows) or Control+click (Mac) the** `HighScoreSubmit MovieClip` **in the Library.**

   In Chapter 5, I show you how to create the `HighScoreSubmit MovieClip` in the Library.

3. **Select Edit Class from the context menu that appears.**

   A new ActionScript class document opens.

4. **Save the document as** HighScoreSubmit.as.

5. **Assign a label to the** `LabelButton` **instance.**

   You gave the `LabelButton` instance the name `submitButton` when you created the `HighScoreSubmit MovieClip` in Chapter 5, so place this code in the class's constructor to alter the label:

```
package
{
    import flash.display.MovieClip;

    public class HighScoreSubmit extends MovieClip
    {
        public function HighScoreSubmit()
        {
            // constructor code
            submitButton.buttonLabel = "Submit";
        }
    }
}
```

6. **Register an event listener for the** `LabelButton` **instance's** `CLICK` **event:**

```
package
{
    import flash.display.MovieClip;

    public class HighScoreSubmit extends MovieClip
    {
        public function HighScoreSubmit()
        {
            // constructor code
            submitButton.buttonLabel = "Submit";
            submitButton.addEventListener( MouseEvent.
            CLICK, onSubmitClick );
        }
    }
}
```

7. **Create a method to handle the** `CLICK` **event that stops the** `CLICK` **event bubbling any further and then dispatches a new** `CHANGE` **event.**

```
package
{
    import flash.display.MovieClip;

    public class HighScoreSubmit extends MovieClip
    {
        public function HighScoreSubmit()
        {
            // constructor code
            submitButton.buttonLabel = "Submit";
            submitButton.addEventListener( MouseEvent.
            CLICK, onSubmitClick );
        }
        private function onSubmitClick( e:Event ) :void
        {
            e.stopImmediatePropagation();
            dispatchEvent( new Event( Event.CHANGE ) );
        }
    }
}
```

This method immediately stops any further bubbling of the event and dispatches a CHANGE event that the main application Document Class can assign a listener to later.

8. **Create an accessor (getter) method for the** TextEntry **instance's** inputText **value.**

```
package
{
    import flash.display.MovieClip;

    public class HighScoreSubmit extends MovieClip
    {
        public function HighScoreSubmit()
        {
            // constructor code
            submitButton.buttonLabel = "Submit";
            submitButton.addEventListener( MouseEvent.
        CLICK, onSubmitClick );
        }
        private function onSubmitClick( e:Event ) :void
        {
            e.stopImmediatePropagation();
            dispatchEvent( new Event( Event.CHANGE ) );
        }
        public function get userName() :String
        {
            return nameField.inputText;
        }
    }
}
```

When the main application receives notification of the CHANGE event, the application needs to access the value that the user entered in the TextEntry MovieClip. By creating a public get method, you can conveniently expose the value the user entered in the TextEntry MovieClip as a property of the HighScoreSubmit MovieClip instance, making it much easier to get.

You can now instantiate an instance of the HighScoreSubmit MovieClip in your application. Add a variable to your SpaceshipZapZap Document Class that will hold the instance, and then initialize it in the class's initialize method. Here how:

1. **Open** SpaceshipZapZap.as **for editing in Flash Professional.**

2. **Declare a new variable called** _highScoreSubmit **below the other variable declarations in** SpaceshipZapZap.as:

```
private var _highScoreSubmit:HighScoreSubmit;
```

You give the variable the type HighScoreSubmit because this is the class name given to the MovieClip and the corresponding code-behind ActionScript file HighScoreSubmit.as.

3. **Initialize the** `_highScoreSubmit` **variable, add the instance to the display list, and register a** `CHANGE` **event listener. Place this code in the** `initialize` **method of the** `SpaceshipZapZap` **Document Class:**

```
private function initialize( e:Event ):void
{
    removeEventListener( Event.ADDED_TO_STAGE,
        initialize );
    displayStartScreen();
    _highScoreSubmit = new HighScoreSubmit();
    addChild( _highScoreSubmit );
    _highScoreSubmit.addEventListener( Event.CHANGE,
        onHighScoreSubmit );
}
```

4. **Assign** *x* **and** *y* **coordinates that will center the** `HighScoreSubmit` `MovieClip` **on the screen.**

   This step is achieved by calculating the center of the stage and then subtracting 50% of the `MovieClip's` width:

```
private function initialize( e:Event ):void
{
    removeEventListener( Event.ADDED_TO_STAGE,
        initialize );
    displayStartScreen();
    _highScoreSubmit = new HighScoreSubmit();
    addChild( _highScoreSubmit );
    _highScoreSubmit.addEventListener( Event.CHANGE,
        onHighScoreSubmit );
    _highScoreSubmit.x = ( stage.stageWidth * .5 ) - (
        _highScoreSubmit.width * .5 );
    _highScoreSubmit.y = ( stage.stageHeight * .5 ) - (
        _highScoreSubmit.height * .5 );
}
```

   The `_highScoreSubmit` `MovieClip` instance retains these values throughout its lifetime, regardless of whether it's in the display list. Assigning the positioning and sizing values here, instead of when the `addChild()` method is called to add `_highScoreSubmit` to the display list, saves on repetition and is therefore more efficient!

5. **Add a new method to the Document Class that handles the** `HighScoreSubmit` `MovieClip's` `CHANGE` **event by removing the** `HighScoreSubmit` `MovieClip` **from the display list.**

```
package
{
    import flash.events.Event;
    import flash.display.MovieClip;

    public class SpaceshipZapZap extends MovieClip
    {
        //...
```

```
public function SpaceshipZapZap()
{
    ..///
}
private function initialize( e:Event ):void
{
    //...
}
private function onHighScoreSubmit( e:Event )
    :void
{
    removeChild( _highScoreSubmit );
}
//...
}
}
```

Your `HighScoreSubmit MovieClip` is now complete and instantiated in your application. Note that it the `MovieClip` is displayed the moment that the application is run — that's just so you can see what it looks like. Simply remove the `addChild( _highScoreSubmit );` line to stop the `MovieClip` from being displayed on startup.

Users can type anything they like, including dollar signs and brackets, in the `HighScoreSubmit MovieClip`. Next, I show you how to validate and restrict the text that users can enter in your text components, to prevent the display of undesirable non-word characters.

There you go; it wasn't too painful, was it? As a plus, you can use the `TextEntry` and `EnterButton MovieClips` elsewhere in your app, without the need to rewrite all the code-behind for them again. You can even use them in other applications; just copy the `MovieClip` into the new Library and ensure that the corresponding class file is in the same directory as the FLA.

Keyboard without the fuss

One of the cool things about packaging applications for Android and iOS is that the hassle of scrolling your application upward to make room for the keyboard is done for you — automagically! If you were to write your application in Objective-C, you'd need to worry about scrolling your application upward by 216 pixels when the keyboard rolled open over the top of input fields on the iPhone, or ensure that your input content was at the top of the screen. Building your application in Flash means that you don't need to compromise on your design or write complex routines to handle the keyboard's presence.

Validating and Restricting Entry

In a perfect world, the user is a highly intelligent individual who not only understands the concept of your application but also the inner workings of it. Reality, however, dictates that this simply isn't the case. Any point where you need the user to enter data should be seen as a major weakness in your application and liable to exploitation — a metaphorical crack in a dam. I'm not suggesting for one moment that you brand your potential customers as malicious hackers, or complete idiots for that matter, but you should implicitly handle anything entered by the user as being incorrect, rather than expecting them to have entered it correctly. Taking this somewhat paranoid approach to form fill can save you from a world of pain when you later recruit people to test your application, and later still, recruit people to buy it.

As an Internet user, I'm sure that you've come across validation issues before. You'd be amazed at some of the websites that won't let me be an O'Rourke and insist that I am ORourke. Although the implementation is poor, valid reasons exist for sites doing this — they think I'm trying to inject script into their forms by inserting an apostrophe. Between the input field and the database insertion, a layer of validation code is executing a set of rules that make sure that I entered a first and last name; I did, so it passed me. At the same time, the validation code checks that my first and last names contain only alphabetical characters; the code decides that my name contains a banned character — so near, yet so far!

Fortunately, code sanitization isn't a major priority for you in ActionScript 3.0 because any number of special characters entered in a `TextField` are treated as a value and not evaluated or interpreted. Because of this, your key priority is just to make sure that what is entered will be useful enough for you to provide the users what they expects. To that end, the following sections explain how to restrict characters in the `TextField` and validate the information that users enter.

Restricting characters

If I want my users to enter a place name, I don't really want them entering numbers or @ signs. Rather than allowing them to do this and then correcting them, it's often easier to stop them from entering them in the first place. TextField exposes a handy property called `restrict` that allows you to specify what a user can enter.

Follow these instructions to add support to the `TextEntry` control to restrict input to specified characters:

1. **Create a new mutator method in the** `TextEntry` **class called** `restrict`.

   It should accept a string as its only parameter:

   ```
   public function set restrict( value:String ) :void
   {
           input.restrict = value;
   }
   ```

   You then assign the value received to the `restrict` property of the `TextField` instance — which you've named `input`.

2. **Open the** `LocationStartScreen` **class.**

3. **Assign an allowed character range to the** `restrict` **property.**

   This step maps to the `restrict` method on the `TextEntry` instance in your `LocationStartScreen` class:

   ```
   locationInput.restrict = "A-Za-z \\-";
   ```

   Only the range A to Z — both uppercase and lowercase — and the hyphen character are allowed.

   Notice that the hyphen needs a double backslash to escape it, because it's a character that normally denotes a range within a `restrict` string.

Validating entry

Despite your best endeavors to deter user error through restricted input only, you find plenty of use cases where input may need to follow a particular pattern. A prime example of this is the golden oldie of all validation examples, the e-mail address. Validation becomes even more important on devices such as the iPhone and Android phones, where users can easily miskey entries on the small keyboard.

Take `hello@jodieorourke.co.uk` for example. The e-mail address can have any number of characters before the @ sign — of which there is only ever one — and then any number of characters for the domain name before a dot, and a further two more characters and another dot before two final characters. My address could also be `hello@jodieorourke.com`, which complicates things further, as there's now just one dot and three characters at the end. Only one tool can efficiently spot these kind of patterns: a regular expression, or RegExp.

The `RegExp` class in ActionScript 3.0 gives you the ability to test strings against complex regular expressions, defined by the same syntax that is used to define regular expressions in other programming languages.

Plenty of patterns exist for testing e-mail addresses. The pattern I've chosen to show you is a pretty hardy one and can check for the following sequence:

- One or more characters that are alphanumeric, a dot, an underscore, or a hyphen

- A single @ sign

- One or more characters that are alphanumeric, a dot, an underscore, or a hyphen

- A single dot

- Between two and four characters within the range of A to Z

These steps show you how you'd test an e-mail address for validity using a regular expression in a test application:

1. **Create a new application in Flash Professional and save it as** RegExp.fla.

   Choose either a new AIR for Android application or a new iOS application.

2. **In the Properties panel, click the wrench icon next to the Class field.**

   The Create ActionScript 3.0 Class dialog box opens.

3. **Type the Class name** Main **and click OK.**

   A new ActionScript 3.0 class opens in Flash Professional.

4. **Press Ctrl+S (Windows) or Command+S (Mac) and save the file as** Main.as.

5. **Declare a** RegExp **instance in** Main.as **and initialize it with a pattern:**

```
package
{
    import flash.display.MovieClip;

    public class Main extends MovieClip
    {
        private var regExp:RegExp = /([a-z0-9._-]+)@([a-
        z0-9.-]+)\.([a-z]{2,4})/;
        public function Main()
        {
            // constructor code
        }
    }
}
```

6. **Use the** `test` **method to verify that the string** `hello@jodieorourke.com` **matches the pattern:**

```
package
{
    import flash.display.MovieClip;

    public class Main extends MovieClip
    {
        private var regExp:RegExp = /([a-z0-9._-]+)@([a-
        z0-9.-]+)\.([a-z]{2,4})/;
        public function Main()
        {
            // constructor code
            trace( regExp.test( "hello@jodieorourke.com"
            ) );
        }
    }
}
```

The `test` method returns `true` if the test passed; otherwise, it returns `false`.

7. **Press Ctrl+Enter (Windows) or Command+Enter (Mac) to test the application in Flash Professional.**

You see "true" displayed in the Output window, meaning the string passed the regular expression test.

You can find a handy online tool for constructing and testing regular expressions at `http://gskinner.com/RegExr`.

Holding Data for Use Later

After you have successfully solicited some input data from a user, you need somewhere to put it. During the lifetime of the application, you can *persist,* or save, data in memory in the form of variables in your application. For example, you might want to remember the name the user entered the last time he used your app so that he doesn't need to enter it again. Using special storage features on the device, you can save these pieces of information so that they're available to the application when it next starts. Persisting data that will still be available after the application has been closed and restarted is very beneficial, particularly on devices like the iPhone, where a user might need to temporarily close the application to perform another task, such as take a call.

SharedObject data types

You can store a variety of different Flash data types in a `SharedObject`:

✔ Array: An object that holds values that are accessible through an index

✔ Object: An object that holds values that are accessible by property names

✔ Vector: Like an array, only the values it holds can be strictly typed

✔ XML: An XML data object

✔ Number: A floating-point positive or negative number

✔ int: A positive or negative integer

✔ uint: A positive integer

✔ String: A string of characters

✔ Date: An object pertaining to a particular date and time

You can persist data locally using your Flash mobile application in two ways. The first is by using Local `SharedObject`, which is a small text file into which the application writes small amounts of data. The second is using a local database, which allows you to store larger amounts of more complex data.

Local SharedObject

Also known to many as the "Flash Cookie," the Local `SharedObject` is not a cookie in the web browser sense but a small text-based file that persists data from a Flash application after it has been closed. The ActionScript 3.0 API for Flash mobile application development makes Local `SharedObject` available to you for use in storing and retrieving small amounts of data.

A Remote `SharedObject` also exists, but it isn't relevant to local data storage on a mobile device. Note that from here on, when I refer to a `SharedObject`, I'm talking about the Local variety!

Because the `SharedObject` is useful for only small amounts of data, you don't want to use it for data in your application that's liable to keep growing. Data items that are capped at a relatively small size, such as the top-ten high scores or a user name, would be perfect candidates. A list of every single score that the user has ever achieved could become problematic over time, as the application will eventually reach a point where it has filled the `SharedObject` — limited to 100K — and won't be allowed to squeeze anything else in. Data whose size needs to be able to scale over time should either be stored remotely or locally in a database — which I talk more about later in this chapter.

Storing data with a SharedObject

Wouldn't it be great if your application stored the top-ten highest scores that the user has achieved playing your game? The game could record the user's score, along with the date that he achieved it and a name that he enters. Because the high-score data is relatively small in size and capped at a maximum of ten entries, it's a perfect candidate for persistent storage in a SharedObject on the client device.

Follow these steps to create a SharedObject instance, retrieve any high score values stored in it, and place those values into an array. Don't worry about not having any high scores stored just yet, I'll show you how to store them after you set up the SharedObject instance:

1. **Open** SpaceshipZapZap.as **for editing in Flash Professional.**

   I show you how to create SpaceshipZapZap.as in Chapter 6.

2. **Declare a** SharedObject **variable called** _sharedObject **directly below all the other variable declarations in** SpaceshipZapZap.as**:**

```
package
{
    import flash.events.Event;
    import flash.display.MovieClip;

    public class SpaceshipZapZap extends MovieClip
    {
        private const ALIEN_PADDING:int = 10;
        private const ALIENS_PER_ROW:int = 6;
        private var _fleetContainer:Sprite;
        private var _aliens:Vector.<MovieClip>;
        private var _startScreen:StartScreen;
        private var _highScoreSubmit:HighScoreSubmit;
        private var _sharedObject:SharedObject;

        public function SpaceshipZapZap()
        {
```

   If your code editor doesn't create the import directive for you, you must add it manually.

3. **Declare an array variable called** _highScoresArray **that will store a mirror of the** SharedObject **data:**

```
private var _sharedObject:SharedObject;
private var _highScores:Array;
```

   With the variable, you can make multiple and extensive changes to the array, then store the array in the SharedObject when you're ready, rather than implementing heavy code to write to the `SharedObject` every time a change is made:

4. **Initialize the** `SharedObject` **instance by calling the** `getLocal()` **method on the** `SharedObject` **class. Pass the string** `spaceship ZapZap` **as the only parameter:**

```
private function initialize( e:Event ):void
{
    removeEventListener( Event.ADDED_TO_STAGE,
        initialize );
    displayStartScreen();
    _highScoreSubmit = new HighScoreSubmit();
    addChild( _highScoreSubmit );
    _highScoreSubmit.addEventListener( Event.CHANGE,
        onHighScoreSubmit );
    _highScoreSubmit.x = ( stage.stageWidth * .5 ) - (
        _highScoreSubmit.width * .5 );
    _highScoreSubmit.y = ( stage.stageHeight * .5 ) - (
        _highScoreSubmit.height * .5 );
    _sharedObject = SharedObject.getLocal(
        "spaceshipZapZap" );
}
```

A new `SharedObject` is created by the app when you reference the static `getLocal` method on the `SharedObject` class, passing in the name you want to give the object. If your app has created an object of this name on the device in the past, the application continues to use that one; otherwise a new one will be created. The best place to put the code is in the `initialize` method of your Document Class:

In the example, the `SharedObject` is named `spaceshipZapZap`. If a `SharedObject` by the same name already exists on the client device, it will be opened for edit. If it doesn't exist, a new one will be created.

5. **Assign the** `highScores` **property from the** `SharedObject` **to the** `_highScores` **array.**

```
_sharedObject = SharedObject.getLocal(
        "spaceshipZapZap" );
_highScores = _sharedObject.data[ "highScores"] as
        Array;
```

If no value exists in the `SharedObject`, the value `_highScores` is null.

6. **Initialize the** `_highScores` **array if the** `SharedObject` **value is null:**

```
_sharedObject = SharedObject.getLocal(
        "spaceshipZapZap" );
_highScores = _sharedObject.data[ "highScores"] as
        Array;
if( !_highScores )
{
    _highScores = [];
}
```

The retrieval of high scores from the SharedObject is complete, but at the moment, no scores are in there. Follow the next set of steps to enhance the onHighScoreSubmit method to store the user's score, name, and the date the user achieved the score in the SharedObject instance:

1. **Declare a new** Array **called** MONTHS **with all the other class variable declarations, and populated it with 12 strings representing each month of the year:**

```
package
{
    //...

    public class SpaceshipZapZap extends MovieClip
    {

        private var _sharedObject:SharedObject;
        private const MONTHS:Array = [ "Jan", "Feb",
          "Mar", "Apr", "May", "Jun", "Jul", "Aug",
          "Sep", "Nov", "Dec" ];

        public function SpaceshipZapZap()
        {
```

2. **Within** onHighScoreSubmit, **create a new local variable called** dateString **and assign today's date formatted as** *DD MON YYYY*:

```
private function onHighScoreSubmit( e:Event ) :void
{
    removeChild( _highScoreSubmit );
    var now:Date = new Date();
    var dateString:String = now.date + " " + MONTHS
        [ now.month ] + " " + now.fullYear;
}
```

3. **Create a new object containing the date string created in the last step, the user's name, and the user's score. Then add this to the** _highScores **array using the** Array.push() **method:**

```
    var now:Date = new Date();
    var dateString:String = now.date + " " + MONTHS
        [ now.month ] + " " + now.fullYear;
    _highScores.push( { userDate: dateString, userName:
        _highScoreSubmit.userName, userScore: _score }
        );
}
```

A shorthand approach for creating a new object is to use {} — curly brace notation — to wrap name/value pairs. Each of these values is accessible on the new object using the name it was paired with.

4. **Sort the** `_highScores` **array so that the highest score is at the start of the array and the lowest is at the end:**

```
    _highScores.push( { userDate: dateString, userName:
        _highScoreSubmit.userName, userScore: _score }
        );
    _highScores.sortOn( "userScore", Array.NUMERIC |
        Array.DESCENDING );
}
```

Using the `Array.sortOn()` method, you provide two parameters. The first is the field, or property, of each object, which is used as the sort value. The second parameter is the sorting behavior. I specify two sorting behaviors in the code — `Array,NUMERIC` and `Array.DESCENDING` — that result in a numerically descending sort.

5. **Use** `Array.pop()` **to remove the last item from the** `_highScores` **array, if more than 10 items are stored in the array:**

```
    _highScores.sortOn( "userScore", Array.NUMERIC |
        Array.DESCENDING );
    if( _highScores.length > _maxHighScores )
    {
        _highScores.pop();
    }
}
```

The `pop()` method simply pops the last item from the array. The only way to add high scores to the `_highScores` array and the `SharedObject` is through the `onHighScoreSubmit` method, so the code can add no more than 11 items into the array before the `pop()` method is called to truncate the array back to 10 entries.

6. **Assign the newly updated** `_highScores` **array to the** `high-Scores` **property on your** `SharedObject` **instance, then call the** `SharedObject.flush()` **method to store the change:**

```
    _highScores.sortOn( "userScore", Array.NUMERIC |
        Array.DESCENDING );
    _sharedObject.data[ "highScores" ] = _highScores;
    _sharedObject.flush();
}
```

The data is now stored in a `SharedObject` file that will persist after the application, and even the device's operating system, has been restarted. If you run your app now on the desktop by pressing Ctrl+Enter (Windows) or Command+Enter (Mac), you can enter your name in the `HighScoreSubmit` `MovieClip`, which your code then stores in the `SharedObject`. You won't see the data being saved, but in the next section, I show you how to read previously stored data, so you can confirm that it's being saved successfully.

Displaying Local SharedObject data back to the user

Retrieving data from a `SharedObject` is easy provided that you know the name of the `SharedObject` and the name of the property whose value you want to retrieve. In the last example, an array called `highScores` was stored in a `SharedObject` called `spaceshipZapZap`. Follow these steps to retrieve that array to a local member variable:

1. **Create a new method in** `SpaceshipZapZap.as` **called** `populate-HighScores`:

```
    _sharedObject.data[ "highScores" ] = _highScores;
    _sharedObject.flush();
}

private function populateHighScores() :void
{
}
```

2. **Create a** `for` **loop that iterates through each object in the** `_highScores` **array and prints the** `userDate`, `userName`, **and** `userScore` **values to the Output window in Flash Professional using the** `trace()` **method:**

```
private function populateHighScores() :void
{
    for each( var score:Object in _highScores )
    {
        trace( score.userDate, score.userName, score.
        userScore );
    }
}
```

3. **Call** `populateHighScores()` **from within the** `initialize()` **method:**

```
    _highScoreSubmit.width * .5 );
    _highScoreSubmit.y = ( stage.stageHeight * .5 ) - (
        _highScoreSubmit.height * .5 );
    populateHighScores();
}
```

Run your app now on the desktop by pressing Ctrl+Enter (Windows) or Command+Enter (Mac). The names and dates stored in the `SharedObject` are printed in the Output console. Scores are not traced out because no was data present for these when they were stored.

In my SpaceshipZapZap application, I display each high score entry in a row comprised of a date, name, and score. When the game is over, I show the user a Hall of Fame, where these high score rows are displayed vertically down the screen. Here's how you build and populate a Hall of Fame screen for your application:

1. **Create a new** `MovieClip` **symbol by pressing Ctrl+F8 (Windows) or Fn+Command+F8 (Mac) and giving it the name** HighScoreRow.

2. **Select the Export for ActionScript check box in the Linkage section, and then click OK.**

 The new `HighScoreRow MovieClip` appears in the Library panel in Flash Professional and the `MovieClip` is opened for editing on the stage.

3. **Use the Rectangle tool to draw a gray (#666666) rectangle on the stage that is 464 pixels wide and 28 pixels high.**

4. **Use the Text tool to draw a dynamic `TextField` 102 pixels wide and 26 pixels high on top of the gray rectangle. Use the Properties panel to modify the following credentials:**

 a. **Assign it the instance name userDate.**

 b. **Set its x value to 0 and its y value to 1.**

 c. **Ensure that the Text Engine selected is Classic Text.**

 d. **Ensure that the text type is Dynamic Text.**

 e. **Set the character family as Arial, the style as Regular, and the size as 18pt.**

 f. **Assign the text (fill) color as white (#FFFFFF).**

 g. **Set the anti-alias to Use Device Fonts.**

 h. **Set the paragraph format as Align Left and the behavior as Single Line.**

5. **Select the `userDate TextField`, press Ctrl+C (Windows) Command+C (Mac) to copy it, then press Ctrl+V (Windows) or Ctrl+V (Mac) to paste a copy of the `TextField` onto the stage.**

6. **Select the copied `TextField` and modify its attributes in the Properties panel as follows:**

 a. **Assign it the instance name userName.**

 b. **Set its x value to 107 and its y value to 1.**

 c. **Set its width to 223 pixels — keep its height as 26 pixels.**

7. **Select the `userDate TextField` again, press Ctrl+C (Windows) Command+C (Mac) to copy it, then press Ctrl+V (Windows) or Ctrl+V (Mac) to paste a copy of the `TextField` onto the stage.**

8. **Select the copied `TextField` and modify its attributes in the Properties panel as follows:**

 a. **Assign it the instance name userScore.**

 b. **Set its x value to 335 and its y value to 1.**

 c. **Set its width to 124 pixels — keep its height as 26 pixels.**

 The user interface for the `HighScoreRow MovieClip` is complete and looks like Figure 7-2.

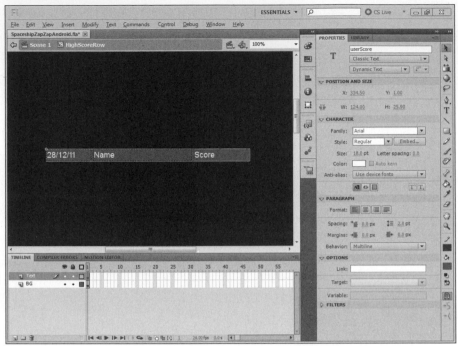

Figure 7-2:
The
HighScore
Row
MovieClip.

Now that you have created the visual elements to display a single high score entry, this next set of steps walks you through the code changes required to display on the screen a vertical list of HighScoreRow instances:

1. **Open** SpaceshipZapZap.as **for editing in Flash Professional.**

2. **Declare a new integer variable called** _position **inside the** populate
   HighScores() **method:**

   ```
   private function populateHighScores() :void
   {
      var _position:int;
      for each( var score:Object in _highScores )
      {
         trace( score.userDate, score.userName, score.
         userScore );
      }
   }
   ```

3. **Delete the** trace **code inside the** for **loop:**

   ```
   private function populateHighScores() :void
   {
      var _position:int;
      for each( var score:Object in _highScores )
      {
      }
   }
   ```

4. **Declare and initialize a new** `HighScoreRow` **variable called** `scoreRow`
inside the for loop:

```
for each( var score:Object in _highScores )
{
        var scoreRow:HighScoreRow = new HighScoreRow();
}
```

5. **Update the** `text` **property of the** `userDate`, `userName`, **and** `user-`
`Score` **instances in** `scoreRow` **with the corresponding values from the**
`score` **object:**

```
var scoreRow:HighScoreRow = new HighScoreRow();
scoreRow.userDate.text = score.userDate;
scoreRow.userName.text = score.userName;
scoreRow.userScore.text = score.userScore;
```

6. **Set** `scoreRow's` *x* **position to** 10 **and its** *y* **position to the value of the**
`position` **variable:**

```
scoreRow.userScore.text = score.userScore;
scoreRow.x = 10;
scoreRow.y = position;
```

7. **Add the** `scoreRow` **instance to the display list:**

```
scoreRow.y = position;
addChild( scoreRow );
```

8. **Increment the value stored in the** `position` **variable by the height of**
the `scoreRow` **user interface, plus 15 pixels of padding to add space**
between rows:

```
addChild( scoreRow );
position += score.height + 15;
```

Your `populateHighScores()` method can now iterate through the high
score objects stored in the `_highScores` array and create a number of rows
that flow vertically down the screen — each one populated with a score, the
date the score was attained, and the name of the user who achieved it.

That's enough about `SharedObjects`. Next, I focus on another local storage
facility available to your Flash mobile application, local databases.

Local databases

Because Flash mobile applications are essentially repackaged AIR applications, you have many of the features that are available to AIR development
at your disposal. One of those features is *local databases.* A local database
allows you to store data locally on the device — in the SQLite database —
and query it from your application using regular SQL (Structured Query

Language) queries. The database is persisted with the application data itself and therefore continues to exist even after the application has been closed and restarted. Even native iOS apps are able to use local SQLite databases, so the translation of this feature by the Flash iPhone Packager is handy. SQLite is a composite part of the Adobe AIR runtime and is included by default with your Flash Professional software — you don't need to download any add-ons.

If you'd like to learn about SQLite in greater detail than I go into here, check out the vast amount of documentation available at `http://sqlite.org`.

In the following sections, I show you how to store data in a local SQLite database.

Setting up the database for use

Before you can write data to a database in your application, you first need to run through a couple of setup procedures which will identify where your database lives and what its table structure will be like.

Follow these steps to set up your database for use:

1. **Create a new application in Flash Professional and save it as** LocalDatabase.fla.

   Choose either a new AIR for Android application or a new iOS application.

2. **In the Properties panel, click the wrench icon next to the Class field.**

   The Create ActionScript 3.0 Class dialog box opens.

3. **Type the Class name LocalDatabase and click OK.**

   A new ActionScript 3.0 class opens in Flash Professional.

4. **Press Ctrl+S (Windows) or Command+S (Mac) and save the file as** LocalDatabase.as.

5. **Declare a database connection object in your** `LocalDatabase.as`:

   ```
   public class LocalDatabase extends MovieClip
   {
       private var _connection:SQLConnection;
       public function LocalDatabase()
       {

   private var connection:SQLConnection;
   ```

6. **Declare a new** `File` **Object called** `database`. **Initialize it with a file in the application's local storage directory called** `data.db`.

   Your data will be written to this file. If the file doesn't exist, it will be automatically created for you:

   ```
   public function LocalDatabase()
   {
   ```

```
    // constructor code
    var database:File = File.applicationDirectory.
        resolvePath( "data.db" );
}
```

7. **Initialize your** SQLConnection **instance:**

```
    var database:File = File.applicationDirectory.
        resolvePath( "data.db" );
    _connection = new SQLConnection();
}
```

8. **Call the** open() **method on the** SQLConnection **instance, providing the** database **variable as a parameter.**

   This step opens a synchronous connection to the database file.

```
    connection = new SQLConnection();
    connection.open( database );
}
```

Now your database is created, and you have an open gateway to it. The next few steps show you how to set up a basic name/value table structure:

1. **Declare and initialize a** SQLStatement **object called** statement:

```
    _connection.open( database );
    var statement:SQLStatement = new SQLStatement();
}
```

2. **Assign your** SQLConnection **instance — called** connection — **to the statement's** sqlConnection **property:**

```
    var statement:SQLStatement = new SQLStatement();
    statement.sqlConnection = _connection;
}
```

3. **Assign a SQL string to** SQLStatement **instance's** text **property that creates a database table called** myAppData **with two columns — one called** property **and one called** value.

   Note that the property column will be the primary key:

```
    statement.sqlConnection = _connection;
    statement.text = " CREATE TABLE IF NOT EXISTS
        myAppData ( 'property' TEXT PRIMARY KEY,
        'value' TEXT )";
}
```

4. **Call the** execute() **method on the** SQLStatement **instance to run the query on the database:**

```
    statement.execute();
```

Synchronous or asynchronous

You can open two kinds of SQLConnections: synchronous and asynchronous. A *synchronous* connection means that no more code in the application is executed until a SQL statement that is executing on the database, via the connection, has completed. You open a synchronous connection using the `SQLConnection.` `open()` method. An *asynchronous* connection doesn't stop the flow of code execution in your application while it is performing a query on the database. The connection notifies the application of its completion through events. To open an asynchronous connection, use `SQLConnection.openAsync()`.

A column that is marked as PRIMARY KEY cannot contain multiple identical values. Attempting an insertion of an identical value results in a runtime exception being thrown by the Flash Player. On the Android and iOS, you should expect the runtime exception to crash your application. Always makes sure to check that the column doesn't first contain a value that's identical to the one you're about to insert.

Reading data from the database

After you've added one or more rows of data to your database, you're going to want to read them back into your application. Are you thinking, "What rows of data ?" Good question. I haven't shown you how to insert data into the database yet. There's a method to my madness: The logic that underpins an insertion of a new row to the database involves being able to determine whether the value being inserted exists in the property column *before* trying to insert it. Remember that property is the primary key in the database table, so duplicate entries aren't allowed and cause nasty errors to be thrown. Because of this requirement, I show you how to read from the database first, and then how to begin adding rows of data to it.

The following steps build on the code you wrote in the previous steps. You can reuse the same SQLConnection and SQLStatement objects you created in the preceding steps and just switch the query to a SELECT statement:

1. **Open** `LocalDatabase.fla` **in Flash Professional.**

2. **Use the Text tool to draw a dynamic** `TextField` **on the stage. Use the Properties panel to modify the following credentials:**

    a. **Assign it the instance name** outputTextField.

    b. **Ensure that the Text Engine selected is Classic Text.**

    c. **Ensure that the text type is Dynamic Text.**

    d. **Set the character family as Arial, the style as Regular, and the size as 18pt.**

    e. **Set the anti-alias to Use Device Fonts.**

3. **Assign a** SELECT **query to the statement's** text **property:**

```
statement.execute();
statement.text = "SELECT * FROM myAppData WHERE
    property='name'";
}
```

4. **Execute the new SQL statement:**

```
statement.text = "SELECT * FROM myAppData WHERE
    property='name'";
statement.execute();
}
```

5. **Declare a local array variable that can accept the results of the** SELECT **query, Assign the array the** data **of the** SQLStatement.get-Result() **method:**

```
statement.execute();
var data:Array = statement.getResult().data;
}
```

The API forces you to use Array here instead of Vector. If you try to assign the data property to a Vector object — an alternative to Array — a *type coercion* error is thrown in your application.

6. **Use an** if **statement to check that the data isn't** null. **If it isn't** null, **assign the** value **field of the first object on the** data **result array to the** text **property of the** TextField **instance you created on the stage:**

```
var data:Array = statement.getResult().data;
if( data )
{
    outputTextField.text = data[ 0 ].value;
}
}
```

Assigning the result to a TextField instance on the stage rather than tracing the result to Output window allows you to verify that your database code is working on your mobile device at this point — something I always recommend doing!

This code doesn't trace anything out at the moment, because you haven't put any data in there yet. This is the perfect time to show you how to do that!

Inserting data into the database

You've created a table in your local database with two columns named property and value and used the SELECT query to retrieve data from the table. Now you can add data to table.

After all the code you've written to create your database table and read from it, the foundations are prepared for the final step of inserting data in the table. One of the most important steps in the process is to first run a query against the database table to check that a *primary key* value you're going to attempt to insert doesn't already exist in the table. By running a SELECT query and checking the resulting data with an if statement, you've already guarded against that risk. Now expand the if statement with an else clause that updates the SQLStatement instance's text property with an INSERT statement. Remember to call the execute() method on your SQLStatement instance; otherwise, the query won't run:

```
    outputTextField.text = data[ 0 ].value;
}
else
{
    statement.text = "INSERT INTO myAppData (
        'property', 'value' ) VALUES( 'name', 'Jodie'
        )";
    statement.execute();
}
```

The string name is the value entered in the property column in the table. This value serves as the primary key for the table, so no other property called name is allowed to be added. The string Jodie is entered in the value column on the same row, so where the property equals *name* in the table, the value equals *Jodie*.

Run the application for yourself by pressing Ctrl+Enter (Windows) or Command+Enter (Mac) and observe that *Jodie* is displayed in the output-TextField instance on the stage. This value has been stored and then retrieved from your database. Good work!

Favoring Vector over Array

The Array object has been the mainstay of indexed-based, typeless data structures in ActionScript since its inception. With the advent of Flash Player 10, Adobe introduced Vector, a new data structure to the ActionScript 3.0 language. Vector is faster than Array for element access and iteration, and it allows developers to specify the type of objects that will be added to it.

Moreover, most of the time you barely notice much change in the syntax, yet you're reaping the benefits of faster code execution. In some tests, Vector has been seen to perform 30 percent to 40 percent faster than Array. Because performance of mobile applications is a primary consideration, you should seek to use Vector instead of Array.

I always choose a Vector object over an Array object, unless the Flash API feature I'm using mandates the use of an Array.

Chapter 8

Sending Data to the Server and Receiving Something Back

In This Chapter

▶ Handling user data with care

▶ Establishing a connection and preparing data for transmission

▶ Sending data and handling a response

▶ Using third-party tools to track user behavior with your application

*i*Phones and Android smartphones can communicate with services beyond the phone itself, over the Internet. Internet connectivity may be available at varying speeds over the cellular network as either a 4G, 3G, Edge (2.5G), or GPRS (2G) connection. Alternatively, connectivity could be supplied by a local Wi-Fi network.

In browser-centric Flash application development, it's largely assumed that the connection will always be there — the users have loaded the application in their web browsers, so they must have an Internet connection, right? With mobile Flash application development, you're exploring a slightly different consumption mechanism — the users have downloaded and installed the app, but when they come to use it, they could be out of range of a network operator's mast or a Wi-Fi hotspot (in a tunnel, for example). Understanding these issues and mitigating against them during development are fundamental parts of developing Internet-connected apps for mobile devices.

This chapter examines how to take advantage of the connectivity available to the application when it's running on the device, how to consume public web services on the Internet that can convert data sent by the application into data that is meaningful to the user (such as converting location coordinates to place-names), how to use the data loaded into the application, and how to deal with fallout from a loss of connectivity.

Understanding Apple's Stance on Transmitting and Storing User Data

Due in part to the cost of lawsuits, Apple takes data protection seriously. With this stance comes a requirement for all developers enlisted in the iOS Developer Program to comply with the clauses in Section 3 of the iOS Developer Agreement (`https://developer.apple.com/membercenter/index.action#agreements`) with regard to the storage and communication of user data, referred to as *transmission*. Most notable is that the onus is placed on the developer to ensure that the way his or her application stores and transmits data complies with all applicable privacy laws and regulations. Does this sound daunting? It is. Certainly the idea of being sued if you get it wrong doesn't seem particularly appetizing, and the majority of applications submitted to Apple that flout "the basics" of data protection rules are batted straight back to the developer by Apple's review process. Following these key principles ensures that your application stays on the right side of Apple's rules and also the law (and gets you into the App Store!):

✔ The users must normally consent to personally identifiable data about them being stored anywhere other than locally on their devices. If you ask for someone's name or e-mail address, you must ask that person's permission before you send the information over the Internet to be stored on a server.

✔ Sensitive user data should be encrypted when stored on the device. If you store a user's credit card number on the device — to speed up purchasing next time — you must encrypt the number so it cannot be accessed by another application.

✔ Personal data must be transmitted across the Internet over a secure protocol, such as Secure Sockets Layer (SSL). You must send data to `HTTPS` URLs instead of regular `HTTP` ones, and have a valid SSL certificate on the web server you're calling. You can read more about SSL security firm Thawte's website (`https://www.thawte.com/resources/ssl-information-center/get-started-with-ssl/index.html`).

✔ It may be illegal or may require the user's consent to store information that your application is collecting on a computer outside of the country in which the user resides. For example, because I live in a country in the European Union, I must explicitly grant an application vendor the right to store my data on a computer located in the United States.

✔ Do not attempt to prevent the display of notifications warning the users that the application is requesting information that may identify them, such as their locations or IP addresses.

For the most part, these rules apply to applications targeting Android too. The only difference is that the approval process for the Android Market is such that serious flaws in the way you manage user data may not be spotted. Self-policing is the best way of ensuring that you're acting professionally when it comes to protecting your users.

Phew! That got a bit serious there for a second, huh? Now that you're mindful of the security considerations about data collection, you can safely start sending and receiving data in your application.

Knowing Whether an Internet Connection Is There

Before attempting to send any data to a remote web server, or load anything in, it's helpful to both you and your user to check whether a network is available. Your application may work perfectly well offline, but you may want to notify the user of the absence of the Internet for additional features. Your application may want to update a set of data it holds locally. For instance, a currency conversion application may persist — that is, save for the next time the application starts — a set of exchange rates locally until it can download a newer set.

Using the URLMonitor class, your application code can determine whether a connection to the Internet is available on the device by periodically attempting to open a connection to the given URL. Once started, the URLMonitor class periodically dispatches a STATUS event — that tells your code whether a connection is available — which you can handle in your ActionScript code. If the status indicates that a connection is available, you can then attempt to send data to a web server over the Internet.

Setting up URLMonitor in Flash Professional

By default, the libraries that include URLMonitor aren't imported when a new AIR project is started. The URLMonitor class is stored inside a file called aircore.swc, which is already lurking on your computer inside the folder that Flash Professional is installed in. In the following steps, you create a new application to test URLMonitor, and then you associate aircore.swc with that application:

1. **Create a new application in Flash Professional and save it as**
URLMonitorExample.fla.

    Choose either a new AIR for Android application or a new iOS application.

2. **In the Properties panel, click the wrench icon next to the Class field.**

    The Create ActionScript 3.0 Class dialog box opens.

3. **Type the Class name** URLMonitorExample **and click OK.**

    A new ActionScript 3.0 class is opened in Flash Professional.

4. **Press Ctrl+S (Windows) or Command+S (Mac) and save the file as**
URLMonitorExample.as.

5. **Switch back to** URLMonitorExample.fla, **and choose File⇨Publish**
Settings.

    The Publish Settings dialog box opens.

6. **Click the Flash (.swf) item in the list on the left.**

7. **Click the ActionScript Settings button (the wrench icon) next to**
ActionScript 3.0.

    The Advanced ActionScript 3.0 Settings dialog box opens.

8. **Click the Library Path tab.**

9. **Click the Browse to SWC File button.**

    This button is the middle icon in the upper-right corner of the SWC files
or folders list. A File Open dialog box opens.

10. **Browse to the aircore.swc file.**

    The file is in /Adobe Flash CS5/AIK2.5/frameworks/libs/air/
aircore.swc. The SWC file appears in the SWC files or folders list.

11. **Click Open.**

12. **Click OK and click OK again to save the changes.**

Creating a URLMonitor instance

Having configured aircore.swc for use with URLMonitor.fla in the preceding section, I'll now show you how to create a URLMonitor instance that
monitors the availability of www.google.com and then updates a Boolean
variable with the result of the availability check. I've chosen Google because
it's a website that responds quickly to requests no matter where in the world
you're located. If your device is able to communicate with http://www.
google.com/, it's safe to say the device has an Internet connection.

The `Boolean` variable serves as a handy way to store the status of the `URLMonitor`'s connection status, which is `true` when connected. Now continue adding to the `URLMonitorExample.fla` application you created in the preceding section by following these steps to create a `URLMonitor` instance.

1. **Open** `URLMonitorExample.as` **in Flash Professional.**

2. **Declare a new** `Boolean` **variable called** `networkAvailable`:

```
public class URLMonitor extends MovieClip
{
    private var _networkAvailable:Boolean;
    public function URLMonitor()
    {
```

3. **Declare a new** `URLMonitor` **instance called** _monitor **and initialize it with a new** `URLRequest` **object whose URL is** `http://www.google.com`:

```
import air.net.URLMonitor;
import flash.net.URLRequest;

public class URLMonitorExample extends MovieClip
{
    private var _networkAvailable:Boolean;
    private var _monitor:URLMonitor = new URLMonitor(
        new URLRequest( "http://www.google.com" ) );
    public function URLMonitor()
    {
```

Don't forget to check that Flash Professional has added the import directives for the `URLMonitor` and `URLRequest` classes at the top of your class. Otherwise, an error will be thrown when you run your app. Type them yourself if you don't see them as shown in the example.

4. **Register an event listener for the** `URLMonitor` **instance's** `STATUS` **event:**

```
public function URLMonitor()
{
    // constructor code
    _monitor.addEventListener( StatusEvent.STATUS,
        onMonitorStatus );
}
```

The `SELECT` event is dispatched by the `URLMonitor` object each time it attempts to access the URL you've provided to it.

5. **Create a method to handle the** `STATUS` **event that assigns the value of the** `available` **property on the event object target to the** `_network Available` **variable:**

```
    _monitor.addEventListener( StatusEvent.STATUS,
        onMonitorStatus );
}

private function onMonitorStatus( e:StatusEvent )
        :void
{
    _networkAvailable = e.target.available;
}
```

The `available` property is `true` if the `URLMonitor` instance was able to contact the URL supplied and `false` if it failed. Check that Flash Professional has added the import directive for the `StatusEvent` class at the top of your class. Type it yourself if you don't see it:

```
package
{
    import flash.display.MovieClip;
    import air.net.URLMonitor;
    import flash.net.URLRequest;
    import flash.events.StatusEvent;

    public class URLMonitorExample extends MovieClip
    {
```

6. **Add a** `trace()` **statement to print the value of the** `networkAvailable` **member variable to the Output panel in Flash Professional:**

```
private function onMonitorStatus( e:StatusEvent )
        :void
{
    networkAvailable = e.target.available;
    trace( 'Status: ' + networkAvailable );
}
```

7. **Start the** `URLMonitor` **by calling its** `start()` **method:**

```
public function URLMonitor()
{
    // constructor code
    _monitor.addEventListener( StatusEvent.STATUS,
        onMonitorStatus );
    _monitor.start();
}
```

The `URLMonitor` instance must be started using its `start()` method before it will begin monitoring the availability of the URL you specified. It can later be stopped by calling its `stop()` method.

With the `URLMonitor` instance in place, your application is now able to determine whether it has a connection to the Internet, to enable it to communicate with web servers. Before making any requests, you can check the value of the networkAvailable variable you created to decide whether it's worthwhile attempting the call.

Preparing Request Data to Be Sent

Perhaps you've harvested a little bit of data from your user that you'd like to send over the Internet to a web server that'll do something with it and then return a response. It sounds quite daunting, but breaking the job into a few manageable stages turns the problem into an enjoyable task.

Preparation of the data is key. I believe that the majority of problems experienced by Flash developers attempting to communicate with third-party web servers are attributable to badly constructed *requests*. The request is essentially a message sent from the application to the server, written in a format that the service running on the server can understand.

You can find loads of free web services — programs that run on web servers and return data responses to requests you make to them — on the Internet. For this example, I've chosen a handy service from a website called Geonames (www.geonames.org/export/ws-overview.html) that enables you to obtain a place-name by providing the latitude and longitude coordinates to it. Although Geonames is free and easy to set up, it does require you to register and activate your account by e-mail before you can use its web services.

After your Geonames account is set up, you need to create a URLRequest object. Follow these steps to get your application to call the Geonames web service with hard-coded location coordinates and then display the resulting place-name in a TextField instance. Continue adding to the URLMonitorExample.as class you started in the "Creating a URLMonitor instance" section:

1. **Create a new method called** getGeonamesService in URLMonitor Example.as:

```
private function onMonitorStatus( e:StatusEvent )
        :void
{
   networkAvailable = e.target.available;
   trace( 'Status: ' + _networkAvailable );
}

private function getGeonamesService() :void
{}
```

2. **Declare a new** URLRequest **instance called** _request, **and initialize it with the URL** http://api.geonames.org/findNearbyPlaceName:

```
private var _request:URLRequest = new URLRequest(
        "http://api.geonames.org/findNearbyPlaceName"
        );
public function URLMonitorExample()
{
```

3. **Declare and initialize a new** URLVariables **instance called** _variables:

```
private var _request:URLRequest = new URLRequest(
        "http://api.geonames.org/findNearbyPlaceName"
        );
private var _variables:URLVariables = new
        URLVariables();
public function URLMonitorExample()
{
```

4. **Inside the** getGeonamesService() **method, set three new properties on the** URLVariables **object. Set one called** lat **and assign it the value** 51.32, **set another called** lng **and assign it the value** 0.5, **and finally set a property called** username **and assign it the value** jodieorourke:

```
private function getGeonamesService() :void
{
    _variables.lat = 51.32;
    _variables.lng = 0.5;
    _variables.username = "jodieorourke";
}
```

5. **Assign the** URLVariables **instance to the** data **property of the** URLRequest **object:**

```
    _variables.username = "jodieorourke";
    _request.data = _variables;
}
```

6. **Set the** method **property of the** URLRequest **object to** URLRequestMethod.GET:

```
    _request.data = _variables;
    _request.method = URLRequestMethod.GET;
}
```

URLRequestMethod is a class that contains a collection of valid values for the URLRequest.method property. In this instance, you've set it as GET. Data sent over HTTP across the Internet is sent as either GET or POST. GET should generally be used when fetching data from a web service — such as the Geonames service — whereas POST should be used for sending data for storage. The Geonames service is just providing information to you, so it prefers the use of GET. With GET, the variables are appended onto the end of the URL, often referred to as a query string.

The preparation is done. Your request data is now assembled and ready for transmission, and you're ready to call the service.

Using URLLoader to Send Form Data to the Server

If you've ever loaded data into an ActionScript 3.0 application, you almost certainly will have come across the URLLoader class. Put simply, the URLLoader class underpins pretty much all data-loading operations that occur in Flash applications. In fact, if you look under the hood of the most Flash applications, you'll find plenty of URLLoader instances in there too.

With the URLRequest and URLVariables objects prepared in the code of the URLMonitorExample.as class — created in the preceding section — then next step is to send latitude and longitude coordinates to the web server that the Geonames service is running on, and then prepare to receive a place-name back.

In the following steps, I further develop the code I wrote in preparing the data to be sent to make a call to the Geonames web service.

Continue working in URLMonitorExample.as. Follow these steps to create a URLLoader instance, and then use it to send data to the Geonames service and finally load the response:

1. **Declare a new** URLLoader **instance inside the** getGeonameService() **method:**

```
    _request.method = URLRequestMethod.GET;
    var loader:URLLoader = new URLLoader();
}
```

2. **Assign a listener to the** URLLoader **instance for the** COMPLETE **event:**

```
    var loader:URLLoader = new URLLoader();
    loader.addEventListener( Event.COMPLETE, onComplete
        );
}
```

3. **Below the** `getGeonamesService` **method, create a new method called** `onComplete` to handle the `URLLoader`'s `COMPLETE` **event:**

```
    var loader:URLLoader = new URLLoader();
    loader.addEventListener( Event.COMPLETE, onComplete
        )
}

private function onComplete( e:Event ) :void
{}
```

4. **Use the** `trace()` **function to write the value of the event object target's** `data` **property to the Output window in Flash Professional:**

```
private function onComplete( e:Event ) :void
{
    trace( e.target.data );
}
```

5. **Invoke the** `load()` **method on your** `URLLoader` **instance, providing the** `_request` **as the parameter.**

   Put the code inside the `getGeonameService()` method:

```
    loader.addEventListener( Event.COMPLETE, onComplete
        );
    loader.load( _request );
}
```

6. **Call the** `getGeonamesService()` **method from inside the** `onMonitorStatus()` **method, using an** `if` **statement to check that** `_networkAvailable` **is** true**:**

```
private function onMonitorStatus( e:StatusEvent )
        :void
{
    _networkAvailable = e.target.available;
    trace( 'Status: ' + _networkAvailable );
    if( _networkAvailable )
    {
        getGeonamesService();
    }
}
```

When the `STATUS` event is handled by `onMonitorStatus`, if the `_networkAvailable` property is set to `true` — because the `URLMonitor` was able to contact `http://www.google.com` — the `getGeonamesService()` method is called, which causes the `URLLoader` to call the remote Geonames server.

At this point, you can quickly publish your Flash application — press Ctrl+Enter (Windows) or Command+Enter (Mac) — to see what's happening. Notice that nothing happens on the stage, but when a response from the Geonames service is received by the application, some XML code appears in the Output panel, as shown here:

```
<?xml version="1.0" encoding="UTF-8" standalone="no"?>
<geonames>
<geoname>
<toponymName>Burham</toponymName>
<name>Burham</name>
<lat>51.33243</lat>
<lng>0.47833</lng>
<geonameId>2654293</geonameId>
<countryCode>GB</countryCode>
<countryName>United Kingdom</countryName>
<fcl>P</fcl>
<fcode>PPL</fcode>
<distance>2.04395</distance>
</geoname>
</geonames>
```

This is the data that's coming back from the service!

Handling and Parsing a Response

After receiving data from the service, it's unlikely to be in a format that is instantly usable in your application. XML doesn't display very nicely in `TextFields`, and you might not want to overload your user with everything that the service returned — some of the data might in fact be irrelevant. To address this, a stage of parsing the response needs to occur before the data is displayed to the user.

In ActionScript 3.0, a handy way of extracting values from loaded XML documents, called *E4X,* was introduced. E4X allows you, the developer, to query the XML data for a particular object with the name you're searching for, using standardized dot notation syntax. The Geonames web service I've been discussing throughout this chapter returns an XML response that contains a place-name string, among other data. E4X enables you to extract the place-name string from the XML with ease, and without needing to consider the other data contained in the XML.

Following the receipt of your service response from the web service, you can now add some code to your `onComplete` event handler to extract the place-name from the body of XML that was returned, which you can then display to the user as the town corresponding to the latitude and longitude coordinates that were sent to the server. Follow these instructions to handle an XML response:

1. **Create a new XML variable called** response **and assign it the value of the event object target's** data **property, converted to an XML object:**

```
private function onComplete( e:Event ) :void
{
    trace( e.target.data );
    var response:XML = XML( e.target.data );
}
```

The data that comes back to your application from the Geonames server is treated by the URLLoader object as text. The data is indeed text, but is formatted as XML markup, so you can convert — or *cast* — it to an XML object. You cast something to XML by placing the object you want to cast inside the parentheses of an XML global function, like this: XML(e.target.data);.

The text response is now treated as XML inside the application, allowing it to be traversed with E4X queries.

2. **Declare and initialize a new** TextField **instance called** outputText:

```
    var response:XML = XML( e.target.data );
    var outputText:TextField = new TextField();
}
```

3. **Assign the value of the** name **property in the** response **XML object to the** text **property of the** TextField **instance:**

```
    var outputText:TextField = new TextField();
    outputText.text = response..name.toString();
}
```

Here is where the E4X comes into play. The name value exists inside the XML object, and using the object notation response..name, the XML hierarchy (or tree) will be explored, and every occurrence of the name node will be pulled out and placed into an XMLList object. In this instance, you see only one occurrence of name in the XML document, so only this one will be returned. Applying a toString() command to the end ensures that only the String value of the node is returned, not the entire XML node itself.

4. **Add the** TextField **instance to the display list:**

```
    outputText.text = response..name.toString();
    addChild( outputText );
}
```

The code that handles the response from the Geonames service is complete! Now test your Flash application in Flash Professional by pressing Ctrl+Enter (Windows) or Command+Enter (Mac) to see what your new changes have done. See that as well as writing the XML response to the Output panel, a `TextField` instance now displays on the stage, as shown in Figure 8-1, with the place-name of location coordinates you sent to the service. Cool stuff, huh?

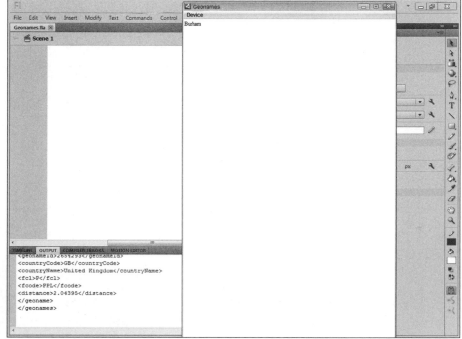

Figure 8-1: A TextField showing the Geonames service result.

Dealing with Loss of Connectivity

Because your application is running on a mobile device, it's highly likely that at times your application will be running when a connection to the Internet is lost. When this happens, you want your user to be let down nicely, not upset with a cataclysmic crash! If your application calls any web server for data, it is doing this asynchronously, and it waits for an event to notify of the load operation completion before continuing. If, while waiting for the remote web server to respond, the mobile device loses its connection with the Internet, the loading operation will never complete. By default, Flash applications throw an error if a load operation exceeds 30 seconds, but these errors occur silently on all but debug versions of the Flash runtime software. The device that your Flash mobile application will run on almost certainly won't invoke

Flash error dialog boxes, and they're rather ugly anyway, so you should handle these failures appropriately by assigning an ErrorEvent listener to your URLLoader instance.

Now you need to register for an ErrorEvent. The following steps add to the URLMonitorExample.as class, which I've been showing you throughout this chapter, to handle a fatal error that terminates the download of data from the Geonames web server:

1. **Open** URLMonitorExample.as **for editing in Flash Professional.**

2. **Register an event listener to the** URLLoader **for the** IO_ERROR **event.**

```
var loader:URLLoader = new URLLoader();
loader.addEventListener( Event.COMPLETE, onComplete
    );
loader.addEventListener( IOErrorEvent.IO_ERROR,
    onIOError );
loader.load( _request );
}
```

3. **Create a method called** onIOError **to handle the event:**

```
        addChild( outputText );
    }

    private function onIOError( e:IOErrorEvent )
      :void
    {
    }
    }
}
```

4. **Declare and initialize a** TextField **instance called** outputText **inside the new** onIOError **method.**

   Declare and initialize a TextField instance called outputText, assign it some text that tells the user that a fault has occurred, and then add it to the display list:

```
private function onIOError( e:IOErrorEvent ) :void
{
    var outputText:TextField = new TextField();
}
```

5. **Assign a string to the** outputText.text **property that tells the user a fault has occurred:**

```
    var outputText:TextField = new TextField();
    outputText.text = "Sorry! Loading failed.";
}
```

6. Add `output` **text to the display list, so that the user sees it onscreen:**

```
function onIOError( e:IOErrorEvent ) :void
{
    var outputText:TextField = new TextField();
    outputText.text = "Sorry! Loading failed.";
    addChild( outputText );
}
```

That's it. Now when the communication between your application and the Geonames web server fails, your application displays a message to users informing them that a problem occurred. In your own applications, you can consider improving the language used in the message or styling in your own way using some of the graphics techniques covered in Chapter 5.

Performing Synchronization

Synchronization is the act of two computers that are remote to each other exchanging pieces of data so that they both hold identical sets of data. In the case of your mobile application, this synchronization will most likely be an application running on your mobile device contacting a remote web server to retrieve data that the application requires to function correctly. Earlier in the chapter, in the discussion of checking whether an Internet connection is present, I mentioned a currency conversion application checking whether an updated version of the exchange rates table is available on startup. Alternatively, you might want some locally stored high scores to be uploaded to the server, so that the server can return the highest score submitted by anyone else playing the game, so that the user can see how his or her score ranks against those of other users.

The synchronization process

The process for synchronizing data between your application and a remote web server is similar to the process covered in the early part of this chapter for sending and receiving data using the Geonames service. To successfully perform synchronization, you need to

✔ Establish that an Internet connection is present using `URLMonitor`

✔ Prepare the data that will be sent to the web server using `URLRequest` and `URLVariables`

✔ Send the data to the server using `URLLoader`

✔ Parse the response sent by the server using E4X queries

Synchronizing high scores

You've been working with the SpaceshipZapZap application throughout the book. Following are the steps required to retrieve the highest score value from the Local `SharedObject`, send it to a web server, and then add a new value to the Local `SharedObject` to store the high score returned from the server. In this example, a check is made to determine whether or not the application can access the `scoreService.php` service running on a remote web server; if the service is available, the application sends data to it and receives a response. The web service you call is just returning a static value, but for the purposes of getting your application built, it will be more than satisfactory:

1. **Associate** `aircore.swc` **with** `SpaceshipZapZap.fla`.

   Follow the steps in the "Setting up URLMonitor in Flash Professional" section, earlier in the chapter.

2. **Reopen** `SpaceshipZapZap.as` **in Flash Professional.**

3. **Declare a** `URLMonitor` **variable called** `_urlMonitor` **with all the other variable declarations:**

```
package
{
    //...

    public class SpaceshipZapZap extends MovieClip
    {

        private var _sharedObject:SharedObject;
        private const MONTHS:Array = [ "Jan", "Feb",
            "Mar", "Apr", "May", "Jun", "Jul", "Aug",
            "Sep", "Nov", "Dec" ];
        private var _urlMonitor:URLMonitor;

        public function SpaceshipZapZap()
        {
```

4. **Declare a** `Boolean` **variable called** `_isSynchronizationComplete`.

```
private var _urlMonitor:URLMonitor;
private var _isSynchronized:Boolean;
```

5. **Initialize the** `URLMonitor` **instance inside the class's** `initialize()` **method, providing the URL** `http://jodieorourke.com/scripts/scoreService.php` **as a new** `URLRequest` **object:**

```
_highScoreSubmit.y = ( stage.stageHeight * .5 ) - (
    _highScoreSubmit.height * .5 );
_sharedObject = SharedObject.getLocal(
    "spaceshipZapZap" );
```

```
      _urlMonitor = new URLMonitor( new URLRequest(
          "http://jodieorourke.com/scripts/scoreService.
          php" ) );
  }
```

6. **Register an event listener for the** URLMonitor **instance's** STATUS **event:**

```
      _urlMonitor = new URLMonitor( new URLRequest(
          "http://jodieorourke.com/scripts/scoreService.
          php" ) );
      _urlMonitor.addEventListener( StatusEvent.STATUS,
          onMonitorStatus );
  }
```

7. **Call the** start() **method on the** URLMonitor **instance:**

```
      urlMonitor.addEventListener( StatusEvent.STATUS,
          onMonitorStatus );
      _urlMonitor.start();
  }
```

8. **Create a method in** SpaceshipZapZap.as **to handle the** STATUS
event called onMonitorStatus **that calls the** populateHigh-
Scores() **method:**

```
      private function populateHighScores() :void
      {
          //...
      }
      private function onMonitorStatus( e:StatusEvent )
          :void
      {
          populateHighScores();
      }
  }
```

The first bit is complete. The next step is to put the value of the highest score
achieved by the user into a URLVariables object and assign this object
to the data property of a URLRequest. The request can then be sent to a
remote web server using a URLLoader instance:

1. **Add an** if **statement to the** onMonitorStatus() **method that checks
whether the** URLLoader.available **property is** true, **the** _highScores
array has a length **value, and the** _isSynchronized **variable is** false:

```
  private function onMonitorStatus() :void
  {
      populateHighScores();
      if( e.target.available && _highScores.length && !_
          isSynchronized )
      {}

      //...
  }
```

2. **Inside the** `if` **statement, declare a new** `URLVariables` **object and create a new property on it called** `userHighScore` — **assigning the value of the first high score in the** `_highScores` **array:**

```
if( e.target.available && _highScores.length && !_
    isSynchronized )
  {
     var variables:URLVariables = new URLVariables();
     variables.userHighScore = _highScores[ 0
       ].userScore;
}
```

3. **Declare a new** `URLRequest` **object, set the method to** `POST`, **assign the** `URLVariables` **instance you created in the last step to the** `URLRequest` **object's** `data` **property, and then set the** `url` **property to** `http://jodieorourke.com/scripts/scoreService.php`:

```
     variables.userHighScore = _highScores[ 0
         ].userScore;
     var request:URLRequest = new URLRequest();
     request.method = URLRequestMethod.POST;
     request.data = variables;
     request.url = " http://jodieorourke.com/scripts/
         scoreService.php ";
}
```

Note that the `userHighScore` variable is assigned the `userScore` value stored in position 0 of the `_highScores` Array. The `userHighScore` value is the user's locally stored highest score.

4. **Declare and initialize new** `URLLoader` **instance:**

```
     request.url = " http://jodieorourke.com/scripts/
         scoreService.php ";
     var loader:URLLoader = new URLLoader();
}
```

5. **Register event listeners to the** `URLLoader` **instance for the** `COMPLETE` **and** `IO_ERROR` **events:**

```
var loader:URLLoader = new URLLoader();
   loader.addEventListener( Event.COMPLETE,
       onLoadComplete );
   loader.addEventListener( IOErrorEvent.IO_ERROR,
       onLoadFailed );
}
```

6. **Call the** `load` **method on the** `URLLoader` **instance:**

```
     loader.addEventListener( IOErrorEvent.IO_ERROR,
         onLoadFailed );
     loader.load( request );
}
```

7. **Set the** `_isSynchronized` **Boolean variable to** `true`:

```
    loader.load( request );
    _isSynchronized = true;
}
```

This code stops any subsequent updates to the `URLMonitor`'s status from causing repeated `load()` calls.

8. **Create a new method called** `onLoadComplete` **to handle the** `COMPLETE` **event, which fires when data comes back from the web server:**

```
    _isSynchronized = true;
}

private function onLoadComplete( e:Event ) :void
{}
```

9. **Assign the value of URLLoader's** `data` **property to a new object on the** `SharedObject` **instance called** `serverHighScore`. **Call the** `flush()` **method on the** `SharedObject` **to save the new data:**

```
private function onLoadComplete( e:Event ) :void
{
    _sharedObject.data[ "serverHighScore" ] = e.target.
        data;
    _sharedObject.flush();
}
```

10. **Call the** `stop()` **method on the** `URLMonitor` **instance:**

```
    _sharedObject.flush();
    urlMonitor.stop();
}
```

After your `URLMonitor` has served its purpose, it's important to stop it from continuing to monitor the presence of an Internet connection. By calling its `stop()` method, you prevent it from perpetually causing your application to synchronize unnecessarily — saving resources on the device the application is running on and saving the user from the expense of unnecessary Internet traffic.

11. **Create a method called** `onLoadFailed` **to handle the** `IO_ERROR` **event. Inside the** `onLoadFailed` **method, you should set the** `_isSynchronized` **variable to** `false`:

```
    urlMonitor.stop();
}

private function onLoadFailed( e:IOErrorEvent ) :void
{
    _isSynchronized = false;
}
```

When the load does fail, the _isSynchronized variable is set back to false to allow the application to attempt to contact the service again later.

That's it! Your application now checks whether it can contact http://jodieorourke.com/scripts/scoreService.php. If it can, it attempts to send and receive high score data from the remote server. A textbook example of synchronization!

Tracking Your Application with Google Analytics

As you wave your application off into the Apple App Store or Android Market (covered in Chapters 19 and 20, respectively), singing "When Will I See You Again?" by Three Degrees, you're certainly hoping that it won't be soon as a result of rejection by the app review process! Assuming that your application sails through to the storefront, is that the last you want to hear from it? Granted, you'll get sales updates from each of the respective stores, but is that all you want to know about your application? Of course it isn't! Google Analytics allows you to track events and interactions that occur when your application is running on a mobile device, and then present all the data collected in ways that help you to see trends in user behavior and spot flaws in the design of your application.

Google Analytics is for harvesting anonymous data about generalized user behavior in your application, such as how many people view a particular screen and where they go next. You should not use it to capture information that can personally identify users or their precise locations — a city is okay but geolocation coordinates are not. Users must always give their express permission for you to store information that can be directly linked to them.

Setting up a new tracking account

Google Analytics is not only one of the strongest web-based tracking and reporting tools available but also free. Signing up is as simple as adding the Analytics product to your existing Google account. Adding a new profile and configuring the tracking URL to call are a little more complicated and are covered in the steps that follow:

1. **Sign in to your Google Account at** http://www.google.com.

2. **Select Analytics from the My Products list.**

   Add Analytics if you don't already have it — it's free.

3. **From the My Analytics Account drop-down list, select Create New Account.**

You are presented with the Getting Started screen.

4. **Click the Sign-Up button.**

The New Account Signup — General Information screen is displayed.

5. **Enter your website URL and friendly account name, and select your location.**

6. **Click Continue.**

The Contact Information screen appears.

7. **Type the required contact information and then click Continue.**

The Accept User Agreement screen appears.

8. **Read the terms, and if you agree to them, select the Yes check box and click Create New Account.**

The Analytics: Tracking Instructions screen appears. The screen asks you to copy and paste JavaScript code into your own web page. Don't bother to do that, because you're not working with web pages, so this code is of no use.

9. **Click Save and Finish.**

The Overview page displays, as shown in Figure 8-2. Next to the website name is an ID code beginning with the letters *UA*. Make a note of it, because this is your tracking ID and is required later when you need to record activity in your application to the Google Analytics servers.

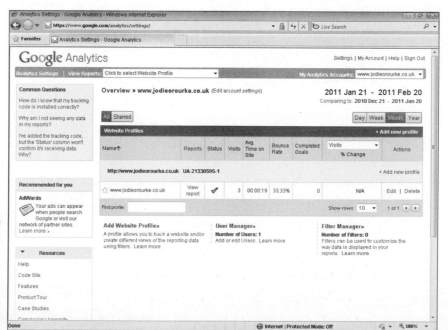

Figure 8-2:
Locating your tracking ID on the Overview page.

Configuring the Google Analytics libraries for Flash Professional

To use Google Analytics in the context of your Flash application, which is quite a different beast from the conventional web page, you first need to download and configure a third-party ActionScript library called Google Analytics for Flash (`gaforflash` libraries), which is hosted on the Google Code website.

The following steps show you how to download and configure Google Analytics for Flash in your own Flash application:

1. **Use your browser to navigate to** `http://code.google.com/p/gaforflash/downloads/list`.

2. **Download the** `gaforflash` **libraries via the latest ZIP file.**

   This ZIP file contains the component that you compile into your application as well as some documentation.

3. **Unzip the archive to a location on your hard drive.**

4. **Open Flash Professional and choose File⇨Publish Settings.**

   The Publish Settings dialog box opens.

5. **Click the Flash (.swf) item in the list on the left**

6. **Click the ActionScript Settings button (the wrench icon) next to ActionScript 3.0.**

   The Advanced ActionScript 3.0 Settings dialog box opens.

7. **Click the Library Path tab.**

8. **Click the Browse to SWC File button.**

   This button is the middle icon in the upper-right corner of the SWC files or folders list.

   A File Open dialog box opens.

9. **Browse to the Google Analytics** `analytics.swc` **file.**

   The file is inside the `lib` directory of the unpacked ZIP archive.

10. **Click Open.**

    On opening, the SWC file appears in the SWC files or folders list.

11. **Click OK and click OK again to save the changes.**

All the classes inside `analytics.swc` are now available to you in Flash Professional and are even included in the code-hinting suggestions when you press Ctrl+spacebar. If you delve into the docs folder of the downloaded archive, you'll also find a comprehensive set of API documentation that provides detailed information about the workings of the Google Analytics for Flash code. Run index.html in the docs folder if you want to view this.

Integrating Google Analytics tracking in Flash applications

Now this is the fun part! You can literally track any event in your application; deciding which ones to track is probably the only difficult part. Having configured Google Analytics for Flash in Flash Professional, you can now add tracking calls at logical points in your application so that you can harvest data about what parts of your application your user is using. When you have a better insight into how people are using your application, you can make more informed decisions about improving functionality that the analytics suggest users aren't using. Conversely, the harvested usage data can save you from spending time altering parts of your application that are already working well.

In the SpaceshipZapZap game, I'm interested in knowing how far my user progresses through the application. For example, how many times a day is the app launched around the world versus how many people submit scores or view the game-over screen at the end of my game? Harvesting these numbers from the application and then calculating the difference would enable me to determine the *dropout rate,* that is, the number of people giving up midgame. If users are dropping out midway through playback, it could be a sign that the game is too difficult to play or not captivating enough. If my analytics alert me to either scenario, I can make improvements.

The following steps show you how to set up an instance for the tracking component inside the SpaceshipZapZap application and then send notifications of in-game events back to the Google Analytics servers:

1. **Open the** SpaceshipZapZap.as **Document Class in Flash Professional.**

   You find out how to create this class in Chapter 6.

2. **Declare a new** GATracker **variable called** _tracker **at the top of the class, along with the other variable declarations:**

```
public class SpaceshipZapZap extends MovieClip
{
    //...
    private var _isSynchronized:Boolean;
    private var _tracker:GATracker;
```

Confirm that Flash Professional automatically creates the `com.google.analytics.GATracker` import directive for you at the top of the class; if not, type it.

3. **Initialize a** `GATracker` **instance in the** `initialize()` **method.**

   Inside the `initialize` method, just above the `displayStartScreen()` line, assign `_tracker` the value of a new `GATracker` object:

   ```
   private function initialize( e:Event ):void
   {
       removeEventListener( Event.ADDED_TO_STAGE,
           initialize );
       _tracker = new GATracker( this, "UA-12345678-9",
           TrackerMode.AS3 );
       displayStartScreen();
       //...
   ```

   The `GATracker` instance needs three required parameters to be able to initialize itself, which you provide inside the brackets. Here's what each of the three parameters does:

   - *Param 1:* A reference to the main application display object, which in this case is the `SpaceshipZapZap` Document Class, referred to using the `this` keyword.

   - *Param 2:* The Account ID string starting with the letters *UA* that was displayed on your Google Analytics account overview screen.

   - *Param 3:* The mode in which the tracker should operate. The two options are Bridge, which requires the Flash application to be embedded in a web page to communicate with Google servers, or AS3, which allows the Flash application to talk directly to web servers. Set the mode to AS3 because the app you're working with is running as a native mobile application, not a Flash Player application embedded in a web page.

4. **Call** `trackPageView` **on the** `GATracker` **instance.**

   I want Google Analytics to treat each event in my application as a page view. In a website, a *page view* occurs each time a web page completes rendering in the browser, enabling the user to see it. In my application, I want to call Google Analytics when certain things happen and have it record the event as a custom page view. Doing this means I can mine this data in a similar way that I would for a conventional website. I can tell Google Analytics to record any event in my application by calling the `trackPageview` method and supplying a unique string that enables me to identify the event when I later browse the data in the Google Analytics online reporting tool. In this example, every time the `displayStartScreen` method is called, the Google Analytics servers receive a page view for `spaceshipzapzap/displayStartScreen`:

```
private function displayStartScreen() :void
{
        addChild( _startScreen );
    _tracker.trackPageview( "spaceshipzapzap/
        displayStartScreen/" );
}
```

You can call trackPageview with many events of your own. For example, if you wanted to track that the user just pressed a button, just change the string you send from spaceshipzapzap/displayStartScreen to spaceshipzapzap/userPressedButtonX — where X is the name of the button. It's a flexible way of tracking user activity, and the reports created for you on the Google Analytics website help you visualize your data in the form of line graphs and pie charts.

That's all there is to it! Now just wait for the tracking data to flood in. You'll see colorful charts forming, and perhaps interesting trends in your users' behavior!

Part III
Adding Extra Bells and Whistles

The 5th Wave   By Rich Tennant

"Of course your current cell phone takes pictures, functions as a walkie-talkie, and browses the Internet. But does it shoot silly string?"

In this part . . .

A 19th-century fairground organ didn't need superfluous bells and whistles to function, but everyone attending the fairs flocked to see it because it was dressed in the full ornamental regalia. The same is true for Flash mobile applications: Add some bells and whistles, and suddenly it's a hit with users.

Chapter 9 looks at how you add audio and video to your application. Chapter 10 introduces you to animation, and Chapter 11 explores the extra features available on mobile devices that your application can use. Chapter 12 looks at how you use a different development tool to build Flash mobile applications faster.

Chapter 9

Enhancing with Video and Audio

*O*nce upon a time, the idea of receiving data as complex as an image on a mobile device seemed like a fairy tale, let alone the prospect of music and video. 3G, and soon 4G, networks have become the norm. These faster networks bring larger data bandwidth capacity, permitting video and audio files to be delivered at speeds comparable to wired broadband connections.

Audio and video have done wonders for the web, making experiences richer and more captivating, and ultimately, making the Internet more human. Bringing audio-visual experiences to a mobile device via Flash is another way to offer an engaging experience to the user.

In this chapter, you find out how to deliver video and audio to users of your application using a variety of different transport protocols. You also become acquainted with the Open Source Media Framework, a powerful code library for developing media players.

Playing Progressive Flash Video Files

Flash Player is able to decode Flash Video (FLV) files without the need for external software or hardware. This independence from any third-party application is one of the primary reasons for Flash's dominance in online media delivery. Users with the Flash Player plug-in in their browser are assured to be able to play Flash video. With Flash mobile applications, the same is true: Your application is able to play FLV files right out of the box!

FLV files downloaded from a conventional web server can be played back in a Flash application as they download, reducing the amount of time the user has to wait before he or she sees or hears the content. This type of delivery is known as *progressive download.*

Although it is possible to import and save a video file in your Flash application FLA, this is bad practice and results in an excessively large application that will be too big to download and install on mobile devices. Instead, follow these steps to play an FLV video using progressive download:

1. **Create a new application in Flash Professional and save it as** Progressive.fla.

   Choose a new AIR for Android or iOS application.

2. **In the Properties panel, click the wrench icon next to the Class field.**

   The Create ActionScript 3.0 Class dialog box opens.

3. **Type the Class name** Progressive **and click OK.**

   A new ActionScript 3.0 class is opened in Flash Professional.

4. **Press Ctrl+S (Windows) or Command+S (Mac) and save the file as** Progressive.as.

5. **Place the following code in the class constructor** function Main() **(the code you type is in bold):**

   ```
   public function Progressive()
   {
       var connection:NetConnection = new NetConnection();
       connection.connect( null );
   }
   ```

   This code declares, initializes, and connects a new instance of the NetConnection object. The null parameter provided to the connect() method simply signifies that a two-way Flash Media Server connection isn't required for this connection. An instance of the NetConnection object manages downloading your video and acts as a virtual pipe between the client (the Flash application) and the remote server along which the video data will pass.

   The NetConnection instance is connected using its connect() method.

6. **Place the following code on the line below the** connection. connect() **code:**

   ```
       connection.connect( null );
       var client:Object = new Object();
   }
   ```

   This code declares and initializes a new object that acts as the target for any video-specific callbacks that arise during playback.

7. **Create a new property on the** `client` **object called** `onMetaData`.

8. **Assign the client object the value** `onMetaData` **— the name of a function you'll create next:**

```
var client:Object = new Object();
client.onMetaData = onMetaData;
}
```

9. **Create a function called** `onMetaData` **to handle the** `onMetaData` **callback assignment:**

```
client.onMetaData = onMetaData;
}

private function onMetaData( info:Object ) :void
{}
```

Whenever something attempts to access `onMetaData` on the client object, that attempt is relayed to a function in your class called `onMetaData`. Although no code will be put in the `onMetaData` method, video playback in Flash requires you to have the method there regardless.

10. **Declare and initialize a new** `NetStream` **instance, and then play it.**

`NetStream` is a representation of the media you want to play through the `NetConnection`. You configure a `NetStream` instance as follows.

   a. **Initialize the** `NetStream` **instance, providing it the reference to the NetConnection instance called** `connection`, **which you just created:**

```
client.onMetaData = onMetaData;
var stream = new NetStream( connection );
}
```

   b. **Assign the client object you created in Step 6 as the client property for the** `NetStream` **instance:**

```
var stream = new NetStream( connection );
stream.client = client;
}
```

   c. **Call the** `play()` **method on** `stream`, **providing the URL of the media you want it to play:**

```
stream.client = client;
stream.play( "http://mywebserver.com/myVideo.
   flv" );
}
```

The `NetStream` object attempts to call the `onMetaData` property on the client object when the video has loaded enough data to start playing. When the property is called, the call is relayed to the `onMetaData()` method, where it can be handled.

11. **Declare and initialize a new** `Video` **object, attach the** `NetStream` **instance, and then add the** `Video` **object to the display list.**

    `Video` is the visual representation of the `NetStream`, the part the users actually see. You use three key steps to set up your `Video` display object ready for insertion into the display list.

    a. **Initialize the** `Video` **object:**

    ```
        stream.play( "http://mywebserver.com/myVideo.
          flv" );
        var video:Video = new Video();
    }
    ```

    b. **Attach the** `NetStream` **instance called** `stream` **to the** `Video` **object using the** `attachNetStream` **method:**

    ```
        var video:Video = new Video();
        video.attachNetStream( stream );
    }
    ```

    c. **Add the** `Video` **instance to the display list using the** `addChild()` **method:**

    ```
        video.attachNetStream( stream );
        addChild( video );
    }
    ```

    Now the `Video` instance will be visible:

Your complete document class code now looks like this:

```
package
{
    import flash.display.MovieClip;
    import flash.net.NetConnection;
    import flash.net.NetStream;
    import flash.media.Video;

    public class Progressive extends MovieClip
    {
        public function Progressive()
        {
            var connection:NetConnection = new
              NetConnection();
            connection.connect( null );

            var client:Object = new Object();
            client.onMetaData = onMetaData;

            var stream = new NetStream( connection );
```

```
                stream.client = client;
                stream.play( " http://mywebserver.com/myVideo.flv
                  " );
                var video:Video = new Video();
                video.attachNetStream( stream );
                addChild( video );
            }

            private function onMetaData( info:Object ) :void
            {}
        }
    }
```

Quick-publish your Flash application by pressing Ctrl+Enter (Windows) or Command+Enter (Mac) to see what your new changes have done. Provided that the URL for the FLV file is correct, the FLV video will play after a short delay for it to buffer. Audio is played through the `NetStream` instance, while video output is displayed in the `Video` instance, as shown in Figure 9-1.

Figure 9-1: An FLV file playing over progressive HTTP download.

Event or callback? Sometimes you'll see these terms used interchangeably, but a difference exists. An *event* is a notification that you're able to subscribe to using `addEventListener()`. You can handle the event in a method that receives the event object as a parameter. If you don't want to bothered by the event, you don't have to subscribe; if you already are subscribed, you can unsubscribe from the notification using `removeEventListener()`. A *callback* is a method that is called by another object when conditions are met. For example, when a file has successfully loaded, a method — the callback — you've provided is called. The callback cannot be prevented. You are required to create the method to which the callback will terminate, regardless of whether you have any need for it.

Playing Audio Files in Your Application

Most people associate sounds emitted from mobile devices as utter annoyances, and they're often right. However, a sound occasionally improves an experience. Used wisely, and in the context of gaming particularly so, sounds can turn an otherwise generic application into a head-turner.

Sounds in your application can be categorized into two types:

- A short notification or alert sound triggered in response to an action by the user or an event in the application. These notifications are typically just a second or two in length.
- Extended audio pieces, such as music, that play for a while.

Determining how to include your sound in your application hinges on which of the two types your sound falls under.

Embedding short notification sounds into your application

A notification or event sound needs to be audible instantaneously, or the moment is lost. If you rely on a network connection to access sounds for your app, your user may end up waiting for notification sounds to load (which is unacceptable to the user's experience). Worse yet, you may render the application useless if a network connection isn't present when sounds are required. Instead, notification or event sounds should be embedded in your application so that they are packaged with it when it is distributed to your users through the Apple App Store and Android Market.

In the SpaceshipZapZap application, I have an MP3 sound that plays when the game starts. Follow these steps to embed your own MP3 sound in the SpaceshipZapZap application that you've been building throughout the book:

1. **Open the SpaceshipZapZap application FLA file in Flash Professional.**

2. **Choose File⇨Import⇨Import to Library.**

   The Import to Library dialog box appears.

3. **Browse to the MP3 audio file that you want to include and select it.**

4. **Click OK.**

   The file appears in the Library panel of your application FLA as a sound.

5. **Right-click (Windows) or Control+click (Mac) Sound Properties.**

6. **Select Properties from the context menu.**

7. **Click to select the Export for ActionScript option.**

8. **Give the sound a class name that you can reference it by in the code.**

   My sound is an alarming shrill to inform users that the game is starting, so I opted to assign mine the class `Alarm`.

9. **Click OK to confirm the changes.**

   A dialog box may appear informing you that the class definition could not be found and that one will be automatically generated during export. This is fine; just click OK.

10. **Open the Document Class** `SpaceshipZapZap.as` **for edit in Flash Professional.**

    This is the ActionScript class that is the root class for the application.

11. **Declare a new instance of the** `Alarm` **sound in the** `onStartSelect` **method and call its** `play()` **method.**

    In Chapter 6, you created a method call `onStartSelect` that handled the event raised when a user pressed the Start button on the start screen of the game. You need to add some code to that method that creates and plays an instance of the sound that you imported to the Library. Open the `onStartSelect` method and type this code:

```
private function onStartSelect( e:Event ) :void
{
   removeChild( _startScreen );
   buildAlienFleet();
   var sound:Alarm = new Alarm();
   sound.play();
}
```

Notice that the sound instance assumes that the object type is identical to the name I assigned it when I set the linkage in Steps 7 and 8. As my Alarm object is a sound, I can access all the methods and properties that are available to the Sound ActionScript class, such as play().

Now quick-publish the SpaceshipZapZap application by pressing Ctrl+Enter (Windows) or Command+Enter (Mac), and then click the Start button on the game's start screen; the sound plays once. Now, imagine the fun you could be having here if you were building a fart app!

Flash Professional is capable of natively importing the following file types into its Library for playback: MP3, ASND SoundBooth, WAV (Windows only), and AIFF (Macintosh only). With QuickTime installed, Flash Professional is also able to handle other file types; check the Adobe Flash Professional documentation at http://help.adobe.com/en_US/flash/cs/using for an up-to-date list.

Loading MP3 files from the Internet

If your audio file is too large to be embedded inside the application, such as a 3MB song, you have to keep the file outside your application and load it in when it's required. Flash lets you load your MP3 file into the application on the fly from the Internet and play it back as it loads. Doing this relies on having network connectivity available to the mobile device.

In the following steps I show you how to load an MP3 file into your Flash mobile application and play it:

1. **Create a new application in Flash Professional and save it as** ProgressiveAudio.fla.

   Choose either a new AIR for Android application or a new iOS application.

2. **In the Properties panel, click the wrench icon next to the Class field.**

   The create ActionScript 3.0 Class dialog box opens.

3. **Type the Class name** ProgressiveAudio **and click OK.**

   A new ActionScript 3.0 class opens in Flash Professional.

4. **Press Ctrl+S (Windows) or Command+S (Mac) and save the file as** ProgressiveAudio.as.

5. **Declare and initialize a new** Sound **instance inside the class constructor method of** ProgressiveAudio.as:

```
public function ProgressiveAudio()
{
    var sound:Sound = new Sound();
}
```

6. **Call the** `Sound` **object's** `load()` **method, using a new** `URLRequest`, **containing the full URL of the MP3 file, as the only parameter:**

```
var sound:Sound = new Sound();
sound.load( new URLRequest( " http://mywebserver.
    com/myMusic.mp3 " ) );
}
```

Remember to add the import directives for the `Sound` and `URLRequest` classes if your code editor doesn't do it for you:

```
import flash.display.MovieClip;
import flash.media.Sound;
import flash.net.URLRequest;

public class ProgressiveAudio extends MovieClip
{
```

7. **Call the** `Sound` **instance's** `play()` **method to start the playback of the sound:**

```
sound.load( new URLRequest( " http://mywebserver.
    com/myMusic.mp3 " ) );
sound.play();
}
```

Now here's the exciting part: Quick-publish the SpaceshipZapZap application by pressing Ctrl+Enter (Windows) or Command+Enter (Mac) and listen to your sound playing. If you don't hear sound, check that you typed the URL correctly in your code.

Streaming Video and Audio Using FMS

Flash Media Server (FMS) is a piece of server-side software that enables audio and video files to be streamed to the Flash Player using *Real-time Media Protocol* (RTMP). The benefits of RTMP are a near-instantaneous playback of media and the ability for the user to seek to any point in the media without waiting for it to completely download. If you want to add to your Flash mobile applications video that will start playing quickly, and you want to download the video data only as the user watches it — as opposed to downloading all the video to the device, as in progressive video — streaming video over RTMP is a great solution.

Most modern mobile devices are able to decode H.264 video playing through your application on the device's graphics processing unit (GPU) hardware. FLV is a format native to just the Flash Player, so the decoding can be done only in the Flash Player using the device's central processing unit (CPU). Software decoding is slower and more prone to errors, so try to favor video formats, such as H.264, that can decode using GPU hardware.

The process for streaming content from FMS involves establishing a connection to the FMS server using a `NetConnection` object and then requesting a particular file to be streamed over the established `NetConnection` using a `NetStream` object.

Follow these steps to create a `NetConnection` to an FMS server:

1. **Create a new application in Flash Professional and save it as Streaming.fla.**

   Choose either a new AIR for Android application or a new iOS application.

2. **In the Properties panel, click the wrench icon next to the Class field.**

   The Create ActionScript 3.0 Class dialog box opens.

3. **Type the Class name** Streaming **and click OK.**

   A new ActionScript 3.0 class opens in Flash Professional.

4. **Press Ctrl+S (Windows) or Command+S (Mac) and save the file as Streaming.as.**

5. **Declare and initialize a new** `NetConnection` **called** `connection` **inside the class constructor function** `Main()`, **then call** `connect()` **on** `connection` **supplying a URL to an FMS server application:**

   ```
   public function Streaming()
   {
       var connection:NetConnection = new NetConnection();
       connection.connect( "rtmp://cp67126.edgefcs.net/
           ondemand" );
   }
   ```

   The RTMP URL I've used in my code is a sample FMS application available from Akamai, a prominent global Content Delivery Network (CDN), for testing purposes. You can use this URL to test your application too.

6. **Register an event listener to the** `NetConnection` **instance for the** `NET_STATUS` **event.**

   ```
   var connection:NetConnection = new
       NetConnection();
   connection.addEventListener( NetStatusEvent.NET_
       STATUS, onNetStatus );
   connection.connect( "rtmp://cp67126.edgefcs.net/
       ondemand" );
   }
   ```

   Before a video can start streaming, you need to wait for a notification from the `NetConnection` instance that it has successfully performed a "handshake" with the FMS server specified.

7. **Create a method called** onNetStatus **to handle the** NET_STATUS **event.**

Inside this method, create a switch statement for the NetStatusEvent object's info.code property. This contains specific information about the type of NetStatusEvent that occurred. Many NetStatusEvent codes can be handled. For a full list, refer to http://help.adobe. com/en_US/FlashPlatform/reference/actionscript/3/flash/ events/NetStatusEvent.html.

For the purposes of this example, I'm concerned only with whether the NetConnection succeeded or failed to connect, so I have two cases in my switch statement:

```
    connection.connect( "rtmp://cp67126.edgefcs.net/
        ondemand" );
}

private function onNetStatus( e:NetStatusEvent ) :void
{
    switch( e.info.code )
    {
        case "NetConnection.Connect.Success":
            // The NetConnection connected!
        break;
        case "NetConnection.Connect.Failed":
            // The NetConnection failed to connect
        break;
    }
}
```

8. **Create a new object called** connectionClient, **set a new property on it called** connectionClient.onBWDone, **and assign it a value of a function called** onBWDone:

```
public function Streaming()
{
    var connection:NetConnection = new NetConnection();
    connection.addEventListener( NetStatusEvent.NET_
        STATUS, onNetStatus );
    var connectionClient:Object = new Object();
    connectionClient.onBWDone = onBWDone;

    connection.connect( "rtmp://cp67126.edgefcs.net/
        ondemand" );
}
```

9. **Assign** connectionClient **to the** client **property of your** NetConnection **instance:**

```
    connectionClient.onBWDone = onBWDone;
    connection.client = connectionClient;
    connection.connect( "rtmp://cp67126.edgefcs.net/
        ondemand" );
}
```

When using `NetConnection` with an FMS server, an automatic attempt to call a method called `onBWDone` is made when a bandwidth detection operation is completed by the `NetConnection.connect` routine. Although it isn't optional for the callback to happen, you can control on which object the callback tries to execute and whether to do anything in the handler method. I find that creating a dedicated client object to handle the `onBWDone` method is cleaner.

10. **Create a new method called** `onBWDone` **to terminate the** `onBWDone` **callback:**

```
    connection.client = connectionClient;
    connection.connect( "rtmp://cp67126.edgefcs.net/
        ondemand" );
}

private function onBWDone() :void
{}
```

The `onBWDone` callback doesn't need to do anything. It's just there to catch the call invoked by the `NetConnection` starting up.

The `NetConnection` is now connected to FMS, so the next step is to create a `NetStream` that will consume an H.264-encoded (MP4) video file from the server using the open `NetConnection`:

1. **Declare and initialize a new** `NetStream` **instance within the** `NetConnection.Connect.Success` **case, providing the** `NetConnection` **object that caused the success as the** `connection` **parameter:**

```
case "NetConnection.Connect.Success":
    // The NetConnection connected!
    var netStream:NetStream = new NetStream( e.target
        as NetConnection );
break;
```

2. **Declare and initialize a new** `Object` **called** `netStreamClient`**:**

```
    var netStream:NetStream = new NetStream( e.target
        as NetConnection );
    var netStreamClient:Object = new Object();
break;
```

3. **Create a dynamic property on** `netStreamClient` **called** `onMetaData` **and give it the value of a function called** `onMetaData` **— which you'll create in the next step:**

```
    var netStreamClient:Object = new Object();
    netStreamClient.onMetaData = onMetaData;
break;
```

4. Create a new method called onMetaData **to terminate the** onMetaData **callback:**

```
private function onBWDone() :void
{}

private function onMetaData() :void
{}
```

5. Assign netStreamClient **to the** client **property of the** NetStream **instance:**

```
    netStreamClient.onMetaData = onMetaData;
    netStream.client = netStreamClient;
break;
```

6. Declare and initialize a new Video **object.**

Video is the visual representation of the NetStream. First, it must be initialized. A NetStream instance is attached to it using the attachNetStream method. Finally, add the Video instance to the display list with the addChild() method:

```
    netStream.client = netStreamClient;
    var video:Video = new Video();
break;
```

7. Call the attachNetStream() **method on** video, **providing the** NetStream **instance as the parameter:**

```
    var video:Video = new Video();
    video.attachNetStream( stream );
break;
```

8. Add video **to the display list:**

```
    var video:Video = new Video();
    video.attachNetStream( stream );
    addChild( video );
break;
```

9. Call the play() **method on the** NetStream **instance, providing the path of a video or audio file.**

```
    var video:Video = new Video();
    video.attachNetStream( stream );
    addChild( video );
    netStream.play( "mp4:mediapm/ovp/content/test/
        video/spacealonehd_sounas_640_300.mp4" );
break;
```

After the `play()` method is called, the `NetStream` communicates to FMS, using the open `NetConnection`, to locate the file specified and stream it back to your application:

```
netStream.play( "mp4:mediapm/ovp/content/test/video/
        spacealonehd_sounas_640_300.mp4" );
```

If you required a streamed audio file, the file path would simply be replaced with the following:

```
netStream.play( "mp3:mediapm/ovp/content/test/video/
        nocc_small" );
```

The file path is the location inside the FMS application's media folder where the file can be found. In the preceding example, the file is nested in a fairly deep directory structure inside that application's media folder. Notice that the MP4 file extension is left on the end of an MP4 file path but omitted from the end of an MP3 path. This behavior is just a nuance in the implementation of the various file formats in Flash Media Server.

MP4 and MP3 file paths loaded from FMS must be prefixed with MP4: and MP3:, respectively. This tells FMS that the file to be streamed is either an MPEG video or MPEG audio file and not a Flash video or audio file — which are the defaults if omitted. An example of a valid MP4 file path is: `mp4:mediapm/ovp/content/test/video/spacealonehd_sounas_640_300.mp4`.

Having completed the steps to create a `NetConnection`,`NetStream` and `Video` object, your `Streaming` class code looks like this:

```
package
{
    import flash.display.MovieClip;
    import flash.net.NetConnection;
    import flash.net.NetStream;
    import flash.media.Video;
    import flash.events.NetStatusEvent;

    public class Streaming extends MovieClip
    {
        public function Streaming()
        {
            var connection:NetConnection = new
              NetConnection();
            connection.addEventListener( NetStatusEvent.NET_
              STATUS, onNetStatus );
            var connectionClient:Object = new Object();
            connectionClient.onBWDone = onBWDone;
            connection.client = connectionClient;
            connection.connect( "rtmp://cp67126.edgefcs.net/
              ondemand" );
        }

        private function onNetStatus( e:NetStatusEvent )
            :void
```

```
    {
        switch( e.info.code )
        {
            case "NetConnection.Connect.Success":
                // The NetConnection connected!

                var netStream:NetStream = new NetStream(
            e.target as NetConnection );
                var netStreamClient:Object = new Object();
                netStreamClient.onMetaData = onMetaData;
                netStream.client = netStreamClient;
                var video:Video = new Video();
                video.attachNetStream( netStream );
                addChild( video );
                netStream.play( "mp4:mediapm/ovp/content/
            test/video/spacealonehd_sounas_640_300.mp4" );
              break;
            case "NetConnection.Connect.Failed":
                // The NetConnection failed to connect
              break;
        }
    }

    private function onBWDone() :void
    {}

    private function onMetaData( info:Object ) :void
    {}

    }
}
```

Quick-publish your Flash application by pressing Ctrl+Enter (Windows) or Command+Enter (Mac) to see the application start in the familiar AIR emulator window on the desktop. The application loads a video that you can see on the stage, as shown in Figure 9-2, and hear through your speakers. That's streaming with FMS!

 Akamai, the global Content Delivery Network, offers some streams for developers to sanity-check their code against. If you're finding that something isn't working and you're unsure whether the problem lies in your code or with the Flash Media Server you're working with, try connecting to one of Akami's streams with your code. If everything works, you can safely say that your code is fine, and the problem is with FMS. Here are a couple of sample RTMP URLs:

- ✓ FMS application: `rtmp://cp67126.edgefcs.net/ondemand`
- ✓ Media file: `mp4:mediapm/ovp/content/test/video/space alonehd_sounas_640_300.mp4`
- ✓ Media file: `mp3:mediapm/ovp/content/test/video/nocc_small`

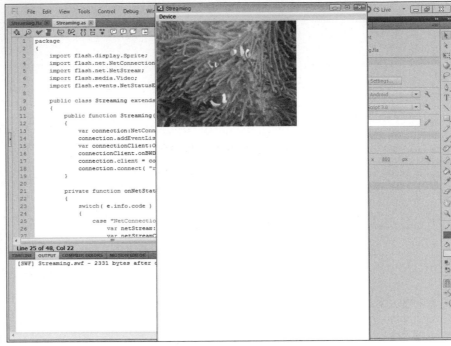

Figure 9-2:
An H.264
video file
streaming
into the
application.

Using Video with the Open Source Media Framework

The Open Source Media Framework (OSMF) is a code library, devised by Adobe, to simplify the efforts of developers when building media playback applications. Using the framework shields you from things such as `NetConnections` and `NetStreams`, affording you more time to think about the aspects of your application that will differentiate it from others. As well as making things simpler, a number of video-related bugs and quirks in Flash have been dealt with in the OSMF API, making it one of the fastest ways to get up and running with video in your Flash mobile application.

Downloading and configuring OSMF for use in Flash Professional

The framework can be downloaded from the OSMF project page on SourceForge, at `http://sourceforge.net/projects/osmf.adobe/files`. Be sure to download the latest release build if you're planning to deploy your application commercially. Sprint, or beta, versions are available for you to try, but these are newer and less mature than the release versions. After downloading, follow these steps to configure OSMF for use with a Flash mobile application:

1. **Create a new application in Flash Professional and save it as** OSMF.fla.

   Choose either a new AIR for Android application or a new iOS application.

2. **In the Properties panel, click the wrench icon next to the Class field.**

   The Create ActionScript 3.0 Class dialog box opens.

3. **Type the Class name** OSMF **and click OK.**

   A new ActionScript 3.0 class opens in Flash Professional.

4. **Press Ctrl+S (Windows) or Command+S (Mac) and save the file as** OSMF.as.

5. **Unzip the OSMF ZIP archive to a location on your computer.**

   Inside the archive is another ZIP archive with the filename OSMF_source.zip.

6. **Unzip** OSMF_source.zip.

7. **In Flash Professional, choose File⇨Publish Settings.**

   The Publish Settings dialog box opens.

8. **Select the Flash (.swf) item in the list on the left.**

9. **Click the ActionScript Settings button — the wrench icon — next to ActionScript 3.0.**

   The Advanced ActionScript 3.0 Settings dialog box opens.

10. **Click the Library Path tab.**

11. **Click the Browse to SWC File button.**

    This is the middle icon in the upper-right corner of the SWC files or folders list.

    A File Open dialog box opens.

12. **Browse to the location of the** OSMF.swc **file.**

    The file is inside the OSMF_source directory of the unpacked ZIP archive.

13. **Click Open.**

    The SWC file appears in the SWC files or folders list.

14. **Click OK and then click OK again to save the changes.**

    OSMF is now ready for use in your application.

Playing a video with OSMF

The great thing about using OSMF instead of hand-coding your playback code is that you don't need to know whether a piece of media is video or audio, streamed or progressively downloaded. OSMF is able to determine how to play the media file based purely on the URL provided for the media. The following steps add to the new application you created in the preceding section to add basic video playback functionality:

1. **Inside the** OSMF() **method — the document class's constructor — declare five new objects, each of them unique to OSMF:**

   - DefaultMediaFactory: This object looks at the URL of a piece of media passed to it and returns a compatible MediaElement object that OSMF can play. Initialize DefaultMediaFactory so that its public methods can be called later:

   ```
   public function OSMF()
   {
       var factory:DefaultMediaFactory = new
       DefaultMediaFactory();
   ```

   - URLResource: This object holds the URL to the media and is passed to DefaultMediaFactory. Initialize the URLResource instance with a URL to a piece of video. I've provided a streaming URL that follows, but a progressively downloaded HTTP URL would work just as well, and no further code changes are required:

   ```
   var factory:DefaultMediaFactory = new
           DefaultMediaFactory();
   var resource:URLResource = new URLResource(  "rtmp://
           cp67126.edgefcs.net/ondemand/mp4:mediapm/
           ovp/content/test/video/spacealonehd_
           sounas_640_300.mp4" );
   ```

   - MediaPlayer: This is the brains of OSMF and is responsible for all the behind-the-scenes operations, such as loading video and notifying the user when video starts and stops. MediaPlayer has no visible presence in your application; visual output is handled by the MediaContainer object — discussed next:

   ```
   var resource:URLResource = new URLResource(  "rtmp://
           cp67126.edgefcs.net/ondemand/mp4:mediapm/
           ovp/content/test/video/spacealonehd_
           sounas_640_300.mp4" );
   var player:MediaPlayer;
   ```

- MediaContainer: This is the visual output of media playing back in your OSMF MediaPlayer. MediaContainer is a display object that you add to your display list using the familiar addChild() method:

```
var player:MediaPlayer;
var display:MediaContainer;
```

- MediaElement: DefaultMediaFactory creates the MediaElement from the URLResource you provide. To get a MediaElement from DefaultMediaFactory, call the createMediaElement() method on it, supplying the URLResource instance you created:

```
var display:MediaContainer;
var media:MediaElement = factory.createMediaElement(
        resource );
```

2. **Pass the** MediaElement **instance you created a moment ago as the constructor parameter:**

```
var media:MediaElement = factory.createMediaElement(
        resource );
player = new MediaPlayer( media );
```

This step initializes the player variable as a new MediaPlayer instance.

3. **Initialize the display variable as a new** MediaContainer **instance:**

```
player = new MediaPlayer( media );
display = new MediaContainer();
```

4. **Add the** MediaElement **instance to the** MediaContainer **using the** addMediaElement() **method:**

```
display = new MediaContainer();
display.addMediaElement( media );
```

You must add the MediaElement to the container using the addMediaElement() method or the MediaContainer won't display a MediaElement when media is being played by the MediaPlayer.

5. **Add the** MediaContainer **to the display list as a child:**

```
display.addMediaElement( media );
addChild( display );
```

The last step is to ensure that video is audible *and* visible during playback.

That's all there is to it! You now have the code necessary to play video and audio over a variety of protocols, including progressive download. Your finished OSMF playback code now looks like this:

```
package
{
    import flash.display.MovieClip;
    import org.osmf.media.DefaultMediaFactory;
    import org.osmf.containers.MediaContainer;
    import org.osmf.media.MediaPlayer;
    import org.osmf.media.MediaElement;
    import org.osmf.media.URLResource;

    public class OSMF extends MovieClip
    {
        public function OSMF()
        {
            var factory:DefaultMediaFactory = new
              DefaultMediaFactory();
            var resource:URLResource = new URLResource(
              "rtmp://cp67126.edgefcs.net/ondemand/
              mp4:mediapm/ovp/content/test/video/
              spacealonehd_sounas_640_300.mp4" );
            var player:MediaPlayer;
            var display:MediaContainer;
            var media:MediaElement = factory.
              createMediaElement( resource );

            player = new MediaPlayer( media );
            display = new MediaContainer();
            display.addMediaElement( media );
            addChild( display );
        }
    }
}
```

Quick-publish your Flash application by pressing Ctrl+Enter (Windows) or Command+Enter (Mac) to see your OSMF-derived player in action. Note that the appearance doesn't suggest much about how it was built and looks largely the same as the hand-coded `NetConnection`/`NetStream` examples. However, the flexibility of the code you've just written allows you to use it in a variety of media playback scenarios, such as streaming H.264 video to an Android smartphone over RTMP or progressively downloading audio files for listening to on an iPhone.

Streaming Video over HTTP

Since version 10.1, the Flash Player API has been able to support streaming of media files, such as H.264 video, over HTTP. Doing this removes the necessity of a Flash Media Server, for the first time permitting video to be streamed using an Apache web server. The video file is broken into many small chunks and delivered piece by piece. The application requesting the chunks knows which chunks it needs by checking a manifest file that is hosted on the server with the video chunks. This manifest file is known as an F4M file.

Using HTTP also helps to bypass network restrictions that might block the ports on which RTMP streaming operates. OSMF works on the client-side (on your user's mobile device) marshaling all the busy network traffic that occurs in the background when a media file is streamed over HTTP. Rather than your head exploding with the idea of trying to piece together hundreds of "chunks" of video served to your application, or worrying about understanding what a complicated video manifest file does, OSMF lets you just provide an HTTP streaming URL. Then OSMF goes off and does the rest for you — the way it should be!

Setting up a file to be streamed over HTTP

Most Apache web servers can be modified to stream media over HTTP using a free Apache Module provided by Adobe. Although going into the ins and outs of installing this are beyond the realms of this book, you can glean a great deal of information from Adobe's online tutorial at `http://help. adobe.com/en_US/HTTPStreaming/1.0/Using`.

For simplicity, in this example, I use HTTP streaming content located on a globally accessible server at `http://mediapm.edgesuite.net/osmf/ content/test/manifest-files/dynamic_Streaming.f4m`.

OSMF makes the trouble of handling HTTP-streamed content on the client disappear. It does all the heavy lifting for you in the background, with the biggest advantage being that by using the generic code created in the section "Playing a video with OSMF," earlier in this chapter, you have to change only the URL! Your OSMF application is able to handle progressive, RTMP-streamed and HTTP-streamed audio or video. Also in the "Playing a video with OSMF" section, I show you how to make a very small OSMF application. To test HTTP streaming for yourself, just reopen `OSMF.as` and change the URL supplied when the `URLResource` object is initialized in your code. If you haven't built the app yet, take a few moments to do so and then head back here when you're done:

```
var resource:URLResource = new URLResource( "http://
        mediapm.edgesuite.net/osmf/content/test/
        manifest-files/dynamic_Streaming.f4m" );
```

Quick-publish your Flash application by pressing Ctrl+Enter (Windows) or Command+Enter (Mac). Your OSMF Flash application loads the F4M file before loading in chunks of video that present themselves in the usual `MediaContainer`.

Making Your User's Experience an Inexpensive One

Remember that many users on cellular networks have limits on the amount of data they're permitted to download each month before extra charges kick in. The last thing they'll want is for your application to download oodles of video over their cellular network. To avert the wrath of damaged bank balances, it is wise to bake in some precautions that prevent your user from having to download anything against his or her will. I suggest that you create your app so that it asks permission to download video (rather than autoplaying it) and looks for a Wi-Fi connection before downloading the video on the cellular network.

Invite the user to play

Never autoplay video. Remembering that one rule can not only save you from costing your user lots of money but also serve as good practice from a user experience perspective.

Whenever you want to present video to a user, always present it in a stopped state with a button that allows the user to initiate playback. Here are two benefits to this practice:

- ✔ Users aren't confused (then frustrated) by audio spontaneously coming from their devices when they may not have expected it.
- ✔ You prevent data transfer from beginning automatically, thus giving the users the final say on whether to download the data (and incur the data costs, if any).

To initiate but not play the video, you need to modify the code created in the section "Playing a video with OSMF," earlier in this chapter. The following steps explain how to set the `autoPlay` property on OSMF `MediaPlayer` to `false` and allow the user to initiate playback when he touches the screen.

Reopen `OSMF.as` in Flash Professional and make the following modifications to the code:

1. **Move the** `player` **variable above the constructor and assign it a** `private` **access modifier:**

```
public class OSMF extends Sprite
{
    private var player:MediaPlayer;

    public function OSMF()
    {
```

The `player` variable is converted into a class member variable instead of a local variable inside the class constructor.

2. **Just after the line that initializes the** `MediaPlayer` **instance, assign a value of** `false` **to the** `MediaPlayer`**'s** `autoPlay` **property:**

```
player = new MediaPlayer( media );
player.autoPlay = false;
display = new MediaContainer();
```

3. **Register a** `CLICK` **event listener to the stage:**

```
addChild( display );
stage.addEventListener( MouseEvent.CLICK,
        onContainerClick );
```

By registering the event listener to the stage, the video will start no matter where the user clicks or touches the application. You may later want to swap that for a button or other metaphor.

4. **Create a method to handle the** `CLICK` **event:**

```
private function onContainerClick( e:MouseEvent )
        :void
{
    player.play();
}
```

Inside this method, a simple call to the `MediaPlayer` instance's `play()` method starts the loading and playback of the file.

Now the OSMF application starts loading content into the mobile device only when the user interacts with the application, making the first step of inviting the user to play complete.

Check for cellular network or Wi-Fi

Using the APIs provided by Adobe AIR, it's possible to determine whether the mobile device has an active Wi-Fi connection, or whether data will instead be sent over the cellular network. Transferring data over Wi-Fi still remains faster and more cost-efficient for users than transferring data over a cellular network (3G or 4G). Given that, you may prefer to only conduct data-heavy operations, such as loading video, when the device is able to use an active Wi-Fi connection.

You can obtain the names and connection statuses of a device's various network interfaces using a class called `NetworkInfo` that lists each device as a `NetworkInterface` object inside a `Vector` object. This list of `NetworkInterface` objects is accessible at any time, and from anywhere within your application, through the `NetworkInfo.networkInfo.findInterfaces()` method. In the following steps, I show you how to set up a basic application that makes a decision on whether to execute a function (for example, streaming video) based upon the `active` status of a `NetworkInterface` reporting itself as "Wi-Fi":

1. **Create a new application in Flash Professional and save it as** DetectWIFI.fla.

   Choose either a new AIR for Android application or a new iOS application.

2. **In the Properties panel, click the wrench icon next to the Class field.**

   The Create ActionScript 3.0 Class dialog box opens.

3. **Type the Class name** DetectWIFI **and click OK.**

   A new ActionScript 3.0 class opens in Flash Professional.

4. **Press Ctrl+S (Windows) or Command+S (Mac) and save the file as** DetectWIFI.as.

5. **Create a new method called** `checkWIFIActive`:

```
public class DetectWIFI extends MovieClip
{
    public function DetectWIFI()
    {}

    private function checkWIFIActive() :Boolean
    {
        return false;
    }
}
```

   This method will be responsible for obtaining a list of `NetworkInterface` objects from the `NetworkInfo` class, finding the one with the `displayName WIFI`, and then returning the value of its `active` property. By default, the method returns a `false` value.

6. **Add an** `if` **statement to the** `checkWIFIActive()` **method to ensure that the device supports** `NetworkInfo`:

```
private function checkWIFIActive() :Boolean
{
    if( NetworkInfo.isSupported )
    {
    }
    return false;
}
```

   Although both iOS and Android OS provide access to `NetworkInfo` by default, a niche device might have this disabled (although this happens rarely). To guard against an error being thrown while your application is running, you should verify that the device your application is running on has access to the `NetworkInfo` API.

7. **Declare a new** `Vector` **variable called** `adaptors` **and initialize it with the list of interfaces list in** `NetworkInfo.networkInfo.`
   `findInterfaces():`

```
private function checkWIFIActive() :Boolean
{
    if( NetworkInfo.isSupported )
    {
        var adaptors:Vector.<NetworkInterface> =
            NetworkInfo.networkInfo.findInterfaces();
    }
    return false;
}
```

8. **Use a** `for-each` **loop to iterate through the list of** `NetworkInterface`
   objects in `adaptors` **and check the** `displayName` **property of each to**
   see whether it matches `WIFI`:

```
var adaptors:Vector.<NetworkInterface> = NetworkInfo.
        networkInfo.findInterfaces();
for each( var adaptor:NetworkInterface in adaptors)
{
    if( adaptor.displayName == "WIFI" )
    {
    }
}
```

9. **Return the active value of the** `WIFI` **interface:**

```
if( adaptor.displayName == "WIFI" )
{
    return adaptor.active;
}
```

10. **Create two new methods, one called** `loadVideo` **and the other called**
    `showApologyScreen`:

```
public function DetectWIFI()
{}

private function loadVideo() :void
{
    // Place code for loading video
}

private function showApologyScreen() :void
{
    /* Place code here to show a screen that explains
        to the user that WiFi is necessary for loading
        video into the application. */
}
```

11. **Add an** `if` **statement to the class constructor that evaluates the** `true`
    or `false` **value returned from** `checkWIFIActive():`

```
public function DetectWIFI()
{
  if( checkWIFIActive() )
  {
    loadVideo();
  }
  else
  {
    showApologyScreen();
  }
}
```

In this simple example, I want to call a `loadVideo()` method if the Wi-Fi interface is active, or call a `showApologyScreen()` method when it isn't. Because `checkWIFIActive()` returns `true` if a Wi-Fi interface is active, evaluating this value as the condition of an `if` statement in the class constructor provides an easy way to decide whether to call the `loadVideo()` method.

The `loadVideo()` and `showApologyScreen()` methods are intentionally left empty, but the comments denote where you place code for each scenario.

12. Press Ctrl+S (Windows) or Command+S (Mac) to save `DetectWIFI.as.`

Your application is now able to detect when an active Wi-Fi connection is available to it on the mobile device. Testing this new feature isn't possible on your computer because it almost certainly won't have a network interface identifying itself as "WIFI." But if you drop your app onto an Android or iPhone device, you'll see the outcome the moment the application starts.

Chapter 10

Bringing Your App to Life with Animation and Transitions

In This Chapter

▶ Animating with Flash Professional

▶ Using code to create animations and detect collisions

▶ Understanding the testing and performance considerations for animation

*I*magine traveling to the bookstore without moving. Imagine arriving at this chapter without having first turned the page. It'd be a little weird, right? Animations and transitions help to support a story, a logical flow or order to events, without which your interpretation of them can become confused. The same is true when the physical world is replaced by the digital one. The balance, however, is important: Too few transitions and your user is lost, too many and your user is overworked.

Flash made itself a name by the way it added movement and sophisticated interactive behavior to a previously bland and lifeless Internet. Often it has been criticized for being good for only novelty animations, but Flash now has a mature programming language — ActionScript 3.0 — and hardware accelerated graphics that make it the best way to get a rich interactive experience in front of users on myriad platforms, particularly mobile devices.

In this chapter, I discuss the techniques for introducing animations and transitions into your application, and describe how to achieve the perfect balance between the capabilities of the device and the desired behaviors of your application.

Paying for Animation

Much as chocolate comes at the price of extra weight around the hips, animation costs CPU usage. Moving graphics around on the display requires the CPU to repeatedly recalculate the position and dimensions of the objects that move and then render the display. This work occurs multiple times each second — perhaps as much as 30 times, depending on the frame rate of your Flash application. When the CPU is crunching numbers and updating the display, it's sucking power out of the battery. The more objects are changing, the harder the CPU has to work, and the more juice it drinks from the battery. Eventually the CPU drinks the battery dry, and your user is left with a dead mobile phone that should've had at least another couple of hours of standby time left in it. Your user is not pleased, and your application just got itself a one-star review. Although this scenario is extreme, it emphasizes an important part in the decision of whether to animate something in your application. Unlike desktop computers the mobile device has a finite power source, and developers must work on the user's behalf to conserve as much of that power as possible.

Making the most of efficiency

Implementing all-singing, all-dancing animation is great. What's better is animation that sings, dances, gets paid less than all its friends, and remembers to turn off the lights before it leaves! I'm always looking for animation that represents good value in terms of how CPU-intensive it is versus what impact it has on the user experience. Very busy animation in a mobile app that does little to aid the user's experience of the application but was left in because the developer thought it looked cool is a real tragedy, and it's something I'm going to help you avoid! In Chapter 6, I cover a technique called bitmap caching, which enables you to delegate the rendering of an object whose shape doesn't change to the graphics processing unit (GPU) instead of the CPU. To make your mobile applications more efficient, you should always embrace techniques that enable you to remove load from the main processor and hand it off to another piece of hardware.

Success is found in delivering the richest and most engaging application that runs with the least resources as possible. With animation, if in doubt, leave it out!

Assessing animation criteria

Here are some points I've put together to help you determine whether animation is appropriate for your application, and whether it adds value to the user's experience of your application:

✔ Does the animation enhance the user experience? If ten users were to sit with you and use the application, would more than five say that the animation improved the way they understood what was happening within the app? Consider testing this with human guinea pigs — your friends are a great resource for this!

✔ Does the animation prevent the user from proceeding at a pace that he is comfortable with? Again, try to undertake some tests with users to see whether the animation throws any problems.

✔ Does the desired animation run smoothly without judders or momentary pauses? Judders and pauses indicate excessive processor load and put your application at risk of crashing.

✔ What is the net effect on battery consumption? Run the animation for a given number of repetitions on the target mobile device and measure the battery depletion. Is it slight — say 10 percent — or considerable?

Animating with Frames

Frame animation is the mainstay of Flash Professional and still one of the easiest ways to arrange intricate effects without needing to touch a line of ActionScript code. You have two ways to create frame animation: frame-by-frame changes and motion tween. I explain both in the following sections.

Frame-by-frame changes

One option for animation is to manually create all the changes you want to make on each individual frame. This method affords you lots of control over the finished article but is a slightly laborious approach. For some situations, frame-by-frame changes may be the simplest way to achieve the desired effect. For example, in the SpaceshipZapZap application, the defender space-craft needs to blink for a short while after a life is lost. Creating the appearance of a blink is as simple as removing and adding the graphic from view on various frames. Doing the same blinking effect with code would be a lot more complicated — requiring you to use timers.

In the following steps, I show you how to apply the blinking effect to a `MovieClip`, using frame-by-frame changes. I suggest importing a PNG image as the content of the `MovieClip` — you can use any image you like or use the reference image I provide in the online source files for the SpaceshipZapZap application at `www.dummies.com/go/flashmobileappdevfd`.

1. **Open the** `SpaceshipZapZap.fla` **file for editing in Flash Professional.**

2. **Create a new** `MovieClip` **symbol and name it** Defender.

   I show you how to create `MovieClips` in Chapter 5.

3. **Click OK.**

   A `MovieClip` is created in the Library, and the view switches so that you are able to edit the contents of the `MovieClip`, as shown in Figure 10-1.

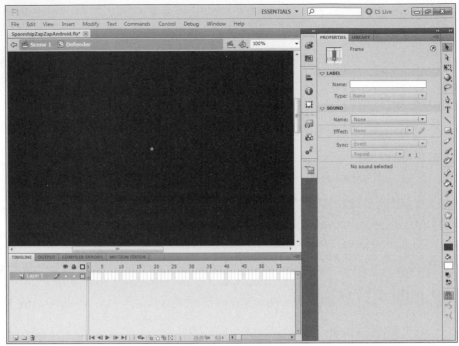

Figure 10-1:
The new
Defender
MovieClip,
ready for
editing.

4. **Choose File⇨Import⇨Import to Stage and select a PNG image to use as the defender spacecraft.**

5. **Click Open.**

6. **Select the Import as a Single Flattened Bitmap option and click OK.**

   The imported image is placed on the stage at 0,0 x and y coordinates. On the Timeline, frame 1 is shaded gray to indicate that the frame has contents visible on the stage.

7. **On the MovieClip's Timeline, right-click (Windows) or Control+click (Mac) frame 9. Then select Insert Keyframe from the context menu that appears.**

   A black dot appears on the selected frame, denoting that it's now a key frame.

8. **Repeat Step 7 for frames 17 and 20.**

9. **On the MovieClip's Timeline, right-click (Windows) or Control+click (Mac) frame 5. Then select Insert Blank Keyframe from the context menu that appears.**

   A white circle appears on the selected frame, denoting that it's now an empty key frame.

10. **Repeat Step 9 for frame 13.**

11. **Add a stop action to frame 20 by pressing F9 (Windows) or fn+Option+F9 (Mac) to open the Actions panel.**

    On line 1 of the Actions panel that opens, type the following:

    ```
    stop();
    ```

12. **Close the Actions panel by again pressing F9 (Windows) or fn+Option+F9 (Mac).**

    The MovieClip is complete and appears as shown in Figure 10-2.

With the Defender MovieClip ready for use, go ahead and create an instance of it on the stage of the SpaceshipZapZap application:

1. **Select and then drag a Defender from the Library to the stage, placing it toward the bottom of the screen.**

    This step creates an instance of the Defender MovieClip on the stage.

2. **Select the Defender MovieClip on the stage, and in the Properties panel, enter the instance name defender.**

3. **Press Ctrl+S (Windows) or Command+S (Mac) to save the FLA file.**

You're done! The Defender MovieClip is now on the stage and accessible through the instance name defender.

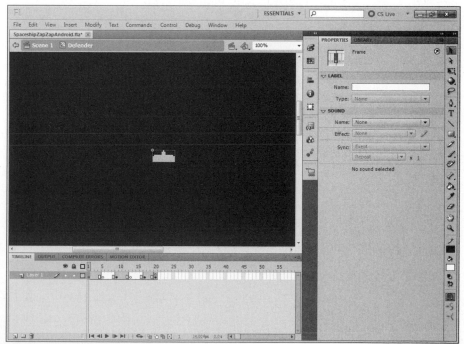

Figure 10-2:
The complete Defender MovieClip.

Motion tween

A *motion tween* is the technique of specifying a start state — normally a position — for a display object, specifying the end state, and allowing Flash Professional to do the heavy lifting to animate between the two. The outcome is a uniform transition that is easily modified. Just change the start or end state, and Flash will fill in the gray matter in the middle again. A classic motion tween is animating a bouncing ball. Follow these steps to create a simple motion tween:

1. **Create a new application in Flash Professional.**

   This can be either an AIR for Android application or an iOS application; see Chapter 4 for details.

2. **Using the drawing tools, draw a circle that is about 80 pixels wide and 80 pixels high on the stage.**

   Note that key frame 1 in the Timeline panel changes from shaded white with a hollow white circle inside to gray with a solid black circle inside. This means that the frame now has content.

3. **Select the shape you just drew.**

4. **Choose Modify⇨Convert to Symbol.**

   The Convert to Symbol dialog box opens.

5. **Type** Ball **in the Name field and click OK.**

   Your shape is converted to a MovieClip.

6. **Select the** Ball MovieClip **on the stage. Then in the Properties panel on the right, type the instance name** ball.

   You now have a Ball MovieClip instance on the stage that can be referenced with the instance name ball, as shown in Figure 10-3.

   Although not essential for this example, naming all your instances is a good practice.

7. **Right-click (Windows) or Control+click (Mac) the key frame at frame 1 and choose Create Motion Tween from the context menu that appears.**

   Flash Professional immediately adds 1 second's worth of frames after the key frame. The new frames are colored blue.

8. **Right-click (Windows) or Control+click (Mac) frame 12 to move the playhead there so that you can create a key frame.**

   I want the entire duration of the animation to be 1 second, so the midpoint of the ball bounce is at frame 12 — or 0.5 seconds.

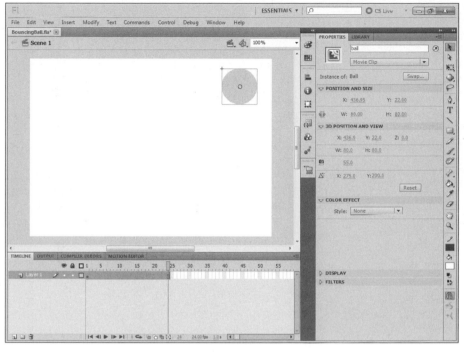

Figure 10-3:
The Ball
MovieClip
with an
instance
name
assigned.

9. **Choose select Insert Keyframe⇨ Position from the context menu.**

   A black diamond appears in frame 12 on the Timeline.

10. **Click and drag the** `Ball MovieClip` **to move to the bottom of the stage.**

    A faint green line with dots on it plots the course of the movement that Flash Professional is creating for your `MovieClip`.

11. **With the ball selected, change the ball height (H) value in the Properties panel to 65.00.**

    Your application in Flash Professional now appears as shown in Figure 10-4.

12. **Move the playhead to the last highlighted frame for the motion tween.**

13. **Right-click (Windows) or Control+click (Mac) and choose Insert Keyframe⇨Position from the context menu that appears.**

    A black diamond appears in frame 24 on the Timeline.

14. **Move the** `Ball MovieClip` **back to where it was at the start of the animation, and restore its height to 80 pixels.**

    This step resets the `Ball MovieClip` to its original size and position.

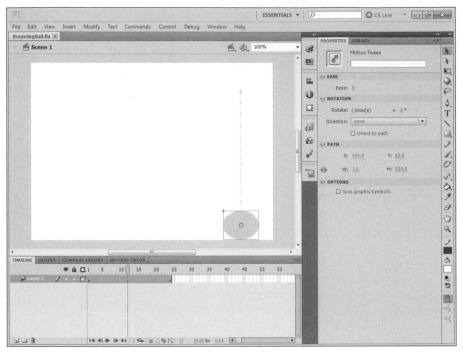

Figure 10-4:
The halfway
point of the
frame
animation.

Press Ctrl+Enter (Windows) or Command+Enter (Mac) to do a quick publish of your application. The application loads and displays the ball bouncing up and down. To expand on this further, you can play around with the movement or the number of key frames, or try increasing and decreasing duration of the animation.

Animating with ActionScript Code

The SpaceshipZapZap game that has been taking shape throughout this book responds to user input; moving the defender spacecraft left or right is dependent on the input value. The two examples of frame animation discussed in the preceding section wouldn't cut it because of the nature in which the display object's position needs to be changed using computed coordinates. The coordinates' values are derived using the object's last known position and the amount of movement required. The answer is to animate using ActionScript code.

Although a scary-sounding prospect, animating purely with ActionScript is actually pretty straightforward, and for tasks like this one, it's far less complicated than the mishmash timeline/code alternative I describe earlier in this chapter.

To move the defender spacecraft left or right, two small procedures must take place:

✔ **Handling the input event:** You must create a function that handles the user input event, such as a left keypress or a left tilt.

✔ **Performing the movement:** You must create a function that can be called repeatedly to incrementally move the target display object based on the input event.

Looking at the SpaceshipZapZap application, I'll put these events into play with some code. Later, I want my game's movement to be controlled by the mobile device's accelerometer (explained in detail in Chapter 11), but I don't have an accelerometer in my computer. Therefore, I need to set up input controls that I can easily operate and test while I develop the animation code with Flash Professional. My keyboard is the most convenient input control to use. Not many developers try and build applications without a keyboard, so I'm going to stick my neck out and presume that you have one too! Follow these steps to wire up the keyboard events to your game:

1. **Open the** `SpaceshipZapZap.as` **Document Class in Flash Professional.**

   I show you how to create this file in Chapter 6.

2. **Create a new method called** `registerInGameEvents`.

   Place this method after the other methods you've created in the class, where all event registrations for in-game user interaction will be placed:

   ```
   private function onStartSelect( e:Event ) :void
   {
       //...
   }

   private function registerInGameEvents() :void
   {}
   ```

3. **Register a listener for the stage's** `KEY_DOWN` **event.**

   This registration causes an event to be handled each time any key on the keyboard is pressed:

   ```
   private function registerInGameEvents() :void
   {
       stage.addEventListener( KeyboardEvent.KEY_DOWN,
           onKeyDownEvent );
   }
   ```

4. **Create the** `onKeyDownEvent` **method to handle the** `KEY_DOWN` **event:**

   ```
   private function registerInGameEvents() :void
   {
       stage.addEventListener( KeyboardEvent.KEY_DOWN,
           onKeyDownEvent );
   ```

```
}

private function onKeyDownEvent( e:KeyboardEvent )
        :void
{
   if( e.keyCode == Keyboard.LEFT )
   {
      moveLeft();
   }
   else if( e.keyCode == Keyboard.RIGHT )
   {
      moveRight();
   }
}
```

When the event is raised, a code corresponding to the key that was pressed is accessible on the event object and passed to the handler method as a parameter. By checking whether the keyCode property is LEFT or RIGHT, a decision can be made on which direction to instigate movement to.

5. **Create** moveLeft **and** moveRight **methods to perform the movement:**

```
private function onKeyDownEvent( e:KeyboardEvent )
        :void
{
   //...
}
private function moveLeft() :void
{
}

private function moveRight() :void
{
}
```

6. **Assign a listener for the** ENTER_FRAME **event inside the** moveLeft **and** moveRight **methods:**

```
private function moveLeft() :void
{
   addEventListener( Event.ENTER_FRAME,
        onDefenderMoveLeft );
}

private function moveRight() :void
{
   addEventListener( Event.ENTER_FRAME,
        onDefenderMoveRight );
}
```

A registration for the ENTER_FRAME event causes a handler method to be called continuously at a rate that's the same as the application's frame rate setting. The frame rate was set in Chapter 4 at a value of 24 FPS, which means that the ENTER_FRAME event is raised and handled 24 times each second. This rate is perfect for animation and will continue to execute until the listener registration is removed.

7. **Create two methods to handle the left and right** ENTER_FRAME **events.**

   These two methods perform the act of moving the target display object, in this case the defender spacecraft, on the stage:

```
private function moveRight() :void
{
    //...
}

private function onDefenderMoveLeft( e:Event ) :void
{
    if( defender.x - 20 >= 0 )
    {
        defender.x -= 20;
    }
}
```

In the onDefenderMoveLeft method, I check first whether moving the defender display object left by 20 pixels will cause it to be off-screen (that is, less than 0 pixels on the *x*-axis). Provided the movement doesn't cause that, I decrease the defender's x value by 20.

In the onDefenderMoveRight method, I want to perform a similar check, but this time I want to make sure that moving the defender won't cause it to be off the far right of the screen. I check this by taking the current x position, adding the defender's width, and then adding the amount by which I'm planning to move the defender to the right. Provided this value is less than the width of the stage, the movement is performed:

```
private function onDefenderMoveLeft( e:Event ) :void
{
    //...
}
private function onDefenderMoveRight( e:Event ) :void
{
    if( defender.x + defender.width + 20 <= stage.
        stageWidth )
    {
        defender.x += 20;
    }
}
```

In both of these cases, the defender display object will keep being moved to the left or the right until the movement results in the defender being off-screen.

8. **Create an new method called** `deregisterInGameEvents()` **to remove the** ENTER_FRAME **event registrations when they're no longer required.**

   Executing code when you don't need to is wasteful on mobile devices, because the computations are still being undertaken by the CPU and therefore using the device's battery. Whenever they're not needed, registrations for ENTER_FRAME events should be removed to improve the efficiency of the application.

   On three occasions, the ENTER_FRAME event registrations need to be removed from your game.

   To cancel all in-game event registrations: When the game or app is no longer being played or used, create a new method called `deregister InGameEvents` to cancel all in-game event registrations:

   ```
   private function onDefenderMoveRight( e:Event ) :void
   {
       //...
   }
   private function deregisterInGameEvents() :void
   {
           removeEventListener( Event.ENTER_FRAME,
           onDefenderMoveLeft );
           removeEventListener( Event.ENTER_FRAME,
           onDefenderMoveRight );
       stage.removeEventListener( KeyboardEvent.KEY_DOWN,
           onKeyDownEvent );
   }
   ```

   To remove the ENTER_FRAME *event listener for moving right whenever the left one is registered:* It's not good for ENTER_FRAME listeners for left and right to execute at the same time, because the net effect will be no movement. To remove the ENTER_FRAME event listener for moving right whenever the left one is registered, add a call to `removeEventListener()` inside the `moveLeft()` method:

   ```
   private function moveLeft() :void
   {
       addEventListener( Event.ENTER_FRAME,
           onDefenderMoveLeft );
       removeEventListener( Event.ENTER_FRAME,
           onDefenderMoveRight );
   }
   ```

To remove the ENTER_FRAME *event listener for moving left whenever the right one is registered:* This item is the converse of the previous one. To remove the ENTER_FRAME event listener for moving left whenever the right one is registered, add a call to removeEventListener() inside the moveRight() method:

```
private function moveRight() :void
{
    addEventListener( Event.ENTER_FRAME,
        onDefenderMoveRight );
    removeEventListener( Event.ENTER_FRAME,
        onDefenderMoveLeft );
}
```

9. **Invoke a call to** registerInGameEvents **from the** onStartSelect **method.**

   You created the onStartSelect() method in Chapter 6 to handle the user pressing the Start Game button on the start screen. After the onStartSelect() method is called, the application is going into in-game mode, so this is the place to call registerInGameEvents() to get all the keyboard interaction set up for use.:

```
private function onStartSelect( e:Event ) :void
{
    removeChild( _startScreen );
    buildAlienFleet();
    var sound:Alarm = new Alarm();
    sound.play();
    registerInGameEvents();
}
```

That's the complete code; now make sure that it's working as expected. Press Ctrl+Enter (Windows) or Command+Enter (Mac) to do a quick-publish. Press the Start Game button after the application loads. The defender and the alien spacecraft fleet appear onscreen, as shown in Figure 10-5. Press the left cursor key and observe the defender animate across the screen to the far left, but stop short of disappearing. Now press the right cursor key and observe the defender move in the opposite direction, again stopping short of vanishing off the right edge. That's all there is to it! You're scripting animations into your application like a pro now!

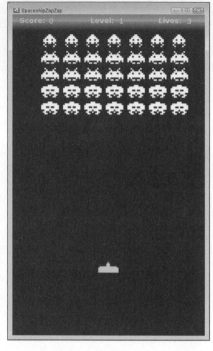

Figure 10-5:
The
defender
and alien
spacecraft
at the start
of game
play.

Using Animation Libraries

Hand-coding your own animations in ActionScript 3.0 is sometimes too complicated and time-consuming to be bothered with. Also, in some circumstances, you have so many individual movements occurring on the screen that discrete ENTER_FRAME listeners for all of them would cause the application to grind to a standstill. For this you need some code in your application that manages them. A good example of some free-to-use code that can handle the animation for you is the GTween animation library.

Setting up GTween

GTween is a lightweight animation library from ActionScript developer Grant Skinner that seeks to reduce the amount of code needed to perform complex animations and centralize the management of timing, so that more and more animation doesn't throttle your application.

First download the library from http://gskinner.com/libraries/ gtween/#download. Then follow these steps to configure GTween for use in your application:

1. **Create a new application in Flash Professional and save it as** GTweenExample.fla.

   Choose either a new AIR for Android application or a new iOS application.

2. **In the Properties panel, click the wrench icon next to the Class field.**

   The Create ActionScript 3.0 Class dialog box opens.

3. **Type the Class name GTweenExample and click OK.**

   A new ActionScript 3.0 class opens in Flash Professional.

4. **Press Ctrl+S (Windows) or Command+S (Mac) and save the file as** GTweenExample.as.

5. **Unzip the archive you downloaded from** http://gskinner.com.

6. **Open the folder** GTween_v2_01, **and then browse to** GTween_v2_01\swc.

   Inside the SWC folder is a single file called GTween_V2_01.swc.

7. **Copy** GTween_V2_01.swc **to the same directory as your** GTweenExample.fla **file.**

8. **In Flash Professional, choose File⇨Publish Settings.**

   The Publish Settings dialog box opens.

9. **Click the Flash (.swf) item in the list on the left.**

10. **Click the ActionScript Settings button (the wrench icon) next to ActionScript 3.0.**

    The Advanced ActionScript 3.0 Settings dialog box opens.

11. **Click the Library Path tab.**

12. **Click the Browse to SWC File button.**

    This is the middle icon at the upper-right corner of the SWC files or folders list.

    A File Open dialog box opens.

13. **Browse to the** GTween_V2_01.swc **file and select Open.**

    The SWC file appears in the SWC files or folders list.

14. **Click OK and click OK again to save the changes.**

    The GTween library is now configured and ready to use.

Animating with GTween

You can create GTween animations with a single line of code, and the structure is relatively intuitive too. A new `GTween` instance animates immediately, unless you tell it to do otherwise. You must supply the `GTween` instance with parameters in the following order:

1. **Target:** The display object instance to be animated.

2. **Duration:** The time in seconds that the animation should take to complete.

3. **Values:** An object containing one or more properties of the display object that are to be altered with the animation, for example, x and y positions or width and height values.

4. **Props:** An object containing one or more additional properties that the GTween code can use during animation. An example of this is specifying an easing function that changes the way the animation changes over time.

Here's an example GTween implementation that animates the width and height of the supplied target display object to 0 over a period of 5 seconds. It conducts the animation using a cubic easing equation:

```
new GTween( myDisplayObject, {width: 0, height: 0},{Cubic.
      easeIn} );
```

Doing is easier than explaining, so it's time to put some of this into practice. Follow these steps to create a simple ball application, where the ball animates to the position on the screen that was clicked (or touched):

1. **Open** `GTweenExample.fla` **in Flash Professional.**

   I showed you how to create this, and configure it for use with GTween, in the preceding section.

2. **Using the drawing tools, draw a circle that is about 50 pixels wide and 50 pixels high on the stage.**

3. **Select the shape you just drew, and choose Modify⇨Convert to Symbol.**

   The Convert to Symbol dialog box opens.

4. **Type** Ball **in the Name field and click OK.**

5. **Select the** `Ball MovieClip` **on the stage. Then in the Properties panel on the right, type the instance name** ball.

   You now have a `Ball MovieClip` instance on the stage that can be referenced with the instance name `ball`.

6. **Open** GTweenExample.as **to edit the code.**

7. **Register a** CLICK **event listener to the stage by placing a single line of code inside the constructor for the class:**

```
public function GTweenExample()
{
    stage.addEventListener( MouseEvent.CLICK,
        onStageClick );
}
```

8. **Create a method called** onStageClick **to handle the** CLICK **event:**

```
public function GTweenExample()
{
    stage.addEventListener( MouseEvent.CLICK,
        onStageClick );
}

private function onStageClick( e:MouseEvent ) :void
{}
```

9. **Create a new** GTween **instance to move the** Ball MovieClip **instance to the position where the** CLICK **event was registered.**

   The localX and localY properties of the MouseEvent object enable you to determine exactly where the click took place. By providing these in an object as x and y values to the GTween instance, the ball instance can be animated to the position of the click:

```
private function onStageClick( e:MouseEvent ) :void
{
    new GTween( ball, 1, {x: e.localX, y: e.localY },
        {ease: Elastic.easeInOut} );
}
```

   Note that the animation duration is specified as 1 second. You can increase this value to make the animation longer in duration. See also that an Elastic.easeInOut is specified in the props parameter object. You can play around with different ease options by specifying other available classes, such as Quadratic, Cubic, and Linear. For a full list of ease classes available to use with GTween, check out www.gskinner.com/libraries/gtween/docs_v2_01/com/gskinner/motion/easing/package-detail.html.

Press Ctrl+Enter (Windows) or Command+Enter (Mac) to do a quick publish of your application. The familiar AIR runtime window opens with your application loaded into it. When you click in the stage, do you see that the ball moves to where you clicked with a fun little bounce?

Understanding Collision Detection

Inevitably when you start moving things around on the screen, you have a heightened risk that these objects may bump into each other. In fact, it's probable that you want this to happen — those collisions may satisfy the playing criteria in a game. In Flash, when display objects bump into each other, this is referred to as a *collision,* and the process of determining when these incidents occur is known as *collision detection.*

The SpaceshipZapZap game that you've witnessed being assembled throughout the course of this book relies heavily on collision detection to know when the defender spacecraft's bullets hit an alien spacecraft. Conversely, the same technique is used to determine when the aliens' bombs hit the defender.

Throughout the book, I introduce elements of the SpaceshipZapZap application. In the steps that follow, I show you how to add collision detection to the alien MovieClips, which I introduced in Chapter 6:

1. **Open** SpaceshipZapZap.as **in Flash Professional.**

   I show you how to create ActionScript 3.0 class in Chapter 6.

2. **Declare the** _bullets Vector **object with all the other class variable declarations at the top:**

```
public class SpaceshipZapZap extends MovieClip
{
    private var _bullets:Vector.<Bullet>;
```

3. **Initialize the** _bullets Vector **object in the class's** initialize() **method:**

```
private function initialize( e:Event ):void
{
    removeEventListener( Event.ADDED_TO_STAGE,
        initialize );
    _bullets = new Vector.<Bullet>();
```

4. **Populate the** Vector **with** Bullet **instances using a** for **loop:**

```
_bullets = new Vector.<Bullet>();
for( var i:int = 0; i<10; i++ )
{
    _bullets.push( new Bullet() );
}
```

5. **Create an object pool of** Bombs.

   a. **Replicating the previous steps for the** Bomb MovieClip, **declare a** Vector **called** _bombs:

```
private var _bullets:Vector.<Bullet>;
private var _bombs:Vector.<Bombs>;
```

b. **Initialize** bombs **in the same place that** _bullets **was initialized, and then populate it with ten** Bomb **instances:**

```
_bullets = new Vector.<Bullet>();
for( var i:int = 0; i<10; i++ )
{
    _bullets.push( new Bullet() );
}

_bombs = new Vector.<Bomb>();
for( var i:int = 0; i<10; i++ )
{
    _bombs.push( new Bomb() );
}
```

6. **Declare a new** Vector **object called** _liveAliens:

```
private var _bombs:Vector.<Bombs>;
private var _liveAliens:Vector.<MovieClip>;
```

The _liveAliens vector stores an exact copy of the _aliens vector, but references to alien spacecraft stored in it will be destroyed when they're hit by a Bullet object. Progressively, the number of alien space-craft references in the vector are reduced until none are left, signifying that the level or game is complete.

7. **Assign the** _liveAliens Vector **a complete copy of — but not a reference to — the** _aliens Vector:

```
private function buildAlienFleet() :void
{
    //...
    _fleetContainer.x = ( stage.stageWidth * .5 ) - (
        _fleetContainer.width * .5 );
    addChild( _fleetContainer );
    _liveAliens = _aliens.slice( 0 );
}
```

You can make a completely new copy of a Vector object by using the Vector.splice() method to "chop out" an exact copy of the data. Place the code on the last line in the method

When you assign the value of one Vector to another Vector — much as when the value of an array is assigned to another array — the second vector simply takes a reference to the first vector. As a consequence, when any changes are made to one vector, they appear in both. For example, if I do the following

```
var vector1:Vector.<String> = new Vector.<String>();
var vector2:Vector.<String> = vector1;
vector2.push( "hello world" );
trace( vector1 );
trace( vector2 );
```

both `vector1` and `vector2` trace out "hello world" to the output panel in Flash Professional. Anything added to `vector2` is actually being added to `vector1` through the reference it was given on the second line.

8. **Register an** `ENTER_FRAME` **listener to the Document Class from inside the** `registerInGameEvents()` **method:**

```
private function registerInGameEvents() :void
{
    stage.addEventListener( KeyboardEvent.KEY_DOWN,
        onKeyDownEvent );
    addEventListener( Event.ENTER_FRAME,
        onBulletEnterFrame );
}
```

As the Document Class extends the `MovieClip` class, it has an internal Timeline running behind the scenes to which you can register a listener to be notified each time the playhead enters a new frame.

9. **Remove the** `ENTER_FRAME` **listener registration in the** `deregisterIn-GameEvents()` **method.**

So that your application isn't chugging away executing code when the game isn't actually being played, remove the listener to prevent the code in the callback from being executed:

```
private function deregisterInGameEvents() :void
{
    removeEventListener( Event.ENTER_FRAME,
        onDefenderMoveLeft );
    removeEventListener( Event.ENTER_FRAME,
        onDefenderMoveRight );
    stage.removeEventListener( KeyboardEvent.KEY_DOWN,
        onKeyDownEvent );
    removeEventListener( Event.ENTER_FRAME,
        onBulletEnterFrame );
}
```

10. **Create a method to handle the** `ENTER_FRAME` **event.**

As you'll have already gleaned from the code you've written, the method is called `onBulletEnterFrame` and takes an `Event` object as its single parameter:

```
private function buildAlienFleet() :void
{
    //...
}
private function onBulletEnterFrame( e:Event ) :void
{
}
```

11. Create a `for...each` **loop that iterates through the** `bullets Vector`:

```
private function onBulletEnterFrame( e:Event ) :void
{
    for each( var bullet:Bullet in _bullets )
    {
    }
}
```

12. Create a nested `for...each` **loop that iterates through the** `_liveAliens Vector`:

```
private function onBulletEnterFrame( e:Event ) :void
{
    for each( var bullet:Bullet in _bullets )
    {
        for each( var alien:MovieClip in _liveAliens )
        {
        }
    }
}
```

13. Use the `hitTestObject()` **method to determine whether the current** `bullet` **and** `alien` **are in collision:**

```
private function onBulletEnterFrame( e:Event ) :void
{
    for each( var bullet:Bullet in _bullets )
    {
        for each( var alien:MovieClip in _liveAliens )
        {
            if( bullet.hitTestObject( alien ) )
            {}
        }
    }
}
```

Using the `hitTestObject()` method, which is available to any display object in Flash, you can check whether two objects are touching each other. The method returns `true` if they are, so it's easy to incorporate into a conditional statement.

14. Use the `removeChild()` **method to remove both the** `alien` **and** `bullet` **from the display list, if the** `hitTestObject()` **method returns** `true`:

```
for each( var alien:MovieClip in _liveAliens )
{
    if( bullet.hitTestObject( alien ) )
    {
        removeChild( bullet );
```

```
        _fleetContainer.removeChild( alien );
    }
}
```

If the return value of `bullet.hitTestObject( alien )` returns `false`, both the bullet and alien are left in the display list.

15. **Use the** `Vector.splice()` **method to remove the** `alien` **that was hit from the** `_liveAliens` **Vector:**

```
    removeChild( bullet );
    _fleetContainer.removeChild( alien );
    _liveAliens.splice( _liveAliens.indexOf( alien ), 1
        );
}
```

Because the alien has been annihilated, it is removed from the `_liveAliens` Vector so that no more collision detection checks are performed against it, and so that the number of aliens in the `_liveAliens` Vector accurately reflects the current state of play.

16. **Break the** `_liveAliens for...each` **loop:**

```
    _liveAliens.splice( _liveAliens.indexOf( alien ), 1
        );
    break;
}
```

As a collision between two objects was detected, no further collisions between those two objects and other objects in the display list are possible, so stop checking for further collisions:

That deals with the logic for detecting collisions between your bullets and your alien spacecrafts. If you want your alien fleet to start dropping bombs on your defender spacecraft, you simply create another loop that iterates through the _bombs object pool that you created in Step 5 to check whether `hitTestObject( defender )` returns `true`.

One thing to bear in mind with animation is that it can only ever be tested manually. That is, the only way to be sure that it runs correctly and doesn't cause noticeable glitches in your application is to run the application on a mobile device and watch the animation with your own eyes.

 Collision detection can be a CPU hog, so be careful how you're using it and be aware that it doesn't scale exceptionally well. Limit the number of checks you have to perform on each ENTER_FRAME event to the absolute minimum necessary. If a display object isn't in the display list, it doesn't need to be included in any collision detection routines. If one type of object's collision with another type of object is irrelevant, you don't need to have code checking this. Performing upwards of 50 detections per frame is likely to gravely affect the functionality of your application.

Chapter 11

Hooking into the Extended Mobile API Features

*O*ne of the most compelling elements to targeting a mobile device is the array of new features that become available to you. I was like an excitable child when I learned that I could hook in the accelerometer to detect movement of the device and to access the device's geolocation data to triangulate where the device is on the planet. Anyone with even the slightest geeky streak in them would think that was pretty cool! As someone who'd become used to regular mouse and key gestures, being able to interact with my device using motion and touch, together with support for multiple simultaneous touch interactions, sparked a whole new wave of ideas in my mind. I'm sure that the same will happen for you, too, as you explore these features.

I begin by looking at reasonably simple concepts, like preventing the device from going to sleep, before moving into slightly more involved, yet highly rewarding tasks, such as handling multitouch gestures — tracking the movement of two or more touch points across the device's screen and translating the movement into a transformation in the objects visible on the screen.

Keeping the Device Awake

Mobile phones are powered by batteries that are able to keep the device running for a finite amount of time. Device manufacturers invest millions in battery technology that will keep the power-hungry CPUs of today's smartphones happy, but this is only half of the work they do. Batteries also power device displays, speakers, and vibrating units. To conserve battery power, the devices will toggle into a sleep or low-power state. Most devices will dim or turn off their display to save on the relatively large power consumption of the backlight.

On most mobile devices, the screen is dimmed by default after a set period of inactivity. The user can configure the time before the device goes to sleep, or disable it completely, by modifying the Auto-lock option on the settings menu. As a developer of applications targeting mobile devices, you can't rely on a user having prevented the screen from dimming, and your application might behave in a way that the user spends long periods looking at the screen but not interacting with it. Watching a movie on a mobile phone is a good example of this case.

Fortunately, you have a way to prevent the mobile device from going to sleep when your application is running — but it comes with a distinct health warning. If your application works in a way that the user may spend long periods watching the screen without interacting with it, you have a justifiable cause to force the device to stay awake. However, keeping your application awake for the sake of being awake is not only unfair to your user — who will suffer shorter battery life on his or her device — but also puts your application at risk of being rejected from the Apple App Store or Android Market.

In the following steps I show you how to set up a new application in Flash Professional. Then I show you the code to keep the device awake:

1. **Create a new application in Flash Professional and save it as** ExtendedFeatures.fla.

   Choose either a new AIR for Android application or a new iOS application.

2. **In the Properties panel, click the wrench icon next to the Class field.**

   The create ActionScript 3.0 Class dialogue box opens.

3. **Type the Class name** ExtendedFeatures **and click OK.**

   A new ActionScript 3.0 class opens in Flash Professional.

4. **Press Ctrl+S (Windows) or Command+S (Mac) and save the file as** ExtendedFeatures.as.

5. **Set the** `NativeApplication's systemIdleMode` **property to** `KEEP_AWAKE`**:**

```
package
{
    import flash.display.MovieClip;
    import flash.desktop.NativeApplication;
    import flash.desktop.SystemIdleMode;

    public class ExtendedFeatures extends MovieClip
    {
    public function ExtendedFeatures()
    {
        NativeApplication.nativeApplication.
         systemIdleMode = SystemIdleMode.KEEP_AWAKE;
        }
    }
}
```

To set the device to go to sleep after a user-configured timeout, use this code instead:

```
NativeApplication.nativeApplication.systemIdleMode =
        SystemIdleMode.NORMAL;
```

If you want to be able to toggle the `systemIdleMode` at various times in your application — for example, you require the device to stay awake only during video playback but not on menu screens — you can switch it back and forth as often as you need to.

Most of the time, I suspect you won't need to modify this `NativeApplication` setting, but I wanted to let you know it was there, just in case!

Initiating Calls, SMS, and Maps

It's easy to forget that today's smartphones are also conventional mobile phones that can make calls and send Short Message Service (SMS) messages. At times, you might have a number in your app that you'd like the user to be able to tap to invoke the native call or SMS dialogs. For example, your app may allow users to look up a local business using geolocation tools. Then, if the information returned includes an address or phone number, it's handy to allow the user to press the phone number to immediately call the business. You're probably thinking I'm going to go all Objective-C on you here, but you'd be wrong: Invoking a call or SMS in your application is surprisingly easy to do. Just use the `navigateToURL` method — a method globally available in Flash applications for navigating to a web page — with the

`URLRequest` object (covered in more detail in Chapter 8) that you would normally use to call a regular web address. But instead of a URL, you use a phone number, and you prefix the number to denote whether you'd like the device to call it or write an SMS message to send to it.

Call

Allowing your users to initiate a call to you from inside your application, with a single tap, can be a useful feature. If you have a dedicated business line, your existing and prospective customers can contact you with minimal fuss. If the line is a personal phone line, however, you might want to consider whether you want the world to have your number and be able to call it instantly.

If the mobile device your application is running on doesn't support calling, as is true with many tablet devices, the calling feature will fail silently.

Using the `tel` URL schema, you can tell the device to call a telephone number. After this method is invoked, it will call the number with no further warning to the user, so be careful how you implement this feature. Follow these steps to make the mobile device call a number after the user touches the screen in your application:

1. **Open** `ExtendedFeatures.fla` **and** `ExtendedFeatures.as` **in Flash Professional.**

   I show you how to create these two files in the preceding section, where I explain how to keep the device awake.

2. **Register an event listener to the stage for the** `CLICK` **event:**

   ```
       addEventListener( MouseEvent.CLICK, onStagePress );
   }
   ```

3. **Create a new method called** `onStagePress` **to handle the event:**

   ```
       addEventListener( MouseEvent.CLICK, onStagePress
           );
   }
   private function onStagePress( e:MouseEvent ) :void
   {}
   ```

4. **Call the** `navigateToURL` **global method, providing the URL** `tel:0123456789` **as a new** `URLRequest` **object:**

   ```
   private function onStagePress( e:MouseEvent ) :void
   {
       navigateToURL( new URLRequest( "tel:0123456789" )
           );
   }
   ```

5. **Save the file as** ExtendedFeatures.as.

That's all there is to it! When you run the application on a mobile device and touch anywhere on the screen, you'll invoke the call dialog on the device. Pressing anywhere on the screen to invoke a call is unpleasant; your application needs a button for the user to press instead (creating buttons is covered in Chapter 5). However, the code to handle the event is the same. Finally, as obvious as it might seem, don't forget to switch the dummy phone number for the real one before you submit your application to the app stores!

If you're populating a `TextField` with `htmlText` and want to make a link within the text initiate a call, your link code would look like this:

```
myTextField.htmlText = '<a href="tel:0123456789">Call us
        today</a>';
```

A handler method is not required in your ActionScript code if you use the `htmlText` technique because `href` is handled automatically, invoking the call.

SMS

As with calling, your application can cause the device to open its default SMS application, already populated with the destination phone number. This feature saves your customers time, but could easily become a burden on you if you don't have a dedicated line for accepting messages. Because of the prevalence of SMS spamming, I suggest that you avoid making your personal number available through this technique.

Looking back at the steps to invoke a phone call in the preceding section, modify Step 4 to invoke SMS behavior, instead of a phone call, on the device:

```
private function onStagePress( e:MouseEvent ) :void
{
    navigateToURL( new URLRequest( "sms:0123456789" )
        );
}
```

To do the same with `htmlText` in a `TextField`, you'd use the following code:

```
<a href="sms:0123456789">Send us an SMS</a>
```

If your application is running on a mobile device that doesn't support SMS (as is the case for many tablet devices), the SMS invocation feature will fail silently.

Maps

Many smartphone apps include a default, or native, mapping application; on Android and iOS the mapping app is Google Maps. As you develop your own mobile applications, you may also want to implement a map feature and open a location in the native Google Maps application. You can call up a map by using an approach similar to invoking calls and SMS, except maps aren't initiated using the same URL schema. Instead, the device is programmed to recognize any Google Maps URL requests (http://maps.google.com) and open the Google Maps application that ships with the device, instead of the default web browser.

Looking back at the steps to invoke a phone call in the previous section, modify Step 4 to open the maps application zoomed into a place called Wichita, instead of invoking a phone call, on the device:

```
private function onStagePress( e:MouseEvent ) :void
{
    navigateToURL( new URLRequest( "http://maps.google.
        com/?q=wichita" ) );
}
```

Using Accelerometer Data

The accelerometer is a unit inside the mobile device that measures the acceleration it experiences in g-force (units of g). At rest, a device lying on a surface has 1 g of upward force exerted on it, but this is countered by exactly 1 g of downward force exerted by the earth's gravity — therefore one cancels the other out. So an accelerometer at rest will register 0 g. If I suddenly lift the device from the surface, upward acceleration is exerted on the device, and depending on the ferocity of the upward motion, the accelerometer will register positive g's. If I were then to throw the device back at the surface I picked it up from, the accelerometer would again register positive g's; then the rapid deceleration as it hits the surface would cause it to register negative g's.

The accelerometer installed inside most mobile devices is able to detect acceleration along three axes of movement: x, y, and z. Figure 11-1 shows how these three axes relate to the orientation of an iPhone; the same is true for Android devices with accelerometers.

So with motion detection possible along three axes of movement, you can capture plenty of types of movement gestures using the accelerometer. A forwards poke with the device held in your hand would register positive g's on the y-axis, whereas holding the device flat in your hand and waving it up and down would cause the accelerometer to register positive g's on the upswing and negative g's on the downswing. By assigning an event listener to an instance of the accelerometer class in your application, your application can be notified of when such movements occur and respond to them accordingly.

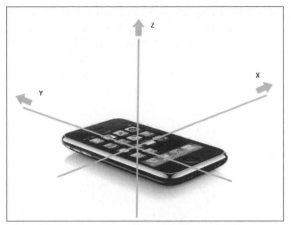

Figure 11-1:
Movement
axes on
the iPhone
accelero-
meter.

The accelerometer features are exposed to your Flash application through the
`Accelerometer` and `AccelerometerEvent` classes. In the SpaceshipZapZap
application you've been watching me assemble over the past chapters, I
thought it'd be pretty cool if the user could move the defender spacecraft left
and right by tilting the device. Here's how you implement it yourself:

1. **In Flash Professional, open the** `SpaceshipZapZap.as` **Document
   Class for editing.**

2. **Declare a new** `Accelerometer` **instance called** `_accelerometer` **and
   a new** `String` **called** `_xStatus`:

   ```
   public class SpaceshipZapZap extends MovieClip
   {
      private var _accelerometer:Accelerometer;
      private var _xStatus:String = "";
   ```

3. **Create a new method in** `SpaceshipZapZap.as` **called**
   `registerAccelerometer`:

   ```
   private function registerAccelerometer() :void
   {}
   ```

4. **Ensure that the device running the application supports the accelerometer feature by evaluating the** `isSupported` **variable with an** `if`
   statement:

   ```
   private function registerAccelerometer() :void
   {
      if( Accelerometer.isSupported )
      {}
   }
   ```

Although your device has an accelerometer, your computer more than likely doesn't. When you test your application on your computer at various stages of development, you don't want runtime exceptions being thrown at you because you're using an API feature that is supported only on mobile devices that have accelerometers.

5. **Initialize the** `Accelerometer` **instance, if the** `isSupported` **property is** `true`:

```
private function registerAccelerometer() :void
{
    if( Accelerometer.isSupported )
    {
        _accelerometer = new Accelerometer();
    }
}
```

After you've established that the accelerometer is supported, you can safely initiate it within your app.

6. **Set the** `setRequestedUpdateInterval` **value:**

```
_accelerometer = new Accelerometer();
_accelerometer.setRequestedUpdateInterval( 50 );
```

The request update interval is the frequency in milliseconds that you'd like the accelerometer to notify your application of updates to its reading. The higher the value, the longer the polling interval between updates to the accelerometer's readings. A higher interval value may help to conserve battery power on the device, but it may also cause delays between the movement of the device and the response in your application.

If the `setRequestUpdateInterval` isn't called, your `Accelerometer` instance will notify of updates at the fastest interval supported by the device — refer to the device manufacturer for the default update interval for a specific device. If the update interval you assign isn't supported by the device, the minimum supported by the device will be used. As a ballpark, an interval of 30–100 milliseconds is sufficient for most applications.

7. **Register an event listener for the** UPDATE **event:**

```
_accelerometer.setRequestedUpdateInterval( 50 );
_accelerometer.addEventListener( AccelerometerEvent.
        UPDATE, onAccelerometerUpdate, false, 0, true
        );
```

8. **Create a new method called** onAccelerometerUpdate **to handle the** UPDATE **event:**

```
_accelerometer.addEventListener( AccelerometerEvent.
        UPDATE, onAccelerometerUpdate, false, 0, true
        );
}

private function onAccelerometerUpdate(
        e:AccelerometerEvent ) :void
{}
```

9. **Evaluate the** AccelerometerEvent.accelerationX **property in an** if **statement to check for acceleration along the** *x*-axis:

```
private function onAccelerometerUpdate(
        e:AccelerometerEvent ) :void
{
    if( e.accelerationX > 0.1 && _xStatus != "left" )
    {
        _xStatus = "left";
        removeEventListener( Event.ENTER_FRAME,
            onDefenderMoveRight );
        addEventListener( Event.ENTER_FRAME,
            onDefenderMoveLeft );
    }
    else if( e.accelerationX < -0.1 && _xStatus !=
        "right" )
    {
        _xStatus = "right";
        removeEventListener( Event.ENTER_FRAME,
            onDefenderMoveLeft );
        addEventListener( Event.ENTER_FRAME,
            onDefenderMoveRight );
    }
    else if( e.accelerationX < 0.1 && e.accelerationX >
        -0.1 )
    {
        _xStatus = "center";
        removeEventListener( Event.ENTER_FRAME,
            onDefenderMoveLeft );
        removeEventListener( Event.ENTER_FRAME,
            onDefenderMoveRight );
    }
}
```

A left tilt registers as negative g's on the *x*-axis, whereas a right tilt registers as a positive g's on the *x*-axis. If a left tilt is detected, the first if clause is `true`, and I register an `ENTER_FRAME` listener that is handled by the `onDefenderMoveLeft()` method. The `_xStatus` variable is set to `left`. Conversely, if a right tilt is detected, the second `if` clause is `true`, and I register an `ENTER_FRAME` listener that is handled by the `onDefenderMoveRight()` method. The `_xStatus` variable is set to `right`. If little or no acceleration is detected in the left or right direction, the third `if` clause is `true` while the preceding two are `false`. The phone is deemed to be "centered," and all animation is stopped — the user doesn't want the defender to move any farther to the left or to the right — so both the left and right `ENTER_FRAME` listeners are removed.

I found that 0.1g or higher was a good threshold for the acceleration, though you might want to experiment with the sensitivity yourself.

10. **Create a new method called** `onDefenderMoveLeft` **that moves** `defender` **left by 20 pixels:**

```
            removeEventListener( Event.ENTER_FRAME,
            onDefenderMoveRight );
    }
}

private function onDefenderMoveLeft( e:Event ) :void
{
    if( defender.x - 20 >= 0 )
    {
        defender.x -= 20;
    }
}
```

11. **Create a new method called** `onDefenderMoveRight` **that moves** `defender` **right by 20 pixels:**

```
        defender.x -= 20;
    }
}

private function onDefenderMoveRight( e:Event ) :void
{
    if( defender.x + defender.width + 20 <= stage.
        stageWidth )
    {
        defender.x += 20;
    }
}
```

The `onDefenderMoveLeft()` and `onDefenderMoveRight()` methods are called on every frame when a listener registration is assigned for them.

12. **Call** registerAccelerometer() **from the** startGame() **method:**

```
private function onStartSelect( e:Event ) :void
{
        removeChild( _startScreen );
    buildAlienFleet();
    var sound:Alarm = new Alarm();
    sound.play();
    registerInGameEvents();
    registerAccelerometer();
}
```

In Chapter 6, I show you how to create a method in the SpaceshipZapZap. as Document Class called onStartSelect() that is called when the user presses the Start Game button to begin using the app. This method is also a logical place to configure the Accelerometer instance.

With the addition of the registerAccelerometer() method, when you tilt your mobile device left or right (provided that it has an accelerometer) the defender spacecraft will move either left or right. Cool, huh? You can capture loads of other movements with an accelerometer, such as shakes, jumps, and spins, so feel free to have a play around and see what you can come up with as well as the silly movements you can get your users to perform!

Using Geolocation Information

With mobile devices offering more and more functionality, the days of stopping someone to ask for directions are limited. At the touch of a button, your phone can quickly establish your position on a map. Most Android and iOS devices are able to figure out where they are using built-in assisted Global Positioning System (GPS) technology. GPS technology allows a device on the earth's surface to triangulate its position using signals transmitted from no fewer than four satellites in a geostationary orbit above the planet. GPS can take up to 40 seconds to triangulate, and in built-up areas, it can take even longer because the signals from the satellites bounce off buildings and other structures. This interference causes fragmenting of the signal and sometimes renders it unusable. To get around this, the Assisted Global Positioning System (A-GPS) was devised to allow cellular devices to be more easily triangulated in built-up areas. Here's how the A-GPS works: Instead of leaving the mobile device on its own to receive signals from the satellites, the cellular transmitters assist in calculating where the mobile device is by using the GPS data received from the device and combining it with satellite data that the cellular transmitter is receiving.

On your Android or iOS mobile device, the geolocation information is available to your application through the `GeoLocation` and `GeoLocationEvent` classes in the Flash API. Geolocation data comes in the WSG-84 standard, which is a location formed of two numbers: latitude in degrees and longitude in degrees. Setting up an application to use this data is very easy. Follow these steps:

1. **Open** `URLMonitorExample.fla` **and** `URLMonitorExample.as` **in Flash Professional.**

   I show you how to create these two files in Chapter 8, where I explain how to monitor the presence of a network connection and call the Geonames web service.

2. **Declare a new** `GeoLocation` **variable called** `_geolocation`:

   ```
   public class URLMonitorExample extends MovieClip
   {
       private var _geolocation:Geolocation;
       private var _networkAvailable:Boolean;
   ```

3. **Declare two new** `Number` **properties called** `_latitude` **and** `_longitude`:

   ```
   private var _geolocation:Geolocation;
   private var _latitude:Number;
   private var _longitude:Number;
   ```

4. **Create a new method in the class called** `registerGeolocation()`:

   ```
   private function registerGeolocation() :void
   {}
   ```

5. **Ensure that the device running the application supports the geolocation feature by evaluating** `Geolocation`'s `isSupported` **variable with an** `if` **statement:**

   ```
   private function registerGeolocation() :void
   {
       if( Geolocation.isSupported )
       {}
   }
   ```

   Like the accelerometer feature, support for geolocation is device specific, so you first need to make sure that the device on which your application is running can support it.

6. **Initialize the** `Geolocation` **instance, if the** `isSupported` **property is** `true`:

   ```
   if( Geolocation.isSupported )
   ```

```
{
    _geolocation = new Geolocation();
}
```

7. **Call the** `setRequestedUpdateInterval()` **method to set the update interval on the** `Geolocation` **instance:**

```
_geolocation = new Geolocation();
_geolocation.setRequestedUpdateInterval( 1000 );
```

This method determines how frequently you'd like the device to notify your application of updates to the geolocation data. The value is milliseconds; I set mine to 1000 (or 1 second).

8. **Register an event listener to the** `Geolocation` **instance for the** `UPDATE` **event:**

```
_geolocation.setRequestedUpdateInterval( 1000 );
_geolocation.addEventListener( GeolocationEvent.
        UPDATE, onGeolocationUpdate, false, 0, true );
```

9. **Create a new method called** `onGeolocationUpdate` **to handle the** `UPDATE` **event:**

```
        _geolocation.addEventListener( GeolocationEvent.
        UPDATE, onGeolocationUpdate, false, 0, true );
    }
}

private function onGeolocationUpdate(
        e:GeolocationEvent ) :void
{}
```

10. **Store the** `latitude` **and** `longitude` **values exposed by the** `GeolocationEvent` **object in your** `_latitude` **and** `_longitude` **variables:**

```
private function onGeolocationUpdate(
        e:GeolocationEvent ) :void
{
    _latitude = e.latitude;
    _longitude = e.longitude;
}
```

After your `_latitude` and `_longitude` properties have updated values, you could initiate a call to a third-party web service (such as the Geonames service introduced in Chapter 8) with the latitude and longitude values from the `GeolocationEvent`. Doing this would allow your application to display the name of the place where the user is located:

```
private function onGeolocationUpdate(
        e:GeolocationEvent ) :void
{
   _latitude = e.latitude;
   _longitude = e.longitude;
   getGeonamesService();
}
```

Then, modify the getGeonamesService method to send the latitude and longitude values instead of the previous hard-coded values (refer to Chapter 8 for the full code):

```
private function getGeonamesService() :void
{
   variables.lat = _latitude;
   variables.lng = _longitude;
   variables.username = "jodieorourke";

   //...
}
```

Now the application is being pretty smart. It's able to triangulate where it is on the planet and then call a service over the Internet to establish the name of the place it's in!

If the user has disabled the geolocation features on the device — or in the case of iOS users, if they decline to allow your application access to the geolocation services when prompted — the geolocation features of your application won't work. Be sure to offer an alternative.

Incorporating Multitouch Gestures

The multitouch capabilities of a touch-screen mobile device allow a user to make gestures on the touch screen using more than one finger simultaneously. The device can then detect advanced pinching gestures, as well as how many digits are touching the screen and whether multiple buttons on a UI are pressed at the same time.

You may not know about some classes that are used specifically for touch interaction in Flash mobile applications yet, but you will become familiar with them as you start to implement complex touch gestures in your applications. Here's a handy list for your reference:

✔ TouchEvent: Raised when a finger is pressed onto the device's touch screen.

✔ GestureEvent:

- PressAndTapGestureEvent: Raised when the user presses down on the touch screen with a finger and taps elsewhere on the screen with another finger.

- TransformGestureEvent: Raised when a user moves one or more fingers across the screen while pressing down.

- GesturePhase: Allows access to the current stage of gesture while it's being performed by the user.

✔ Multitouch: A convenience class for determining the touch capabilities of the mobile device on which your application is running.

- MultitouchInputMode: Defines the settings you can use to control the type of touch inputs that your application accepts.

I explain each of these in more detail, and give an example of implementation, so that you can see how you'd wire them in your application.

TouchEvent

TouchEvent is an event type specific to touch-screen devices. Although most of the single-touch behavior is adequately represented by MouseEvents, the real purpose of TouchEvent is to be able to track multiple contact points on the touch screen. Say that I were to create two separate applications. Inside one, I register an event listener for TouchEvent.TOUCH_BEGIN, and in the other one, I register an event listener for MouseEvent.MOUSE_DOWN. In each, I then count the number of times these events fire when I put one, two, three, and then four fingers down on the touch screen. When I test this on my iPhone, I see that MouseEvent.MOUSE_DOWN fired only when I put the first finger down, whereas TouchEvent.TOUCH_BEGIN is fired when I put the first finger down and on each successive finger.

MouseEvents are executed faster than TouchEvents. If the interaction you're trying to capture can be achieved with a single touch point, you're better off using MouseEvent.

With multiple touch points being registered and tracked, you're able to track not only how these points move in relation to your DisplayObjects but also how they move relative to each other. This is where the complex GestureEvent classes can help.

GestureEvent

GestureEvents are simply a consolidation of a number of events that occur in close succession, which together represent a gesture. An example would be the swipe gesture. This starts as a touch and then continues with a movement of the touch point across the screen. Manually writing all the logic to track the individual events that comprise a gesture like swipe is not only painful but also regularly unnecessary. Native software running on a mobile device is able to notify the ActionScript API — on which your application is running — that a gesture has occurred, and you just need to write the code that responds as a result of the gesture.

The best way to see how all the gestures on your device work is to create a quick Hello Event application that can tell you when they occur. That way, you can perform the gesture you'd like to use, then see which event it is mapped to. Follow these steps to create a Hello Event application:

1. **Create a new application in Flash Professional.**

   This can be either an AIR for Android application or an iOS application; see Chapter 4 for how to create a new application.

2. **Create two dynamic** TextField **instances on the stage, and give one the instance name** supportedGesture **and the other the name** gesture.

3. **In the Properties panel, change the** supportedGesture TextField **behavior to Multiline.**

   Now the TextField can accept a list of gestures from the supported Gestures Vector.

4. **Create a new ActionScript 3.0 class called** Main **and save it as** Main.as **in the same directory as your application FLA.**

5. **In the Properties panel, type** Main **as the Document Class of your application.**

6. **Set the input mode to** GESTURE **by putting the following code in the constructor of the Document Class:**

```
public function Main()
{
    Multitouch.inputMode = MultitouchInputMode.GESTURE;
}
```

7. **Assign the supported gestures to a local** Vector:

```
    Multitouch.inputMode = MultitouchInputMode.GESTURE;
    var supported:Vector.<String>  = Multitouch.
        supportedGestures;
}
```

8. Iterate through the supported gesture events, registering an event listener for each to the stage:

```
var supported:Vector.<String>  = Multitouch.
    supportedGestures;
for each( var item:String in supported )
{
    supportedGesture.appendText( "\n"+item );
    stage.addEventListener( item, onGesture );
}
}
```

9. Create a new method called `onGesture` **to handle the events:**

```
        stage.addEventListener( item, onGesture );
    }
}

private function onGesture( e:Event ):void
{
    gesture.text = e.type;
}
```

This single method can accept any event type and display it in the `TextField` instance on the stage.

When you put the compiled application onto your mobile device, you can see the range of gestures that it supports, as well as perform those gestures yourself on the touch screen and see the event types being raised in the `TextField`.

Here's what the complete code for the Hello Event application looks like:

```
package
{
    import flash.display.MovieClip;
    import flash.ui.Multitouch;
    import flash.ui.MultitouchInputMode;
    import flash.events.Event;

    public class Main extends MovieClip
    {
        public function Main()
        {
            Multitouch.inputMode = MultitouchInputMode.
            GESTURE;
            var supported:Vector.<String>  = Multitouch.
            supportedGestures;
            for each( var item:String in supported )
            {
                supportedGesture.appendText( "\n"+item );
                stage.addEventListener( item, onGesture );
```

```
        }
    }

    private function onGesture( e:Event ) :void
    {
        gesture.text = e.type;
    }
  }
}
```

10. Save the application as HelloEvent.fla **and publish it.**

To see the outcome, you need to put the application on your mobile device. I show you how to do this in Chapter 13 for Android devices and Chapters 16 and 17 for iOS devices. When the application is running on your device, press, tap, swipe, and rotate your fingers on the device's touch screen and see the output in the `TextField` instance on the stage.

PressAndTapGestureEvent

As the name might suggest, `PressAndTapGestureEvent` is an event dispatched in response to a user pressing on the touch screen with one finger and then tapping with another, while holding the first finger in place. As a subclass of the `GestureEvent`, it is commonly used to open context menus, like the menu that would pop up on a web page if you right-clicked a hyperlink.

The `PressAndTapGestureEvent` object exposes four properties that allow you to access the coordinates that the tap touch occurred, from within the event handler:

✔ `tapLocalX`: The horizontal position along the *x*-axis at which the tap took place, relative to the position of the initial press gesture

✔ `tapLocalY`: The vertical position along the *y*-axis at which the tap took place, relative to the position of the initial press gesture

✔ `tapStageX`: Like `tapLocalX`, except this is an absolute horizontal position on the stage, not a relative one

✔ `tapStageY`: Like `tapLocalY`, except this is an absolute vertical position on the stage, not a relative one

Using these properties, you can determine where the tap occurred in an `InteractiveObject`'s internal coordinates, as well as translate that action to the wider application's coordinate system. You may find that you don't need to interrogate these properties when the event is raised; just handle the event as you would any other event. Nevertheless, I want to make you aware that they exist on the event object, in case you want to made sure the tap happened within a given number of pixels of the press.

Here's how you create a press and tap gesture in the Hello Event application, which you created in the last section:

1. **Register an event listener for the** GESTURE_PRESS_AND_TAP **event:**

```
public function Main()
{
    addEventListener( PressAndTapGestureEvent.GESTURE_
        PRESS_AND_TAP, onPressAndTap );
    Multitouch.inputMode = MultitouchInputMode.GESTURE;
```

2. **Create a new method called** onPressAndTap **to handle the** PressAndTapGestureEvent:

```
}
private function onPressAndTap(
        e:PressAndTapGestureEvent ) :void
{
    // do something here
}
```

TransformGestureEvent

The gestures defined by TransformGestureEvent are likely to be the ones you use the most in your applications, as swipe, rotate, and zoom are all event types of this class.

In the following example, you see how to add a rotation gesture to a simple rectangle display object on the stage:

1. **Create a new application in Flash Professional and save it as** TransformGestureEvent.fla.

   This can be either an AIR for Android application or an iOS application; see Chapter 4 for how to create a new application.

2. **Use the Rectangle tool to draw a rectangle that is about 200 pixels wide by 200 pixels high on the stage.**

3. **Press F8 (Windows) or fn+F8 (Mac OS) to invoke the Convert to Symbol dialog box.**

4. **In the Convert to Symbol dialog box, type** MyRectangle **in the Name field.**

   The rectangle is converted to a MovieClip.

5. **Select the rectangle, and then in the Properties panel, type** MyRectangle **in the Instance name field.**

6. **Double-click the** MyRectangle MovieClip **instance on the stage to open the internals of the** MovieClip **for editing.**

7. **Drag the rectangle shape so that the small center circle denoting its center point aligns with the crosshair that denotes the** MovieClip's **registration point.**

8. **Click the Scene 1 link on the breadcrumb trail at the upper-left corner of the stage view to exit.**

9. **Move the `MovieClip` to the center of the stage for tidiness.**

10. **Create a new ActionScript 3.0 class called `Main` and save it as `Main.as` in the same directory as your application FLA.**

    This class will be the Document Class for your small application.

11. **Register an event listener to the stage for the `GESTURE_ROTATE` event, by placing this code inside the constructor:**

```
public function Main()
{
   stage.addEventListener(TransformGestureEvent.
        GESTURE_ROTATE, onRotate );
}
```

12. **Create a method called `onRotate` to handle the `GESTURE_ROTATE` event.**

    The `rotation` property of the `MyRectangle MovieClip` instance — referenced through the `myRectangle` instance name — is then incremented by the value of the `TransformGestureEvent`'s `rotation` property. Incrementing is achieved using += instead of just the = sign, which would just assign the current value of rotation, rather than add it on:

```
private function onRotate( e:TransformGestureEvent )
        :void
{
    myRectangle.rotation += e.rotation;
}
```

    Your Document Class code in its entirety now looks like this:

```
package
{
    import flash.display.MovieClip;
    import flash.events.TransformGestureEvent;

    public class Main extends MovieClip
    {
       public function Main()
       {
       stage.addEventListener(TransformGestureEvent.
         GESTURE_ROTATE, onRotate );
       }

       private function onRotate(
         e:TransformGestureEvent ) :void
       {
           myRectangle.rotation += e.rotation;
       }
    }
}
```

13. **Deselect everything on the stage.**

14. **In the Properties panel, type** Main **as the Document Class of your application.**

15. **Publish your application to a mobile device to test the effect.**

    I show you how to compile and install your application in Chapter 13 for Android devices and Chapters 16 and 17 for iOS devices.

    To test, place two fingers on the screen and then rotate them. You should see the rectangle rotating.

GesturePhase

The GesturePhase class is simply used to store public constant properties that represent the varying phases, or stages, of a gesture. The values are used with the phase property of the GestureEvent, TransformGestureEvent, and PressAndTapGestureEvent classes.

If you dig out the Hello Event application from earlier in the chapter, you can easily modify it to output the phase of the event too:

1. **Add an additional dynamic** TextField **to the stage and give it the instance name** phase.

   You can shrink the other TextFields if you need to make some room.

2. **Assign the** phase **property of the** GestureEvent **object to the phase** TextField.

   In the onGesture event handler, just below the line where you assign the event type to the gesture TextField, add the following:

```
    gesture.text = e.type;
    phase.text = ( e as GestureEvent ).phase;
}
```

When you run this application on your mobile device, you can observe the various phases that each GestureEvent reports. Note how TranformGestureEvent.GESTURE_SWIPE and GestureEvent.TWO_FINGER_TAP show only the event phase all. These two gestures are not comprised of individual phases; the entire gesture is completed in a single phase.

Detecting Orientation Change

A fun aspect to working with mobile devices is that they know which way is up! In addition to detecting acceleration/deceleration along three axes, the accelerometer that is built in is also able to detect orientation changes. As the user turns the device from a portrait to a landscape orientation, a StageOrientationEvent object is dispatched in your application. You can register an event listener to the stage for this, so you can get your application to perform logic each time it occurs.

In the preceding section you created an application called `TransformGestureEvent.fla`. In the following steps, I show you how to build upon the code in that application to add detection for orientation change:

1. **Open** `Main.as` **in Flash Professional.**

   This is the Document Class associated with `TransformGesture Event.fla`.

2. **Register an event listener to the stage for the** `ORIENTATION_CHANGE` **event:**

   ```
   public function Main()
   {
       stage.addEventListener(TransformGestureEvent.
           GESTURE_ROTATE, onRotate );
       stage.addEventListener( StageOrientationEvent.
           ORIENTATION_CHANGE,
   onStageOrientationChange );
   }
   ```

3. **Create a new method called** `onOrientationChange` **to handle the** `ORIENTATION_CHANGE` **event:**

   ```
       stage.addEventListener( StageOrientationEvent.
           ORIENTATION_CHANGE, onStageOrientationChange
           );
   }

   private function onOrientationChange(
           e:StageOrientationEvent ) :void
   {}
   ```

4. **Create a** `switch` **statement that evaluates the four possible orientations of the device, which are accessed using the** `afterOrientation` **property of the event object:**

   ```
   private function onOrientationChange(
           e:StageOrientationEvent ) :void
   {
       switch( e.afterOrientation )
       {
       case StageOrientation.DEFAULT:
       // The device is the right way up - the home
         button is at the bottom
       break;
       case StageOrientation.ROTATED_RIGHT:
       // The device has been rotated to the right
       break;
       case StageOrientation.ROTATED_LEFT:
   ```

```
        // The device has been rotated to the left
        break;
        case StageOrientation.UPSIDE_DOWN:
        // The device is upside down - the home button
          is at the top
        break;
    }
}
```

After the ORIENTATION_CHANGE event is raised, if the device has been rotated to the right, the e.afterOrientation property carries the value ROTATED_RIGHT, which you can then act upon to cause display objects on the screen to slide to the right. Were the device turned upside down, consider rotating display objects on the stage by 180 degrees, so that the user can still view them correctly.

The Stage object also exposes a Boolean property to allow you to check whether the device supports orientation changes. Although this property is true on most Android and iOS devices, it's good practice to put a check in place before your listener assignment, just in case you later decide to repackage your application for another type of device.

Looking at the code you just wrote to handle the ORIENTATION_CHANGE event, wrap the event registration with an if statement that evaluates the Stage.supportsOrientationChange property:

```
if( Stage.supportsOrientationChange )
{
    stage.addEventListener( StageOrientationEvent.
            ORIENTATION_CHANGE,
onStageOrientationChange );
}
```

Multitouch

The Multitouch class provides information about the device's support for contact that involves two or more touch points on the screen. It also manages how multitouch and gesture events are handled at runtime, as well as how many touch points the device on which your application is running supports.

Checking for TouchEvent support

The Multitouch class has a static Boolean property called supports TouchEvents that will return true if the device that your application is running on can dispatch TouchEvents.

I write my applications on a computer, and perform a fair amount of testing on my computer before I install the application on my mobile device for testing. My computer doesn't have a touch screen, so my application can dispatch only `MouseEvents`. Rather than rewriting code each time I move my application between these two environments, I use the `supportsTouch-Events` property to determine whether my application should set up event listeners for mouse or touch interaction.

Earlier in this chapter, I show you how to create an application called `HelloEvent`. Reopen `Main.as` — the Document Class associated with this application — in Flash Professional. Wrap all the code that is currently inside the constructor with an `if` statement that evaluates the `Multitouch.supportsTouchEvents` property. If it evaluates `true`, it's fine to register for touch events. Otherwise, the `else` clause is executed, which in my example prints *Touch events not supported* to the `supportedGesture` `TextField`:

```
public function Main()
{
    if( Multitouch.supportsTouchEvents )
    {
        addEventListener( PressAndTapGestureEvent.GESTURE_
            PRESS_AND_TAP, onPressAndTap );
        Multitouch.inputMode = MultitouchInputMode.GESTURE;
        var supported:Vector.<String>  = Multitouch.
            supportedGestures;
        for each (var item:String in supported)
        {
            supportedGesture.appendText( "\n"+item );
            stage.addEventListener( item, onGesture );
        }
    }
    else
    {
        supportedGesture.text = "Touch events not
            supported";
    }
}
```

The `supportsTouchEvents` Boolean will always return `true` on touch-screen devices.

Checking for GestureEvent support

Just as you need to check whether the mobile device supports `TouchEvents` before registering event listeners for them, you also need to check for `GestureEvents`. The property is exposed as a static Boolean called `supportsGestureEvents`.

In the previous code example, I show you how to create an `if` statement in the `HelloEvent.as` constructor to determine whether touch events are supported. Modify that code to instead check whether gesture events are supported:

```
public function Main()
{
   if( Multitouch.supportsGestureEvents )
   {
      //...
   }
   else
   {
      supportedGesture.text = "Gesture events not
         supported";
   }
}
```

This property will return `true` on touch-screen Android and iOS devices and return `false` on a computer.

Checking which gestures are supported

The Flash API defines a list of common touch gestures that are largely supported by the big device manufacturers (see `http://help.adobe.com/en_US/FlashPlatform/reference/actionscript/3/flash/events/GestureEvent.html` for an up-to-date list). Some devices may support all the gestures defined in the Flash API, whereas others may support only a subset. Because of this, it is important to verify that the `GestureEvent` you're going to register a listener for is in the list of supported gestures. This is exposed as a static `Vector` property of the `Multitouch` class.

In the following code, I'm iterating through the supported gestures. If the swipe gesture is supported, I add an event listener for it:

```
var supported:Vector.<String>  = Multitouch.
         supportedGestures;
for each( var item:String in supported )
{
   if( item == TransformGestureEvent.GESTURE_SWIPE )
   {
      addEventListener( TransformGestureEvent.GESTURE_
         SWIPE, onSwipe );
   }
}
```

If the gesture you want to use isn't supported by the device, you could consider using an alternative input gesture. However, you may find that your application simply won't work as you intended without the required gestures; in that case, display a message onscreen informing the user of this.

Checking how many touch points are supported

I've heard it said that the average person has less than five fingers per hand — perhaps 4.99 — but for the sake of simplicity, I'll round it to five.

Conveniently, both Android and iOS support a maximum of five simultaneous touch points. For those with more dexterity than me, this may come as a disappointment. But believe me, if you have more than five fingers and thumbs on the screen, I can't imagine you can see much of it!

The `Multitouch` class exposes a static property that tells you how many simultaneous touch points the device your application is running on supports, allowing you to verify that the user will be able to interact in the way you intended. You can read the maximum number of touch points supported by the mobile device like this:

```
var maxPoints:int = Multitouch.maxTouchPoints;
```

You can reference `Multitouch.maxTouchPoints` from most places in your code, so the placement of this code depends more on where you need to know the maximum touch points supported by the device than on where I tell you to put it. As you'd expect, this value changes only as you move your application onto a different model of device.

MultitouchInput mode

This class simply provides the valid values that can be assigned to the `inputMode` property of the `Multitouch` class. You can assign three values:

- ✔ NONE: All user contact with the touch screen is interpreted as a `MouseEvent`.

- ✔ TOUCH_POINT: Only the basic set of events defined by the `TouchEvent` class are dispatched.

- ✔ GESTURE: `ComplexTransform`, `PressAndTap`, and other `GestureEvent` events are dispatched, whereas simple `TouchEvents` such as `TOUCH_BEGIN` and `TAP` are interpreted as `MouseEvents`.

If you wanted your application to support just the basic `TouchEvents`, but not have them treated as `MouseEvents`, you'd set the multitouch input mode to `TOUCH_POINT`. Reopen the HelloEvent application you created earlier in this chapter, and modify it to use the `inputMode` `TOUCH_POINT`. Locate the line:

```
Multitouch.inputMode = MultitouchInputMode.GESTURE;
```

Change the line to:

```
MultiTouch.inputMode = MultitouchInputMode.TOUCH_POINT;
```

The application will now dispatch only TouchEvents. In most cases, you'll find the default setting GESTURE works perfectly well for your needs; in other words, you won't need to change inputMode.

By default, your application will have multitouch input mode set to GESTURE, meaning that all basic TouchEvents will be translated to and dispatched as MouseEvents. If you're listening for only MouseEvents in your application, you do not need to worry about configuring the multitouch input mode.

In this chapter, you've had a whistle-stop introduction to the enhanced APIs available to you when targeting mobile devices. If you are used to traditional input devices, the additional sensors make for a great deal of fun when developing your application.

Chapter 12

Building Mobile Flex Applications with Flash Builder

In This Chapter

▶ Introducing the Flex SDK and Flash Builder

▶ Building a Flex mobile application with Flash Builder

▶ Viewing and debugging the application on iOS and Android devices

*T*here comes a time in any Flash application's existence where the code-management features provided by the Flash Professional development environment become insufficient for your needs. Sometimes a less visual and more code-centric approach to the development of your application is required to maintain some law and order in large projects.

Flex is an open source software development kit (SDK), so you can download the SDK and compiler for free from Adobe and create applications in a text editor of your choice. As the developer, you are then free to distribute your application as you choose. Flash Builder 4.5 — from here on I'll call it Flash Builder — is an integrated development environment (IDE) that makes the development of Flash applications much easier than if they were written in Notepad, TextEdit, or even Flash Professional. For example, Flash Builder can compile your application as you're writing your code, informing you of errors. It also provides code hints as you type, making the speed at which you can write code impressive!

In this chapter, I show you how to use the Flash Builder IDE and walk you through some of the benefits of the Flex SDK — a library of ActionScript 3.0 visual components and classes that can help you to develop your Flash mobile applications faster. I focus on the newly introduced components that are optimized to run on mobile devices. I also explain how to use Flash Builder's advanced debugging tools to problem-solve your Flex application directly on an Android mobile device.

Introducing Mobile Application Development with the Flex SDK

Until now, you've been familiar with developing your applications by writing ActionScript 3.0 code in Adobe Flash Professional. As you become more experienced in Flash mobile application development, you will begin to find that you repeat tasks — duplicating code — in different projects and will want to look at ways to avoid this repetition. In this next section, I explain how using the Flex SDK in Flash Builder helps you to build applications faster.

What is Flex?

Adobe Flex is a software development kit (SDK) that allows you to build Flash applications rapidly using a set of precanned visual components and data objects. Think of Flex less like the creative and time-consuming "from scratch" carving of an ornate table (pure Flash application) and more like the assembly of an Ikea table. The finished article is functional and highly usable, but to get that extra level of individuality, you need to spend some extra time styling it to make it your own.

The emphasis of Flex applications has always been on loading and displaying data back to users; Flex executes those actions like a dream. Most of the elements, or components, you need in your application are provided for you to include in your code, such as data-loading components, buttons, containers, and lists. You can be confident that the Flex SDK code has gone through a sufficient amount of testing to leave you assured that it'll "just work"!

In the display list, Flex also works its magic, managing the layout of the visual elements in your application using layout rules defined by you, and applying a look and feel throughout your application with style rules that can be defined in a regular Cascading Style Sheet (CSS) document.

What makes the development of Flex applications so different from the development of pure ActionScript 3.0 Flash applications is the capability to assemble components by writing MXML (Macromedia eXtensible Markup Language), an XML-based declarative markup language. The bare bones of a Flex application can take shape quickly, with data and styling laid over the top later. Flex is extremely flexible, and after you're comfortable with the basics, I'm confident that you'll find working with Flex a civilized affair!

In the context of Flex application development, you'll often hear two names bandied around a lot: Halo and Spark. Halo was the original component set that came into existence when Flex 2 was launched back in 2006. With the arrival of Flex 4, a newer component set called Spark was made available alongside the older Halo components. The two sets of components are distinguished in MXML by the *MX* namespace prefix for Halo components and the *S* namespace prefix for Spark components. With this in mind, you can tell that this code declares a Halo button:

```
<mx:Button/>
```

whereas this code declares a Spark button

```
<s:Button/>
```

For mobile application development, it's important to use the subset of Spark components that have been optimized for use on mobile devices. Flash Builder warns you if your component selection isn't appropriate for mobile use.

Although MXML and CSS cover pretty much everything with your layout and styling, you write the logic of your Flex application in good old ActionScript 3.0. Whether you're handling an event triggered by a component or accessing geolocation information from the phone, you need to write this logic in ActionScript 3.0. What I've explained here is the *separation of concerns* process that is found in many SDKs, as well as in Flex. You create two conceptual layers in your application. The *presentation layer* is written in MXML and is responsible purely with what the user sees. The *business logic layer* is written in ActionScript 3.0 and is responsible for functionality that the application performs. Keeping to this concept of separation helps to remove the complexities in building large applications.

IDs in MXML are the same as variable names in pure ActionScript 3.0 code and instance names in Flash Professional. IDs act as a unique way of referencing a single component in your application. Whenever you declare a new MXML component in your markup, be sure to assign a value to its `id` attribute to enable easy access to the component and its properties in your accompanying ActionScript.

Acquiring the necessary tools

In 2005, Adobe launched Flex Builder 2, the first ActionScript 3.0 and Flex development tool to be built on the Eclipse IDE, software with which Java developers are familiar writing code. Flex Builder 2 went on to huge success; its name was later changed to Flash Builder.

You can download Flash Builder on a trial basis from `www.adobe.com/go/ try_flashbuilder`. After the trial period has expired, you'll need to purchase a license to continue using the software.

After downloading the software, run the installer application, which will take you through the installation of Flash Builder on your operating system.

Starting a Project in Flash Builder

Flash Builder has a host of preconfigured applications that can be set up in just a few clicks through the wizard process. After opening Flash Builder for the first time, follow these steps to begin a new Flex mobile project:

1. **Choose File⇨New⇨Flex Mobile Project.**

   The Create a Flex Mobile AIR Project dialog box opens, as shown in Figure 12-1.

2. **In the Project Name text box, type** MyFirstMobileProject.

3. **Click Next.**

   The Mobile Settings wizard screen appears.

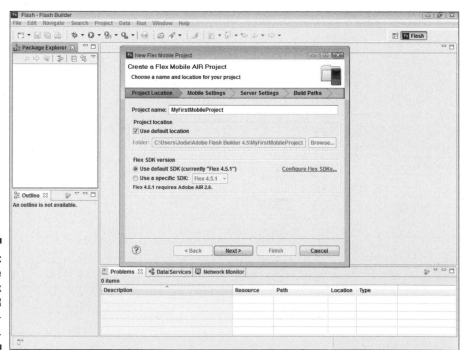

Figure 12-1:
The Create a Flex Mobile AIR Project dialog box.

4. Deselect BlackBerry Tablet OS from the target platforms section.

Flash Builder can compile your application for Apple iOS, BlackBerry Tablet OS, and Android. In my example, I have opted not to compile my application for BlackBerry Tablet OS, though you may later decide to support it, if you want.

5. Click the Application Template tab and select Tabbed Application.

6. In the Tabs text box, type News **and click the Add button.**

News appears in the list.

7. Repeat Step 6 to create a tab called Weather.

Your Tabbed Application template looks identical to Figure 12-2.

8. Click the Permissions tab, select Google Android from the Platform drop-down list, and select INTERNET and ACCESS_FINE_LOCATION.

Apple iOS, unlike Google Android, does not require permissions to be set on applications this way — as you'll see in the text that appears if you select the Apple iOS option from the platform drop-down.

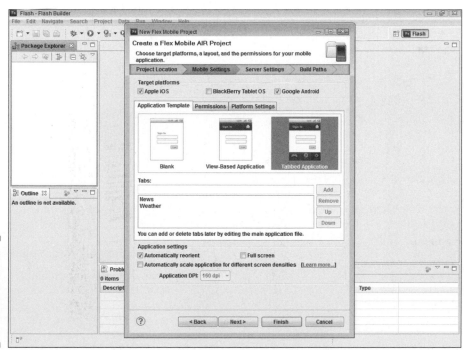

Figure 12-2: Tabs added to the Tabbed Application template.

9. Click Finish.

All the other settings can be left at their defaults.

Flash Builder creates your new application and presents you with `NewsView.mxml`, ready for editing in the editor window. The main application document `MyFirstMobileProject.mxml` is also opened but not currently selected for editing, as shown in Figure 12-3.

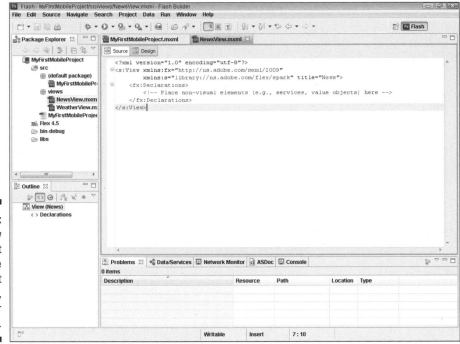

Figure 12-3:
The new MyFirst Mobile Project application, ready for editing.

If at any time you want to add or remove compiling your application for Apple iOS, BlackBerry Tablet OS, or Google Android, simply choose Project ➪ Properties➪Flex Build Packaging. Select the platform you want to add or remove support for, select or deselect the Enable This Target Platform option, and then click Apply.

Finding your bearings in the Flash Builder development environment

When your project first loads, you may be forgiven for feeling a little daunted by the various panels and labels that you're presented with. Fear not; the project workspace really isn't as bad as it looks, and you won't need too many of these options until you're far into developing Flex applications. Even so, it's a good idea to familiarize yourself with the most-used elements of Flash Builder, so I explain those in the list that follows. Figure 12-4 shows the location of each element on your screen.

- ✓ **Package Explorer:** Occupying the upper-left panel, this element shows the structure of your project and all the dependent files. At the very top of the hierarchy is the name of the project. Expanding the tree by clicking the + icon exposes a folder called `src`, where all the code you create for your application lives. Next, the Flex 4.5 SDK link library is denoted by an icon of a stack of books. Expanding the Flex 4.5 item by clicking the + icon exposes the various Flex libraries available to your application. At this stage, it's necessary to know only that they're there; I won't be asking you to do anything with them. Another folder, called `bin-debug`, is where the compiler in Flash Builder will build the SWF files. Finally, the `libs` folder is where you can place any third-party code libraries in the form of SWC files.

- ✓ **Outline:** Below the Package Explorer, the Outline panel provides an overview of all the properties and methods inside an MXML or ActionScript file. As MXML documents and AS 3.0 classes become lengthier and more complex, you can save time locating a particular method by using the Outline panel instead of skimming through the entire document.

- ✓ **Editor window:** The largest of all the panels, the Editor window is where you find the main application MXML document and type your code. To the far left is a gray line running vertically down the window. Right-click (Windows) or Control+click (Mac) and select Show Line Numbers from the context menu. See the line numbers appear? This feature is handy when you're trying to find a particular part of your code. You can turn off line numbers at any time by repeating this step.

- ✓ **Problems:** On face value, Problems doesn't sound like a particularly nice panel. No one likes problems! This one is actually welcome, because it displays a list of issues that Flash Builder detects in your code. By double-clicking a particular issue, you go directly to the site of the problem and can resolve it. No code has been written yet, so the Problems panel should display 0 items.

- ✓ **Run icon:** When you're ready to test an application with Flash Builder, you can run it by clicking the Run icon, which appears on the Launch toolbar as a green circle with a Play icon. You can also press Ctrl+F11 (Windows) or Command+F11 (Mac) or choose Run⇨Run from the main menu.

- ✓ **Debug icon:** Clicking this button does everything the Run icon does, plus more. Running your application with the debugger in Flash Builder allows you to insert breakpoints (markers you place on a line a code to stop the running of the application at that point so you can inspect all its properties) and view the output of any `trace()` messages you place in your code. Advanced debugging features, which are discussed at the end of this chapter, enable you to run your application on a connected mobile device while debugging it in Flash Builder. You can also press F11 on both Windows and Mac to run your application in debug mode.

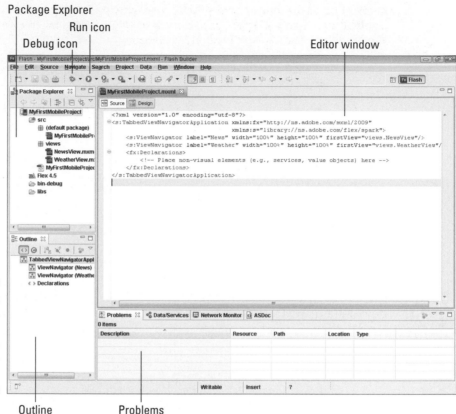

Package Explorer

Run icon

Debug icon

Editor window

Figure 12-4:
The work-
space
elements
in Flash
Builder.

Outline

Problems

The preceding list covers the panel essentials. You can find out more about the features of the Flash Builder development environment at http://help.adobe.com/en_US/flashbuilder/using/index.html.

Running an application

When you run the MyFirstMobileProject application — that Flash Builder generated in the previous steps — for the first time, Flash Builder invokes the Run Configurations dialog box and prompts you with Select a launch method. You can launch the application in the AIR runtime installed on your computer, or install the application on an attached mobile device as an AIR for Android application, a process known as *remote debugging*. Although it's possible to remote-debug an iOS application, Flash Builder cannot install the application on the iOS device for you — as it can with Android. You must install the application yourself; I explain how in Chapter 17.

In the following example, you specify a desktop run configuration for your application; later, you may opt to switch to running on a mobile device. Set the launch method by following these steps:

1. **In the Run Configurations dialog box, select On Desktop as the launch method.**

2. **From the Choose Device to Simulate drop-down list, select Google Nexus One.**

3. **Click the Apply button.**

   Your settings are saved.

4. **Click the Run button.**

   The application launches in an AIR application window on top of Flash Builder, as shown in Figure 12-5.

Congratulations! You've just compiled and run your first mobile Flex application.

You can change the run configurations for your application by clicking the downward-pointing arrow next to the Run button on the Launch toolbar and selecting Run Configurations from the menu.

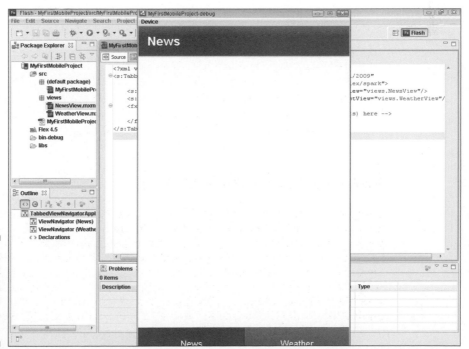

Figure 12-5:
The Flex mobile application running on the desktop.

Creating a Simple Flex Mobile Application

One of the simplest types of applications you can build that demonstrates the capabilities of the Flex framework is a feed reader. A feed reader loads an RSS- or Atom-formatted XML document and displays the contents in a more visually digestible way. In the following steps, I show you how to add to the MyFirstMobileProject application, which you created earlier in the chapter, to create a simple news-reading application for the BBC News:

1. **Open** `NewView.mxml` **for editing in Flash Builder.**

   If the file isn't already open and its contents displayed, double-click `NewsView.mxml` in the `src\views\` package in the Package Explorer panel.

2. **Using MXML, declare a new** `List` **instance nested inside the** `<s:View>` **tags. Give it the** id `newsList` **and set the** `width` **and** `height` **attributes to 100%:**

   ```
       </fx:Declarations>
       <s:List id="newsList" width="100%" height="100%"/>
   </s:View>
   ```

   A `List` is a precanned Flex component that displays a list of items vertically and is populated by assigning a sequence of data to its `data Provider` property.

   Setting the width and height to these values makes the component as big as its parent container, in this case, the full width and height of the `TabbedViewNavigtorApplication`'s content pane.

3. **Declare a** `HTTPService` **instance inside the** `<fx:Declarations>` **tags. Assign the** `id` **attribute as** `newsService`, **the** `resultFormat` **attribute to** `e4x`, **and the** `url` **attribute to** `http://feeds.bbci.co.uk/news/ rss.xml`:

   ```
   <fx:Declarations>
       <!-- Place non-visual elements (e.g., services,
           value objects) here -->
       <s:HTTPService id="newsService" url="http://feeds.
           bbci.co.uk/news/rss.xml" resultFormat="e4x"/>
   </fx:Declarations>
   ```

The `HTTPService` component can load data in a variety of formats and from numerous types of services. For feeds, the data is almost always XML formatted, and `HTTPService` handles it perfectly. Setting the `resultFormat` to `e4x` treats the loaded data as XML that can be queried using E4X syntax. I discuss E4X in Chapter 8.

4. **Place the mouse cursor at the end of** `<s:HTTPService`, **then press the spacebar.**

   A list of autocompletion options is displayed below the cursor.

5. **Type** result **and press Enter.**

   A new attribute called `result` is created in your `HTTPService` MXML declaration. The autocompletion list appears again, this time with a single option, Generate Result Handler.

6. **Press Enter.**

   Flash Builder automatically creates a `<fx:Script>` block in your document and adds a new ActionScript 3.0 method to it called `newsService_ resultHandler()`. A reference to this method is also added to the `result` attribute of the `HTTPService` MXML declaration.

7. **Being careful not to click anywhere else, type** onNewsServiceResult.

   The name of the ActionScript 3.0 method is automatically changed when you type within the `result` attribute, as shown in the following code:

```
<?xml version="1.0" encoding="utf-8"?>
<s:View xmlns:fx="http://ns.adobe.com/mxml/2009"
        xmlns:s="library://ns.adobe.com/flex/spark"
        title="News">
   <fx:Script>
      <![CDATA[
         import mx.rpc.events.ResultEvent;
         protected function onNewsServiceResult(event:
         ResultEvent):void
         {
             // TODO Auto-generated method stub
         }
      ]]>
   </fx:Script>
   <fx:Declarations>
      <!-- Place non-visual elements (e.g., services,
         value objects) here -->
      <s:HTTPService result="onNewsServiceResult(ev
         ent)" id="newsService" url="http://feeds.bbci.
         co.uk/news/rss.xml" resultFormat="e4x"/>
   </fx:Declarations>
   <s:List id="newsList" width="100%" height="100%"/>
</s:View>
```

If typing a new method name into the `result` attribute doesn't rename the ActionScript 3.0 method in the script block, just manually change them both to the same name, and your code will work fine.

8. **Create a new** XMLListCollection **object from the news article titles returned from the service; then assign it to the** dataProvider **property of the** newsList.

```
protected function onNewsServiceResult(event:ResultEve
        nt):void
{
   var collection:XMLListCollection = new
        XMLListCollection( event.result.channel.item.
        title );
   newsList.dataProvider = collection;
}
```

When E4X queries are used to extract values from a larger XML document, the results are put into an object called an XMLList. By creating a
new XMLListCollection object, and providing the XMLList from the
E4X query as the source, the data can be provided to any List component for display.

If you run your application using the steps described in the preceding section, you see that the List component on the News tab is populated with a
list of news articles from the BBC. You can scroll through the list by swiping
up and down. Note that an Internet connection is required to load the data.

You can get Flash Builder to generate almost all of your result handler methods for you. When the Generate Result Handler option is selected, pressing
Ctrl+spacebar (Windows) or Command+spacebar (Mac) while the cursor is
inside the quotation marks of an MXML component's event handler assignment invokes the code completion tooltip. Pressing Enter causes Flash Builder
to automatically create the ActionScript for an event handler in the script
block of your MXML document. Flash Builder places a reference to the event
handler between the quotation marks. All that's left for you to do is to modify
the name of the handler.

With your feed reader app built, the next step is to let the user select a news
item from the List component and be taken to the full article on the BBC
News website in the web browser on his or her mobile device. Follow these
steps to add click and navigational functionality to the Flex mobile application:

 1. **Declare a new** Vector **member variable inside the** <s:Script> **block
    of your application, just below the two** import **statements, to store
    each of the articles' URLs:**

    ```
    import mx.rpc.events.ResultEvent;
    private var links:Vector.<String>;
    protected function onNewsServiceResult(event:ResultEve
            nt):void
    ```

    Along with a title, each item that comes back in the XML feed from the
    BBC has a corresponding URL. Creating a Vector object accessible
    from anywhere within the NewsView component allows a series of links
    added to the Vector to be referenced later.

2. **Initialize the** `links Vector` **object from inside the** `onNewsService Result()` **method:**

```
protected function onNewsServiceResult(event:Result
        Event):void
{
   links = new Vector.<String>();
   var collection:XMLListCollection = new
        XMLListCollection( event.result.channel.item.
        title );
   newsList.dataProvider = collection;
}
```

3. **Declare a new** `XMLList` **variable called** `newsServiceLinks,` **and assign it all the URLs received in the loaded BBC XML feed — presented in the feed as the** `link` **property of each** `item`**:**

```
links = new Vector.<String>();
var newsServiceLinks:XMLList = event.result.channel.
        item.link;
```

4. **Iterate through the** `XMLList`**, and "push" each URL value from the** `XMLList` **onto the** `links Vector` **instance:**

```
var newsServiceLinks:XMLList = event.result.channel.
        item.link;
for each( var item:XML in newsServiceLinks )
{
   links.push( item.toString() );
}
```

5. **Place the mouse cursor at the end of** `<s:List`**, then press the spacebar.**

   A list of autocompletion options is displayed below the cursor.

6. **Type** click **and press Enter.**

   A new attribute called `click` is created in your `List` MXML declaration. The autocompletion list appears again, this time with a single option, Generate Result Handler.

7. **Press Enter.**

   Flash Builder adds a new ActionScript 3.0 method to the script block called `newsList_clickHandler()`. A reference to this method is also added to the `click` attribute of the `List` MXML declaration.

8. **Being careful not to click anywhere else, type** onNewsListClick.

   The name of the ActionScript 3.0 method is automatically changed when you type within the `click` attribute. Your `List` markup appears like this:

```
    </fx:Declarations>
    <s:List click="onNewsListClick(event)"
        id="newsList"  width="100%" height="100%"/>
</s:View>
```

In your script block, the new autogenerated click event handler looks identical to this:

```
protected function onNewsListClick(event:MouseEvent):v
        oid
{
    // TODO Auto-generated method stub
}
```

9. **Inside the** `onNewListClick()` **method, invoke the device's web browser using the ActionScript 3.0** `navigateToURL()` **method. Supply a URL from the** `links` **Vector object that exists at the same index as the** `selectedIndex` **value of the** `newsList`:

```
protected function onNewsListClick(event:MouseEvent):v
        oid
{
    navigateToURL( new URLRequest( links[ event.
        currentTarget.selectedIndex ] ) );
}
```

Because the URLs in the `Vector` and the items in the `List` component are in the same order, an item at position 0 in the `List` corresponds to the URL at position 0 in the `Vector`. Because of this relationship, I can use the `selectedIndex` property of the `List` — accessed through the `event.currentTarget` property — to select the correct URL from the `Vector` and supply it to the `URLRequest`, which is in turn used to invoke the `navigateToURL()` method.

Run your application to see what it now does. Press Ctrl+F11 (Windows) or Command+F11 (Mac) and watch the application load on the desktop to the News screen, with the `List` populated with news items. Click one of the items and observe it open a new web browser window and navigate to the chosen article on the BBC News website. Although you can see that the application is running on the desktop, don't take my word for it that it runs on your mobile device. The next stage is to verify that all these features work as expected on the target device.

Setting Up a Debugging Session for an Android Device

One handy feature in Flash Builder is the capability to debug applications directly on a mobile device. If you have a bug that seems to crop up only when the application is running on the mobile device, this feature could save you hours of poking around in your code.

From Flash Builder, you can compile, install, and launch your application onto a connected mobile device; then you allow the application to connect back to Flash Builder so it can insert breakpoints and read any trace() statements placed in the code. Follow these steps to run your application on a mobile device and check it with the debugger in Flash Builder:

1. **Connect your device to your computer using a USB cable.**

2. **Ensure that the USB Connected notification appears in the status bar of your Android device.**

3. **On the mobile device, navigate to Settings⇨Applications⇨Development and select USB Debugging.**

   A notification is shown in the status bar on the device, as shown in Figure 12-6.

4. **Press the down-facing arrow next to the Debug button on the Launch toolbar (refer to Figure 12-4).**

   A context menu appears.

Figure 12-6: USB Connected and Debugging notifications on the Android status bar.

5. **Choose Debug Configurations from the context menu.**

   The Debug Configurations dialog box opens, as shown in Figure 12-7.

   If a launch configuration for your application doesn't exist when you open the Run or Debug Configuration dialog box, simply double-click the Mobile Application label in the list on the left. A new launch configuration is created for your application.

6. **Select Google Android from the target platform drop-down list.**

7. **Select On Device as the launch method.**

8. **Select Debug via USB (Recommended).**

9. **Press Apply to save the new configuration.**

10. **Press Debug to start the debug process.**

    A progress bar appears at the lower-right corner to notify you that Flash Builder is compiling and launching. After a short delay, the application is installed and launched on the connected Android device, as shown in Figure 12-8.

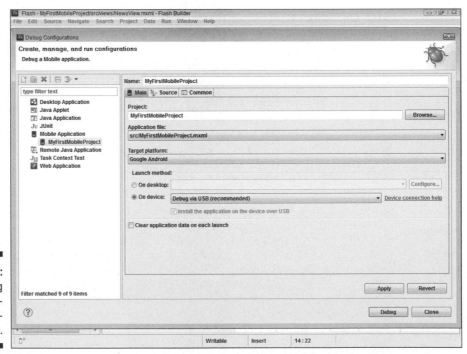

Figure 12-7: The Debug Configurations dialog box.

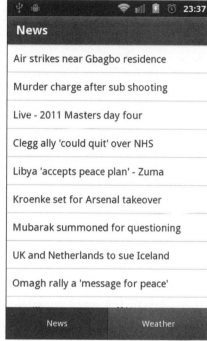

Figure 12-8:
The MyFirst
Mobile
Project app
running on
an Android
device.

Now that your debugging session has begun, you can skip to the section about debugging code after your application is running.

Setting up a debugging session for an iOS device

Unlike on Android, debugging on iOS devices is a little more convoluted because Apple doesn't allow applications other than iTunes to install application files onto iOS devices. There is also no mechanism on iOS to allow Flash Builder and your application to share runtime debugging information over a USB cable. Fortunately, the clever people at Adobe have programmed the iOS Flash application container and Flash Builder so that they can conduct a debugging session over a local Wi-Fi network — a process called *remote debugging*. Provided your device and computer are connected to the same local network, and your computer isn't hiding behind and overly aggressive firewall application, you can debug your Flex mobile application on your iOS device using the remote debugging technique.

Preparing your application for debugging on iOS

Follow these steps to prepare Flash Builder and your application for remote debugging:

1. **Click the down-facing arrow next to the Debug button on the Launch toolbar (refer to Figure 12-4).**

   A context menu appears.

2. **Select Debug Configurations from the context menu.**

   The Debug Configurations dialog box opens (refer to Figure 12-7).

3. **Select Apple iOS from the target platform drop-down list.**

4. **Select On Device as the launch method.**

5. **Select Standard as the packing method.**

   Selecting the other option — Fast — causes Flash Builder to package the application more quickly, but the iOS application it creates hasn't undergone additional optimization steps in the packaging process. Applications you submit to the App Store should be packaged through the Standard packaging method, so it makes sense to use this method during device testing too.

   Below the packaging method you can see two messages: One informs you that you must manually install the application on the device, and the other warns you that packaging settings have not been configured.

6. **Click Configure.**

   The Flex Build Packaging properties for Apple iOS dialog window opens, as shown in Figure 12-9.

7. **Browse to the location of your iOS P12 Certificate.**

   I show you how to obtain a digital certificate from Apple in Chapter 15 and how to convert an Apple certificate to a P12 certificate in Chapter 16.

8. **Browse to the location of your iOS Provisioning Profile.**

   I show you how to obtain a Provisioning Profile in Chapter 15. If you haven't yet provisioned the iOS device you want to debug your application on, follow the steps in Chapter 15.

9. **Click Apply and then click OK.**

   The Flex Build Packaging properties for Apple iOS dialog window closes, and the packaging settings warning message in the Debug Configurations dialog is removed.

10. **Click Configure Network Debugging.**

    A dialog box displays the settings for network debugging.

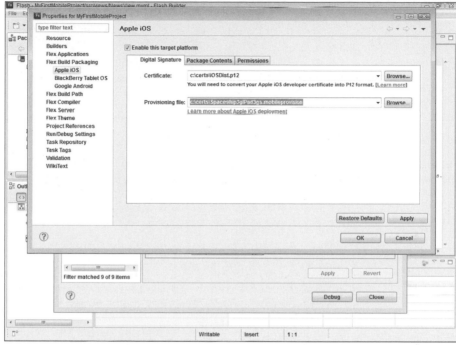

Figure 12-9:
Configuring
the Flex
Build
Packaging
properties
for Apple
iOS.

11. **Select the network interface — the hardware that your network connection enters your computer through — from the drop-down list.**

    If you're unsure which one to select, often the one you need will have a number in brackets that starts with 192.168. If you don't see this, refer to your computer manufacturers documentation for support.

12. **Click Apply, then click OK.**

    The dialog box closes.

Starting the iOS debugging process

After following the previous set of steps to configure the packaging and network settings for your application, follow these steps to compile a debug version of your application, install it on your iOS device, and connect a Flash Builder debugging session to it:

1. **Click Debug on Debug Configurations.**

    The Certificate Password dialog box is displayed.

2. **Enter the password you set for your P12 certificate and click OK.**

    The Packaging dialog box informs you that your application is being packaged, and that it may take several minutes. When the packaging is complete, the dialog box changes to ask you to install the application on your iOS device.

3. **Click Show Package in Explorer (Windows) or Show Package in Finder (Mac) — item 3 in the steps listed in the dialog box.**

   A new window opens on your operating system, displaying files created during the packaging process. The important file is the .IPA file.

4. **Connect your iOS device to your computer's USB port.**

5. **Open iTunes on your computer.**

6. **Drag the .IPA file — presented to you in Step 3 — into iTunes.**

   Your application is listed in the applications section of your iTunes library.

7. **Right-click (Windows) or Command+click (Mac) and choose Sync from the context menu.**

   iTunes performs a synchronization with your connected iOS device.

8. **Launch the application on the device.**

   Flash Builder connects to the application running on the iOS device, and the Waiting for Debugger Connection dialog closes.

After the application is running on the iOS device and Flash Builder is connected to it, you can start debugging your code, which I cover in the next section.

Debugging code after your application is running on a mobile device

After you've completed the steps to set up a debugging session for either an Android or iOS device, you can begin adding breakpoints to your code and observing the output of `trace()` statements while the application is running on the device. Follow these steps to debug the MyFirstMobileProject application, which you built earlier in this chapter:

1. **Open** `NewsView.mxml` **in Flash Builder.**

2. **Double-click the line number for the line where the** `navigateToURL` **method is called inside the** `onNewsListClick()` **method.**

   In my code, this is line number 27, so I click the 27 in the left margin. A blue dot appears denoting that a breakpoint is in place.

3. **On the mobile device running the application, press one of the news items in the list.**

   Flash Builder immediately responds with a Confirm Perspective Switch dialog box, which requests your permission to switch to the debugging perspective.

4. **Press Yes.**

   Flash Builder changes to the debug perspective and highlights the line of code at which the breakpoint occurred, as shown in Figure 12-10.

5. **Press F8 to make the application continue past the breakpoint.**

   Selecting another item in the list triggers the breakpoint again, unless you double-click the blue dot next to your code to remove the breakpoint.

Later, you can debug the application again by pressing F11 or clicking the Debug button on the Launch toolbar (refer to Figure 12-4).

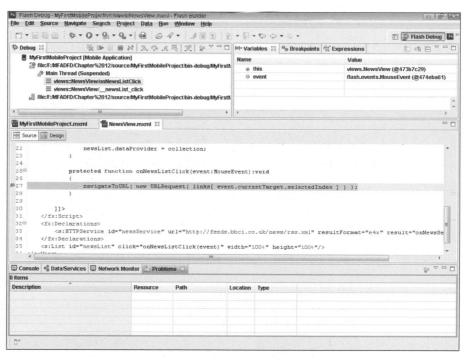

Figure 12-10: A breakpoint triggered in Flash Builder.

Flash Builder relies on the Google Android SDK and drivers installed on your computer to be kept up to date with the feverish pace at which Google releases changes to the Android operating system. You should run the Google SDK Manager — covered in more detail in Chapter 14 — once a week. That way, you won't find yourself trying to debug and wondering why Flash Builder claims it cannot find a connected mobile device!

Part IV
Getting Your App onto a Mobile Device

The 5th Wave   By Rich Tennant

"Other than this little glitch with the landscape view, I really love my iPhone."

In this part . . .

Part IV is the place where your Flash mobile application and your mobile device meet for the first time. Sounds quite romantic, doesn't it?

Chapter 13 looks at compiling a Flash mobile application and running it on Android devices. Chapter 14 looks at how to use Google's tools to manage applications on an Android device. Chapter 15 focuses on the process of signing up for the Apple iOS Developer Program, and how to set up your iOS devices for testing your application. Chapter 16 looks at how you cross-compile a Flash mobile application for iOS. Chapter 17 explains the process for installing an iOS application on an iOS device.

Chapter 13

Compiling and Packaging an AIR for Android Application

In This Chapter

▶ Preparing your application for publishing

▶ Making manual changes to the application's configuration file

▶ Signing the application with a self-signing certificate

▶ Compiling your Flash application for Android

*I*magine if users had to download all your application's contents individually and then ensure that it was all placed in the correct locations on their mobile device's file system before they could use your application. I doubt that scenario would make you or your app particularly popular. Instead, now that you've designed the user interface and written the code for your mobile Flash application, you need to assemble everything into a single tidy file, an APK, that can be easily distributed to your users. This process is referred to as *compiling and packaging*.

Since Adobe introduced the AIR for Android packager to Flash Professional, the workflow of creating an application and running it on your Android device has become a breeze. Without needing to leave Flash Professional, you can compile, package, and then install your application on a device for testing in just a few minutes.

In this chapter, I explain the packaging workflow for AIR for Android applications, including how to attach the all-important Menu icon.

Creating the Icon Artwork

If you've used an Android OS device, you already know that installed applications are represented by a small square graphic accompanied by the application's name. These applications are almost always displayed in a grid layout, across multiple scrolling screens.

If you package your application without specifying icon files, Android OS will use a default icon instead. Although the default icon is acceptable when you're developing and testing the application, it's not acceptable for submission to the Android Market — your app will be rejected for looking incomplete. The icon sizes required for applications targeting Android OS are 36x36 pixels, 48x48 pixels, and 72x72 pixels. Only one of the three will be required by the mobile device, but all three must be present in the application so that Android OS can determine the appropriate dimensions based on the device's screen resolution. Follow these steps to create the icon PNG images for your AIR for Android application:

1. **Go to the directory of your application FLA and create a new folder called** `icons`.

   This new directory is where you'll save the file you're about to create.

2. **Create a new PNG image measuring 512 pixels by 512 pixels.**

   You can use any graphics creation software to make your image, as long as it can output the image as a PNG file. I prefer using Fireworks or Photoshop; you might have your own preference.

   Creating source (or reference) artwork at the largest size means that quality is retained if the artwork is scaled down. Starting with the smallest size and then attempting to scale up causes distortions in the artwork.

   I suggest creating your new image at 512x512 pixels because that is the largest icon size required by both Android and iOS. Even though this chapter focuses on Android and you may not plan to deploy to iOS at this time, it's best to keep all your assets in a state that permits reuse across both platforms, in case you change your mind. By creating your reference graphics at the 512x512-pixel size, you can be sure that you won't have additional scaling rework to do in the future.

   Keep your icon design simple. The icons are small on the device, so intricate designs are likely to be lost when scaled down to 36x36 pixels.

3. **Save the image as** `icon512x512.png`.

   The 512x512-pixel image I created for my application is shown in Figure 13-1.

4. **Resize the graphic to 72 pixels by 72 pixels.**

5. **Save it as** `icon72x72.png`.

6. **Resize the graphic to 48 pixels by 48 pixels.**

7. **Save it as** `icon48x48.png`.

8. **Resize the graphic to 36 pixels by 36 pixels.**

9. **Save it as** `icon36x36.png`.

You should have four PNG files in the `icons` folder.

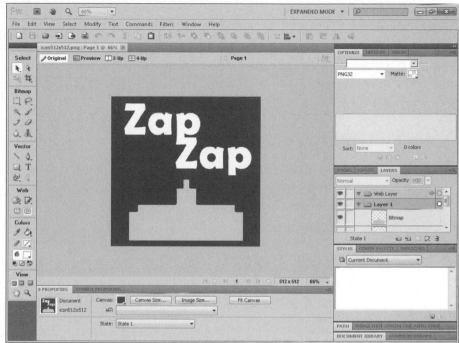

Figure 13-1:
An example
512x512-
pixel icon.

Your icons are now complete. In the next section, I show you how to include these icons in your Flash application so that they appear when your application is installed on an Android device.

Unlike iOS, Android doesn't add rounded corners or glass effects to your icons. If you'd like your icons to appear the same as they do on iOS devices, you need to include the rounded corners and glass effects in your own artwork. Remember to make the PNG background transparent when exporting, or the rounded corners won't appear as desired against the device background.

Modifying the AIR for Android Publish Settings in Flash Professional

You'll configure the main publish settings for your Android application in the AIR for Android Publish Settings dialog box. Open Flash Professional and choose File⇨AIR for Android Settings. The AIR for Android Settings dialog box opens, as shown in Figure 13-2.

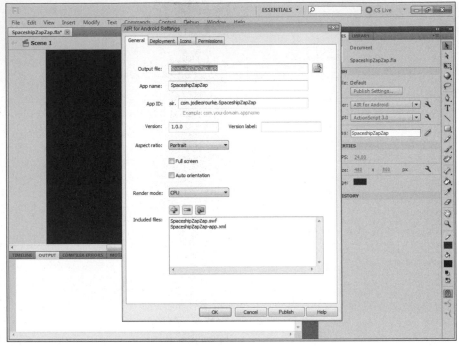

Figure 13-2:
AIR for
Android
Settings dia-
log box.

The General tab

The General tab is the first tab presented to you when you open the AIR for Android Settings dialog box. The fields on this tab contain the fundamental configuration settings for your AIR for Android application:

✔ **Output File:** The filename you give to the APK application file when it is generated. By default, Flash Professional assigns this file the same name as your application FLA, but gives it an APK file extension instead. If the default name isn't to your liking, you can change it by entering a new name.

✔ **App Name:** The friendly name for your application, which will appear below the icon on Android devices. Try to keep it between 12 and 14 characters in length or it will be truncated.

✔ **App ID:** A unique name for your app. No other application in the Android Marketplace should have the same ID as your app.

To prevent name collisions, you can use reverse domain notation, where you take a website domain name that you own and assemble it backward and then put your application name on the end. For example:

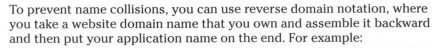

```
com.jodieorourke.SpaceshipZapZap
```

✔ **Version:** The version number you assign to each release of your application. Each time you make a modification, a new IPA is generated for submission to Apple.

✔ **Version Label:** An optional friendly tag to the application version, enabling you to identify the changes made in it.

✔ **Aspect Ratio:** The display orientation for your application upon startup. This drop-down list is set to Portrait by default, though you can change this to Landscape if you'd rather have your application start in Landscape mode.

✔ **Full Screen:** The display area for your application. The application will appear with the phone's status bar at the top or in the device's entire viewable display area. Gaming applications tend to operate in full-screen mode, whereas utility and productivity applications tend to operate with the device status bar remaining visible. The setting is largely up to you.

✔ **Auto Orientation:** Automatically reorient the application when the device is rotated from a portrait (upright) hold to a landscape (sideways) hold.

✔ **Render Mode:** Render display objects on the target device. You have three possible selections from the drop-down list:

   • *CPU:* The application uses the CPU (central processing unit) to render all display objects. No hardware acceleration is used.

   • *GPU:* The application uses the mobile device's GPU (graphics processing unit) to render bitmaps.

   • *Auto:* (At the time this book was published, the Auto option was not properly implemented in Flash Professional.) Currently, this option does the same as the CPU setting. In the future, the intention is that this setting will allow your application to make the decision whether to render graphics using the CPU or GPU. For the time being, this setting is best avoided.

As a general rule, select GPU so that your application will use the enhanced performance of the mobile device's dedicated graphics hardware as opposed to all rendering computation having to be handled by the device's CPU. This is particularly important for gaming applications, where objects move around the display rapidly and change frequently.

✔ **Included Files:** The files that will be included in the resulting APK file. Unless you're packaging additional files of your own into the Android application, such as a custom database file, you don't need to modify the Included Files settings from the default.

The Deployment tab

The Deployment tab, shown in Figure 13-3, contains the settings required by the AIR for Android packager part of the publishing process. The top section requests the information required to digitally sign your AIR for Android application, the middle section determines what type of application the packager should create, and the bottom section determines what to do with the application after it has been created.

The following list describes the fields that you see on the Deployment tab:

- ✔ **Certificate:** The path to the P12 certificate file that you will use to sign your application. Because you're able to self-sign your Android application, it's easiest to click the Create button to open the Create Self-Signed Digital Certificate dialog box, which generates a valid certificate for you. Creating the certificate and applying it in Flash Professional are discussed in more detail in the "Signing the Application" section, later in this chapter.

- ✔ **Password:** The password assigned to the P12 certificate. The password is required to be able to use the certificate. Selecting the Remember Password for This Session check box means that you won't be required to enter the password again until Flash Professional is closed and restarted.

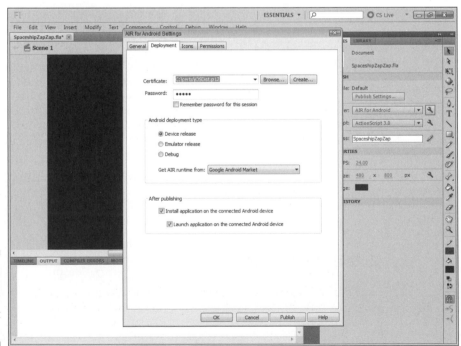

Figure 13-3:
The AIR
for Android
Deployment
settings.

✔ **Android Deployment Type:** The type of APK application file that Flash Professional will build when you publish your application. You have three settings to choose from:

- *Device Release:* Compiles the application to run on an Android device.

- *Emulator Release:* Compiles the application to run on the Android Emulator desktop software. You can find out more about the Android Emulator at `http://developer.android.com/guide/developing/tools/emulator.html`.

- *Debug:* Compiles the application to run on an Android device and also carry additional tools so that the Flash Professional debugger console can receive `trace()` output from the application when it's running on the Android device.

- *Get AIR runtime from:* The user receives the AIR runtime from Google Android Market or Amazon Appstore — a competing Android app store run by Internet retailer Amazon. (When a user installs your application on a device but doesn't have the AIR runtime installed, the user is prompted to download it.) My preference is to select Google Android Market.

✔ **After Publishing:** What Flash Professional does with your application after it has been packaged:

- *Install application on the connected Android device:* Removes the need for you to use command-line tools to perform the installation manually. With this option selected, after the APK file for your application has been created, it is automatically installed on an Android device that is connected to your computer (via USB). The device must be recognized as being connected by the computer, and the device should show a USB Connection notification on the status bar.

- *Launch Application on the Connected Android Device:* Automatically launches the application on the connected Android device after installation.

The Icons tab

The Icons tab carries the information relating to the icon files that will be packaged into the APK application file. This tab also shows a list of the all the required icon sizes for your AIR for Android application. For applications targeting Android OS devices, you are required to supply icons at 36x36, 48x48, and 72x72 pixels in size, as shown in Figure 13-4.

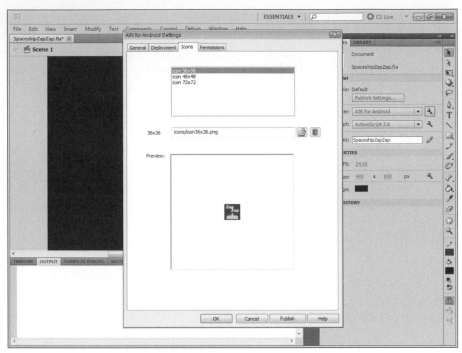

Figure 13-4:
Setting AIR
for Android
icons.

Follow these steps to associate the icon files created earlier in this chapter with each of the sizes in the list:

1. **Select icon 36x36 from the list.**

   36x36 appears next to the file-path text box.

2. **Click the Open File icon to the left of the file-path text box.**

   A system File Open dialog box opens.

3. **Browse to the `icons` folder and select `icon36x36.png`.**

   Earlier, in the "Creating the Icon Artwork" section, you created a selection of icons specifically for AIR for Android applications. Select the 36x36-pixel icon you created. You can see the path to the icon (refer to Figure 13-4).

4. **Repeat Steps 1–3 for the other icons shown in the list.**

After you've configured your icons, you don't need to do it again unless you change the icons that you want to associate with your application. Flash Professional saves the icon associations with your application FLA file.

The Permissions tab

This Permissions tab in the AIR for Android Settings dialog box, shown in Figure 13-5, manages things that you want the Android operating system to allow your application to do, such as using the extended ActionScript 3.0 features afforded to mobile devices.

When users install the application for the first time, they are notified of the permissions that the application is requesting, and they can accept or decline the application. Your application's default permissions do not allow it to access the Internet or use features such as geolocation — you must ask for these permissions. It is also important to request only the permissions that your application will use, rather than simply selecting them all, because users are less likely to install an application that is requesting all manner of permissions. Applications that request a full set of permissions on a device often raise the suspicion of being malicious. Remember that you're asking permission because the user is taking a risk or giving up something in return for granting it to you, so try not to ask for too much from the user!

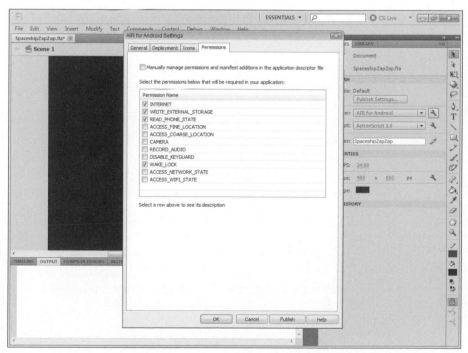

Figure 13-5: Add or remove Android permissions.

Permissions are chosen by selecting the check box next to them in the list. The following is a summary of what enabling each of the permissions does:

- **INTERNET:** Allows the application to communicate with the Internet, if available. This option also permits AIR applications to display HTML content loaded from the Internet, using the `HTMLLoader` class. If your application needs to communicate with the outside world, you need to select this option.

- **WRITE_EXTERNAL_STORAGE:** Allows the application to write data to a file on the local file system, such as to a database file. If your application writes data to a local file, you should enable this option.

- **READ_PHONE_STATE:** Allows the application to see changes in the device's status, such as an incoming call, so that it can mute audio that might be playing. Out of courtesy to your user, if your application plays audio, you should enable this.

- **ACCESS_FINE_LOCATION:** Permits the application to access the GPS data corresponding to the device's location. If your application requires device GPS coordinates — using the Geolocation classes — you need to select this option.

- **ACCESS_COARSE_LOCATION:** Permits the application to access less precise location data using the device's proximity to a cell tower or Wi-Fi network. If your application uses ActionScript features that require access to basic location data from the device, you should enable this option.

- **CAMERA:** Allows the application to access the device's camera. If your application captures pictures or video from the camera, you need to select this option.

- **RECORD_AUDIO:** Allows the application to access the device's microphone. If you're capturing audio from the user, you should select this option.

- **DISABLE_KEYGUARD:** Permits the application to disable the phone from invoking the key guard (screen lock) while it is running. If you expect your user to be viewing your application for extended periods of time without needing to touch the screen, you should select this option.

- **WAKE_LOCK:** Allows your application to prevent the phone's processor from going to sleep or the screen from dimming during periods of inactivity when your application is running. Again, if you think your user will continue to view your application for extended periods of time without interacting with the touch screen, you should select this option.

- **ACCESS_NETWORK_STATE:** Allows your application to access information about the network interfaces running on the device. If your application requires information such as the device's IP address on the current network, you should select this option.

- **ACCESS_WIFI_STATE:** Allows the application to access information about the Wi-Fi network to which the device is connected. If your app needs information about the Wi-Fi network's name (SSID), select this option.

At the top of the Permissions tab is a check box called Manually Manage Permissions and Manifest Additions in the Application Descriptor File. Leave this option deselected, unless you're feeling adventurous and want to modify the code inside the application descriptor XML file yourself.

At least one permission must be selected from the list of available permissions for your application to be compiled and packaged. Clicking Publish without first selecting one or more permissions will result in an error dialog box informing you that the application has not specified its permission requirements in `application.xml`.

After they are set, these permission settings are saved with your application FLA file, so they need to be modified only when the permissions required by your application change.

Modifying the Application Descriptor File

The Application Descriptor File is an XML document that accompanies all AIR applications. This file stores the settings that you configure using the friendly AIR for Android Settings dialog box in Flash Professional.

Sometimes you may want to edit the Application Descriptor File manually. Advanced or new Android settings that aren't offered in Flash Professional may have to be added to the XML file by hand. Editing the file isn't hard, but I'm going to walk you through changing a few properties in it so that you feel comfortable should you need to edit it on your own later.

Earlier in the chapter, you modified the permissions for your application using the Application & Installer Settings dialog box in Flash Professional. When you select permissions from the list on the Permissions tab, XML is written to the Application Descriptor File to indicate that your application should request that permission when the app is installed. You can remove these permissions by modifying the Application Descriptor File directly. To do that, follow these steps:

1. **Browse to the directory on your file system containing your AIR for Android application FLA.**

2. **Open the Application Descriptor File.**

   The name of this file is automatically constructed by Flash Professional using the name of your application FLA file, with a `-app.xml` suffix.

   If you cannot locate the file, you may need to execute the Test Movie feature in Flash Professional by pressing Ctrl+Enter (Windows) or Command+Enter (Mac). Doing this causes Flash Professional to generate the Application Descriptor File for the first time.

Before making changes to the XML file, make a backup copy of the old file. That way, if something undesirable happens as a result of changing the file, you can simply restore the original from the copy.

3. **Locate the** `<android>` **XML node in the code.**

You can find it lurking toward the bottom of the XML document. It looks similar to this:

```
<android>
    <manifestAdditions>
        <![CDATA[<manifest>
        <uses-permission android:name="android.
          permission.INTERNET"/>
        <uses-permission android:name="android.
          permission.WRITE_EXTERNAL_STORAGE"/>
        <uses-permission android:name="android.
          permission.READ_PHONE_STATE"/>
        <uses-permission android:name="android.
          permission.ACCESS_FINE_LOCATION"/>
        <uses-permission android:name="android.
          permission.ACCESS_COARSE_LOCATION"/>
        <uses-permission android:name="android.
          permission.WAKE_LOCK"/>
        <uses-permission android:name="android.
          permission.ACCESS_NETWORK_STATE"/>
        <uses-permission android:name="android.
          permission.ACCESS_WIFI_STATE"/>
        </manifest>]]>
    </manifestAdditions>
</android>
```

4. **Select and delete the code** `<uses-permission android:name="android.permission.INTERNET"/>`.

5. **Save the XML file.**

Saving this file overwrites the previous version. The next time you package the application, the changes made in the Application Descriptor File will be included.

After saving the changes to the Application Descriptor File, if you return to Flash Professional and view the Permissions tab in the Application & Installer Settings dialog box, you can see that the INTERNET permission is now deselected. The changes that you made to the XML document have been picked up by Flash Professional.

Signing the Application

To package an AIR for Android application, you must first digitally sign it. Unlike applications targeting iOS, you do not need to obtain a signing certificate from a third party and then convert it for use with your Flash application; Flash Professional is able to handle the creation of a license for you. The certificate created is a P12, which is the file extension for the Personal Information Exchange format.

Create a certificate to sign your AIR for Android application by following these steps:

1. **From the main menu in Flash Professional, choose File⇨AIR for Android Settings.**

   The AIR for Android Settings dialog box opens.

2. **Click the Deployment tab.**

   The certificate and password options appear at the top of the panel that appears.

3. **Click Create.**

   The Create Self-Signed Digital Certificate dialog box is displayed, as shown in Figure 13-6.

4. **Fill in the Publisher Name field.**

   If you're an individual, enter your name. If you're a company, enter your company's trading name or brand.

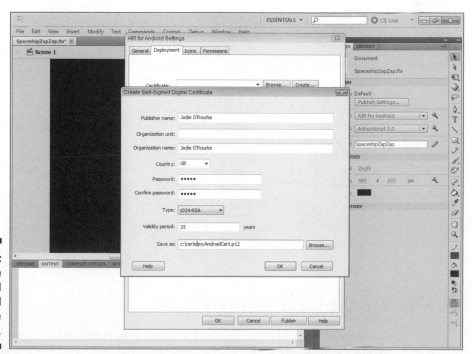

Figure 13-6:
The Create
Self-Signed
Digital
Certificate
dialog box.

5. **Fill in the Organization Unit field.**

   This is the department in your company where you work. You may leave this blank if not applicable.

6. **Fill in the Organization Name field.**

   This is the registered name of your company. You can leave this blank if you aren't operating as an incorporated company, or you can enter your own name here.

7. **Choose a country from the drop-down menu.**

   I'm a Brit, so I selected GB (for Great Britain).

8. **Fill in the Password field.**

   This is the password that will be used to lock your certificate. Make a note of it — either mentally or written — as you'll be asked for it whenever you use your certificate.

9. **Retype your password in the Confirm Password field.**

   As an added level of validation, you're asked to repeat the password that you entered previously.

10. **Select 1024-RSA from the Type drop-down menu.**

    Flash Professional can create two types of certificates for you:

    - *1024-RSA* is the industry-standard 80-bit key length and is used in most secure web applications.

    - *2048-RSA* is a longer key (112-bit) and is considered more secure than its 1024-RSA counterpart. The trade-off is that it requires more processing power to generate.

11. **Fill in the Validity Period field.**

    Google mandates that applications submitted to the Android Market are signed with a certificate that is valid for at least 25 years. Google has chosen this arbitrary value to prevent any applications in the Market becoming invalid through expired certificates. Their rationale is that an application built today is unlikely to be relevant in 25 years, so your certificate will outlive your application.

12. **In the Save As text box, type the location and filename that you want to be assigned to your certificate.**

    I suggest saving your certificate in the same directory as your application FLA or, to be tidier, in a new directory called `certificates`.

13. **Click OK.**

That's it! Your application is now signed and ready to be packaged as an AIR for Android APK file that you can then either deploy to your Android device or submit to the Marketplace.

Compiling an APK Using the AIR for Android Packager

When your application is in a position where it compiles and runs without throwing any errors in Flash Professional, you can deploy it to your Android device to see how well it behaves there. Packaging an APK and putting it onto your device really is a walk in the park using Flash Professional's publishing tools. To do this, you just follow these simple steps:

1. **Connect your Android device to your computer via USB.**

2. **Open Flash Professional.**

3. **Choose File⇨AIR for Android Settings.**

   The AIR for Android Settings dialog box appears.

4. **Select the Deployment tab.**

5. **Under Android Deployment Type, select Device Release.**

6. **Under After Publishing, select Install Application on the Connected Android device.**

7. **Click the Publish button.**

   Flash Professional begins to compile your application, packaging it as an AIR for Android application, and then installs it on the connected Android device.

   A small dialog box appears at the end to inform you that the process is complete.

After your application is packaged and installed, you can find it listed on the Applications menu of your Android device. If the application already existed on your device, it is overwritten with the new one.

The APK file is also placed in the directory where you saved your application FLA file. The next step is to manually install this APK file on Android devices using tools provided by Google. You can flip to Chapter 14 for more information on that process.

Chapter 14

Getting Your App onto an Android Device

*F*lash Professional provides all the tools you need to compile and deploy an AIR for Android application. (In Chapter 13, I show you how Flash Professional can launch an AIR for Android application on a connected device after it has been compiled.) What Flash Professional doesn't provide is the same flexibility you find with the Android development tools from Google. As a developer targeting the Android platform, it's handy to have a basic appreciation of the tools provided by Google — the Android platform manufacturer — to perform tasks such as checking whether an Android device is successfully connected to your computer, installing an AIR for Android application without Flash Professional, and uninstalling an application from a connected device. That way, should Flash Professional report an error in the packaging or installation process, you have a set of backup tools to help you get to the seat of the problem. So although you use Flash Professional to build your application, you can use the supplementary tools I describe in this chapter to help you be even more productive.

In this chapter, I cover the steps necessary to get Google's Android Developer tools running on your computer, how to install an APK file you previously compiled in Flash Professional on a connected Android device, and how to grab a screen shot from your Android device.

Installing the Android SDK and Debug Bridge

Google provides a software development kit (SDK) to help developers easily write applications in Android's native language, Java. The SDK also supplies some useful tools that allow developers targeting the platform with other languages to be able to perform read and write operations on a connected device. At the time of this writing, the tools are available to install on Windows, Mac OS, and Linux. In the steps that follow, I explain how to get up and running with the Google Android tools on Windows and Mac OS:

1. **Navigate to** `http://developer.android.com/sdk`.

2. **Download the Google SDK package for your operating system.**

   Windows users will find it easier to install the `.exe` installer rather than the ZIP archive.

   Mac users must download a ZIP archive and choose where to save/unpack it.

3. **Run the file that you downloaded.**

   Windows users will find the application in the Program Files directory.

   Mac users can choose where to unzip the downloaded archive. For these examples, unzip it to your `documents` folder.

After you have the required files installed on your computer, you need to run the Android SDK Manager application to install the latest SDK and supporting tools on your system. The following sections explain how to do that for both Windows and Mac OS.

Windows

Follow these steps to run the Android SDK Manager application and install the Android SDK and developer tools on your Windows computer:

1. **Navigate to** `C:\Program Files\Android\android-sdk-windows`, **and then double-click that file to start the SDK Manager.**

   If you can't locate this folder on your computer, do a Windows search for *Android*.

   The Android SDK and AVD Manager dialog box appears, as shown in Figure 14-1.

2. **Select Installed Packages from the left menu.**

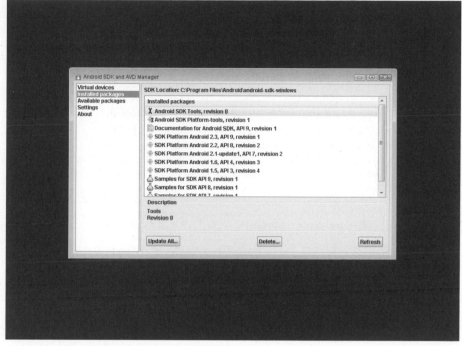

3. **Click the Update All button.**

   The Choose Packages to Install dialog box opens. The Packages list is populated with the latest versions of the SDK and supporting tools, as shown in Figure 14-2.

4. **Select the Accept All radio button.**

5. **Click the Install button.**

   The Installing Archives dialog box displays the progress of the download and the installation of each of the packages. This process will take several minutes.

With the Android SDK and tools installed, you can now configure your Windows operating system to be able to use it from the command line. Setting an *environment variable* is a time-saving step that permits applications in the `platform-tools` directory to be executed by their names, no matter what the current directory of the Command Prompt window is. Setting up the environment variable allows you to run ADB in the context of your mobile application's directory, meaning you type considerably less at the command line:

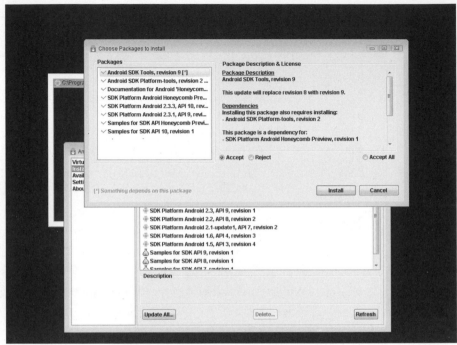

Figure 14-2:
Choosing
packages
to install
using SDK
Manager.

1. **From the Start menu, right-click Computer and then select Properties.**

   The System window opens.

2. **Click Advanced System Settings.**

   The classic System Properties dialog box opens with the Advanced tab already selected.

3. **Click Environment Variables.**

   The Environment Variables dialog box opens listing variable and value pairs for the current user account and for the system as a whole.

4. **Click New under the user variables list.**

   The New User Variable entry box opens.

5. **Enter the variable name** ANDROIDTOOLS.

6. **Enter the variable value as the path to the Android tools directory.**

   For most Windows installations, this is `C:\Program Files\Android\android-sdk-windows\platform-tools`.

   If you're running a 64-bit version of Windows, it might instead be in `C:\Program Files (x86)\Android\android-sdk-windows\platform-tools`.

7. **Click OK.**

   The variable is now stored.

8. **Select the user variable called PATH from the list.**

9. **Click Edit.**

   The Edit User Variable dialog box opens, already populated with information. You may see values already entered in the Variable value field; if so, be sure to leave them intact.

10. **Add the ANDROIDTOOLS variable to the PATH variable.**

    If a value already exists in the field, type a semicolon after the last character of the existing value and then type **%ANDROIDTOOLS%**, as shown in Figure 14-3.

11. **Click OK.**

    The PATH variable is now appended with the ANDROIDTOOLS variable.

12. **Click OK to save and close the System Properties dialog box.**

13. **Open the Windows Command Prompt and type the following:**

    ```
    adb version
    ```

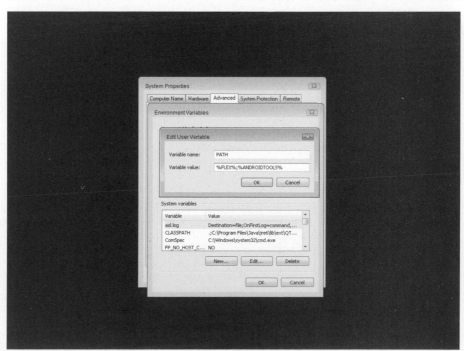

Figure 14-3:
Adding the Android tools path to the environment variables.

14. **Press Enter.**

    The text `Android Debug Bridge version 1.0.26` is displayed in the Command Prompt — your version number may be higher than mine, because Google regularly updates the SDK and tools. The environment variable is correctly configured!

Your Windows computer is now able to communicate with connected Android devices using the Command Prompt.

Mac OS

Follow these steps to run the Android SDK Manager application and install the Android SDK and developer tools on your Mac OS computer:

1. **Navigate to** `Users/<yourusername>/documents/android-sdk-mac_x86/tools` **to find the Android SDK Manager application.**

2. **Double-click the Terminal application called Android.**

    A Terminal window opens, and shortly afterwards, the SDK Manager application opens.

3. **Select Installed Packages and click Update All.**

    The Choose Packages to Install dialog box opens. The Packages list is populated with the latest versions of the SDK and supporting tools.

4. **Select the Accept All radio button and click Install.**

    The Installing Archives dialog box displays the progress of the download and the installation of each of the packages. This process will take several minutes.

You can run the Android Debug Bridge tool in command-line applications such as Terminal and Command Prompt in two ways. The first method is to type the full file path to the ADB application, such as `~/documents/android-sdk-mac_x86/platform-tools`. The other method is to configure a PATH variable that allows you to reference the ADB application using the name `adb`. The advantage of this method is that you can run ADB from your Android application directory; you don't need to use the `cd` command before running ADB. Regrettably, unlike Windows, configuring the PATH variable in Mac OS is a complicated task way beyond the limits of a *For Dummies* book. For simplicity's sake, I prefer to use the full path to the `platform-tools` directory.

After the Android SDK files have been downloaded and installed, follow these steps to test whether you can run the Android Debug Bridge tool:

1. **From the main menu, choose Applications➪Utilities to open Terminal.**

2. **Change the current directory to the** `platform-tools` **directory.**

3. **At the Terminal prompt, type the following:**

   ```
   cd ~/documents/android-sdk-mac_x86/platform-tools
   ```

   The current directory for the Terminal session is changed to the `platform-tools` directory.

4. **Run the ADB application from the Terminal screen by typing the following into the Terminal prompt:**

   ```
   ./adb version
   ```

   `Android Debug Bridge version 1.0.26` is displayed. The environment variable is correctly configured!

Your Mac OS computer is now able to communicate with connected Android devices using the Terminal application.

Connecting Your Android Device

The Android Debug Bridge (ADB) command-line tool provides functionality to determine whether a compatible Android device is connected to the computer. Follow these steps to connect your device and verify that the ADB tool can "see" it:

1. **Connect your Android device to your computer using a USB cable.**

2. **Confirm that the USB Connected notification icon appears on the status bar of your Android device.**

   The USB Connected notification icon is shown in Figure 14-4.

3. **On the device, navigate to Settings➪Applications➪Development and select USB Debugging.**

   A Debugging Enabled notification icon is shown on the status bar on the device (refer to Figure 14-4).

4. **Open the Command Prompt (Windows) or Terminal (Mac OS).**

   On Mac OS, change the current directory to `platform-tools` as follows (Windows users who configured the environment variable for ADB earlier in this chapter can skip this):

   ```
   cd ~/documents/android-sdk-mac_x86/platform-tools
   ```

USB connected

Debugging enabled

USB
Connected
and
Debugging
notifications
on the
Android
status bar.

Figure 14-4:
USB
Connected
and
Debugging
notifications
on the
Android
status bar.

5. List the connected devices.

In Windows, enter the following in the Command Prompt window:

```
adb devices
```

On Mac OS, enter the following in the Terminal window:

```
./adb devices
```

A list of attached devices is shown. Each device attached to the computer is represented in the list as a serial number and the word *device* next to it, as Figure 14-5 shows. This list indicates that the Android Debug Bridge is able to "see" your Android device.

Anytime you need to check whether your computer can "see" your connected Android device correctly, just follow the previous steps. The ADB tool will list the Android devices it believes are attached to the computer.

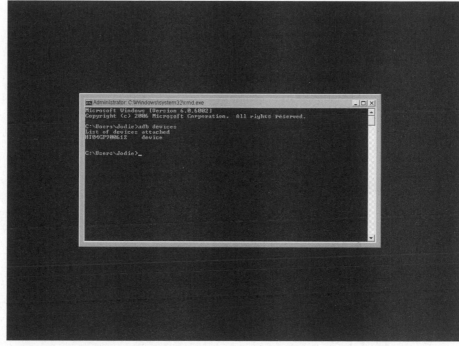

Figure 14-5:
ADB lists
connected
Android
devices.

Installing Your App on an Android Device

You'll often want to install an APK file that was compiled by Flash Professional on multiple devices, for testing. You obviously don't want to have to go through the rigmarole of compiling and packaging the application for each device. Besides, your tests will be reliable only if the same APK file is being tested on each device. To side-step the need to publish your application from Flash Professional to install it onto a device, you can use the ADB tool (demonstrated in the preceding section) to install the file directly onto the connected Android device(s). Here's how:

1. **Open the Command Prompt (Windows) or Terminal (Mac OS).**

   On Mac OS, change the current directory to `platform-tools` as follows (Windows users who configured the environment variable for ABD earlier in this chapter can skip this):

   ```
   cd ~/documents/android-sdk-mac_x86/platform-tools
   ```

2. **Type the** `adb install` **command, providing the file system path to the APK file to install.**

   My APK file is on my Windows desktop, so I entered the following in the Command Prompt window:

   ```
   adb install C:\Users\jodie\Desktop\MyApplication.apk
   ```

   On Mac OS, and assuming my APK file is on my desktop, I would enter the following in the Terminal window:

   ```
   ./adb install ~/desktop/MyApplication.apk
   ```

   The ADB application installs the APK application file on the connected Android mobile device.

Do not disconnect your device until the command line reports that the installation was successful. After a few moments, the display will update with information about the file size of the application being installed, the location it is being installed to on the Android device, and then the all-important `Success` line, as shown in Figure 14-6. Your application is now installed on the connected device and can be found in the device's applications menu. At this point, it is safe to disconnect the device from the USB port.

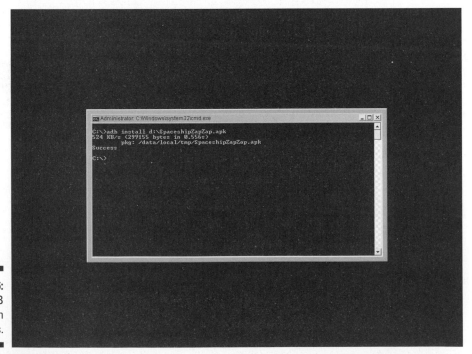

Figure 14-6: ADB installation success.

Capturing a Screen Shot from an Android Device

The Android Market requires developers to submit a minimum of two screen shots when they upload an application. Although you could mock up a couple of screens in a graphics-editing package, you may find it easier to simply grab images from the device while your application is running.

Follow these steps to capture a screen shot from the Android device connected to your computer:

1. **Connect your device to your computer using a USB cable.**

2. **Confirm that the USB Connected notification icon (refer to Figure 14-4) appears on the status bar of your Android device.**

3. **On the device, navigate to Settings⇨Applications⇨Development.**

4. **Select USB Debugging.**

5. **On your computer, navigate to Android SDK⇨Tools.**

6. **Double-click DDMS (Dalvik Debug Monitor Service).**

   After a short delay, the DDMS application opens, as shown in Figure 14-7.

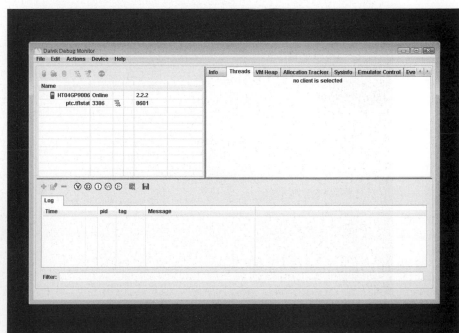

Figure 14-7:
The Dalvik Debug Monitor Service (DDMS) application.

7. **Click the Phone icon shown in the Name column on the left to select the attached Android device.**

   The row turns gray.

8. **Choose Device⇨Screen Capture.**

   The Device Screen Capture window opens, as shown in Figure 14-8. The image displayed is from the screen of the attached Android device.

9. **On the Android device, navigate to a screen that you want to capture.**

10. **Click the Refresh button to update the image.**

    The image displayed in the Device Screen Capture window will change only when you refresh it.

11. **Click the Save button.**

12. **Select the location on your computer where you want to save the PNG image.**

Figure 14-8:
The Device
Screen
Capture
window.

Now you can capture screens of your application to include with your Android Market submission. While you're using your application, just have your device connected to your computer and the Dalvik Debug Monitor Service application running in the background; then capture a screen whenever you like.

No one wants his or her expensive mobile phone to become nothing but an overpriced paperweight, so remember to never disconnect your device from your computer's USB port during reading and writing operations. If data transfer is unexpectedly interrupted by a cable being unplugged, files on the mobile device can become corrupted.

Now that you're comfortable with installing your AIR for Android application, and taking screen shots from it, pop over to Chapter 19 to find out how to submit it to the Android Market for distribution to your users!

Chapter 15

Registering as an iOS Developer and Provisioning Your iOS Device

In This Chapter

▶ Subscribing to the iOS Developer Program

▶ Creating a Certificate Signing Request file on your computer

▶ Generating and downloading provisioning profiles and certificates

Arguably one of the most taxing parts of the Flash mobile device development process is the interaction you must have with the iOS Developer Program, an entirely web-based resource that provides you with the vital ingredients required to deploy apps to an iOS device and the App Store.

The idea behind the iOS Developer Program is to create a way to validate that the code running on an iOS device comes from a verifiable source, to which Apple has name and contact details. You validate your application by signing it with a digital certificate, which you obtain from Apple after providing Apple with some information about yourself. Some would suggest that this is a commendable way of safeguarding the iOS platform from malicious code. Others familiar with the relative freedom of developing applications for the web browser would argue that it creates excessive barriers to entry. Whatever your view on the matter, you have to enroll in the iOS Developer Program before you can put your iOS Flash application onto the iOS device.

I won't make excuses for Apple; its website is very Mac-centric. Because of this, at times it may seem that certain tasks cannot be performed unless you have a Mac. In fact, Windows users do just fine. I'll steer you through it all; just follow the steps in this chapter that are relevant to your platform.

Registering as an iOS Developer

Becoming an iOS Developer is free. Like you, I was reasonably excited by this; alas, it's not free if you want to put your iOS Flash applications onto an iOS device. To do that, you need to be a paid-up member of the iOS Developer

Program. For a reasonable yearly fee, you can sign up for the full enchilada, which affords you the tools and certificates required to get an app onto a device.

Registering as an iOS Developer can be a little confusing. In the steps ahead, I do my best to help you through the minefield. To begin your journey, just follow my lead:

1. **Using your web browser, navigate to the Apple iOS device Developer home page, shown in Figure 15-1, at** `http://developer.apple.com/devcenter/ios/index.action`.

2. **Click the Register link.**

   The page that follows is an intermediary page explaining why you should become an iOS device Developer, despite the fact that you already made the decision to register!

3. **Click Get Started.**

   A page appears asking if you'd like to create a new Apple ID or use an existing one:

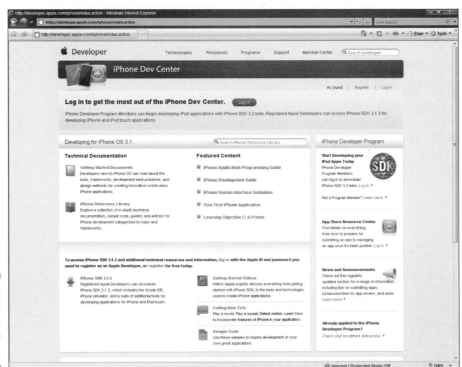

Figure 15-1:
The Apple iOS device Developer home page.

- If you have an iTunes account, you can use your iTunes ID to register as an iOS Developer.

- Alternatively, you can register a new ID, as shown in Figure 15-2. Follow the site's instructions to create a new Apple ID, agree to the license, and verify the e-mail address you register with.

4. Click Continue.

You'll receive a verification e-mail from Apple confirming your new Apple ID. A page appears, requesting that you enter the verification code included in the e-mail.

5. In the appropriate space, type the verification code from the e-mail message.

6. Click Continue.

You are presented with a screen confirming your registration as an Apple Developer.

7. Click Continue.

The Apple Member Center page loads.

8. Click the iOS link listed under Dev Centers.

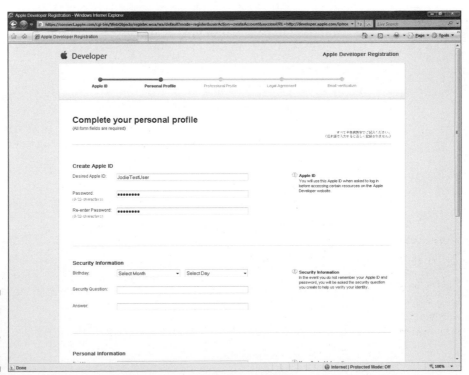

Figure 15-2:
Registration
for a new
Apple ID.

Now that you're registered as an iOS Developer, you can access all the tools and services that conventional iOS Developers have at their disposal. Because you're building your iOS application with Flash and not Objective-C, you aren't what Apple would class a conventional iOS device developer, so you do not need to be concerned at the moment with the tools Apple provides.

Joining the iOS Developer Program

The iOS Developer Program is a tier of privileges that allows you access to the iOS device software development kit (SDK), as well as gives you the files required to compile an iOS device application and run it on your iOS device. Browse to `https://developer.apple.com/devcenter/ios/index.action` and follow these steps to get your golden ticket:

1. **Click the Learn More link under the iOS Developer Program section.**

   A welcome page displays, highlighting the benefits of the iOS Developer Program.

2. **Click the Enroll Now button to start the application process.**

   A page appears explaining the process you're about to complete.

   You'll find a number of different pricing tiers for joining the iOS Developer Program. Whether you plan to develop and distribute your app as an organization or an individual will ultimately dictate which tier you subscribe to.

3. **Click Continue.**

   You see a page asking whether you are a new or registered Apple Developer, as shown in Figure 15-3.

4. **Select the I'm Registered as a Developer with Apple and Would Like to Enroll in a Paid Apple Developer Program radio button (under Existing Apple Developer).**

5. **Click Continue.**

   You see a page asking whether you'd like to register as an individual or as a company.

6. **Choose either Individual or Company.**

   If you aren't planning to market your application through an incorporated business, you can register as an individual. If you would like your company name to appear as the creator of the application in the App Store, you should register as a company.

   Registering for the program is instantaneous for individuals. Businesses may be called upon to submit extra identification documents, which may delay the process.

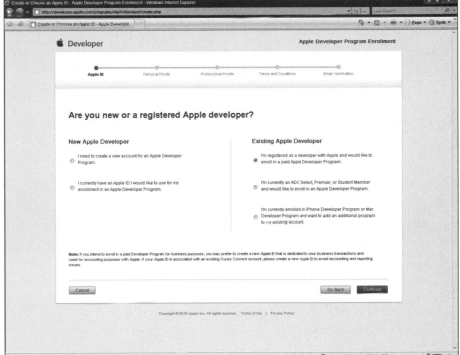

Figure 15-3:
The new or
existing
Apple
Developer
registration
page.

7. **Confirm your account information and click Continue.**

   You arrive at the page shown in Figure 15-4, asking you to select your program.

8. **Select iOS Developer Program and click Continue.**

   A page appears asking you to review your enrollment information.

9. **Review the information to ensure accuracy, and then click Submit.**

10. **Continue with the remainder of the payment process.**

    When the process is complete, you arrive back at the iOS Dev Center home page. Notice that a menu called iOS Developer Program has appeared at the top of the right column — this is where you'll go to download files that you'll need to include in your application.

You've completed the sign-up process. You can now begin using the online tools provided by the iOS Developer Program to create provisioning profiles for your iOS device and create certificates to sign your applications.

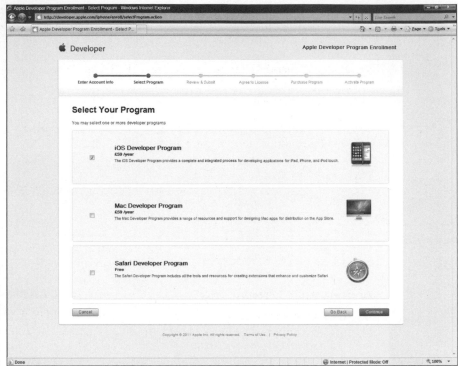

Figure 15-4:
Selecting
the iOS
Developer
Program.

Generating a Certificate Signing Request

A Certificate Signing Request (CSR) is a file you generate and send to a certifying authority — in this case, Apple — to apply for a digital identity certificate. This step adds an extra layer of security and integrity to the developer certificate and profile generation process. The CSR file contains information identifying you, as well as a public key that has been generated by you using a private key. The details inside the CSR file are then used to generate the certificate or profile you're applying for, making them unique to you and difficult to forge.

CSRs are required whenever you need to generate a new provisioning profile or certificate though the iOS Provisioning Portal. I suggest generating your CSR before you get knee-deep in creating your provisioning profile or certificate.

Generating a Certificate Signing Request in Windows

Unsurprisingly, the process for generating a Certificate Signing Request for a Windows PC is a little more complicated than that for a Mac. The process requires the installation of a small application called OpenSSL, and then you use OpenSSL to create a private key that the program then uses to generate the signing request for you.

Download and install OpenSSL (Win32 OpenSSL Light). You can obtain it free from

```
www.slproweb.com/products/Win32OpenSSL.html
```

If you are prompted to install Microsoft Visual C++ 2008 Redistributables, you can download and install this small package from

```
www.microsoft.com/downloads/details.
        aspx?familyid=9B2DA534-3E03-4391-8A4D-
        074B9F2BC1BF
```

The OpenSSL installer prompts you for a location where you want to install the application. By default, `c:\openssl` is selected. All the following examples assume that OpenSSL has been installed at this location.

Creating the private key file

The first step in creating a CSR is creating a private key file. This file is generated by OpenSSL using cryptographic algorithms and is used to validate that the CSR came from you and hasn't been tampered with. Follow these steps to create the private key file:

1. **Open the Windows Command Prompt.**

2. **Type** cd c:\openssl\bin **to change the directory to the OpenSSL bin directory.**

3. **Type** openssl genrsa -out mykey.key 2048 **to create a 2048-bit RSA private key with OpenSSL.**

   The `genrsa` command instructs the OpenSSL application to create an RSA key. The digits 2048 after the key name denote the length in bits that the key must be. Apple requires all CSRs to be 2048-bits in length. If successful, the Command Prompt window displays output similar to that shown in Figure 15-5.

Keep your private key safe. You need this exact key when it's time to sign your applications for deployment to an iOS device. If you mistakenly overwrite or delete your private key, you will need to repeat the steps for creating a provisioning profile and a certificate. After the private key and the CSR are generated, it's best to copy them to another location outside the OpenSSL bin directory.

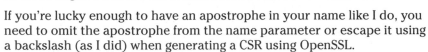

Figure 15-5:
Successful
private key
generation.

Creating the signing request file

With a private key file already generated, you can then generate your CSR file.
The following steps show you how to do that:

1. **Open the Windows Command Prompt.**

2. **Type the following:**

```
openssl req -new -key mykey.key -out
        CertificateSigningRequest.certSigningRequest
        -subj /emailAddress=youremail@youremail.
        com<mailto:/emailAddress= youremail@youremail.
        com>, CN=Jodie O\'Rourke, C=GB
```

Substitute the value of the `emailAddress` parameter for your Apple ID,
`CN` as your name, and `C` as your country code. The country code value
must be an ISO 3166-1 complaint code — you can find your country code
in the listing at `http://en.wikipedia.org/wiki/ISO_3166-1`.

If you're lucky enough to have an apostrophe in your name like I do, you
need to omit the apostrophe from the name parameter or escape it using
a backslash (as I did) when generating a CSR using OpenSSL.

3. **Press Enter.**

The Command Prompt window displays the output shown in Figure 15-6.
A file called `CertificateSigningRequest.certSigningRequest`
is created in the `c:\openssl\bin` directory. This is the file you should
upload when prompted by the Development Provisioning Assistant.

You can create a batch file to save time producing CSRs. A batch file is simply
a text file that runs a set of instructions at the Windows Command Prompt.
The simplest way to create one is to change the file extension of a text file
from `.txt` to `.bat`.

Just save the following code as Windows batch file (`*.bat`) on your desktop:

```
@echo off
SET /p email=Enter publisher email address:
SET /p name=Enter publisher name:
SET /p country=Enter publisher country code:
cd c:\openssl\bin
```

```
openssl genrsa -out mykey.key 2048
pause
openssl req -new -key mykey.key -out
        CertificateSigningRequest.certSigningRequest
        -subj "/emailAddress=%email%<mailto:/
        emailAddress=%email%>, CN=%name%, C=%country%"
pause
```

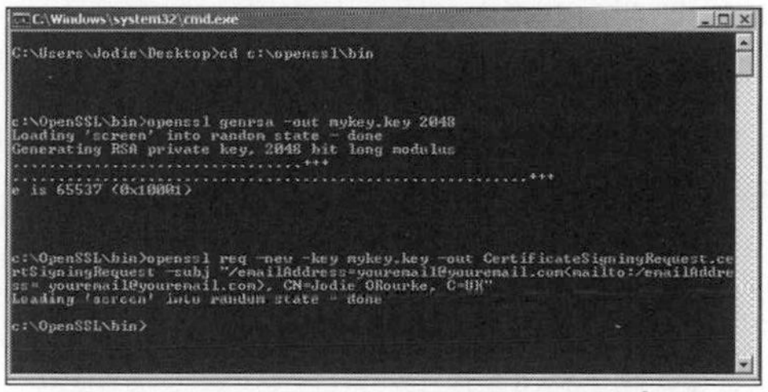

Figure 15-6:
OpenSSL
has
generated
the CSR.

Now, each time you want to generate a CSR for an iOS device provisioning profile, you can simply double-click this file on the desktop and enter the information as prompted, and a CSR file is created in `c:\openssl\bin`.

Generating a Certificate Signing Request on Mac OS

Generating signing requests is slightly less painful for Mac OS users. The Keychain Access application handles the creation of the private key — a file that is used to validate that the CSR came from you and hasn't been tampered with — and then generates the CSR file. Here's the process to follow:

1. **Open the Keychain Access utility.**

    You can find this utility in the Applications⇨Utilities folder in Mac OS X.

2. **Choose Keychain Access⇨Preferences from the menu.**

    The Preferences dialog box opens.

3. **Click the Certificates tab from the Preferences dialog box.**

4. **Set the Online Certificate Status Protocol and Certificate Revocation List drop-down lists to Off.**

5. **Close the dialog box.**

6. **Choose Keychain Access⇨Certificate Assistant⇨Request a Certificate from a Certificate Authority.**

    The Certificate Assistant dialog box opens.

7. **Type your e-mail address and your name in the text boxes provided.**

   Use the same information you used to register for the iOS Developer Program. Leave the CA Email Address text box empty.

8. **Select the Saved to Disk option, and click Continue.**

   A Save As dialog box appears.

9. **Type a filename and click Save.**

   Remember to keep the file extension .certSigningRequest when typing the filename. The CSR file is saved to your computer.

You're done. Your CSR file is now ready to use with the iOS Developer Program website, something I'll show you how to do in the next section.

Obtaining a Provisioning Profile

All iOS device applications must be associated with a provisioning profile when they are compiled. Some profiles also have to be manually installed on the iOS device to allow the applications they're associated with to run. iOS devices are also able to store multiple provisioning profiles, allowing you to test other developers' applications, as well as your own.

You can deploy your application with one of three types of provisioning profiles:

- ✔ Development Provisioning Profile: Can be associated with only one device and is typically used to test your application on a device during development.

- ✔ Distribution Provisioning Profile — Ad Hoc: Can be associated with up to 100 devices and is typically used for larger-scale testing of your application after the development is completed.

- ✔ Distribution Provisioning Profile — App Store: Allows your application to be installed on any iOS device, via the Apple App Store. Typically, you use the App Store profile after you have completed testing with the Ad-Hoc profile and are ready to submit your application to the App Store.

 You need a CSR to create a provisioning profile or certificate. If you haven't generated your CSR, I suggest going to the section "Generating a Certificate Signing Request," earlier in this chapter, and completing those steps before you move forward.

Getting your Device ID

Before you begin generating provisioning profiles, you need to make a note of the Device ID of the iOS device you're generating a profile for. Follow these steps:

1. **Connect your iOS device to your computer using a USB cable.**

2. **Open iTunes on your computer.**

3. **Select your iOS device from the list of devices in the left column.**

   A summary screen for your iOS device is displayed.

4. **Click the serial number.**

   The serial number is transformed into a Unique Device ID (UDID). This 40-character alphanumeric string is your Device ID.

5. **Press Ctrl+C (Windows) or Command+C (Mac) to copy the UDID to the Clipboard.**

6. **Save the ID in a text file.**

   Notepad or similar will suffice.

Your Device ID is now stored somewhere handy, ready for when you're asked to enter it at the Apple website during profile and certificate creation.

Creating a Development Provisioning Profile

A Development Provisioning Profile is a small file installed on an iOS device that allows a developer to install an application on an iOS device without App Store approval (particularly handy when testing). The Development Provisioning Profile contains the unique Device ID of the iOS device onto which it can be installed, as well as the certificate that is to be used to sign the iOS device application. A Development Provisioning Profile gives you the freedom to test your app on your phone whenever you want, but it prevents you from circumventing the App Store in two ways:

- The Development Provisioning Profile is useful only on an iOS device for which it carries the Device ID.

- Only applications signed with the certificate that was used to sign the Development Provisioning Profile will work.

Apple accepts for the App Store only applications that have been built using an App Store Distribution Provisioning Profile. Apps built with any other profile type are instantly rejected.

Here's the process for generating a Development Distribution Profile:

1. **Use your browser to navigate to** `http://developer.apple.com/membercenter/index.action`.

2. **Log in using the credentials you used during your iOS Developer Program registration.**

Earlier in this chapter, I showed you how to join the iOS Developer Program. If you haven't yet registered, follow those steps first and then resume from here when you're done.

The iOS device Developer home page appears (refer to Figure 15-1).

3. **Click the link to the iOS Provisioning Portal.**

   The iOS Provisioning Portal home page appears, as shown Figure 15-7.

4. **Click Launch Assistant.**

   A modal window launches the Development Provisioning Assistant, as shown in Figure 15-8.

5. **Click Continue.**

   The Choose App ID screen asks you to enter an App ID.

6. **Type your choice of alphanumeric App ID.**

   The App ID is your unique identifier for your application. You can type any string you like, up to a limit of 50 alphanumerical characters, but with no special characters such as @, $, or ".

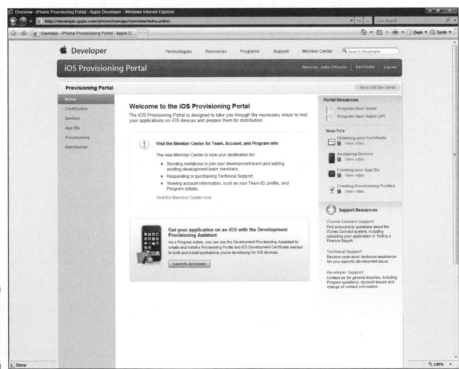

Figure 15-7:
The iOS
Provisioning
Portal.

Your App ID is a unique identifier used by any iOS device to identify your application, once installed. Don't worry if you haven't decided on your App ID while you're still developing. You have to create a Distribution Provisioning Profile (covered in the next section) for distributing your app, so you can use a made-up placeholder ID until you're ready to deploy.

7. **Click Continue.**

   The dialog box shown in Figure 15-9 appears.

8. **In the Device Description field, type the name of the device where you're installing this Development Provisioning Profile.**

A selection of Development Provisioning Profiles, all with the title *iOS device,* can become difficult to manage. Using developers' names or the iOS device serial number in a device description can simplify the task of managing many profiles.

9. **In the Device ID field, type the Device ID of the iOS device where you're installing this Development Provisioning Profile.**

   You can find your Device ID by following the steps in the previous section in this chapter.

A Device ID is unique to an iOS device and must be entered carefully to ensure that the Provisioning Profile works correctly.

Figure 15-8: The Development Provisioning Assistant.

Figure 15-9:
Assigning
a devel-
opment
device.

10. **Click Continue.**

    The screen shown in Figure 15-10 asks you to generate a Certificate Signing Request (CSR). Windows users should ignore the steps to Launch Keychain Access.

    Earlier in this chapter I demonstrated how to create a CSR file, ready for uploading to the iOS Developer Program website. If you haven't yet completed those steps, head back to the section "Generating a Certificate Signing Request in Windows" or "Generating a Certificate Signing Request on Mac OS," earlier in this chapter, for instructions on how to generate a certificate for your chosen development platform. When you're done, come back here to continue.

11. **Click Continue.**

    The Submit Certificate Signing Request screen appears.

12. **Click the Browse button and find and select your CSR file.**

    The CSR file is uploaded to the iOS Provisioning Portal. The screen shown in Figure 15-11 appears, asking you to name your Development Provisioning Profile.

    If the CSR file upload is unsuccessful, your certificate will not be created. Try uploading again. If problems persist, click the Support link at the top of the screen.

Figure 15-10:
Upload a
Certificate
Signing
Request.

Figure 15-11:
Name your
Development
Provisioning
Profile.

13. **Type the name you want to give your Development Provisioning Profile, and then click Generate.**

    The requested credentials are checked off, and you see the confirmation screen shown in Figure 15-12, telling you that a Development Provisioning Profile has been generated.

14. **Click Continue.**

    On the final page of the process, which is shown in Figure 15-13, you can download the Development Provisioning Profile to your computer.

15. **Download your profile now or later.**

    Decide whether you want to download your profile now by clicking Download Now or leave your profile on the portal and download it later by clicking Cancel to close the dialog box.

You can delete certificates from Apple's system. You may have a large number of certificates and provisioning profiles from old or defunct projects that are just causing clutter. Clutter causes chaos, and before you know it you have an application that's been compiled using the wrong certificate. You can *revoke* a certificate at any time by visiting the Certificates section of the iOS Developer Program Portal and then clicking the Revoke link next to the certificate you want to destroy.

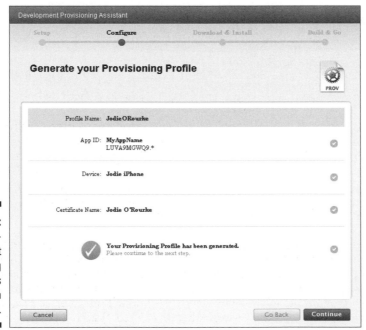

Figure 15-12:
A Development Provisioning Profile has been created.

Figure 15-13:
Download
your
Development
Provisioning
Profile.

Creating a Distribution Provisioning Profile

A Distribution Provisioning Profile is required if

- ✔ You want to put your application on multiple devices for testing
- ✔ You want to submit your application for distribution in the iTunes App Store

After you've reached the stage where you need to extend the testing of your application to a number of people, or you're ready to offer your application to the public, you have to return to the iOS Provisioning Portal website — `https://developer.apple.com/ios/manage/overview/index.action` — to generate a different provisioning profile. If you already have a Development Provisioning Profile in place, the process of creating a Distribution Provisioning Profile is relatively straightforward.

Use the correct profile (Ad Hoc Distribution Provisioning Profile or App Store Distribution Provisioning Profile) for the type of distribution you're planning for your application. You also need to create a Development Provisioning Profile for your application before you can proceed to creating a Distribution Provisioning Profile for it. If you haven't yet done that, head back to the "Creating a Development Provisioning Profile" section in this chapter.

Ad Hoc Distribution Provisioning Profile

This is the profile you require if you'd like to install your application on more than one iOS device for testing purposes. Perhaps your peers are developing applications that they'd like you to test for them, and in return, they test yours for you. In these situations, an Ad Hoc Distribution Provisioning Profile could be just the ticket. Like the Development Provisioning Profile, the Ad Hoc Distribution Provisioning Profile must be manually installed onto each iOS device that the application will be tested on.

The following steps show you how to create an Ad Hoc Distribution Provisioning Profile:

1. **Navigate to the iOS Provisioning Portal at** `https://developer.apple.com/ios/manage/overview/index.action`, **and log in if requested.**

   The iOS Provisioning Portal home page is displayed.

2. **Click the Provisioning link on the left.**

   A screen with a set of tabs appears.

3. **Click the Distribution tab.**

   The Distribution Provisioning Profiles page is displayed.

4. **Click New Profile.**

5. **Select Ad Hoc as the distribution method.**

6. **Type a name for the profile in the text box provided.**

7. **Select the ID of your app from the drop-down list.**

   If your app isn't listed, you first need to create a Development Provisioning Profile for it. Follow the steps earlier in this chapter for doing this, and then return here to continue.

8. **Select the check box next to each device on which you want to install this provisioning profile.**

9. **Click Submit.**

   The Distribution Provisioning Profiles page appears, listing your new Ad Hoc Distribution Provisioning Profile as Active.

10. **Download the provisioning profile and save it in a dedicated folder on your computer that you can save all of your certificates and provisioning profiles in.**

App Store Distribution Provisioning Profile

The App Store Distribution Provisioning Profile is the profile you use when you're ready to submit your application to the App Store. Unlike the Development Provisioning Profile and the Ad Hoc Distribution Provisioning Profile, this one is preinstalled on all iOS devices, but only applications that are distributed by the App Store will work using it.

The following steps show you how to create an App Store Distribution Provisioning Profile:

1. **Navigate to the iOS Provisioning Portal at** `https://developer.apple.com/ios/manage/overview/index.action`**, and log in if requested.**

   The iOS Provisioning Portal home page is displayed.

2. **Click the Provisioning link on the left.**

   A screen with a set of tabs appears.

3. **Click the Distribution tab.**

   The Distribution Provisioning Profiles page displays.

4. **Click New Profile.**

5. **Select App Store as the distribution method.**

6. **Type the name you want to give the profile.**

7. **Select the ID of your app from the drop-down list.**

   If your app isn't listed, you first need to create a Development Provisioning Profile for it. Follow the steps earlier in this chapter for doing this, and then return here to continue.

8. **Click Submit.**

   The Distribution Provisioning Profiles page appears, listing your App Store Distribution Provisioning Profile as Pending. Reload the page, and the Provisioning Profile will eventually be processed by the system and become Active. In periods of exceptional demand, the profile may remain as Pending for a few hours.

9. **Download the provisioning profile in a dedicated folder on your computer in which you can save all your certificates and provisioning profiles.**

Obtaining a Certificate

All iOS applications must be signed by a valid certificate before they can be run on an Apple device.

All iOS applications must be signed by a valid digital certificate — obtained from Apple — before they can be installed on an iOS device. Certificates differ to Provisioning Profiles because they verify the authenticity of your application, whereas Provisioning Profiles simply determine on which devices your digitally signed application is allowed to run. You can choose one of two types of certificates to sign your application:

✔ Developer Certificate

✔ Distribution Certificate

The main distinction between the two, and the way I find it easiest to remember, is that the Developer Certificate is the one you use during development and testing. The Distribution Certificate is the one you use to sign your application before submitting it to the App Store.

Obtaining a Developer Certificate

A Developer Certificate is automatically generated for you when you complete the process of creating a Development Provisioning Profile, discussed earlier in this chapter. You can download this certificate by clicking the Certificates link on the iOS Developer Program Portal page and clicking the Download button next to your certificate name on the Development tab, as shown in Figure 15-14.

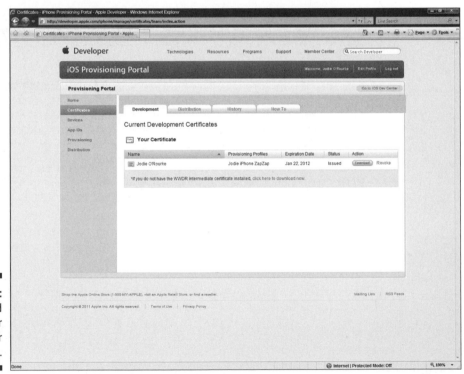

Figure 15-14:
Download
your
Developer
Certificate.

Obtaining a Distribution Certificate

Unlike its Developer counterpart, the Distribution Certificate is not automatically generated when you create a provisioning profile. The following steps describe how to create and download a Distribution Certificate:

1. **Navigate to the iOS Provisioning Portal at** `http://developer.apple.com/ios/manage/overview/index.action`, **and log in if requested.**

   The iOS Provisioning Portal home page is displayed.

2. **Click the Certificates link.**

3. **Click the Distribution tab.**

   A message appears, as shown in Figure 15-15, and tells you that you don't currently have a valid Distribution Certificate.

4. **Click the Request Certificate button.**

   The Create Distribution Certificate page appears, as shown in Figure 15-16.

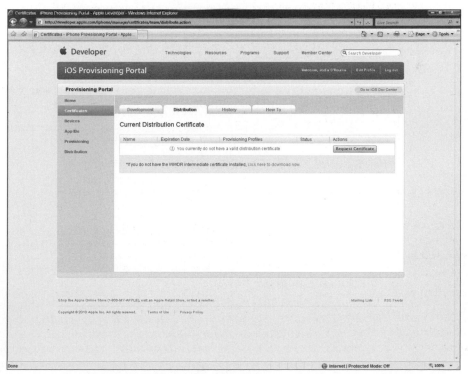

Figure 15-15: No Distribution Certificates are available.

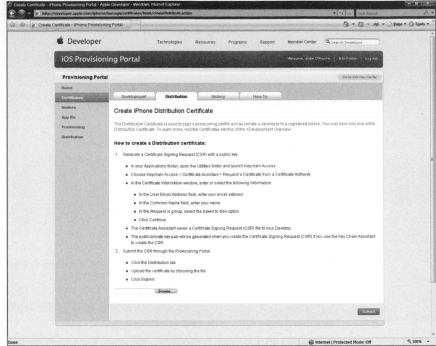

Figure 15-16:
The Create
Distribution
Certificate
screen.

5. Click the Browse button and choose your CSR file from the location you saved it on your computer.

This file is the same certificate signing request file you created and uploaded for your Development Provisioning Profile.

If the CSR file is uploaded to the iOS Provisioning Portal, you're returned to the Current Distribution Certificate page, where you see the Certificate name you just created, together with Pending Approval in the status column, as shown in Figure 15-17.

If the CSR file upload is unsuccessful, your certificate is not created. Try uploading again. If problems persist, click the Support link at the top of the screen.

6. Click the Approve button.

The page refreshes, and you see that the message in the status column changes to Pending Issuance. This simply means that the certificate is being generated on the Apple servers. The issuing process can be immediate or it can take longer. You can check whether the Distribution Certificate has been generated by reloading the page or waiting for a notification e-mail from the Apple Developer Program.

After the certificate is issued, it's ready to be downloaded, as shown in Figure 15-18.

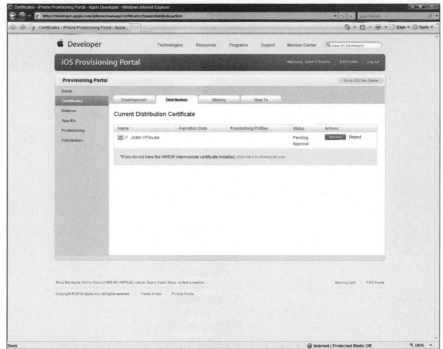

Figure 15-17:
A new Distribution Certificate pending approval.

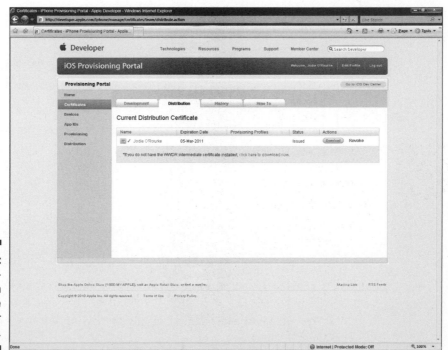

Figure 15-18:
A Distribution Certificate ready for downloading.

You may be wondering why you need to approve your own certificate requests. The reason is that multiple users are permitted to request distribution certificates on some iOS Developer Program subscriptions. However, only the primary account holder (or Program Admin) is allowed to approve these requests. For an individual subscription, you are the Program Admin.

I try to resist the urge to download my certificates the moment I generate them. Instead, I find it easier to leave all my certificates on the iOS Developer Program Portal and just download them when I need to sign my applications. Holding loads of certificates on your local machine can be quite confusing!

Installing a Provisioning Profile on an iOS Device

Whether you're using Windows or a Mac, to provision your iOS device, you need to connect your device to your computer using the sync cable supplied. Software on your computer then copies the provisioning profile you generated in the iOS Provisioning Portal to the device. In the next sections, I explain how to complete this process for both Windows and Mac.

Using Windows to provision your iOS device

With your iOS device connected to your Windows computer with a USB cable, follow these steps to provision your iOS:

1. **Open the iPhone Configuration Utility for Windows.**

   This utility normally comes with a standard iOS device/iTunes installation. If you find you don't have it installed, you can download it from http://support.apple.com/kb/DL926.

2. **Choose Library⇨Devices and check that your iOS device is listed, as shown in Figure 15-19.**

   A connected device has a green light icon to the left of its name. If your device isn't listed, or doesn't have a green light icon next to it, check that the device is connected to the computer's USB port. If it's already connected, try disconnecting it from the USB port and then reconnecting it.

3. **Choose Library⇨Provisioning Profiles, as shown in Figure 15-20.**

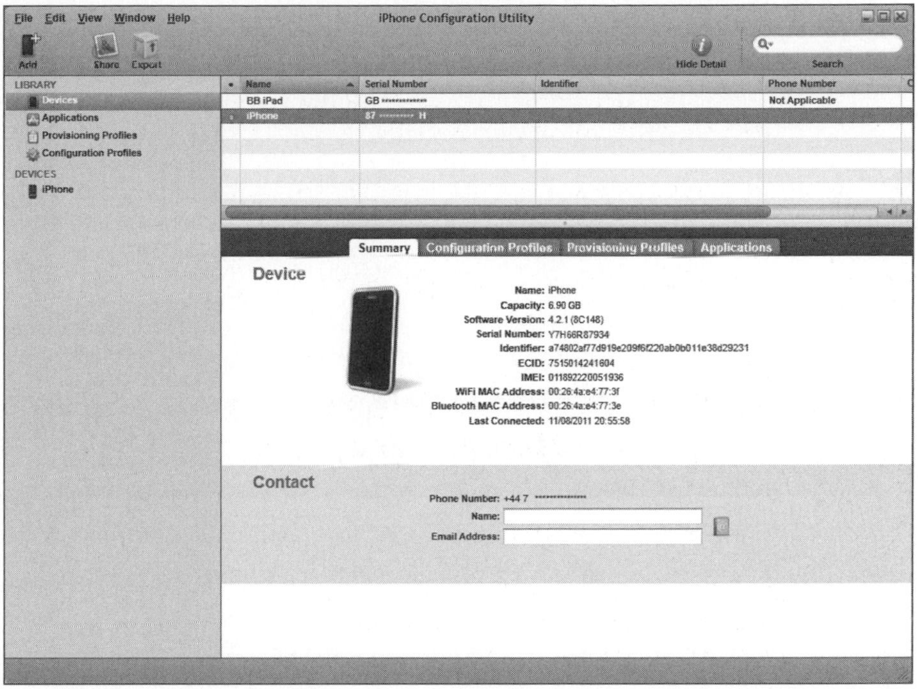

Figure 15-19:
The list of available devices in the iPhone Configuration Utility.

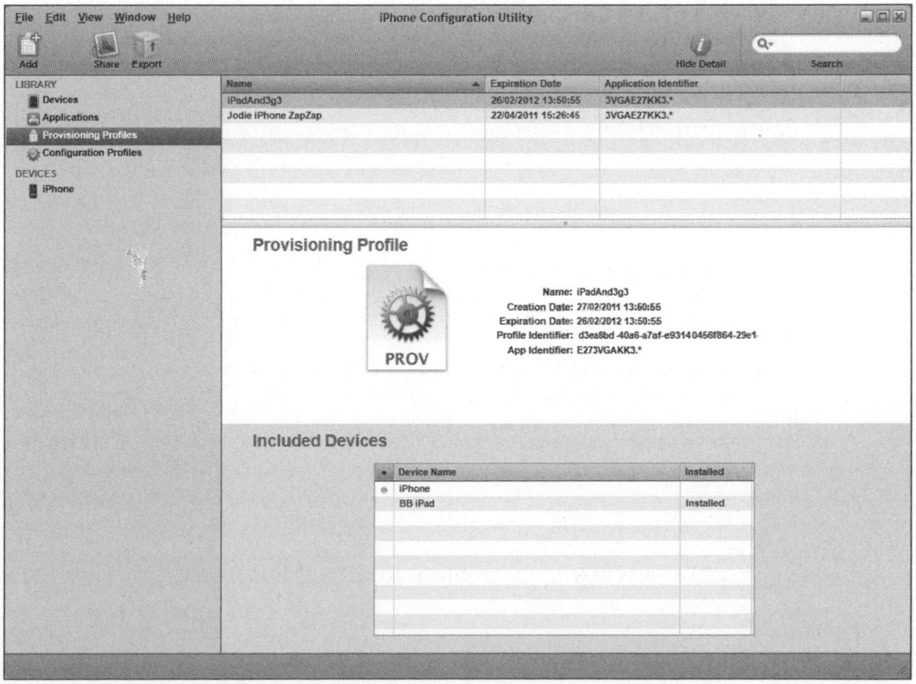

Figure 15-20:
The provisioning profiles in the iPhone Configuration Utility.

4. Click the Add button (at the top-left of the screen).

A file browser dialog box opens.

5. Select the .mobileprovision file you downloaded from the iOS Developer Program Portal.

The .mobileprovision file appears in the list.

6. Check that your iOS device is listed in the included devices.

If the device isn't listed, it's likely you have a provisioning profile for another iOS device, which means that the device identifier in the profile doesn't match your iOS device. Head back to the iOS Provisioning Portal to download the provisioning profile that contains your device ID.

7. Select your iOS device listed under Devices in the left-hand menu.

8. Click the Provisioning Profiles tab.

A list of installed provisioning profiles is displayed, as shown in Figure 15-21.

9. Click the Install button next to the profile you imported in Step 5.

The provisioning profile is installed onto the connected iOS device.

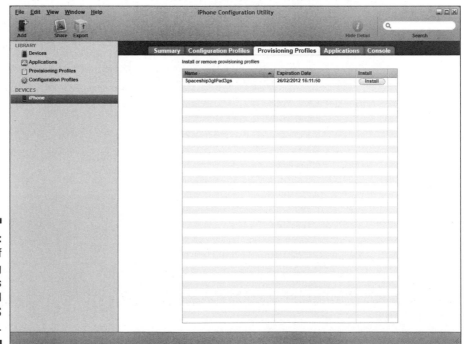

Figure 15-21:
A list of provisioning profiles installed on an iOS device.

10. **Click Devices in the left-hand menu.**

11. **Click the Provisioning Profiles tab.**

    You see the profile you just installed in the list of Installed Provisioning Profiles, as shown in Figure 15-22.

12. **Close the iPhone Configuration Utility.**

Congratulations! You've just provisioned your iOS device ready to accept your first iOS Flash app.

Using a Mac to provision your iOS device

Installing a provisioning profile on an iOS device using a Mac is a little simpler than it is for Windows. Just connect your device to your Mac with a USB cable and follow these steps:

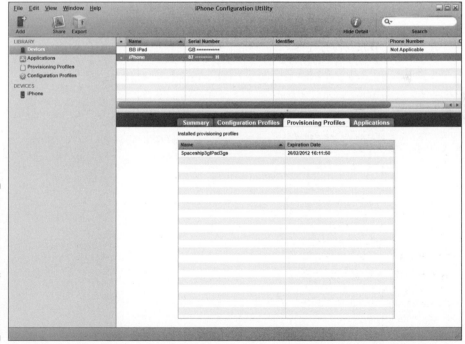

Figure 15-22:
A provisioning profile added to the list of installed provisioning profiles.

1. **Open the Finder to show your** `.mobileprovision` **file.**

2. **Drag the** `.mobileprovision` **file you downloaded from the iOS device Provisioning Portal onto the iTunes icon in the dock.**

3. **Select the iOS device in iTunes.**

4. **Click Sync.**

Having installed your provisioning profile on your iOS device, the next step is to package your Flash application as an iOS application ready for installation, as described in Chapter 16.

Chapter 16

Compiling and Packaging an Application for iOS

Many similarities exist between packaging an application for iOS and AIR for Android. Like any proprietary platform, some nuances must also be addressed to ensure success. Like AIR for Android, Flash applications targeting iOS need to be packaged into a single distributable file, and for iOS, this is called an IPA file.

Flash Professional handles all the compiling and packaging of an IPA for you, using a friendly graphical user interface, so you find no command-line packaging here! With just a few tweaks here and a couple of certificates there, you'll have your first iOS application sitting on your hard drive waiting to be installed on a device.

In this chapter, I explain the processes for creating and associating your icons with your application FLA file, modifying the iOS settings, and creating the iOS application file.

Creating the Icon and Startup Screen Images

Without icons and a start screen image, you can't install your application on an iOS device, such as an iPhone. You need to design four images (three app icons and a start screen), size them according to Apple specifications, save them to specific locations relative to your application FLA file, and then specify each in the AIR for iOS Settings dialog box in Flash Professional. Although it's beyond the scope of this book to explain how to design an icon from scratch, I do give you Apple's icon size requirements and tell you how to resize your icons and how and where to save them. I also explain how to use an image for your startup screen artwork and save it properly.

Resizing your existing icons

iOS requires application icons to be specific sizes: 29x29 pixels, 57x57 pixels, 114x114 pixels, and 512x512 pixels. If you want to also target the iPad, an additional two icons are required, measuring 48x48 pixels and 72x72 pixels. For simplicity, I'll demonstrate the steps used to create icons for an iOS application:

1. **Browse to the directory of your application FLA and create a new directory called** `icons`.

2. **Using graphics-creation software like Fireworks or Photoshop, create a new image that is 512 pixels by 512 pixels (the largest size required for an iOS deployment).**

   Creating source (or reference) artwork at the largest size means quality is retained as scaling down occurs. Starting with the smallest size and then attempting to scale up will cause distortions to appear.

3. **Save the image as** `icon512x512.png` **in the** `icons` **folder you created in Step 1.**

   The 512x512-pixel image I created for my SpaceshipZapZap application is shown in Figure 16-1.

4. **Resize the graphic to 114 pixels by 114 pixels.**

5. **Save the file as** `icon114x114.png` **in the** `icons` **folder you created in Step 1.**

6. **Resize the graphic to 57 pixels by 57 pixels. Then save the file as** `icon57x57.png` **in the** `icons` **folder.**

7. **Resize the graphic to 29 pixels by 29 pixels. Then save the file as** `icon29x29.png` **in the** `icons` **folder.**

iOS automatically adds rounded corners and the glass effect to your icons; you do not need to include this in your own icon artwork.

Where are all these icons used?

The various icon sizes are used as follows:

✔ icon 29x29: Used by Spotlight search results on the iPhone and iPod touch

✔ icon 48x48: Used by Spotlight search results on the iPad

✔ icon 57x57: Used by the iPhone and iPod touch home screens

✔ icon 72x72: Used by the iPad home screen

✔ icon 114x114: Displayed on iOS devices with high-resolution screens (since the iPhone 4).

✔ icon 512x512: Displayed by iTunes

The 512-pixel PNG file is used only for testing development versions of your application. When you submit the final application to the Apple App Store, submit the 512x512 image separately, as a JPG file. Do not include it in the IPA file you submit.

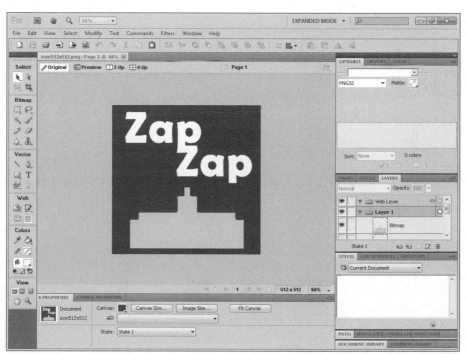

Figure 16-1: An example 512x512-pixel icon.

Choosing your start screen

To be approved for distribution in the App Store, your application must display a start screen when the application is initializing. A start screen is like a splash screen that many desktop software applications display to the user when they're starting. Many applications, including some of Apple's own iOS apps, give the impression that the application has loaded quicker than it actually has by simply displaying a start screen that is a screen shot of the first screen the users see when the application has loaded. The downside is that the users might think the app is hanging or is buggy when starting, because they still need to wait for the application to initialize before they can interact with it. The alternative is to use a start screen that acts as a "welcome" or "hang on a moment" message, while your application is initializing behind the scenes. I tend to favor the latter approach, because it doesn't pretend to be anything that it isn't! However, in the following sections, I explain how to use both a screen shot and a custom splash screen for your app's startup screen.

Capturing a screen shot for use as a start screen

To use a screen shot of the first screen that users see in your application as your app's main startup screen, you need to capture a screen shot from your iOS device, transfer it to your development computer, and include it in the IPA file. Simply follow these steps:

1. **Open your application on the iOS device.**

   Refer to Chapter 17 for information about how to transfer your application to your iOS device. Wait until the first screen of the user interface appears.

2. **Press and hold the Home button (below the screen) and the Power/Sleep button (at the top of the device) at the same time.**

   This action takes a screen shot and sends it to the Camera Roll.

3. **Transfer the image to your development computer.**

   E-mail is the simplest and most effective way to transfer the image:

   a. **Open the Camera application on your iOS device.**

   b. **Open the Camera Roll by tapping on the small picture in the lower-left corner.**

      The most recent picture or screen shot you took appears. You can use the arrow at the bottom of the screen to scroll through your pictures until you come to the one you want to use.

   c. **When you've found the image you want to mail, tap the Forward button (an arrow coming out of a box) in the lower-left corner.**

   d. **Press the Email Photo button and send the image to yourself.**

4. **After you receive the picture via e-mail, open the file in a graphics-editing application and save it as** `Default.png` **in the same directory as your iOS application FLA file.**

   Note that the filename is case sensitive and requires a capital *D*.

5. **Open Flash Professional.**

6. **Choose File⇨AIR for iOS Settings.**

   The AIR for iOS Settings dialog box appears. You can read more about the tabs and settings for this dialog box in the section "Modifying the AIR for iOS Publish Settings in Flash Professional," later in this chapter.

7. **On the General tab, click the plus sign above the Included Files list.**

8. **Browse to the directory containing your** `Default.png` **file.**

9. **Double-click the filename to add it to the Included Files list.**

10. **Click OK.**

   The AIR for iOS Settings dialog box closes. The next time you publish your application, `Default.png` will be included in the IPA file.

Creating a custom splash screen

A custom splash screen allows you to be a little more creative than if you simply used a screen shot. To create a custom splash screen, you need to use a graphics-editing application (such as Photoshop or Fireworks) to create an image from scratch. The important thing to remember as you create your image is that the start screen image must be 320 pixels wide by 480 pixels high. In addition to the strictly enforced dimensions, the PNG file created must be named `Default.png` (with a capital *D*) and saved to the same directory as your iOS FLA file. Any other ideas are up to you! You can create a logo, use graphics from your application, and even insert a little credit to yourself if you like! My completed start screen is shown in Figure 16-2.

Having generated your start screen PNG file and placed it in the same directory as your application FLA file, you need to set the `Default.png` file as a file that Flash Professional will include in the IPA file it generates. The following steps explain how:

1. **Open Flash Professional.**

2. **Choose File⇨AIR for iOS Settings.**

   The AIR for iOS Settings dialog box appears. You can read more about the tabs and settings for this dialog box in the next section.

3. **On the General tab, click the plus sign next to Included Files.**

4. **Browse to the directory containing your** `Default.png` **file.**

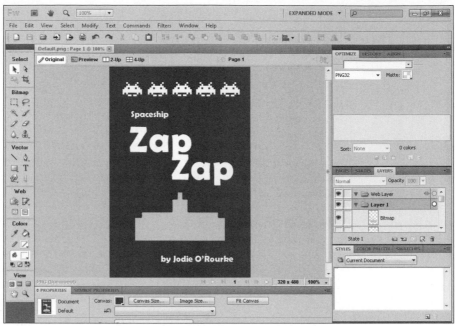

Figure 16-2:
My start
screen
image.

5. **Double-click the filename to add it to the Included Files list.**

6. **Click OK.**

   The AIR for iOS Settings dialog box closes. The next time you publish
   your application, `Default.png` will be included in the IPA file.

Modifying the AIR for iOS Publish Settings in Flash Professional

The AIR for iOS Settings dialog box is where you configure the main publish
settings for your iOS application. To invoke the dialog box, choose File➪AIR
for iOS Settings in Flash Professional. The AIR for iOS Settings dialog box
opens, as shown in Figure 16-3. I explain each of the publish settings tabs
and their options in the upcoming sections.

General tab

The General tab contains the fundamental configuration settings for your
application; each setting is explained as follows:

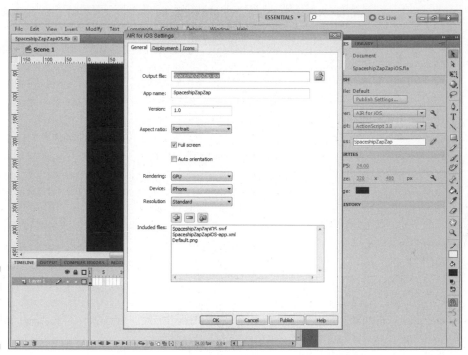

Figure 16-3:
The AIR for
iOS Settings
dialog box.

✔ **Output File:** The filename you give to the IPA application file when it is generated. By default, Flash Professional will assign your IPA the same name as your application FLA, but with an IPA file extension. If the default doesn't float your boat, you can change it here to anything you choose.

✔ **App Name:** The friendly name for your application, which will appear below the icon on iOS devices and in iTunes. Try to keep it between 12 and 14 characters in length or it will be truncated.

✔ **Version:** The version number you assign to each release of your application. Each time modifications are made, a new IPA is generated for submission to Apple and you must attach a new version number.

✔ **Aspect Ratio:** The display orientation your application will operate in when it starts on the mobile device. The Aspect Ratio drop-down list is set to Portrait by default, though you can change this to Landscape if you'd rather have your application start up in landscape mode.

✔ **Full Screen:** The display area for your application. The application will appear with the phone's status bar at the top or in the device's entire viewable display area. Gaming applications tend to operate in full-screen mode, whereas utility/productivity applications tend to operate with the device status bar remaining visible. The setting is largely up to you.

✔ **Auto Orientation.** Automatically reorient the application display when the device is rotated from a portrait (upright) hold to a landscape (sideways) hold.

✔ **Rendering:** Render display objects on the target device in one of three ways:

- *CPU:* The application uses the CPU (central processing unit) to render all display objects. No hardware acceleration is used.

- *GPU:* The application uses the device GPU (graphics processing unit) to render bitmaps.

- *Auto:* (At the time this book was published, the Auto option was not properly implemented in Flash Professional.) Currently does the same as the CPU setting. The intention is that this setting will allow your application to make the decision whether to render graphics using the CPU or GPU. For the time being, this setting is best avoided.

As a general rule, select GPU so that your application will use the enhanced performance of the mobile device's dedicated graphics hardware as opposed to the rendering computation having to be handled by the device's CPU. Choosing GPU over CPU is particularly important for gaming applications where objects move around the display rapidly and change frequently.

✔ **Resolution:** How your application graphics are drawn on high-resolution displays (such as those in the iPad and newer iPhones). Choosing Standard from the list means your application graphics are drawn at a lower resolution but are rendered faster. Choosing High draws graphics with the greatest level of detail, but rendering may take longer. I recommend choosing Standard, unless you are targeting the iPad.

✔ **Device:** The class of iOS device that you want to target with your application. You can select from three options:

- *iPhone:* Compile an IPA file that is compatible with the iPhone; includes all iPod touch devices.

- *iPad:* Compile an IPA file that is compatible with the iPad tablet device.

- *iPhone and iPad:* Compile an IPA file that is compatible with iPhone, iPod touch, and iPad devices.

✔ **Included Files:** This files that will be included in the resulting IPA file. For iOS applications, it's important to include `Default.png`, which I explain a little earlier in the chapter. To include the `Default.png` image, click the (+) icon and then browse to the directory containing the `Default.png` file for your application. Double-click the filename to add it to the Included Files list.

Deployment tab

The Deployment tab contains the settings required by the Packager for iOS part of the publishing process and is shown in Figure 16-4.

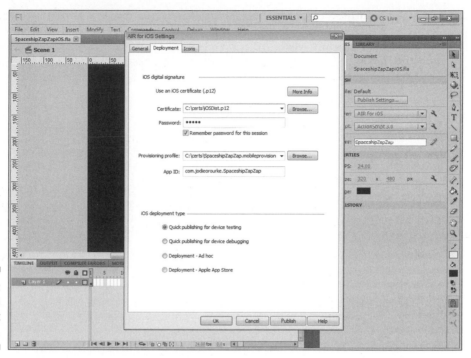

Figure 16-4:
AIR for iOS
Deployment
settings.

The iOS Digital Signature section (at the top) solicits the information required to digitally sign your iOS application. Then the iOS Deployment Type section (at the bottom) determines what type of application the packager should create. The following list explains each of your options:

- ✔ **Certificate:** The path to the P12 certificate file that you will use to sign your application. If you simply want to package your application for testing on your iOS device, you can use a Development Certificate. If you want to submit your application to the App Store, or distribute your IPA to a group of testers, you'll need to specify a Distribution Certificate here. I cover obtaining Development and Distribution certificates from Apple in Chapter 15. I show you how to convert them to P12 files, which are compatible with Flash Professional, later in this chapter.

- ✔ **Password:** The password assigned to the P12 certificate. The password is required to be able to use the certificate. Selecting the Remember Password for This Session check box means that you won't be required to enter the password again until Flash Professional is closed and restarted.

- ✔ **Provisioning Profile:** The information you provide in this field is determined by what you entered in the Certificate field. If you specified a Development Certificate in the Certificate field, enter the path to the Development Distribution Profile * . mobileprovision file. If you specified a Distribution Certificate in the Certificate field, enter a Distribution Provisioning Profile.

✔ **App ID:** A unique name to assign to your app. No other application in the Apple App Store should have the same ID as your app. To prevent name collisions, you can use reverse domain notation, where you take a website domain name that you own, assemble it backward, and then put your application name on the end. For example: `com.jodieorourke.SpaceshipZapZap`.

✔ **iOS Deployment Type:** The possible deployment formats for your application:

- *Quick Publishing for Device Testing:* Quickly compile a version of the application for testing on your developer iOS device.

- *Quick Publishing for Device Debugging:* The same as the first option, but the application is packaged so that the Flash Professional debugger console can receive `trace()` output from the application when it's running on the iOS device.

- *Deployment — Ad Hoc:* Create an application for ad hoc deployment. Use this option when you're distributing the application to a select number of testers.

- *Deployment — Apple App Store:* Create a final version of the IPA file for deployment to the Apple App Store.

Development and Distribution Certificates, along with Development and Distribution Provisioning Profiles, are obtained from the iOS Provisioning Portal as part of your iOS Developer Program subscription. Registering and obtaining certificates and provisioning profiles are detailed in Chapter 15. I show you how to convert your certificates for use in Flash Professional later in this chapter.

Icons tab

The Icons tab contains the information relating to the icons you want to package into the application. As you can see in Figure 16-5, this tab has a list of all the required icon sizes for your iOS application. For applications targeting iPhone and iPod touch devices, you are required to supply icons at 29x29, 57x57, 114x114, and 512x512 pixels in size. For the iPad, you are additionally required to submit icons at 48x48 and 72x72 pixels.

It's no coincidence that the 114x114 icon is twice the size of the standard 57x57 icon. A high-resolution display on an iOS device is composed of twice as many pixels as a lower resolution iOS device, so the high-resolution display uses the 114x114 icon.

Follow these steps to associate the icon files created earlier in this chapter with each of the sizes in the list:

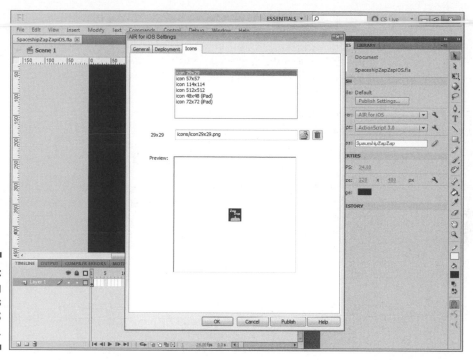

Figure 16-5:
Specifying
the icons
for your iOS
application.

1. **Select icon 29x29 from the list.**

   29x29 appears next to the file-path text box.

2. **Click the Open File icon to the right of the file-path text box.**

   A System File Open dialog box opens.

3. **Browse to the** `icons` **folder and select** `icon29x29.png`.

   Earlier, in the "Resizing your existing icons" section, you created a selection of icons specifically for iOS applications. Select the 29x29-pixel icon you created. (The path to the icon is shown in Figure 16-5.)

4. **Repeat Steps 1–3 for the other icons shown in the list.**

You need to specify only the 48x48-pixel and 72x72-pixel images if you intend to distribute your application to the iPad.

Modifying the Application Descriptor File

The Application Descriptor File is an XML document that accompanies all AIR applications. This file stores the settings that you configure using the friendly AIR for iOS Settings dialog box in Flash Professional.

Sometimes you may want to edit the Application Descriptor File manually. Advanced or new iOS settings that aren't offered in Flash Professional may have to be added to the XML file by hand. Editing it isn't hard, but I'm going to walk you through changing a couple of properties in it so that you feel comfortable should you need to edit it on your own later.

Changing the description in the Application Descriptor File

What if you wanted to add a description to your application that is displayed in iTunes? Although Flash Professional doesn't currently provide a way of doing this, you can manually add it to the descriptor XML file. Follow these steps to manually edit the app name for your iOS application in the Application Descriptor XML File:

1. **Browse to the directory containing your iOS application FLA.**

2. **Open the Application Descriptor XML File.**

   The name of this file is automatically constructed by Flash Professional using the name of your application FLA file, with a `-app.xml` suffix.

   If you cannot locate the file, you may need to execute the Test Movie feature in Flash Professional by pressing Ctrl+Enter (Windows) or Command+Enter (Mac). Doing this causes Flash Professional to generate the Application Descriptor File for the first time.

3. **Right-click (Windows) or Control+click (Mac) the file and select Open With to open the file with a text editor of your choice.**

   Before making changes to the file, make a backup copy of the old file. That way, if something undesirable happens as a result of changing the file, you can simply restore the original from the copy.

4. **Locate the** `<escription>` **XML node in the code.**

   You can find it nested in the `<application>` tag, directly below the filename node:

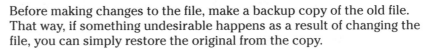

```
<filename>SpaceshipZapZapiOS</filename>
<description/>
<!-- To localize the description, use the following
        format for the description element.
<description>
    <text xml:lang="en">English App description goes
        here</text>
    <text xml:lang="fr">French App description goes
        here</text>
    <text xml:lang="ja">Japanese App description goes
        here</text>
</description>-->
```

Note that the second description block beneath has sample content in it. The `<!--` and `-->` tags wrapping this content mean that it's *commented out* and will be ignored during compilation and packaging.

5. **Select and delete the code** `<description/>`.

6. **Delete the content surrounding the** `<description>` **and** `<description/>` **tags so that you're left with the following XML:**

```
<description>
    <text xml:lang="en">English App description goes
        here</text>
    <text xml:lang="fr">French App description goes
        here</text>
    <text xml:lang="ja">Japanese App description goes
        here</text>
</description>
```

7. **Modify the English node contents by entering your description in the** `<text>` **node with the** `xml:lang="en"` **attribute.**

You'll notice that it's possible to specify descriptions in many different languages — Flash Professional automatically creates placeholders for English, French, and Japanese — though in this instance, I'm going to just specify an English description.

8. **Save the XML file so that it overwrites the previous version.**

The next time you package the application, the changes you made in the Application Descriptor File will be included.

Converting Your Apple Certificate to a P12 Certificate

A somewhat painful step in targeting iOS is the need to convert the Developer Certificate, which is a `.cer` file, into a `.p12` file for use with Flash Professional. P12 is the file extension for the Personal Information Exchange format.

Before you can convert your Developer Certificate to a P12, you need to download it from the iOS Provisioning Portal (`https://developer.apple.com/ios/manage/overview/index.action`). After you've downloaded the Developer Certificate, follow the steps for either Windows or Mac to convert the file to a P12 certificate that you can then specify in the AIR for iOS Settings dialog box in Flash Professional.

Windows

You need to take three main steps in Windows: convert the CER file to a temporary PEM file, convert the PEM file into a P12 file, and then configure a password for the P12 file. You need OpenSSL installed for your Windows Command Prompt application (introduced in Chapter 15) to complete the following steps. With Command Prompt open, follow these steps to perform the certificate conversion:

1. **Use the OpenSSL command-line tool (see Chapter 15) to enter the following code, where** `developer_identity.cer` **is the certificate you downloaded from the iOS Provisioning Portal:**

   ```
   openssl x509 -in developer_identity.cer -inform DER
           -out developer_identity.pem -outform PEM
   ```

   This code converts the CER file to an intermediary PEM file.

2. **At the OpenSSL command line, enter the following code to convert your temporary PEM file into the P12 file required by Flash Professional:**

   ```
   openssl pkcs12 -export -inkey mykey.key -in developer_
           identity.pem -out iphone_dev.p12
   ```

   Note that `mykey.key` must be the same 2048-bit RSA key you used to generate a Certificate Signing Request with in Chapter 15.

3. **Enter and verify the password for the new P12 certificate.**

   When a P12 file is generated, a password must be set up, which must be specified whenever the certificate is used. After verifying the password, the P12 certificate is ready to use in Flash Professional.

Don't forget your password! Try to make your password easy to remember or write it down if you can't. If you do forget the password for your P12, all is not lost. Just repeat the steps to convert your Apple Certificate to a P12 certificate and you'll be up and running again.

To save time, I've created a batch-file script that you can save to your Windows computer and then run when you want to convert a CER file to a P12 file.

1. **Open Notepad.**

2. **Copy the following code into Notepad:**

   ```
   @echo off
   SET OPENSSLBIN=c:\openssl\bin
   SET P12NAME=iphone_dev.p12
   cd /d %OPENSSLBIN%
   SET /p CERT=Enter certificate file name (*.cer):
   SET /p KEY=Enter key file name (*.key):

   ECHO Creating PEM
   openssl x509 -in %CERT% -inform DER -out developer_
           identity.pem -outform PEM
   ```

```
ECHO Creating P12
openssl pkcs12 -export -inkey %KEY% -in developer_
        identity.pem -out %P12NAME%

ECHO Your .P12 (%P12NAME%) file is now in %OPENSSLBIN%
PAUSE
```

3. **Press Ctrl+S to invoke the save as dialog.**

4. **Browse to the desktop folder.**

4. **Type the filename** ConvertAppleToP12.bat.

5. **Choose the Save as type as All Files (*.*).**

6. **Click Save.**

When you need to convert an Apple certificate to a P12 certificate, just double-click the ConvertAppleToP12.bat icon on your desktop. When the batch file has completed successfully, your command window screen appears as shown in Figure 16-6.

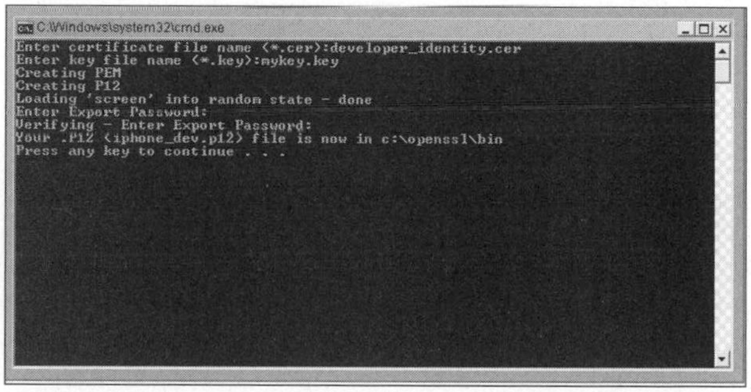

Figure 16-6:
Successful
certificate
conversion.

Mac OS

Converting Apple certificates to P12 certificates on a Mac is a little easier than it is on Windows computers. The Keychain Access application bundled with Mac OS can perform the conversion in a few easy clicks. Follow these steps to convert your certificate:

1. **Open the Keychain Access utility.**

   You can find this utility in the Applications➪Utilities folder in Mac OS X.

2. **Choose File➪Import Items.**

3. **Navigate to the certificate file (the CER file) that you downloaded from the iOS Provisioning Portal.**

4. **Select the Keys category in Keychain Access.**

5. **Select the private key that you used to generate the Certificate Signing Request for your iOS Development Certificate.**

6. **Choose File⇨Export Items.**

   A Save As dialog box opens.

7. **Enter a filename for the P12 certificate, and select where you want to save it. Choose the file format** `Personal Information Exchange (.p12)` **and click Save.**

   You are prompted to create a password that is used when you attempt to import this key to another computer.

8. **Enter a password, verify it, and then click OK.**

   The Keychain Access application generates the P12 certificate file and saves it to the location you specified.

 As with all your digital certificates, be sure to store your P12 certificate in a safe place on your computer, ideally a place where it cannot be mistakenly overwritten by the utility that created it. I find a good place to store all of my Apple certificates is on an external USB flash drive.

Signing the Application

Digitally signing your iOS application is a required step of the development process. It adds safeguards to the distribution process that go some way to reassuring the user of your application that the app came from a verifiable source.

Having followed the steps for obtaining a provisioning profile and certificate in Chapter 15, and then converting your Apple Developer Certificate into a P12 certificate in this chapter, now you can digitally sign your iOS Flash application. Follow these steps to do so:

1. **Open your iOS application FLA in Flash Professional.**

2. **Choose File⇨AIR for iOS Settings.**

3. **Click the Deployment tab.**

   The iOS Digital Signature section appears at the top of the screen.

4. **Click the Browse button next to the Certificate text box and browse to your saved P12 certificate.**

5. **Select the P12 certificate file and click Open.**

6. **Enter the password.**

   You provided this password when you converted your CER file into a P12 file. You can optionally select the Remember Password for This Session check box to keep from having to enter the password.

7. **Click Browse next to the Provisioning Profile field and select your Ad Hoc Distribution Provisioning Profile file from its location on your computer.**

   This is the Development Provisioning Profile `mobileprovision` file you created on the iOS Provisioning Portal using the Provisioning Assistant. The steps for obtaining this are detailed in Chapter 15.

8. **Enter an App ID.**

   By default, this field is populated with the name of your application FLA, but you shouldn't leave it as that. See the earlier section "Modifying the AIR for iOS Publish Settings in Flash Professional" to devise a unique ID for your application and the reasons why you should. If you've already set the App ID, you can leave this field as it is.

Your application is now signed with a Developer Certificate and has a Developer Provisioning Profile associated with it. After it is compiled, the application can be run on an iOS device that has the same Development Provisioning Profile installed on it. I show you how to install a provisioning profile on an iOS device in Chapter 15.

It is important to ensure that the Development Provisioning Profile and the Developer Certificate that you are compiling your application against were both generated using the same Certificate Signing Request (CSR). The application will not be correctly packaged if mismatched provisioning profiles and certificates are used. By default, the iOS Provisioning Portal creates a Developer Certificate for each Development Provisioning Profile it creates.

Compiling an IPA Using the AIR Packager for iOS

After your application is compiling and running in Flash Professional without throwing any errors, you can deploy it to your iOS device to see how well it behaves there. Packaging an IPA and putting it onto your device is easy using Flash Professional's publishing tools. To deploy your app to your iOS device, follow these simple steps:

1. **In Flash Professional, choose File⇨AIR for iOS Settings.**

2. **Click the Deployment tab.**

3. **Ensure that the iOS certificate and provisioning profile are already filled in.**

   Remember to enter your password for your P12 certificate. If you don't yet have a certificate or provisioning profile, see Chapter 15 for the steps to obtain these.

 4. **Under iOS Deployment Type, select Quick Publishing for Device Testing.**

 5. **Click the Publish Button.**

    Flash Professional begins working away compiling your application, packaging it as an iOS application. A dialog box appears at the end to inform you that the process is complete.

 The IPA file — the iOS app — is automatically saved to the directory in which your application FLA file is saved.

Chapter 17

Getting Your App onto an iOS Device

In This Chapter

▶ Installing your application on your iOS device with iTunes

▶ Deleting your application from your iOS device

▶ Compiling your application so that others can test it

*T*here comes a point in every baking process where it's time to sample the product. Having crafted the user interface (UI) and toiled over the code, it's time to see what your application looks like on an iOS device. You will inevitably need to make some tweaks, but rest assured that even the world's best chefs take multiple attempts to perfect their recipes.

Installation to iOS devices isn't the automated delight that you experience with AIR for Android applications. Sadly, Flash Professional has to yield to Apple's iTunes software for the act of installing your IPA (iOS application file) onto your device. Although this extra step lengthens the deployment process, it does afford you the ability to manage your installed applications using a nice graphical user interface.

In this chapter, I cover the steps for installing your compiled iOS application file onto your iOS device, seeing how to remove it, and then knowing how to get others in on the act of testing your application.

Using iTunes to Install Your App on an iOS Device

iTunes is the only approved route of getting your application onto your iOS device without invalidating your device warranty or breaching the iOS Developer Program terms, so it's best to stick with it — and it isn't all that bad! Follow this short set of steps to install your IPA file on your iOS device:

1. **Connect your iOS device to your computer with a USB cable.**

2. **Launch iTunes.**

3. **Confirm that the iOS device connected to your computer is listed on the left side under Devices.**

   If the device isn't listed, try disconnecting and then reconnecting the USB cable.

4. **Choose File⇨Add File to Library.**

   A file browser dialog box opens.

5. **Browse to the directory where you published your IPA file.**

   By default, your IPA file is published to the same directory as your application FLA file.

6. **Select the IPA file and click Open.**

   The application is imported to iTunes, and iTunes switches to the Apps Library view to show you your application, as shown in Figure 17-1.

Figure 17-1: An iOS application imported into the iTunes Library.

SpaceshipZapZap imported to my iTunes library

Now that you've uploaded your application to iTunes, it's time to sync it with your device. Right-click (Windows) or Control+click (Mac) the device listed under Devices on the left side of iTunes. Select Sync from the context menu that opens. iTunes notifies you that it is syncing with the attached device. After syncing is complete, you can find your application icon in the list of installed apps on the iOS device.

After the application is on the device, you can run it like any other iOS application. Give it a go and see how well your app performs!

Removing an App from Your iOS Device

It stands to reason that if I tell you how to put an application on your device, you're going to want to know how to remove it, right? You can remove an app in two ways, both of which you'll be familiar with if you're an iPhone or iPod touch user. You can delete the app either directly from the device or via iTunes. I explain each option in the next sections.

Delete the app from the device

The easiest way of getting rid of an installed iOS application is to do it directly on the device. Follow these instructions to delete an app from your device:

1. **Press and hold the app icon of the application you want to remove.**

   The app icon and all the surrounding app icons vibrate, and each has an X assigned to its upper-right corner.

2. **Press the X on the app.**

   The application is deleted.

3. **Press the Main Menu button (the round one at the bottom of the device) to exit Delete mode.**

   All the app icons stop vibrating.

A flaw exists in this process, though: The next time you sync this device with iTunes, the app will come back. This situation can sometimes make you question your sanity: "I deleted that, didn't I?" I prefer to do any installation or removal using iTunes, which stops my iPhone from playing mind games with me!

Delete the app using iTunes

You used iTunes to get the application on the device, so why not use it to get the app off too? Connect your iOS device to your computer with a USB cable and open iTunes; then follow these steps to delete the application from your device:

1. **Select Apps — under the Library list on the left side of iTunes.**

   iTunes switches to Apps view, and you see a list of all your iOS applications.

2. **Right-click (Windows) or Control+click (Mac) the app you want to delete.**

3. **Choose Delete from the context menu that appears.**

   A warning dialog box appears asking you to confirm your delete action.

4. **Click Remove.**

   A second dialog box appears asking whether you want to leave the IPA file in the Mobile Applications folder. Because you have a local copy of this application in your Flash application's project directory, you can safely remove the IPA file.

5. **Click Move to Trash.**

   The application is removed from the list of apps in the Library.

6. **Sync your iOS device.**

   The application is removed from the attached device.

Distributing Your iOS App to Other Testers

Having satisfied yourself that your application is good enough for the world to see, it's time to get a few extra pairs of eyes (and hands) on your application. Given the cost of acquiring just one iOS device isn't trivial, the cost of acquiring multiple devices could prove prohibitive to most. Fortunately, most of us have friends and colleagues who sport a variety of models and generations of iOS devices. Now wouldn't it be useful if you had a way to get these folks to play with your application without going through a full-fledged deployment to the Apple App Store? Enter the Ad Hoc Distribution Provisioning Profile and the Distribution Certificate.

Ad Hoc Distribution allows you to supply a version of your application that works only on the devices whose IDs have been specified in the Distribution Provisioning Profile, and where that provisioning profile has also been installed on the device. By implementing this method, Apple prevents your application from being freely distributed and installed on iOS devices outside of the App Store while allowing you to test your application on various devices.

Add your testers' devices to the iOS Provisioning Portal

The ID of each device you want to test your application on must be included in the Ad Hoc Distribution Provisioning Profile. For this to happen, each of the devices needs to be registered in the Devices section on the iOS Provisioning Portal. So, the first thing you need to do is request the 40-character Device ID from each of your testers. To find the Device ID, follow these steps:

1. **Connect the iOS device to the computer with a USB cable.**

2. **Open iTunes.**

3. **Click the iOS device listed under Devices in the left navigation pane in iTunes.**

   The Summary screen for that device appears in the main area of iTunes.

4. **Click the serial number to toggle to the Unique Device ID (UDID).**

   This is the Device ID.

5. **Choose Edit⇨Copy.**

   The Device ID is copied to the Clipboard.

At this point, have your friends send you the Device ID (or make a note of the ID if you're registering your own device) so that you can register the devices on the Provisioning Portal. When you're ready to register the devices with the Provisioning Portal, follow these instructions:

1. **Navigate to the iOS Provisioning Portal at** `https://developer.apple.com/ios/manage/overview/index.action`.

2. **Click the Devices link on the left.**

3. **Select the Manage**

   The Current Registered Devices list is shown.

4. **Click Add Devices.**

   The Add Devices screen appears, with empty Device Name and Device ID text boxes.

5. **Type each device name.**

   It's best to enter the tester's name and his or her device type, for example, **Tony Blair's iPhone**. (Obviously, Tony has to do something with his time now that he's no longer the British Prime Minister.)

6. **Type the Device ID.**

   Enter the 40-character ID that the tester gave you.

7. **Click Submit.**

   The device is added to the Current Registered Devices list.

After registering all the devices, the next step is to create a Distribution Certificate. I explain that process in the next section.

Obtaining a Distribution Certificate

A Distribution Certificate is the digital certificate you use to sign your application to install it on multiple test devices or before submitting it to the App Store. Unlike its Developer counterpart, the Distribution Certificate is not automatically generated when a Provisioning Profile is generated. The following steps describe how to create and download a Distribution Certificate:

1. **Navigate to the iOS Provisioning Portal at** `https://developer.apple.com/ios/manage/overview/index.action`.

2. **Click the Certificates link on the left.**

3. **Click the Distribution tab.**

    A message tells you that you don't currently have a valid Distribution Certificate.

4. **Click the Request Certificate button.**

    The Create iOS Distribution Certificate page appears, as shown in Figure 17-2.

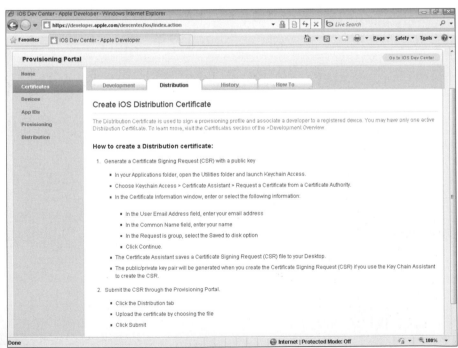

Figure 17-2:
The Create iOS Distribution Certificate screen.

5. **Upload the Certificate Signing Request file**.

   This is the same file you created and uploaded for your Development Provisioning Profile, which I cover in Chapter 15.

   If your upload was successful, you're returned to the Distribution Certificate page, where you see the name of the certificate you just requested, together with `Pending Approval` in the status column.

6. **Click the Approve button.**

The page refreshes, and the message in the status column changes to `Pending Issuance`, as shown in Figure 17-3. This simply means that the certificate is being generated on the Apple servers. The issuing process can be immediate, but it may be slower at busy periods. You can check whether your certificate request has been generated by reloading the page or waiting for a notification e-mail from the Apple Developer Program.

You may wonder why you need to approve your own certificate requests. On some iOS Developer Program subscriptions, multiple users are permitted to request Distribution Certificates. However, only the primary account holder, or Program Admin, is allowed to approve these requests. For an individual subscription, you are the Program Admin.

After the Distribution Certificate is issued, you see a completed certificate ready to be downloaded, as shown in Figure 17-4.

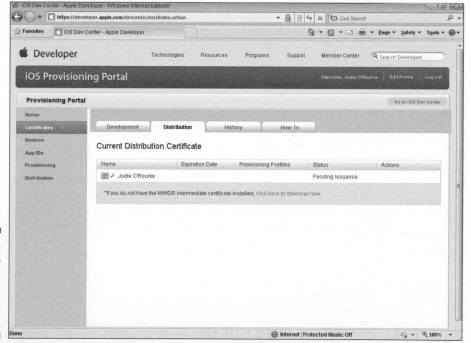

Figure 17-3:
A new Distribution Certificate pending issuance.

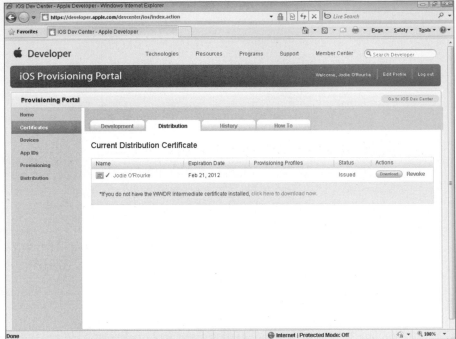

Figure 17-4:
A Distri-
bution
Certificate
ready for
downloading.

Click the Download button to save the Distribution Certificate to your computer, and then follow the steps in Chapter 16 to convert the .cer file you downloaded into a .P12 certificate that you can use in Flash Professional.

The next step after obtaining your Distribution Certificate is to obtain an Ad Hoc Provisioning Profile, which you include with your application, and install it on the iOS devices on which you want to test your application.

Ad Hoc Distribution Provisioning Profile

If you'd like to install your application on more than one iOS device for testing, you'll need an Ad Hoc Distribution Provisioning Profile. Perhaps your peers are developing applications that they'd like you to test for them, and in return they test yours for you. In these situations, an Ad Hoc Distribution Provisioning Profile could be just the ticket. Like the Development Provisioning Profile, this profile must be manually installed on each iOS device on which the application will be tested.

The following steps show you how to create an Ad Hoc Distribution Provisioning Profile:

1. **Navigate to the iOS Provisioning Portal at** `https://developer.apple.com/ios/manage/overview/index.action`.

2. **Click the Provisioning link on the left.**

   A screen with a set of tabs appears.

3. **Click the Distribution tab.**

   The Distribution Provisioning Profiles page displays.

4. **Click New Profile.**

5. **Select Ad Hoc as the distribution method.**

6. **Type a name of your choice for the profile.**

7. **Select the ID of your app from the drop-down list.**

   If your app isn't listed, you first need to create a Development Provisioning Profile for it. Follow the steps described earlier in this chapter for creating a Development Provisioning Profile; then return here to continue.

8. **Select the check box next to each device you want to install this Provisioning Profile on.**

9. **Click Submit.**

   The Distribution Provisioning Profiles page appears, listing your new Ad Hoc Provisioning Profile as Active.

10. **Click the Download button, and save the new Ad Hoc Distribution Provisioning Profile to your computer.**

Recompile for ad hoc distribution

The trusty old IPA file that you've been using for testing on your own device now needs to be retired in favor of one that is compiled as an Ad Hoc Distribution IPA. Switching out the files allows the app to be installed on up to 100 devices listed in the Ad Hoc Distribution Provisioning Profile. To switch from using your original IPA file to using an Ad Hoc Distribution IPA file, follow these steps:

1. **Open your iOS application FLA in Flash Professional.**

2. **Choose File⇨AIR for iOS Settings.**

   The AIR for iOS Settings dialog box appears.

3. **Click the Deployment tab.**

   A new screen appears with a section for iOS Digital Signature.

4. **Click the folder icon next to the Certificate text box.**

5. **Browse to the location on your computer where you have saved your P12 certificate file, select the file, and click Open.**

   You're asked for a password.

6. **Type your password.**

   This is the password you provided when you converted your `.cer` file into a `.P12` file. You can select the Remember Password check box so that you don't have to keep entering the password.

7. **Click Browse next to the Provisioning Profile field and select your Ad Hoc Distribution Provisioning Profile file from its location on your computer.**

   You created the Ad Hoc Distribution Provisioning Profile `mobileprovision` file earlier in this chapter using the iOS Provisioning Portal.

8. **Select Deployment — Ad Hoc as the iOS deployment type, and click Publish.**

   After a short delay, the new IPA file for Ad Hoc Distribution is created in the same directory as the application FLA.

After you have compiled your new IPA file, you can distribute it to testers, whose device IDs have been included in the Ad Hoc Distribution Provisioning Profile, to install on their devices. In the next section, I tell you how to do this.

Distribute to your testers

Your testers need to install two files on their iOS devices to be able to test your application:

- ✔ The Ad Hoc Distribution Provisioning Profile
- ✔ The Ad Hoc Distribution IPA file

You'll need to provide both of these files to them — you can send them by e-mail or on a USB flash drive.

Advise the tester to first install the provisioning profile on his or her iOS device, following the steps laid out in Chapter 15. Then install the application on the device, following the instructions provided in the section "Using iTunes to Install Your App on an iOS Device," earlier in this chapter.

After installing the two files on their devices, your testers will be able to use your application in the same way that they would any other iOS application on their devices. With luck, they'll provide you with some invaluable feedback! For a start, you could consider asking them to look out for performance bugs, in addition to obvious crashes. Ask whether they felt the features and functionality of your application are what they would expect, and whether they felt the presentation was usable and aesthetically pleasing. To ensure your application gets tested in its entirety, it's often helpful to provide a set of tasks that your testers should complete using your application.

Part V

Testing and Sending Your App to Market

The 5th Wave   By Rich Tennant

"Marketing said they'd make these things levitate off retailers' shelves. Apparently, someone in engineering heard them first."

In this part . . .

"This little piggy went to market, this little piggy stayed at home, this little piggy had roast beef . . ." To be honest, I'm interested only in the piggy that went to market, because he probably earned his owner some money. If piggy were an app, I'd like him to go to market and be downloaded a million times. Part V is about taking the fruits of your labor and displaying them in the app stores for the world to see and, I hope, buy!

Chapter18 looks at the all-important but often overlooked task of rigorously testing your application before you ship it. Chapter 19 walks you through the process of submitting your AIR for Android application to the Google Android Market. Chapter 20 looks at the steps for submitting your Flash iOS application to the fabled Apple App Store.

Chapter 18

Performance Is Key: Testing the Application

Getting something right the first time is one of those hugely satisfying yet rare experiences for all of us. The more complicated the task, the less likely you are to get it right on the first attempt. In software development, the number of variables in play makes the probability of building an entire application without a single bug very low. Were you to defy the odds and create a bug-free application, how would you know? The answer is through testing.

Testing allows you to verify the completeness and suitability of an application against a set of criteria that are usually defined in advance of the application's development. Testing also enables scenarios that might not have been envisaged by the developer to be run on the application to see whether they expose bugs.

This chapter presents you with the tools available in your arsenal to spot bugs, consistently reproduce them, and understand why they might arise in the first place. I show you how to use Device Central, a software application for testing mobile applications, and then how to use the debugging tools in both Flash Professional and Flash Builder. After you've successfully identified where a bug is happening, you can fix it in your application's code.

Identifying and Isolating Potential Bottlenecks

One of the most troubling types of bugs for mobile application developers is one that occurs not because of a coding defect in the application, but because of a lack of resources on the host device to be able to handle the amount of logic it is being asked to process. Although this is a challenge seldom faced by a Flash developer targeting the web, it's hugely pertinent to a Flash developer building applications for mobile devices. Fortunately, you have a toolbox at your disposal to mitigate against hangs and crashes on mobile devices. To make sure that you get the most out of these tools, it helps to know what you can do to get a good first run through testing and then know how put your application under stress. Two of the most basic things you can do to ensure your success are rereading your code and then trying to break your code.

Rereading your code

It might sound like I've put this here to fill a bit of space on the page, but I'm convinced that any developer who goes back over the code he wrote a couple of days — or weeks — ago will find modifications he can make. It's similar to writing an essay. Although a first draft might not have any spelling or grammatical errors, you may find plenty of ways to put a point across more eloquently when you reread and edit that draft. I believe that the same is true for code. As you review your code, ask yourself whether you need to loop that many times, whether you need to keep creating new instances of the same object type, or whether an object pool would work better.

Add comments — inline notes that have no bearing on the way your code executes — to your code to improve is readability and to highlight areas that may require further attention. In the following example, my comments tell me the purpose of loadMethod(), and a reminder tells me I need to come back later and check whether this was the best way to write the code:

```
/* Initiates a request for data from the remote service
 * in the E4X format. Calls onLoadComplete() when done.
 *
 * TODO: There may be a faster way to do this.
 * Check, and then delete this comment.
 */
private function loadData() :void
{
    //...
}
```

Everything inside the /* */ comment markers is a comment and ignored when your application runs.

Check that your event listener registrations are being removed each time an object is being discarded, or consider using weakly referenced listeners. After you've made these modifications, your application is going into testing with a far higher level of confidence.

Trying to break your code

Whether you're testing your application on a device, in a testing tool such as Adobe Device Central, or on your computer desktop, try to deviate from the "happy path" as much as you can. Bear in mind that your users won't necessarily use the application the way you intended, and your application needs to be able to cope with some real abuse. iOS and Android devices support multiple touch points, so start by pressing all the buttons in your application at the same time. Try to perform multiple gestures. Give the device a good long shake to get the accelerometer functionality working hard. If you find that your application hangs or crashes, congratulate yourself on a job well done — you've just saved one of your users from finding that bug.

Testing Your Application with Device Central

Adobe Device Central is an emulation tool that helps developers to see how their applications will run on a variety of mobile devices. The software comes preloaded with hundreds of common device profiles, that is, the characteristics of the hardware and software and the performance of a device. By selecting one of these device profiles and then selecting the Flash application to run, Device Central attempts to run the application as though it were running on the device itself. It is easy to switch between device profiles, so a developer can use Device Central to emulate the behavior of his application on a number of mobile devices with very little effort.

Tools such as Device Central are massively helpful in identifying issues that may floor an application across a range of devices, and should be included in the testing plan for your application. What Device Central doesn't do is replace testing on the device itself. Before making a decision to support a particular device, it is still important to install the application on a physical mobile device and verify that the functionality of your application is as expected.

Device Central is packaged with Flash Professional and Creative Suite products. It can be found in the Program menu (Windows) or the Applications folder (Mac). If you can't find Device Central on your computer, or need further information about it, visit `www.adobe.com/products/devicecentral.html`.

Selecting a device profile

Before you can test your application in Device Central, you have to select a device profile against which you'll run your test. The following steps show how to select an AIR device profile:

1. **Open Device Central on your computer.**

   The application opens to the Welcome screen.

2. **Click Browse Devices.**

   This option is just below the Device Profiles heading on the Welcome screen. If at any time the Welcome screen is not present, click the Browse link at the upper-right corner of the application.

   The Device Library window opens, listing hundreds of device profiles for you to choose from.

3. **Use the search box at the top of the list to search for AIR.**

   As you type, a filter is immediately applied to the list, leaving only a few device profiles.

4. **Select the device listing named AIR 2.5 32 480x800 Multitouch — if multiple devices have the same name, select the one with Adobe listed as the creator — and then right-click (Windows) or Command+click (Mac) and select Download Device Profile.**

   The device profile is downloaded from the Internet to your computer. The icon in the location column changes from a planet to a smaller planet with a computer next to it.

5. **From the list, select and then drag the newly downloaded AIR 2.5 32 480x800 Multitouch device profile to the AIR list in the Test Devices panel at the far left.**

   The device is added to the list of available test devices.

6. **Double-click the AIR 2.5 32 480x800 Multitouch item in the Test Devices list to select it.**

   The Mobile Device icon changes to an orange-and-black circle, indicating that it is the active device profile. A selected AIR 2.5 32 480x800 Multitouch device profile is shown in Figure 18-1.

With a device profile configured and selected for use, you can now move on to prepare and then open your Flash mobile application in Device Central.

Preparing and opening an application

After you select a device profile for use, you can open an application in Device Central and begin testing its behavior and resource usage. Device Central is able to test the SWF file that Flash Professional generates as a by-product of the compiling operations. However, Device Central tests the application in the context of an embedded Flash file, not as an AIR application. So before you start your Device Central testing, be sure to wrap any AIR-specific code in the application in conditions that check whether the player type is desktop, which means the AIR runtime. Follow these steps to update the code you've written for the SpaceshipZapZap application to run safely on both browser-based Flash Player plug-ins (like the one used in Device Central) and on AIR for Android/iOS:

1. **Open** `SpaceshipZapZap.as` **for edit in Flash Professional.**

2. **Press Ctrl+F (Windows) or Command+F (Mac) to invoke the Find and Replace dialog box.**

   A small window displaying a Find What text box appears.

3. **Type** NativeApplication **into the Find What text box and press Find Next.**

4. **Wrap** NativeApplication **references with an** if **statement that takes the** Capabilities.playerType **condition:**

```
if( Capabilities.playerType == "Desktop" )
{
    NativeApplication.nativeApplication.
        addEventListener( Event.DEACTIVATE,
        onApplicationFocusLost );
    NativeApplication.nativeApplication.systemIdleMode
        = SystemIdleMode.KEEP_AWAKE;
}
```

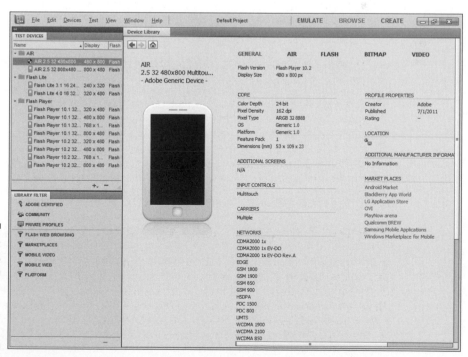

Figure 18-1:
An AIR 2.5 32 480x800 Multitouch device profile ready for testing.

When the SpaceshipZapZap application starts, the `initialize` method is run. This method contains two lines of code responsible for checking when the application loses focus, and stopping the application from going to sleep. Both of these operations are dependent on the application running as an AIR application, and they will cause errors when the application is run in any other Flash runtime, such as a browser-based Flash Player. Use `Capabilities.playerType` to check whether the player type is desktop, and if it is, allow the two lines of code to be run.

If you added references to `NativeApplication` in any other classes associated with the project, be sure to open those, too, and wrap the `NativeApplication` references with a player type check.

5. **Press Ctrl+Enter (Windows) or Command+Enter (Mac) to run the application in Flash Professional.**

   The application compiles and launches in an AIR application window. Additionally, if you look in the folder where your application FLA file is saved, a new SWF file has been generated. Checking the date the file was modified confirms that the file has just been updated.

6. **Launch the Device Central application from the Programs menu (Windows) or the Applications folder (Mac).**

   The program opens to the Welcome screen.

7. **Choose File⇨Open file.**

   Alternatively, press Ctrl+O (Windows) or Command+O (Mac). A system file browser dialog box opens.

8. **Browse to the directory of your SpaceshipZapZap application FLA file and double-click the SWF file with the same name.**

   The SWF file is loaded into Device Central, and its graphical output appears in the device window, as shown in Figure 18-2.

The application is now loaded into Device Central against a device profile, so the fun of testing how the application performs can now begin.

Simulating accelerometer data

Desktop computers aren't designed to be waved around in the same manner as mobile devices, so desktop computer manufacturers leave out input components such as accelerometers — a motion-sensing component in mobile devices, which I introduced in Chapter 11. As you'll have found throughout the development of your application in Flash Professional, this creates a bit of a problem when your application relies on the accelerometer data as user input. Fear not; the people behind Device Central realized this and built in an accelerometer controller so that the party can continue! By modifying the degrees of rotation on one of the three accelerometer axes, you can mimic the physical act of moving the phone along one of these axes. Follow these steps in Device Central to simulate a right and left rotation of a mobile device:

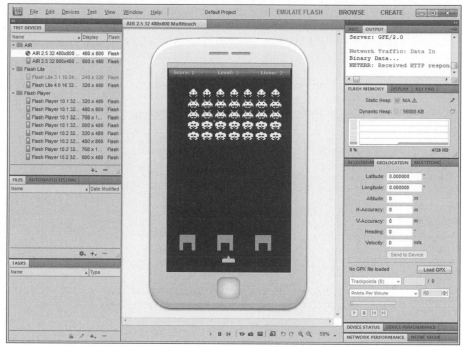

Figure 18-2:
A Flash application loaded into Device Central.

1. **Ensure that the device profile is selected and that the Flash application is loaded.**

   Follow the steps in the earlier sections "Selecting a device profile" and "Preparing and opening an application," if you haven't already done this.

2. **Choose Window➪Flash➪Accelerometer.**

   The Accelerometer panel appears on the right side of the screen.

3. **At the top of the Accelerometer panel, select the Upright radio button.**

4. **In the Z text box, type a value of** –70.

   The device shown in the Accelerometer panel immediately rotates to the left, as does the device displaying your application in the AIR 2.5 32 480x80 Multitouch panel. Any behavior in your application associated with the accelerometer is also triggered. For example, the defender spacecraft in my SpaceshipZapZap application has moved to the far left of the screen, as shown in Figure 18-3.

5. **Enter a value of** 70 **into the Z text box.**

   The device now rotates to the right and triggers any behavior coded into your application associated with this movement.

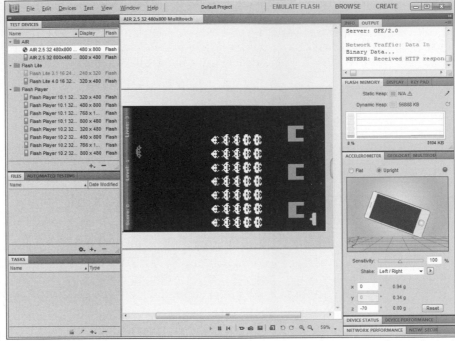

Figure 18-3:
Simulating
a left
rotation
using
Device
Central.

You'll find that being able to test accelerometer behavior, without needing to deploy the application to a mobile device, is a real time-saver.

The Accelerometer panel also allows you to simulate movement on the x and y axes. Just enter the degrees of rotation you want to apply to each of the axis, then observe the change. You can also simulate rapid left/right, up/down and back/forth shakes by making a selection from the Shake drop-down list and pressing the adjacent Play button.

Testing on a Device

Device Central serves as a handy testing environment when you're developing your application, but it doesn't replace the eventual need for you to test your application on the target device(s). You can deploy an application to an Android device for testing directly in Flash Professional. Unlike on Android, debugging on iOS devices is a little more convoluted because Apple doesn't allow applications other than iTunes to install application files onto iOS devices. In addition, iOS has no mechanism to allow Flash Professional and your application to share runtime debugging information over a USB cable. Fortunately, Adobe has programmed the iOS Flash application container and Flash Professional so that they can conduct a debugging session over a local Wi-Fi network, in a process called *remote debugging*. Provided your device and computer are connected to the same local network, and your computer isn't hiding behind an overly aggressive firewall application, you can debug your Flash mobile application on your iOS device using the remote debugging technique.

In this section, I show you how to prepare and debug your AIR for iOS application on an iOS device and then your AIR for Android application on an Android device. You can decide which is easiest!

Publishing an AIR for iOS application for debug

Before you can debug a Flash application on an iOS mobile device, you must first publish and package the app within Flash Professional. Follow these quick steps to create a debug IPA file:

1. **Open an iOS Flash application** `fla` **file in Flash Professional.**

2. **Choose File⇨iPhone OS Settings.**

   The iPhone OS Settings dialog box appears.

3. **From the four options available under iPhone Deployment Type, select Quick Publishing for Device Debugging.**

4. **Click Publish.**

   Flash Professional compiles and packages the iOS application file (IPA).

5. **Deploy to the connected iOS device.**

   Follow the steps covered in Chapter 17 if you're not sure how to install the application on your connected device.

That covers the preparation of your application for debugging on the device. The next step is to launch the application and connect it to the debugger.

Debugging an AIR for iOS application using Flash Professional

Your iOS debugging application and Flash Professional are able to communicate with each other over a local Wi-Fi network. Follow these steps to initiate a debugging session between your application running on your iOS device and Flash Professional:

1. **In Flash Professional, choose Debug⇨Begin Remote Debug Session⇨ ActionScript 3.0.**

   The Output panel displays the message Waiting for Player to connect.

2. **Launch the application on the iOS device.**

   As the application launches, a Flash Debugger prompt displays on the iOS device, requesting you to enter the IP address or hostname, as shown in Figure 18-4.

3. **Type the network IP address of your development computer.**

   To find out your development computer's IP address, open the command prompt and type **ipconfig** (Windows) or open Terminal and type **ifconfig** (Mac). The address usually begins with 192.168.

4. **Click OK.**

   The Flash iOS application attempts to make contact with Flash Professional over the local network. When the connection has succeeded, the SWF filename and the file size after compression are displayed in the Output panel in Flash Professional.

5. **Interact with your application and view the results in the Output panel.**

   Placing trace() statements inside your application code causes these to be written to the Output panel, as shown in Figure 18-5.

Remote debugging gives you the ability to test your iOS applications directly on the target device, while retaining the ability to see what is going on under the hood, which is helpful when you're trying to isolate a device-specific bug!

Figure 18-4:
A debug application requesting the IP address or hostname.

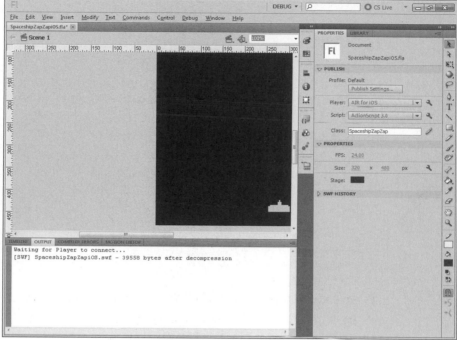

Figure 18-5:
Trace
output from
a remote
iOS app
being
logged
in Flash
Professional.

Publishing and debugging an AIR for Android application using Flash Professional

Flash Professional makes debugging on an Android device easy. The process is as simple as connecting your device and then selecting the debug option in Flash Professional. Follow these steps to debug your AIR for Android application in your device via USB:

1. **Connect your Android device to your computer via USB.**

2. **Open Flash Professional.**

3. **Choose File⇨AIR for Android Settings.**

   The AIR for Android Settings dialog box appears.

4. **Ensure both the Certificate and Password fields are completed, and select the Remember Password for This Session check box.**

   I explain how to complete these two fields in Chapter 13.

5. **Click OK.**

   The AIR for Android Settings dialog box closes.

6. **Choose Debug⇨Debug Movie⇨On device via USB.**

   The publishing activity dialog box appears, then closes when publishing is complete. Your application opens on your Android device, and at the same time the following text can be seen in the Output panel in Flash Professional:

   ```
   Waiting for Player to connect...
   [SWF] TheNameOfMyApp.swf - 9610 bytes after
         decompression
   ```

   This text indicates that Flash Professional and your application running on the Android device are now communicating with each other.

7. **Perform your debugging tests.**

   You may be trying to see what's happening in your code when the application appears unresponsive; in debug mode, you can see the error messages that are hidden when your application is running on a device. Alternatively, you may have put `trace()` statements in your AS3.0 code, and want to see those while the application is running.

8. **Close your application on the connected Android device.**

   The message `Debugging session terminated` appears in the Output panel in Flash Professional.

Using the Network Monitor in Flash Builder

If, instead of Flash Professional, you've used Flash Builder to build your mobile application — using the Flex framework — then some extra features in Flash Builder can help you to quickly and easily find the cause of problems in your application. The Network Monitor is a feature of Flash Builder — I give a comprehensive introduction to Flash Builder in Chapter 12 — which enables you see any outbound and inbound communication that your application is making with various web servers and data services. Files that are loaded into your application at runtime, as well as XML responses received in response to service requests, appear in a real-time list with Network Monitor. If you find that your application isn't behaving as you expect when loading a remote resource — such as an XML file hosted on a web server — the list that the Network Monitor generates allows you to see what requests your application is making and what data it's getting back. The Network Monitor may help you to see that a request for the XML isn't made at all, or that a request is being made, but the data isn't coming back to the application in a format you're expecting. It's tools like these that make Flash Builder a better code developer tool than Flash Professional — my sanity has been saved by this tool on more than one occasion!

You can launch the Network Monitor when your application is being run or debugged in Flash Builder, but you first need a working project in Flash

Builder. In Chapter 12, I show you how to create a Flex project in Flash Builder called MyFirstFlexProject. If you haven't built that application yet, head back to Chapter 12 now, then resume from here when you're done.

Although the following steps show you how to use the Network Monitor against that Flex project, the steps are identical for any Flex mobile project:

1. **Launch Flash Builder and open** MyFirstFlexProject.

   I show you how to create the MyFirstFlexProject application in Chapter 12.

2. **Click the Network Monitor tab.**

   By default, Flash Builder displays the Problems tab at the bottom of the Flash Perspective. The third tab is the Network Monitor tab. Currently, the label below the tab states Disabled for project MyFirstMobileProject.

3. **Click the small icon depicting a computer screen with a green tick.**

   This icon is on the far right of the Network Monitor tab.

   The icon changes to a computer screen with a disable/cancel symbol. The label below the tab changes to Enabled for project MyFirstMobileProject.

4. **Press Ctrl+F11 (Windows) or Command+F11 (Mac) to run the application.**

   Alternatively, choose Run⇨Run. The application launches in the familiar AIR window, and the Network Monitor displays the text Recording.

5. **Explore the Response tab for the** HTTPService **call.**

   The MyFirstMobileProject application makes a single HTTP request when it tries to load an RSS feed from the BBC News website. The HTTP request is logged in the list on the left side of the Network Monitor panel, while the details for each item are viewed on the right, as shown in Figure 18-6.

   Looking inside an HTTP response is a bit like unstacking a Russian doll — the response is made up of layer upon layer of nested objects that you have to open to discover the next. In Flash Builder's Network Monitor, click the Response tab, and then expand the Response body by clicking it to reveal child items. Keep going until you can't drill down any further.

6. **Switch to Raw view by clicking the middle of three icons sitting to the far right of the Request and Response tabs.**

   By default, the Network Monitor presents the contents of the Request and Response tabs as a tree view. Sometimes it may be easier to view the data that was sent to the server and what was returned as a simple text file — I certainly find it easier to read myself!

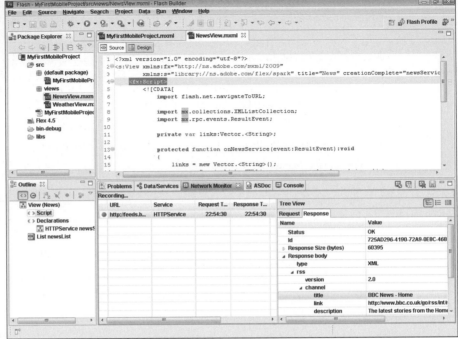

Figure 18-6:
The
Network
Monitor
displaying
an
HTTPService
request.

As you build more complicated applications in Flash Builder, the Network
Monitor list will fill with requests made to various locations. You can analyze
all the requests in detail, which gives you yet another way to isolate any bugs
in your application, or the service data for that matter.

Using the Performance Profiler in Flash Builder

In the past, one of the trickiest aspects of Flash application development
was knowing what was going on inside your application when things weren't
behaving quite as they should. Flash Builder solved that problem not only
with line-by-line debugging of your code but by also allowing you to inspect
the performance of the various components of your application using a built-
in tool called the Performance Profiler. The Performance Profiler enables you
to see how much memory your application is using and which objects are
responsible for any *leakage,* which occurs when an incident of an object is
no longer required but is not cleared from memory when a new incident is
generated. Tools such as the Performance Profiler set Flash Builder ahead of
Flash Professional as a more helpful and user-friendly developer tool.

Starting a profiling session

To use the Performance Profiler, you first need an application to profile. In Chapter 12, I show you how to create a Flex project in Flash Builder called `MyFirstFlexProject`. If you haven't built that application yet, head back to Chapter 12 and then resume from here when you're done. Although the following steps show you how to use the Performance Profiler against that Flex project, these steps are identical for any Flex mobile project:

1. **Launch Flash Builder 4.5 and open MyFirstFlexProject.**

2. **Choose Run⇨Profile.**

   After a short wait while Flash Builder compiles your application, the Connection Established dialog box appears.

3. **Click Resume.**

   Flash Builder launches the application in an AIR window and toggles to the Flash Profile screen, as shown in Figure 18-7.

Understanding the Flash Builder Profile screen

After you have the Performance Profiler up and running in Flash Builder, the set of panels that are displayed to you on the Flash Profile screen of Flash Builder can at first appear a little daunting. Although the data is presented well, you'll often find that you're searching for only a particular piece of information, so not all the features and displays will be applicable. Working clockwise around the Flash Profile screen from the upper left, here's what you have:

- ✔ **Profile panel:** This panels states the path of the file currently running as well as the file paths of any sessions that were previously profiled but not deleted. Selecting a profile enables a set of icons above that allow you to control the profiling activity.

- ✔ **Memory Usage panel:** This graphical panel plots the change in memory usage in your application over a 100-second period. The most recent memory events in your application appear from the right, and the oldest events move off the right side of the chart. The Peak Memory (red) line indicates the highest usage of memory since profiling started. The Current Memory (blue) line shows the amount of memory the application is currently using. It's normal to see these lines diverge and converge from time to time.

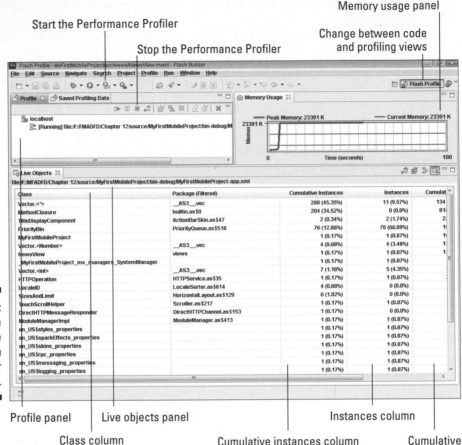

Memory usage panel

Change between code and profiling views

Start the Performance Profiler

Stop the Performance Profiler

Figure 18-7:
The
Performance
Profiler in
Flash Builder
after launch.

Profile panel   Live objects panel

Class column

Cumulative instances column

Instances column

Cumulative column

✔ **Live Objects panel:** The largest of all the panels on this screen, the Live Objects panel lists all the objects created in the application since profiling started. Some of the columns contain useful information; others are helpful only in niche circumstances. The fundamentals are as follows:

- The Class column lists the type of object.

- The Cumulative Instances column displays the total number of times an object of that type has been created since profiling started.

- The Instances column states how many objects of that type are "live" in the application right now.

- The Memory column on the far right (not shown in Figure 18-7) displays how much memory all the instances of an object type are occupying. The value in brackets is the percentage of the total memory used by the application.

What does a memory leak look like?

A memory leak occurs when your application is using an ever-increasing amount of the available system memory, until it reaches a point where the system is no longer able to allocate any more memory to the application and the application crashes. Leakages may originate from a single problematic component in your application, or they might come from a number of components. Generally speaking, the greatest cause of memory leaks in Flash applications is the failure to remove listener registrations from an object before the object is discarded.

Using the Performance Profiler in Flash Builder, you can keep an eye on the number of instances of a particular type of object versus the number of cumulative instances. If these values steadily increase and retain parity throughout the lifetime of the application, it's worth looking at whether all the instances in existence are needed, or whether the application is failing to clean up discarded objects.

Sort the Memory column in the Profiler to display memory usage in descending order. Objects that are occupying the most memory appear at the top. Anything that is genuinely leaking memory will eventually float to the top of the Memory column, if left long enough.

Ending a profiling session

After you've seen all you need to see in the Performance Profiler, you'll most likely want to return to the code development view see your code again. Here's how you terminate your active profiling session:

1. **Select the file that is [Running] in the Profile panel.**

2. **Click the red square (the Stop button).**

   This icon is in the Profile panel just above the file you selected in Step 1.

   [Terminated] is displayed next to the file path.

3. **Click the X to the right side of the Profile panel.**

   The profile session is deleted.

4. **Click the X at the upper-right corner (Windows) or upper-left corner (Mac) to close the AIR application window.**

5. **Choose the Flash perspective from the upper right.**

   Alternatively, choose Window⇨Open Perspective⇨Flash.

Chapter 19

Submitting Your App to the Android Market

In This Chapter

▶ Signing up as a publisher in the Android Market

▶ Preparing your application listing

▶ Uploading your AIR for Android application to the Android Market

You've toiled night and day, fixing bugs and polishing UIs, and now you've reached the point where you stand back and declare your project finished. Congratulations, the majority of the hard work is behind you, and you should be humbled by your achievements! It's not quite time to go home yet though, as leaving off here would mean that no one but you would see the application. You need to deploy it.

The final stage in the development life cycle of your mobile Flash application is deployment. To deploy your application in the Android Market, you need to enlist as a publisher and then upload your compiled and tested APK file.

After uploading, your application takes a place of pride in the Android Market alongside the other Fart and Flashlight applications. It'll appear in search results, and if it's the best Fart application Google has ever seen, it could even become a featured app!

Creating an Android Market Developer Profile

Before you can upload your application to the Android Market, you first need to set up a Publisher Account. Head to http://market.android.com/publish to register as an Android Market Publisher. If you already have a Google ID, such as for a Gmail account, this is as simple as signing in with your credentials. If you don't have a Google ID, click the Create an Account

Now link to create one; then return to the Publisher page to continue with these steps to create a Developer Profile:

1. **Enter a name in the Developer Name field.**

   Developer Names must be unique, so if your first preference is already taken, consider adding an extra initial or arbitrary word — your Developer Name is not a legally binding name. Note, however, that this name will be shown to users of your application.

2. **Enter a contact e-mail address.**

   This address doesn't need to be the same e-mail address as your Google account ID. You might want e-mail concerning your applications in the Android Market sent to another address.

3. **Provide a link to your website.**

   This field is optional. If you do enter a URL, ensure that it points to a site that is easily recognizable as your own — your website home page is fine, but your Facebook or Twitter page is not appropriate.

4. **Enter your phone number.**

   Don't worry; this phone number isn't published on public pages in the Android Market. The number is used internally by Google, in the rare event that Google needs to contact you.

5. **Click to select whether you want to receive marketing communication from Google.**

6. **Click the Google Checkout button and pay your registration fee.**

   Sadly, becoming a publisher for the Android Market is not free, but it's also not as pricey as other developer programs you can join.

7. **Read the Developer Distribution Agreement.**

   It's not as big as Apple's, and these documents are always worth a read before you pour your heart and soul into an application that contravenes the Market's rules.

8. **Select the check box that says you've read the Developer Distribution Agreement and agree to those terms of service.**

You're in, and you can begin submitting applications immediately!

Uploading an App to the Android Market

The process of submitting an application to the Android Market is considerably easier than it is for the Apple App Store. You'll also find that your application propagates onto the live Android Market servers very quickly.

On the Android Market home page, `http://market.android.com/`, click the Upload Application button to start the process of submitting your AIR for Android APK file. You are presented with the Upload an Application screen, as shown in Figure 19-1.

The myriad file upload boxes and text fields may look daunting at first, but this page isn't as scary as it looks, and it is completed fairly quickly. I explain each of the fields in the list that follows.

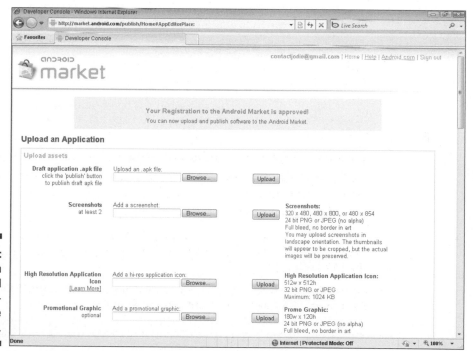

Figure 19-1:
Upload an Android application to the Market.

Upload Assets section

The Upload Assets section contains the collection of files that you upload to the Market servers when you submit the Upload an Application form. Following is a description of each of those fields:

- ✔ **Draft Application .apk File:** This file is the APK file published by Flash Professional that you tested to be working fine on your Android device. This is a required field. Click the Browse button to select the APK file on your computer, and then click the Upload button to the right.

- ✔ **Screenshots:** You must submit a minimum of two and a maximum of six screen shots with your application. The files must be either PNG or JPEG. The resolution must be 320x480, 480x800, or 480x854 pixels; these dimensions match the three most common screen resolutions found on Android devices. These screen shots are displayed in the Market so that users can gain an appreciation of what your application looks like in use.

  Click the Browse button to select the PNG or JPEG file on your computer, and then click the Upload button to the right.

- ✔ **High Resolution Application Icon:** This icon is a 512-pixel x512-pixel image of your application's icon. The design of this image should be identical to the three images specified when you compiled your AIR from Android APK file in Flash Professional. The creation of the icons for your application is covered in Chapter 13.

  Click the Browse button to select the PNG or JPEG file on your computer, and then click the Upload button to the right.

- ✔ **Promotional Graphic:** You can upload this optional image with your application; the image must be 180 pixels wide by 120 pixels high. The promotional graphic is displayed in various locations in the Android Market.

  If desired, the image may have a transparent background, which is useful if you want to give the image rounded corners that integrate seamlessly with the background of the web page on which the image is embedded. This effect, however, can causes problems when the web page background is the same color as your image. My view on transparency is that it's good only when you have control over the background that the image will sit on; if you don't have that control — as is the case with the Promotional Graphic option — don't use transparency.

  Click the Browse button to select the PNG or JPEG file on your computer, and then click the Upload button to the right.

✔ **Feature Graphic:** If your application is awesome (of course it is), you could well expect it to appear in the Featured section of the Android Market. Applications are selected on merit by the editorial team behind the Android Market. If you want your application to be considered, you should include a PNG or JPEG image that is 1024 pixels wide by 500 pixels high. The image should not have a transparent background, and all important content (such as text) should not be within 50 pixels of the edges of the image. An example of an acceptable feature graphic is shown in Figure 19-2; I placed a red bounding box in the image to show the mandatory 50-pixel padding.

Click the Browse button to select the PNG or JPEG file on your computer, and then click the Upload button to the right.

✔ **Promotional Video:** Here you can provide a link to a video on YouTube, produced by you, that promotes your application. This field is optional.

✔ **Marketing Opt-Out:** Selecting this check box means that Google (Android's parent company) will not promote your application outside the Google network of websites and mobile applications. Opting out of marketing means that your application would not be featured in an Android marketing campaign on TV or in a magazine, for example. In effect, this means little because Google is likely to promote your application only through the online channels it owns; the numbers and reach of these are considerable enough. At any rate, if you do not want your application to be marketed on non-Google-owned properties, select this check box.

Figure 19-2: An example feature graphic.

Listing Details section

In the Listing Details section of the Upload an Application screen, you enter all the contextual information (or metadata) about your application. This information is displayed to users on your application's Market page and will be used in searches. Here's what each of the fields is responsible for:

✔ **Language:** This field refers to the languages in which your application is available. If your application contains text that is only in English, you can skip this step, leaving the preselected default value of English (en). If your application is available in multiple languages, click the Add Language link and select the languages that are applicable to your app. Additional links for each of the selected languages are then displayed next to the default language. You can flip the listing details among the languages, enabling you to enter details in those languages. An example of a multilingual listing is shown in Figure 19-3.

Note that you can't submit the form until all the listing details for each of the selected languages are completed.

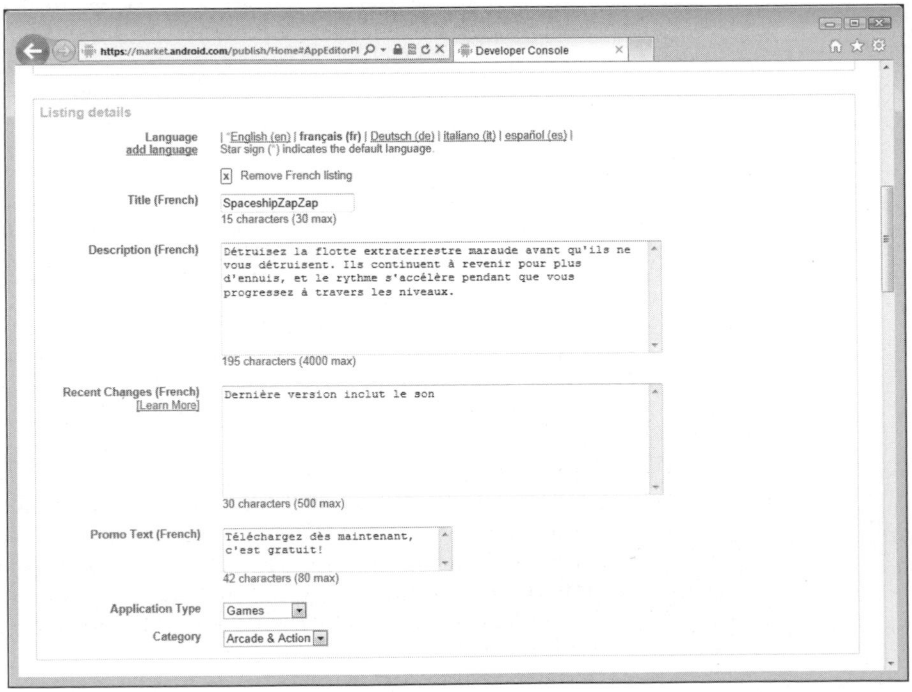

Figure 19-3: Configuring a multi-lingual Android Market listing.

✔ **Title:** This field is the title of your application and is limited to 30 characters.

✔ **Description:** In this field, you can let the marketing professional in you come out! Promote and glorify your application like it's the best application anyone has ever seen in the Android Market. Don't make any false claims, but don't hold back either.

✔ **Recent Changes:** If you're updating an application that you have previously distributed through the Android Market, this is the place to list enhancements and bug fixes that can entice users to update.

✔ **Promo Text:** The information you provide here will accompany the promotional graphic you may have uploaded in the Upload Assets section. The promo text is optional, but it must be less than 80 characters.

✔ **Application Type:** You find two options in the drop-down list: Applications and Games. If your application is a game, select Game; otherwise, select Application.

✔ **Category:** After making an Application Type selection, the Category drop-down list becomes enabled. Select the primary category that best describes your application or game.

✔ **Price:** By default, your application is made available in the Android Market for free, though you can set up a merchant account with the Google Checkout service to enable you to receive payment for your application at a set price. You can set up a merchant account by clicking the link at the bottom of the Publisher home page: `http://market.android.com/publish/Home`.

Publishing Options section

In the Publishing Options section, you configure the availability of your application. This availability covers protecting your application from being copied and redistributed, availability to minors, and the territories in which you want to market your application. This section contains the following fields:

✔ **Copy Protection:** When selected, this setting prevents users from being able to copy your application from their devices, having downloaded it from the Android Market, to their computers. To download the application to a different Android device, they must first be logged in to this device with the same Google account. If you deselect copy protection, users can copy the application from their devices to their computers and install it on other Android devices.

At the time of this writing, Google announced plans to replace this feature with a more complex Digital Rights Management (DRM) licensing system. The service it plans to offer allows you to enforce licensing policies for paid applications published through the Android Market. When your applications are run on the original Android device that downloaded the app, they call the Android Market servers to obtain their licensing status for the current user, and then allow or disallow further use as appropriate. If you'd like to learn more about this way of protecting your application, visit `http://developer.android.com/guide/publishing/licensing.html`. As with all DRM, pitfalls exist, such as being unable to use an application if it can't access the license server when the device has no Internet connectivity.

✓ **Content Rating:** Correctly rating the content of your application is important; no one wants the wrath of a nation's parents heading his or her way. If your application content is universally suitable for audiences of all ages, you can select the All radio button. If, on the other hand, your application contains content that is unsuitable for teenagers and preteen children, select the Mature radio button.

✓ **Locations:** By default, your application will be made available to Android Market users in all the territories in which the Android Market is available. Deselect the All Locations check box to see the entire list of countries to which your application will be available after it's uploaded.

You may decide that you want to distribute your application only in certain countries, perhaps because of licensing restrictions, because web services you call won't work in those countries, or because it is villegal in your country for you to trade with that territory.

Google makes a point of telling you that it is up to you as the developer of the application to determine whether your local laws permit you to distribute or sell your content to the countries listed. If you're unsure, and sufficiently paranoid, I recommend seeking legal counsel to advise you.

Contact Information and Consent sections

The last two short sections — Contact Information and Consent — ask you to provide the contact information that will be used for people who want to make inquiries about your application. The Consent section is where you sign (or check-box) your life away by agreeing to the terms of the program and United States export laws. The following list details what each of the fields does:

✔ **Web Site:** This option refers to the website that specifically relates to the your application, or at the very least, to the developer of the application. It's often helpful to have a dedicated page set up on your website that can provide answers to common support queries that may arise from your application (for example, a FAQs list).

✔ **Email:** This is a support e-mail address that customers can use to submit queries relating to this application. Note that this e-mail address will be visible to the world in the Android Market.

Should Google want to contact you about your application submission, it will use this e-mail address to reach you, so be sure to supply one that works!

✔ **Phone:** This field is optional. It's rare that Google needs to contact you by telephone about your application without first having sent you an e-mail. Because the phone number you share here is published in the Android Market for the world to see, I would advise against supplying this information.

✔ **Consent to the Android Content Guidelines:** These guidelines are considerably shorter than those relating to iOS, and they can be reviewed at `www.android.com/us/developer-content-policy.html`. Rules being rules, bear in mind that you are unable to submit an application to the Android Market without accepting these terms.

✔ **Acknowledge the Export Compliance:** Because your application will live on Google servers, and Google is a company incorporated in the United States, your application may be subject to U.S. export laws. Your application could fall afoul of these laws if it uses encryption libraries that are beyond what U.S. government officials deem acceptable. By selecting that you acknowledge the export compliance, you also acknowledge that Google won't distribute your application to countries that are subject to U.S. trade embargoes.

Phew! After completing all of that, you're ready to click the Publish button at the bottom of the screen. If you find that you don't have all the information you need, you can click the Save button to store your partially complete form for later submission. When you click Publish, your application is uploaded to the Android Market, and within a period of minutes to hours — dependent on system conditions at the time of the upload — your application appears in search results in the Market and is available for download. Your application also gets its own URL on the Android Market website. You can send this URL to prospective customers in an e-mail. Better still, the link opens in the Market app on Android devices, with only an additional tap being required to complete the installation!

Chapter 20

Submitting to the Apple App Store

Congratulations! You've worked extremely hard to get this far, and you should already be feeling a massive sense of achievement; you've created an application that is now running on your iOS device. Having gotten this far, it would be a crying shame for the world to not see the fruits of your labor. To guard against such a travesty, submit your compiled IPA to the Apple App Store and bask in the glory of five-star reviews.

The final stage in the development life cycle of your Flash mobile application is going live. The deployment mechanism to Live for iOS applications is the process of uploading your iOS application to the Apple App Store for review.

In this chapter, I walk you through the final steps of configuring your application for deployment, capturing those all-important screen shots for your prospective users to see, and submitting your application using iTunes Connect. Later in the chapter, I give a few helpful hints on deciding what to charge for your application. Finally, I describe how you can avoid the dreaded rejection e-mail from Apple. I recommend that you read the entire chapter before you submit your application to the App Store.

Getting Your Ducks in a Row

Before your application can go to the Apple App Store, you need to have several things in place. To start, the IPA has to be recompiled against a different certificate and provisioning profile. This recompiling is necessary because the ones you've been using up until now have been specifically for you to test your application on your iOS device. Then you recompile your app specifically for distribution in the Apple App Store. When that's done, you need to gather your screen shots and ready them for submission. The next three sections explain how to achieve these tasks.

Apple accepts to the App Store only applications that have been built using an App Store Distribution Provisioning Profile. Apps built with any other profile type will be instantly rejected.

At the end of Chapter 17, I show you how to generate a Distribution Certificate using the iOS Provisioning Portal. If you haven't yet obtained a Distribution Certificate and converted it to a compatible P12 certificate, head back there now and then carry on from here when you're done.

Obtaining a Distribution Provisioning Profile

Up to this point, your application has been compiled using provisioning profiles that tie your application to specific devices, through the specification and selection of Device IDs in the iOS Provisioning Portal. You're now at the stage where you no longer want your application to be tied to a handful of known devices; you want to open it up to the masses. Follow these steps to generate an App Store Distribution Provisioning Profile in the iOS Provisioning Portal to allow your application to be installed on any iOS device, via the Apple App Store:

1. **Point your browser to the iOS Provisioning Portal at** `https://developer.apple.com/ios/manage/overview/index.action`, **and log in, if requested.**

   The iOS Provisioning Portal home page is displayed.

2. **Click the Provisioning link on the left.**

   A screen with a set of tabs appears.

3. **Click the Distribution tab.**

   The Distribution Provisioning Profiles page displays.

4. **Click New Profile.**

   The Create iOS Distribution Provisioning Profile screen loads.

5. **Select the App Store radio button as the distribution method.**

6. **Type a name of your choice for the profile.**

7. **Select the ID of your app from the drop-down list.**

   If your app isn't listed, you first need to create a Development Provisioning Profile for it. Follow the steps in Chapter 15 for doing this, and then return here to continue.

8. **Click Submit.**

   The Distribution Provisioning Profiles page appears, listing your new App Store Provisioning Profile as Active.

9. **Download the new App Store Provisioning Profile.**

   Save the file somewhere safe on your computer, alongside your other certificates.

Recompiling for distribution

When compiling an application for submission to the Apple App Store, it must be compiled specifically for this method of distribution. Fortunately, it's all baked into Flash Professional, and when you have a Distribution Certificate and a Distribution Provisioning Profile in place, you can follow these steps to perform the final compilation of your application:

1. **Open your iOS application FLA in Flash Professional.**

2. **Choose File➪AIR for iOS Settings.**

3. **Click the Deployment tab.**

   At the top of the screen that appears, you see the section for iPhone Digital Signature.

4. **Next to the Certificate text box, click the button with a Folder icon on it and browse to the location on your computer where you have saved your P12 certificate file.**

5. **Select the file and click Open.**

6. **Enter the password.**

   You provided this password when you converted your CER file to a P12 file (refer to Chapter 16 for more information on the conversion process).

You can select the Remember Password for This Session check box to avoid having to keep entering the password.

7. **Click the Browse button next to the Provisioning Profile text box and browse to your saved Distribution** `mobileprovision` **file.**

   I show you how to create and download the `mobileprovision` file in the preceding section.

8. **Select the** `mobileprovision` **file and click Open.**

9. **Set the iOS deployment type to Deployment — App Store.**

10. **Click Publish.**

    After a short delay, the new IPA for App Store distribution is created in the same directory as the application FLA.

Gathering screen shots

An integral part to your App Store submission is a collection of screen shots that depict to the user what your app looks like in operation. Not only are these screen shots important to Apple, but they're also an excellent way to promote your application to potential customers. What is it they say? — "A picture speaks a thousand words." In this context, it could well mean the difference between your app being consistently overlooked by users or downloaded thousands of times.

In Chapter 16, I show you how to capture a screen shot from your iOS device and transfer it to your computer. Follow the steps covered in that chapter to gather as many images of your application in action as you can — if you capture a lot of images, you will have more images to choose from later.

Submitting Your App to the Apple App Store

After you've published your Flash mobile application for the App Store and gathered your screen shots on your computer, you can start the online App Store submission process. In this section I explain the process of defining a new application profile on the iTunes Connect website.

Adding a new application to iTunes Connect

The first step in submitting your application to the App Store is to add all the details about your application to the iTunes Connect website.

Throughout the process of adding a new application on iTunes Connect, clicking the Question Mark icon to the right of any form field reveals additional information about the type of data that Apple requires you to enter.

Follow these steps to begin the Add a New App Wizard using your iTunes Connect account:

1. **Point your browser to** `http://itunesconnect.apple.com`.

   The iTunes Connect login screen appears.

2. **Enter your iOS Developer Program login information and click Sign-in to continue.**

   This is the same Apple ID and password you set up when you registered as an iOS Developer. If you haven't registered yet, refer to Chapter 15 for more information.

   The iTunes Connect welcome page appears, as shown in Figure 20-1.

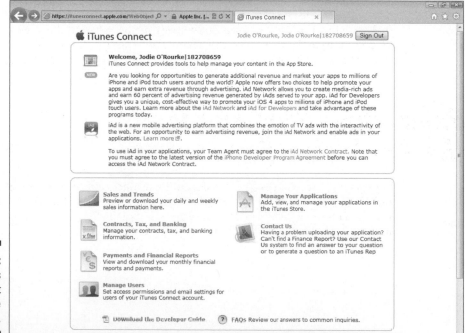

Figure 20-1:
The iTunes Connect welcome page.

3. **Click Manage Your Applications.**

   The Manage Your Apps screen appears. As you don't currently have any applications, the list is empty.

4. **Click Add New App.**

   This button is located at the upper-left corner of the screen.

   The New Application screen appears.

5. **Select the primary language, type a company name, and click Continue.**

   If you're an individual, simply type your own name in the Company Name text box.

   The App Information screen is displayed, as shown in Figure 20-2.

6. **Type the app name.**

   This is the friendly name you want users to see.

7. **Type the SKU number.**

   The SKU, or Stock-Keeping Unit number, is a unique identifier for the version of the application you're submitting and should not clash with any other app in the App Store.

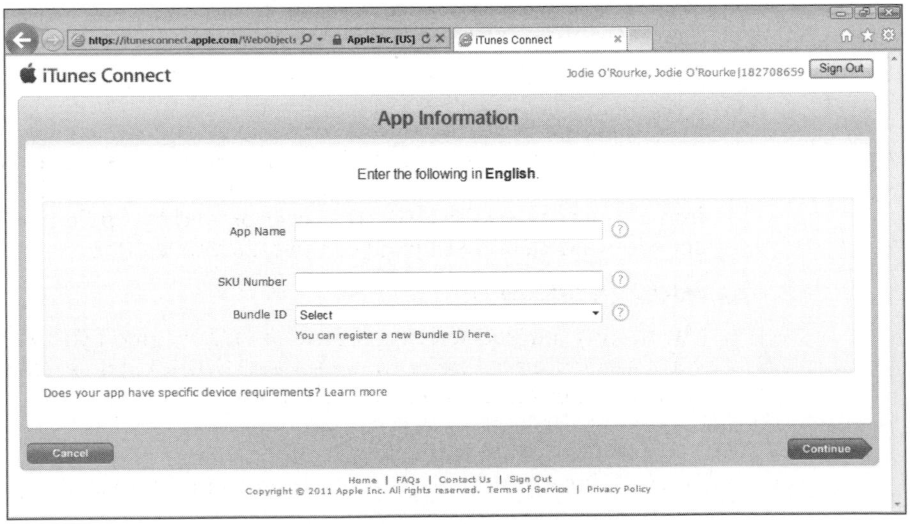

Figure 20-2:
The App
Information
screen
in iTunes
Connect.

I suggest using reverse domain notation to concatenate a string and then prefixing it with a version number, like this:

```
0001.com.jodieorourke.spaceshipzapzap
```

Because a domain name you own is unique to you, a clash with someone else in the App Store is easily avoided.

8. **Use the Bundle ID drop-down list to find the app name that you previously configured in the iOS Provisioning Portal.**

   A new text field called Bundle Suffix ID appears below your Bundle ID selection.

9. **Type the name of your Flash iOS application FLA file — excluding the `.fla` extension — in the Bundle ID Suffix field.**

   For conventional iOS development, this value can be varied in a manifest — or descriptor — file called `plist.info`. In Flash iOS application development, the developer is never exposed to this file; Flash Professional generates it during the packaging process and places it inside the IPA. It always assigns the name of your application as the Bundle ID. For example, my application has the filename `Spaceship ZapZap.fla`, so Flash Professional gives the packaged IPA file the bundle ID suffix `SpaceshipZapZap`, which I enter in the Bundle ID Suffix field in iTunes Connect.

10. **Click Continue.**

    The availability date and pricing tier page loads.

11. **Select the availability date.**

    The availability date is the date when you want users to be able to download your application from the App Store. This is preselected as today's date, meaning that your application will be available for download from the App Store the moment it is approved by Apple. You can schedule a date more than a year away, if you need to.

12. **Select the pricing tier.**

    The pricing tier you select will depend on how much you want to sell your application for. Refer to the section "Deciding on a Price Point," later in this chapter, for more tips on this.

13. **Click Continue.**

    The Metadata page is displayed, as shown in Figure 20-3.

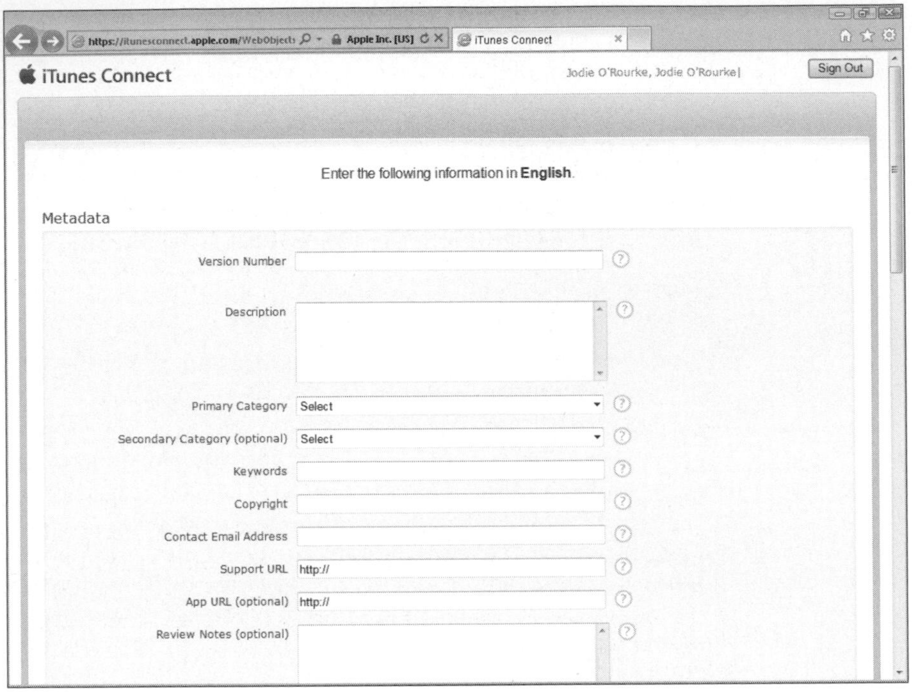

Figure 20-3:
The
Metadata
page in
iTunes
Connect.

Adding your application metadata

The next step to adding your application to the iTunes Connect website is to specify the metadata for your application. Metadata is the information you provide that describes the content of your application. The Metadata web page, which is quite long, is divided into four sections: Metadata, Rating, EULA, and Uploads. Guidance on each of the fields and what data to enter follows:

- **Version Number:** This number is the version of the application you're submitting and should be the same as the version specified in the iPhone OS settings in Flash Professional. The standard format for a version number is Major.Release.Build, so the first submission would have the version number 1.0.0.

- **Description:** This text is displayed in the App Store to describe your application to users. Keep it concise and informative, but hold back on making wild or unsubstantiated claims.

- **Primary Category:** Enter the category under which your application is best filed. If your app falls under more than one category, select the one that describes it best — or flip a coin! After you select a primary category from the list, the Secondary Category menu is enabled.

✔ **Secondary Category:** A selection from this category is optional and necessary only if you feel it will better categorize the app in the App Store. For example, if you choose Games as the primary category, specifying the type of game in the secondary category will help prospective users locate your app when perusing the thousands of games already in the App Store.

✔ **Keywords:** Enter one or more single keywords, each separated by a comma, to further help Apple to classify your app. Enter only keywords that are directly related to your app. Do not enter phrases as keywords; for example, type `football, scores` instead of `football scores`. Do not enter trademarks or keywords unrelated to your application. If in doubt, leave it out.

✔ **Copyright:** Type the name of the company or individual claiming copyright for the application. It's customary to type the year in which the application was created followed by the name of the copyright holder. For example, for my application, I entered **2011 Jodie O'Rourke**.

✔ **Contact Email Address:** This address is one that customers can use to contact you and the address that will be published in the App Store for all to see. It is advisable not to enter your personal e-mail address in this field. My recommendation is to set up a new e-mail alias or a new account with a provider like Gmail, specifically to receive your App Store customer support queries.

✔ **Support URL:** If users are spending money on your application, they often want to make sure that the entity they're dealing with is legitimate and contactable. By providing a support URL you provide your customers with some reassurance that they're dealing with a trustworthy and reliable developer. If your app is good, people will want to know who's behind it. You may find that businesses looking for developers to build apps for them will approach you through this channel. If you don't have a website, you can quickly set up a free blog at sites such as WordPress (`https://en.wordpress.com/signup/`) or Blogger (`http://www.blogger.com/`) and use the resulting blog URL as your support URL.

✔ **App URL:** If you end up getting flamed by users in your app reviews, it can prove beneficial to be able to respond to these comments on a website that you have control over. The optional URL you provide here should be specifically about your app and not be a generic web page, such as your blog home page. If you don't have a website but you followed the suggestion in the preceding paragraph to create a WordPress or Blogger site for the support URL, you can create a new blog entry for your application and then use the resulting URL as your app URL.

✔ **Review Notes:** In this field, include important information that the reviewer at Apple may need to approve your application. If the application incorporates licensing content from a third party, has specific test criteria, or has supporting documentation, this is the place to notify the reviewer of this and tell him who to contact to verify it.

Scroll down the page to reveal the Rating metadata fields you need to complete.

Rating your app

In the next section, you are asked by Apple to rate the content of your own application. For each of the content descriptions, make a selection from None, Infrequent/Mild, or Frequent/Intense.

Apple requires that "Apps must not contain any obscene, pornographic, offensive or defamatory content or materials of any kind . . ." To maximize the chances of your application being accepted, I suggest you avoid making a selection of Frequent/Intense for any of Apple's content descriptions.

EULA

Users of your application are bound by the EULA (End User License Agreement) when using your application. The EULA contains statements of liability; you should have it reviewed by a qualified lawyer if you see terms that you do not understand. By default, the standard Apple EULA applies to your application. You can opt to provide your own, though your own version must include the Minimum Terms stated at `http://www.apple.com/legal/itunes/appstore/dev/minterms`.

Uploads

The final part of the application process is to upload some images: a large application icon and some screen shots to accompany your metadata:

✔ **Large 512x512 icon:** This application icon PNG image must measure 512 pixels wide by 512 pixels high. Creating this icon is covered in Chapter 16.

Click the Choose File button, and then double-click the image file to upload from the file browser dialog box.

✔ **iPhone and iPod touch-screen shots:** In Chapter 16, I explain how to capture screen shots from your application running on an iOS device. This is the point where you include those screen shots with your App Store submission to help you promote your app.

Click the Choose File button, and then double-click the file to upload from the file browser dialog box. You can repeat this process to add multiple screen shots.

After completing the uploads, click the Save button to store your application data. Now you can move on to uploading your application file to iTunes Connect.

Uploading Your Application

To verify that your application is ready for upload, browse to the Manage Your Applications page on the iTunes Connect website (`https://itunes connect.apple.com/`), log in, and then click your application listed under Recent Activity. The status of the current version is `Prepare for Upload`, as shown in Figure 20-4.

Now you're ready to upload the application binary using Application Loader in Mac OS. Application Loader is a free Mac OS application that uploads your iOS IPA file to iTunes Connect. The app is bundled with Apple's XCode software, which as a registered iOS Developer you can download for free from `http://developer.apple.com/xcode/index.php`.

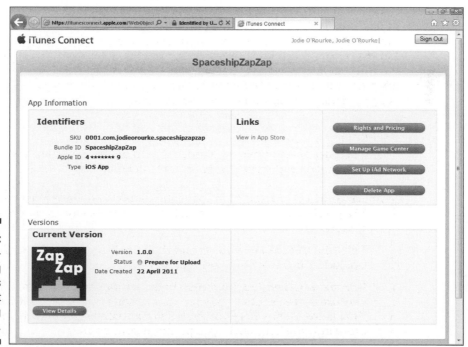

Figure 20-4:
An application listing in iTunes Connect awaiting upload.

"Mac OS you say? But I've developed my application in Windows!" Ah, yes. There is a catch with developing Flash iOS applications in Windows. Although you are able to do everything a Mac OS user can do during the development and testing of your application, as a Windows user you cannot upload the application to the App Store without the Application Loader software, which Apple makes available only to Mac users. No other mechanism exists to upload your app. Fortunately, everyone has a friend or an acquaintance who has a Mac! The finished application file just needs to be transported to any Mac computer and uploaded from there.

If you are a Windows user, you'll need to undertake the steps in the "Windows users" section that follows, then move on to the "Uploading with Application Loader" section. Mac users can skip straight to the "Uploading with Application Loader" section.

Windows users

Because Mac OS doesn't understand the compression used to generate the IPA file in Windows, when Application Loader uploads the IPA file in Mac OS, it's unable to look inside it for all the required files. Application Loader throws an error complaining that it's unable to unzip the archive. Follow these quick steps after transferring your IPA file from your Windows development machine to a Mac OS computer to recompress it:

1. **Transfer the compiled IPA file to a computer running Mac OS.**

   Either e-mail the file to your friend with a Mac OS computer or transport it yourself on a USB storage key.

2. **Select the file and press Enter to edit the name of the file.**

3. **Use the cursor keys to move to the end of the filename extension, and then delete the letters *ipa* and replace them with *zip*.**

4. **Press Enter.**

   A warning dialog box appears asking you to confirm that you want to change the extension from .ipa to .zip.

5. **Click Use .zip.**

6. **Double-click the file to extract it.**

   A folder called Payload is created.

7. **Open the Payload folder.**

   Inside is the file with the same name as your application.

8. **Select the file with the same name as your application, Control+click, and then select Compress.**

   A ZIP file is created alongside the original file. This new ZIP file can now be uploaded to the Apple App Store using Application Loader.

At this point, you can continue to the next section and complete the upload process with Application Loader on a Mac computer.

Uploading with Application Loader

Although Macs don't come with Application Loader software installed, it's free and easy to download. Follow these steps to install Application Loader on Mac OS and then upload your application:

1. **Download and install Xcode from** `http://developer.apple.com/xcode/index.php` **and install it on a computer running Mac OS.**

   Xcode is a development tool Apple provides to iOS developers. It contains software called Application Loader that enables you to upload your IPA file to iTunes Connect.

2. **Open the Finder in Mac OS and type** Application Loader **in the search box in the upper-right corner.**

   Application Loader appears in the results list.

3. **Double-click the Application Loader app icon to launch it.**

   The login screen appears.

4. **Log in with your iTunes Connect credentials.**

   This is the same Apple ID and password that you use for the iTunes Connect website and the iOS Developer Program website.

5. **Click Next.**

   The Choose an Application screen appears, as shown in Figure 20-5.

6. **Select your application from the drop-down list and click Next.**

   The Application Information screen is displayed.

Figure 20-5:
Choose an
application
listing.

SpaceshipZapZapiOS.zip

Choose an application.

Please select the application you're adding to the iTunes Store:

Choose...

Cancel   Next

If you see the message `No eligible applications were found`, instead of a drop-down list, review the details you entered on the iTunes Connect website and verify that the status of the current version is `Prepare for Upload`. If everything appears fine on iTunes Connect, click the Contact Us link at the bottom of the page in iTunes Connect to ask Apple for support.

7. **Click the Choose button at the lower-right corner of the dialog box and select the application IPA file if you developed the application in Mac OS, or the newly converted ZIP file if you transferred your application from a Windows development machine.**

If you're purely a Mac OS user, or a Windows user following the previous Windows steps, but you see the error message `Unable to unzip application`, this may be because your certificates have in some way become invalid. If you generated and downloaded your certificate some time ago, you should return to the iOS Provisioning Portal, revoke your existing Distribution Certificate, add a new one, download it, and then recompile your application against it. I explain the process of obtaining certificates from the iOS Provisioning Portal in Chapter 15.

8. **Click Next.**

The validation and upload of your application file take a few minutes, after which a dialog box confirming your submission to the App Store appears, as shown in Figure 20-6.

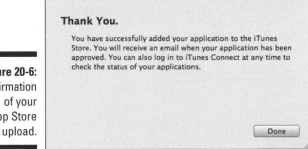

Figure 20-6: Confirmation of your App Store upload.

At this point, you need to confirm that your application's status is `Waiting For Review`. To do that, log in to the iTunes Connect website. Click the Manage Your Applications link, and then below the Recent Activity section, click your application. See that the status of the current version has changed to `Waiting For Review`, as shown in Figure 20-7. This message means that your application was successfully uploaded and is now in a queue to be reviewed by Apple.

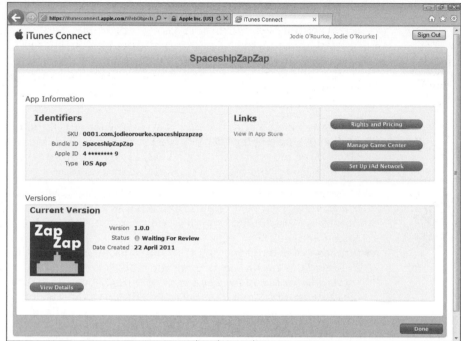

Figure 20-7:
iTunes
Connect
status
showing
Waiting For
Review.

Waiting for Approval

The next step is out of your hands. Your application is placed in a queue for Apple personnel to review against the criteria laid out in the iOS Review Guidelines and the Human Interface Guidelines (HIG). Although Apple provides no guarantees as to how long the review process will take, you should typically expect your app to be approved or rejected within ten working days.

Apple provides a review status indicator on the iOS Developer Program website that states the percentage of apps being reviewed within seven days. You can view this data on the App Store Approval Process page at `http://developer.apple.com/appstore/resources/approval`. Typically, the lower the percentage, the higher the number of apps going in for review, and the longer you should expect Apple to take to review yours. At low-traffic periods, you can expect this figure to be in the high 80s.

When Apple makes a decision regarding your app, it sends an e-mail to you notifying you of the change to your application's status on iTunes Connect.

You can log in to iTunes Connect to check the status of your application at any time.

If you haven't heard anything from Apple after waiting a couple of weeks, you may want to prod Apple by using the Contact Us link on the iTunes Connect home page to send a note to an iTunes representative. Remember to be nice!

Deciding on a Price Point

Deciding what to charge for your application might be as easy as giving it away, or it might be a complicated process of calculating what it costs to produce and maintain your application. Whatever your pricing requirements, don't forget to factor in the following points:

- ✔ **Apple's cut:** Whatever price you charge for your app, Apple will take a 30 percent cut of it. This is Apple's fee for providing the App Store service as a method for you to distribute your app. Like death and taxes (I talk about taxes in a moment), you simply have to accept Apple's cut. If your app is free, Apple gets nothing, too.

- ✔ **Overhead:** What did it cost you to build your application? Time is money, so make sure that your app price includes a sensible mark-up for the investment of time you put into it. How much is upkeep on the application? These are factors that you need to take into account when deciding on your price point. You may be using a third-party API that charges a fixed monthly fee for unlimited use, or you may be charged for the number of API calls your application makes. If your costs aren't fixed, you need to include the additional cost you incur in the price of each app you sell.

- ✔ **Competitors:** What's the price of similar apps in the App Store or in other stores like the Android Market? Unless you can rationalize a higher price with different or enhanced functionality, you should consider setting your app price at the median price of your competitors. If you fancy starting a price war, consider undercutting them!

- ✔ **Credibility:** Charging a nominal fee for your application often helps to raise the credibility of you and your application in the eyes of the consumer. The idea behind this theory is that if you're charging something for your app, the belief arises that the application must be properly built, unlike a lot of the free ones. Charging also nurtures the belief that the consumer is buying a product from an organization that will stand by its product. Some of the most popular applications in the Apple App Store have followed a similar approach and managed to become profitable out of the sheer volume of purchases.

✔ **Taxes:** Remember that revenue from the App Store is liable to taxation in your local jurisdiction. If you're an individual, the revenue will generally be regarded as income, so to stay on the right side of your taxman, be sure to query how you should report your App Store income before submitting your return. Taxation and its potential additional complication are two reasons why many developers simply choose to give their apps away rather than charge for them.

Avoiding Rejection

Rejection from the App Store can and does happen, so it shouldn't be seen as the end of the world if your app isn't accepted. With that said, Apple rejects applications for plenty of reasons. I've noted some of these reasons in the following list, and by reviewing them, you can be confident that you have done everything in your power to ensure that your application doesn't fall over where so many do:

✔ **Excessive bandwidth usage over cellular networks:** As a mobile application developer, you should be conscious that your user will frequently use your application out of range of Wi-Fi, requiring any data to be carried by the cellular network to which he or she subscribes. Applications that load excessive amounts of data over the cellular network place a heavy load on the network in a given "cell," restricting the use of other network subscribers in that cell. Heavy network use is discouraged by cellular network providers, and they apply severe cost penalties on those who use excessive amounts of data. That means your user could pay a heavy price just for using your application.

If your application loads video or audio or performs other tasks that require persistently high-data bandwidth, you should restrict the application to do this only over Wi-Fi. In Chapter 9, I show you how to determine whether a Wi-Fi connection is available to your application.

✔ **Human Interface Guidelines (HIG) violation:** Apple prides itself on the usability of iOS, and it requires applications to conform to the guidelines that it lays down in the Human Interface Guidelines (HIG) document. Applications that challenge user interface design and metaphors that are already covered in the HIG are rejected on these grounds. I cover HIG in more detail in Chapter 5.

✔ **Objectionable content:** Like most large organizations, Apple has a corporate responsibility not to offend. "Objectionable content" goes a little further than what is in the public's interest, though. As a general rule, it means "content that Apple finds objectionable." As much as Apple would have a problem with your application if the content was gratuitously sexual or violent, it would also have a problem with your application if the content was in any way stepping on the toes of its iTunes business model or appearing to be doing something better than iOS does natively.

After making sure that your application isn't obscene to the point that Apple won't allow it in the App Store even with a content rating, you then need to make sure that your application doesn't try to subvert Apple's money-making channels or make iOS look anything other than delightful.

✔ **Application description:** This one seems kind of obvious: Don't state that your application can do things that it doesn't actually do. Sadly, many developers get carried away when they're "bigging up" their application in iTunes Connect. Apple's reviewers will seek to ensure that your application does everything it purports and reject it when it doesn't.

To avoid overegging the pudding on the description, review and confirm that every statement made is 100 percent true; if it's not, remove it. Resist the urge to mention forthcoming features or future plans; these again have no relevance to the current submission.

✔ **App Store keywords:** Much like the application description, do not insert keywords in your metadata that do not apply to your application. If your application is about cricket, don't add *football* to your list of keywords in the hope that some sports fans will cross over. Apple rejects submissions that do this.

The web was a horrible place when metasearch engines returned web pages that merely mentioned your search term in their keywords' metadata. Apple is doing its utmost to ensure that the same thing doesn't happen to searches in the App Store.

✔ **Internet connectivity:** It is important to handle the lack of Internet connectivity in a manner that degrades correctly. Apple expect your app to behave gracefully, irrespective of whether it's able to connect to the Internet. Because of this, it's safe to assume that the Apple reviewer of your app will test it entirely without Internet connectivity, so if your app depends on a connection to the Internet to function, make sure that your app displays a message to the user informing him or her of this requirement, or expect rejection.

If your application doesn't depend on an Internet connection, ensure that as connectivity comes in and out of availability, your application is able to handle it effectively. If your app falls over when a connection is lost, expect the reviewer to reject it.

✔ **Handling of user data:** If your application solicits information from users about themselves and transmits this to a server, your application must tell the users what is about to happen and give them the ability to cancel if they do not want you to proceed. Sensitive user information, such as data collected during a sign-up process, must be sent over the secure HTTPS protocol to prevent interception by third parties.

If your application sends user-generated data to a remote server — even data like high scores — and fails to notify the user of this behavior, Apple will reject your application.

✔ **Copyrighted content:** When submitting your application to the App Store for review, you state to Apple that you own the copyright of the content in your application, or have the permission of the copyright owner to use the content. If Apple believes that your application infringes on a third party's copyright, it will reject your app.

If you have copyrighted material in your app to which the copyright holder has granted you permission to use, it's advisable to provide Apple with this information in the Reviewer Notes section when you add your application to the iTunes Connect website.

Part VI
The Part of Tens

In this part . . .

No *For Dummies* book is complete without a Part of Tens — chapters featuring ten tips apiece to, in this case, make your Flash mobile application development experience a great one.

Chapter 21 looks at the top ten ways to improve the performance of your application when it's running on a mobile device. Chapter 22 focuses on the fluffier side of mobile applications, offering ten ways to improve the user experience of your Flash mobile application. Chapter 23 offers my top ten tips for maximizing your application's chance of being approved for inclusion in the Apple App Store.

Chapter 21

Top Ten Performance Tips

In This Chapter

▶ Squeezing the most out of the graphics hardware on a mobile device

▶ Making sure that the processor isn't overworked

▶ Testing with the correct tools

Some chores you do, not because you enjoy them but because the long-term consequences of forgetting them far outweigh the hassle of doing them. When I had a car, I had it regularly serviced. The time and cost of this were nothing compared to the hassle and cost I'd have incurred with a breakdown.

With Flash mobile application development, you can either address or choose to overlook plenty of chores. Addressing them makes your application perform better and stand the test of time on myriad devices. Assuming, like I do, that you don't have all the time in the world to meticulously polish every line of code in your application, the following sections describe the ten performance issues that I always tackle first when developing a mobile Flash application.

Favoring Preauthored Graphics over the Drawing API

The drawing API in Flash Professional uses computation — handled by the central processing unit (CPU) on the mobile device — to create the graphics that your users see in your app. Processors on mobile devices are not only slower than those in desktop computers but also attached to a limited power supply. These restrictions mean that it's important to carefully evaluate whether the graphics you're using in your application absolutely need to be drawn using code or whether you can draw them yourself in Flash before you compile your application. Preauthored graphics remove the need for the application to put a heavy burden on the mobile device's CPU. Because the CPU isn't being used for programmatic drawing, it is freed for other tasks, making your application run faster and smoother. If your application uses the CPU less, the battery on the mobile device will be conserved.

Preauthored graphics can come in three forms: graphics drawn directly in Flash Professional using the drawing tools, images imported into the Library in Flash Professional and compiled into the application, and images that are loaded from the Internet into the application when it is running. For the most part, you'll find that drawing graphics in Flash Professional with the drawing tools satisfies most tasks, while images imported to the Library are suitable for photos and other complicated graphics. If the number of images in your application is such that the file size of the compiled application is huge — more than 20MB — you should consider the third option of loading the images at runtime over the device's Internet connection.

Recycling Objects

Resources in the world are scarce, and the experts tell us that we need to recycle to be able to sustain ourselves into the future. The same is also frighteningly true for mobile application development. I've said it so many times before that this is likely to grate: Resources on mobile devices are scarce, so it's important to do everything you can to conserve them. As much as I recycle at home, I've also managed to find a way to incorporate recycling into my Flash mobile applications. The trick is not to throw anything away that you might be able to reuse. If I built a game that threw projectiles at a target, my approach might be to create new projectiles each time the user pressed the Fire button and then destroy them when they weren't needed. Although I'm being good in cleaning up the objects when I'm done with them, I'm actually requiring the CPU to work harder than it needs to. Each time that I create a new projectile, the application has to create a new object instance, memory has to be allocated, and pointers to this memory have to be generated — all of which requires time from the CPU, time it could spend doing something else.

A better approach would be for me to work out the maximum number of projectiles that could appear onscreen at any one time, have the application create exactly that number of projectiles, and then store them in an `Array` (or a `Vector` object). Then, each time I need a projectile, I can take one from the `Array` and add it to the display list. When I no longer want the projectile, I can remove it from the display list but leave it in the `Array` to use again later. This concept is called *object pooling,* and a code example is provided in Chapter 6, where I talk about cleaning up after yourself.

Avoiding Bubble Events

The event model in Flash works with a concept called *bubbling*. When certain events — particularly keyboard and mouse events — are dispatched from objects, the events rise to the parent object. Where an object is nested deeply inside many other objects — think of the smallest doll inside of a stack of Russian dolls — the event dispatched by the innermost object can travel (or bubble) all the way through to the outermost parent. This is the Russian-doll equivalent of the smallest one inside saying "Hello" and then each doll sequentially hearing this and saying "Hello" too. If the smallest doll only wanted to say hello to the next largest one — its parent — the ensuing echo of greetings would be pointless and a waste of effort for the others. You can save on unnecessary bubbling in your application by stopping the event from propagating any further than the object that needs to be notified. I give you a full explanation of how to stop bubbling in your code in Chapter 6, where I discuss event handling.

Paying for Every Pixel Drawn

Modern mobile devices are blessed with a dedicated graphics processing unit (GPU) that removes the need for the CPU to handle rendering graphics to the screen and makes graphical applications run faster as a result. Even so, the GPU in a mobile phone isn't nearly as powerful as the one found in the average desktop computer, so it's important to understand how not to upset it!

The best way to think about the visual output of your application is to consider that if an object is in the display list, the GPU has to deal with it. Even if the object is occluded by another object, the GPU is going to need to crunch the geometry. This "stacking" of objects is somewhat wasteful and can quickly become a problem when lots of stacked objects need to be rendered multiple times per second. The situation becomes all the more exacerbated during fast game-play, where momentary freezes — caused by the GPU struggling to keep up and asking the CPU to help — lead to interruptions that end the game. You can help the GPU by having it render only objects that the user is able to see. If an object is no longer needed, pull it out of the display list using the `removeChild()` method (you can see it in use in Chapter 10). If you know that the current state of your application means that some objects are not visible — perhaps because you've added a large display object on top of them that obscures them from view — rather than leave those objects stacked underneath, remove them from the display list and add them again later. The GPU will thank you by rendering that a little bit quicker.

Try to keep your display list as flat as possible. By this I mean try not to nest many `MovieClips` and `Sprites` inside each other in the display list. Approaching the development of your app in this way can further help you to avoid stacking display objects.

Reducing Frame Rate

Flash works using a system of frames, with each frame responsible for executing code and updating animation changes — in Chapter 4, I explain frames and show you how to configure the frame rate for your application. The more frames per second your application runs at, the more calculations per second the CPU has to perform. Naturally, the more the CPU has to do per second, the more likely it is to become overworked. An overworked CPU manifests itself as momentary hangs in your application's user interface — or crashes if things get really bad — and rapid battery depletion on the device.

When deciding on a frame rate, choose the lowest frame rate possible that will satisfy all the animation and/or code requirements of your application. For example, most stop-frame animation is perceived by the eye below 24 frames per second (FPS) — a phenomenon called *persistence of vision* — so you'll need to set your frame rate to at least 24 FPS. If your application doesn't rely on any animation, you can get away with a far lower frame rate. For example, the playback of loaded video isn't affected by the frame rate that the Flash application is running at, so if your application is a video player, you can drop the frame rate to just 1 FPS and give the CPU a break!

Keeping Code Activity to a Minimum During Video

Although modern smartphones are perfectly capable of rendering high-quality video, it shouldn't be considered a trivial task. Behind the scenes, the device's GPU is busy decoding the video and rendering video at a rate of 25–30 frames per second onto the screen. The CPU is on standby to help when things get a bit busy over in the graphics department. For the user, the most important thing is the video that he or she has selected to watch and is now engaged with. If the video starts juddering or distorting, it becomes unwatchable, and the user experience has been compromised. It may be tempting to have other tasks being performed in the background during video playback, but I advise keeping those to an absolute minimum on a mobile device. Loading and parsing web service responses, for example, is not something to do while a video is being played.

Updating items in the display list should be undertaken before the video starts or after it ends.

Deploying and Testing on the Same Device

Device Central (introduced in Chapter 18) is extremely useful in helping developers to rapidly test features as they develop them, but it is in no way a substitute for testing on the real thing. I have a few reasons for saying this. First, although the engineers who create the emulators are highly skilled in mimicking mobile device behavior on another operating system (your computer), the operating system and hardware on your computer aren't the same as those on your mobile device. No amount of software is going to be able to replicate some of the race conditions — that is, bugs caused by timing and environmental nuances — that are thrown up by niche mobile device hardware.

Second, desktop emulators don't have touch screens like the target mobile devices do. Even with software simulation of multiple touch points, the behavior and outcome of actions can often be different when you test on the mobile device.

Finally, you have to consider the usability of the application. On a large desktop display, with a mouse as the primary input device, the application might appear both understandable and usable. Shrink the display to ⅟₂₀ the size and make touch the primary form of input, and suddenly the application seems confusing to the user. Some of the interaction points are either missed or too small for the average finger. Only by putting an application on a mobile device early in the development process will flaws such as these present themselves.

Caching as Bitmap

In Chapter 5, I discuss the creation of graphics in your application and introduce a technique called Bitmap Caching. In a nutshell, if your display object doesn't animate internally and you don't resize it frequently, you can get better rendering performance by setting its `cacheAsBitmap` property to `true`. Setting this property causes the GPU on the mobile device to create a bitmap representation of the vector graphics in the display object, allowing it to be rendered faster than if the vector was left as it was.

However, if the display object does have animated contents or is resized a lot when the application is running, it's important not to turn on `cacheAs Bitmap`. To disable Bitmap Caching, either set the property to `false` in the ActionScript code that implements the object, or with the object selected on the stage, change the Renderer option in the Display section of the Properties panel from Cache as Bitmap to Original (No change). This is because the GPU will have to recache the display object each time the dimensions — or internal contents of the object — change, leading to slower rendering than if the `cacheAsBitmap` property wasn't set (or `false`).

Limiting the Use of Filters

Filters allow you to programmatically apply effects like blurs and drop shadows to display objects in your application. Although they're very cool and easy to use, they cost a lot in terms of computation and rendering. The device that your app is running on is rather constrained by the amount of computation and rendering it can do at any one time, so you should decide whether you need those effects. I take the view that if I can achieve a similar appearance using predrawn graphics, I'll opt not to use programmatic effects in my ActionScript code. In Chapter 5, I demonstrate how to use the drawing tools in Flash Professional to mimic a drop shadow effect.

Toggling Display Object Visibility Instead of Alpha

When you toggle a display object's `alpha` property from 1 to 0 to make it invisible, the object still remains in the display list and is still marked for rendering. When the `visible` property of a display object is toggled from `true` to `false`, the object is hidden from view but also causes the object to be ignored when it comes to rendering. Be kind to the GPU on the mobile device by hiding all your display objects using the `visible` property instead of the `alpha` property. In return, the GPU renders your application faster.

Chapter 22

Top Ten Ways to Please Your User

In This Chapter

▶ Understanding how good design avoids annoyance

▶ Sensing what is acceptable to ask of your user

▶ Making a reliable app that nurtures confidence

How many times have you gone to plug a USB key into your computer and found you had it the wrong way around and had to turn it around the other way before it goes in? If it were designed to perfection, the humble USB key would go in the first time, every time, and there'd be no need to take a look at the slot before you tried for a second time! Have you found yourself annoyed with the way something works and wondered who on earth decided to design it like that? When it comes to your Flash mobile application, your attention to user interface, design, and function can be the determining factors of your app's success. The last thing you want is your user ruing the day that he or she installed your app and cursing you as the user presses the Uninstall button.

Pleasing your user is as important as coming up with a unique proposition for a mobile application. Get the formula right and you've perfectly executed your perfect idea. Get the implementation wrong and you've put your cards down on the table for the world to see, leaving the way clear for a competing app to come in and do what your app is doing, only better! It'd be a shame for your app to fall victim to poor execution, so I've assembled a hit list of points that can help you keep your users happy and your competitors at bay.

Justify Location Requests

I like using mobile apps that use my geographic location to provide location-specific features — it's really cool. Those apps save me from needing to know where I am and having to enter my location via the touch-screen keypad. What's not cool is when the application I'm using wants to know my location but doesn't provide any features associated with the location request. Suddenly I feel as though the data I'm sharing (or is being collected by default) is being used for someone else's benefit rather than my own. Perhaps the application is sending data about me back to a marketing database, or maybe it's completely benign and just an oversight by the developer; either way, I don't know and I'm not comfortable with it. The consequence may be that I delete the app.

Avoid breeding mistrust and suspicion in your users by requesting their location only if the outcome will be of clear benefit to them. It's okay to store their location if they explicitly consent to it — and you comply with data protection legislation — but make sure that in providing their location, your users derives some benefit too.

Adjust the User Interface for Fat Fingers

Screens on mobile devices are intentionally small — they wouldn't be particularly mobile if they weren't — and require users to interact using their fingers (and thumbs). Like you, my digits are a bit wider than just a couple of pixels, so hitting an area that's just a couple of pixels wide on a touch screen is an extremely tricky business. After a while, it can become pretty frustrating!

Make sure that your buttons and hit areas — hidden active areas that surround visual cues — are large enough to comfortably fit the tip of a finger on them, and then add a little bit more. It sounds a little accusatory, but don't assume for a moment that your fingers are normal! Some people have really fat fingers; others have much skinnier digits. All need to be able to use your application's UI without frustration. Get a few people to test the interactive parts of your app and watch closely for any repeated presses or apparent failures of the application to respond to the press — these are indicative of hit areas being too small.

Isolate Code Bottlenecks to Improve the User Interface

Crunching numbers and loading data from the Internet keep a mobile device's central processing unit (CPU) extremely busy. If your application is performing these processes while animation is occurring on the screen, a bottleneck may arise that causes less critical tasks in your application to be dropped in an attempt to prevent the application from crashing. An example of tasks that get dropped are intermediary frames. These frames are queued to be rendered on a screen when your application is animating from one state to another. When things get too busy, the mobile device decides that as long as the view is rendered to the final state it's supposed to be in, the steps that occur in between can be dropped. From a stability perspective, this is great, because the device has managed your application's hungry demands sufficiently to keep it from crashing. The downside is that the animation appears ugly to the users and leaves them thinking it's struggling to work on their devices.

Take time to isolate code bottlenecks in your application, where too many tasks are being attempted at the same time. Consider whether the tasks can be performed at different times to spread out the load. Avoid intensive computation and loading/parsing data from the Internet while you're animating objects in the display list.

Test Your Application to Avoid Crashes

"You crashed my device!" are words you don't want to hear from your user. Sometimes, even when you try to avoid code bottlenecks, they happen, and the mobile device eventually screams, "No more" and shuts down your app. Crashes are a serious bug, because they tell the user that the application has been written in a way that can challenge the integrity of the device's operating system. As much as users dislike buggy applications, developers dislike being responsible for them — we're a proud bunch. Make sure you've exhausted all available resources to test that the app is as bug-free as possible before you release it for your users to install on their devices.

I've stressed it plenty of times throughout the book, and I'll mention it again here. Mobile devices are resource constrained, so crashes are a lot more likely to occur than on desktop computers. Because you develop mobile apps on a desktop computer, it's all too easy to miss problems. The answer is deploying your application to mobile devices that are attached to your development computer as frequently as possible. Test your app through the entire building process — particularly when you've added big changes. I can't stress this enough: As soon as the code can be compiled, get it onto the device to see how it performs. Chapter 18 covers the aspects of testing your application as well as some tools that can help you do this.

React Positively to App Store Comments

Both the Android Market and Apple App Store allow users to write short reviews of your app and award it a rating (from one to five stars). You can do one of two things with this data: Take offense at every criticism and ignore anything but the most beaming of reviews, or carefully analyze the comments for trends and respond to them by modifying your app.

Every app — even the most popular ones — gather negative reviews from time to time. If those negative reviews are isolated grumbles about nothing in particular, it's safe to park them for now and see whether anyone else moans about the same thing. If you're getting continuous reviews suggesting that you add the same feature, it would make sense to put that feature high on the list of development goals for the next release of the app.

Be on the alert for users complaining of crashes. If you can glean from their comments the device and version of the operating system they're using, that makes it easier for you to reproduce the issue on your device.

When it comes to responding to individual comments, avoid it as best as you can! Resist using your app description text in the store, on your official app website, or in other public forums to respond to individual people. Instead, when pushing out a release, include release notes in the app description that allow the users to see what's in the latest version. Taking note of common issues, fixing them, and then providing accurate release notes are the most positive responses to criticism.

Release Updates to Increase Stickiness

If you're already an Android or iPhone user, you already know that when an update is available for your installed applications, you receive a notification. Now I don't know about you, but I frequently forget about some of the applications I have installed on my device. Perhaps I used them once or twice, didn't think they had much value yet, and simply forgot about them. When an update notification comes along, I'm reminded that the app is installed on my device, and I'm also being told it's improved (I hope). I download the update and then open the app to see what's new. This phenomenon is the mobile app equivalent of a repeat visit to a website — the *stickiness* of a website is its ability to generate repeat visits from the same user. Unlike the web, you have a hook into a device that users carry with them all the time. By releasing a new version of your app, you bring it to the users' attention once again and increase the likelihood that they will open and use it.

Provide Just Enough Information

Even when I'm working on a desktop computer with a large screen, I dislike websites that bombard me with too much text, or those portal websites that have information about anything you want to know neatly arranged into 650 small squares. To me, this is information overload, and I switch off or click away. Now consider this same approach on an even smaller screen: loads of things going on and even less real estate. Your user is likely to close the application (or worse, uninstall it).

Successful mobile applications carefully balance the need to provide relevant and sufficiently detailed information, while avoiding putting too much on screen. Perfecting the balance between too little and too much information is a fine art, but the one rule that I stand by when working out how much is too much is "If in doubt, leave it out." If the content in your application doesn't make sense when the user reads it, you haven't provided enough information. If the user gets bored — or his eyes start to hurt — halfway through reading content, you've included too much information.

Use Device Fonts for Legibility

Mobile devices come with a great set of fonts already installed that your Flash mobile application can use. These fonts have been specifically tailored by the operating system manufacturer (Google or Apple) to render well on small screens and be easily read. Although Flash includes the capability to include embedded fonts in your application, you have a couple of reasons to avoid using these. First, choosing to use the device's default font ensures that your text is rendered using the most legible means available. Anti-aliased fonts look nice in Flash on the web but don't render well on disparate mobile device screens. Second, many fonts are provided to you under license, and one of the common restrictions of the license is not to distribute the font without authorization to do so. Packaging a font in your application for distribution to mobile devices is a form of distribution that requires you to review your font's license.

I provide more information about using fonts in your Flash mobile application in Chapter 5.

Maintain Functionality without Requiring Connectivity

A mobile app is a package that is downloaded and installed on a mobile device. Unlike a web application, mobile apps can run without needing to access the Internet through an available connection on the device. Wherever possible, take advantage of this capability to work in offline mode, and allow your user to use your application irrespective of their capability to receive data over a cellular or Wi-Fi network. Doing this maximizes the scenarios in which users will run your app on their devices — on an airplane, a subway, or even on a ship out at sea!

Consider this example: If your application searches for the cheapest airfare to a destination entered by the user, an Internet connection is likely to be mandatory for the user to get the latest prices. What if the user had searched earlier and reopened the app to view the price results from the earlier search? Should the application have cleared the results and mandated a new search — even when an Internet connection isn't available — or should it display the data from the last search and advise the user that the search is old and that the prices can't be updated because the device can't access the web? My feeling is that it should do the latter. The ability to store reasonably large amounts of data on the device — using the local SQLite database, covered in Chapter 7 — means that even apps that pull data from the web are able to offer some functionality (albeit a little restricted) to users, even when disconnected.

Use Existing User Interface Metaphors

You could try to reinvent the wheel, if you really wanted to, though I'm confident you'll be there a long time and come up with something not quite as good as the wheel. The same is true for common user interface components that have stood the test of time — they're used all over the place for a reason.

If you see a text box with a border around it and a down-pointing arrow to the right, you instinctively think it's a drop-down menu (or combo box). When you interact with a drop-down menu, you are accustomed to clicking the down arrow and seeing a list of selectable items appear. What if clicking the down arrow caused a new browser window to launch? You'd probably be surprised, and quite possibly annoyed — particularly if you were actually in the middle of entering some data.

Now think about an app where a Next button is placed at the lower-right corner of the screen. When the button is pressed, the current screen slides away to the right and a new screen slides in from the left. In most applications on mobile devices, the left-to-right slide transition is reserved for a backward step. A next (or forward) step is generally represented by a right-to-left transition. The user is left confused by the apparent direction of progress through the app, challenging what he has seen using other apps. Wherever possible, seek to follow existing conventions for interaction that embrace rather than challenge the behaviors that your user has become accustomed to.

Chapter 23

Top Ten Tips for Apple App Store Success

In This Chapter

▶ Getting through the App Store review process with ease

▶ Dealing with your customers

▶ Maximizing your apps appeal

*I*f iOS is the Crown Jewels, the Apple App Store is surely the Tower of London. Compliant visitors are welcomed on a daily basis to view the treasures within, while hostile characters are left contemplating scaling the impossibly high outer walls.

Getting into the App Store isn't as hard as many would have you believe but is a lot tougher than getting into the Android Market. The key to success is understanding the up-to-date list of things Apple does and doesn't like. That list changes frequently, so keeping abreast of news from the iOS stable can ensure that you don't get caught by moving goalposts. I've compiled a list of ten tips, and if you keep them in mind, I believe you'll have no trouble getting your app accepted into the Apple App Store on the first attempt.

Read the Submission Criteria Thoroughly before You Develop

Nothing is worse than spending hours putting something together only to find that it's not fit for the intended purpose. Before embarking on an application bound for the Apple App Store, you should understand the specifications and requirements that your application will be subjected to on submission. I recommend that you take the time to read two documents before you start work on an app targeting iOS:

✔ The iOS Human Interface Guidelines (HIG): `http://developer.apple.com/library/ios/#documentation/userexperience/conceptual/mobilehig/Introduction/Introduction.html`

✔ The App Store Review Guidelines: `https://developer.apple.com/appstore/resources/approval/guidelines.html`

Although both documents are long and rather boring, they contain essential information on what is and isn't acceptable in terms of the content and appearance of your app. I urge you to take the time to review both against the working version of your application. This extra check ensures that parts of the guidelines weren't overlooked or ignored in the melee of development.

Allow Time in Your Schedule for the App Store Process

Although building an app might take only four or five days to complete, the App Store review process takes at least a week. Given that delay, if a client comes to you and asks you to build an application and have it available in the App Store in one week, you'd have to indicate that the earliest you could realistically have the app available in the App Store is two weeks.

Be careful about committing to a fixed date for availability in the Apple App Store, as acceptance is ultimately at Apple's behest. Always be mindful that the time of delivery for an application includes the development and test time plus the time to go through the Apple review process.

Ensure That Your App Does Everything the Title and Description Claim

It's all too easy to overstate the abilities of your application when you're trying to come up with an appealing title and description. In its testing of your application, Apple is careful to assess whether your application can do all that it claims. If it finds that it doesn't — or it finds a subjective statement that it disagrees with — your application will be rejected from the review process. This is hugely disappointing, as it's one of the most avoidable reasons for rejection. Double-check your title and description, and remove any subjective claims.

Don't Write Your App Page Editorial As an Afterthought

I'm as guilty as the next person for leaving things until the last minute and sometimes racing to meet deadlines. This is all well and good if the rush is to complete things that are tucked away under the hood of an application, but rush anything that the user sees at your peril. One case in point is your app's description that will be seen in the App Store.

When it comes to the words you use to market your application, a carefully written application description has proven time and again to be pivotal in how successful an app is. As you write your app's description, try to convey what the app does in the first sentence. If you spark the user's interest immediately, she is more likely to read on; if you don't, she's unlikely to spend time digging through the rest of your description to understand what your app is for. Your choice of words is often key to creating a concise and meaningful description. For example, a game where the user controls a spacecraft and shoots aliens to score points would benefit from having the words *game, spacecraft,* and *shoot* in the first sentence. Using those keywords, I'd construct my first sentence as "Navigating the spacecraft and shooting the aliens are the objects of this fast-paced game." In the sentences that follow, you can provide a more verbose narrative about specific features.

Use Screen Shots to Influence Users

If your app looks cool — which I'm sure it does — you should be screaming about it to potential users in the App Store. You can tell potential users until you're blue in the face that the user interface is a sight to behold, but are they going to believe you? Probably not as much as they would if you substantiated your excited claims with some screen shots of the application in action! Capturing screen shots on iOS devices is as simple as pressing a couple of buttons at the same time and then e-mailing the screen shots to yourself — the complete steps to do this are provided in Chapter 20.

iTunes Connect allows you to specify as many as five images to use as screen shots, and I encourage you to take advantage of that — these images are the best advertising slot available for your app. Although the images you provide must include a screen shot of the application, the orientation, border, and overlay art you put on there are entirely up to you. This is your chance to visually appeal to your prospective users — be creative!

Set Up a Website to Respond to User Feedback

The App Store is a bit one-sided in that it allows users to make comments about your app, but you're unable to respond. When I suggest setting up a website to respond to feedback, I don't mean for you to create a web page with retorts to individual comments — that would be suicidal! Instead, I encourage you to create a web page that allows you to present your application to users in the way you want it to be seen, using the tone of voice you want to have associated with your app, all outside the Apple realm. When you make updates to your application, you can say things like, "After a large number of users voiced concerns about X, they'll be pleased to hear that I've now implemented Y in the latest version!" You're responding to the comments users are making, not allowing yourself to be drawn into a war of words with any single user. Because Apple can mandate what you say only in the App Store, you're free to say as much or as little as you choose on your own site; you're no longer gagged if you receive unfair feedback.

Test to Avoid Rejection

If you submit your app for review and then realize you have an error in the binary code you uploaded, you can fix and then resubmit your app by using the Developer Reject option. The downside is that when you do this, you go to the back of the Waiting for Review queue — which means that you can add on another seven days before the app will be live. As tempting as it is to let an error or issue ride and hope that Apple's testers don't spot it, they probably will. Worse still, if they don't spot it, your users surely will, and they'll slam you with bad reviews and one-star ratings. So what's the answer? The trick is to get it right the first time by making sure that you upload binary to Apple only after it has been subjected to numerous and rigorous rounds of testing.

 If, despite all your testing efforts, you find a flaw in the app while it's awaiting review, upload a new binary file with the fix and accept the seven-day hit in return for getting things right for your users.

Get Approval for Updates

You'd be forgiven for thinking that because your app has already been accepted into the App Store, any subsequent revisions to the app go through a different review process, but this isn't the case. Apple treats every submission to the App Store as though it's the first time it has seen it. Updates will reach your users as soon as Apple approves them, but you'll be queued behind apps that don't yet have their first approval. Your updated app will be subjected to the same rigorous testing it endured in the first approval process — the whole app, not just the new features. You may also find that because your app is tested by different people on the Apple side, bugs that got through in an earlier version are flagged in the newer version. That's bad luck when that happens. Just accept that it's a fair cop that should have been snagged earlier and move on — Apple detests whiny e-mails from developers!

Use Easter Eggs but Tell Apple!

Surprisingly, Apple is okay with you putting jovial booby traps — colloquially referred to as *Easter eggs* — into your applications, so if you want a silly picture to magically appear when your users interact in a particular way, this treat won't prevent your application from being accepted into the App Store. One caveat that Apple places on Easter eggs is that you need to warn the testers that the Easter eggs are there. If you submit an app and don't warn Apple about an Easter egg, when testers find it, they'll treat it as a bug and reject the app. It's also imperative that the booby traps are entirely benign in nature. If Apple perceives them to be in any way malicious, you'll get your knuckles rapped!

Decide on Your Application Price

Some of the best and most successful applications in the Apple App Store aren't free. The idea that your app will be popular only if you give it away is wrong. iOS users spend in excess of $2 billion on apps each year, so plenty of users are out there willing to part with cash for a decent app. A "magic price point" exists at which apps sell in the millions; the sub-$1 app seems to be a real moneymaker. From a consumer's perspective, a 99-cent app brings a slightly elevated expectation of quality compared to a free app. On the flip side, the price is so low that consumers are willing to take a punt on it. As a developer, your 99-cent application is perceived to be less inferior to a free app while still being able to command high numbers of downloads. The profit is to be found in the sheer volume of sales.

Index

• X •